THE CAROLINE ISLANDS

N.W. ANGLE OF CYCLOPEAN ENCLOSURE ON LELE ISLAND

THE TOKOSA, OR KING OF THE ISLAND, IN FOREGROUND

From a Photo by Dr. Channon

THE
CAROLINE ISLANDS

TRAVEL IN THE SEA OF THE LITTLE LANDS

F. W. CHRISTIAN

*" I am haunted by numberless islands and
many a Danaan shore."*—W. B. YEATS.

*" Go little book and wish to all
Flowers in the garden, meat in the hall."*
—R. L. STEVENSON

FRANK CASS & CO. LTD.
1967

Published by
FRANK CASS AND COMPANY LIMITED
67 Great Russell Street, London WC1
by arrangement with Methuen & Co. Ltd.

First edition   1899
New impression   1967

Printed in Great Britain by
Thomas Nelson (Printers) Ltd., London and Edinburgh

TO HIS EXCELLENCY

THE RIGHT HON. THE EARL OF RANFURLY

K.C.M.G.

GOVERNOR OF NEW ZEALAND

WHO, FOLLOWING THE EXAMPLE OF HIS GREAT PREDECESSOR, THE LATE
SIR GEORGE GREY, HAS TAKEN SO LIVELY AND PRACTICAL AN
INTEREST IN THE WELFARE OF THE MAORIS AND
THEIR CLOSELY-RELATED NEIGHBOURS OF THE
VAST POLYNESIAN AREA, THIS BOOK
ON THE CAROLINE ISLANDS
IS VERY CORDIALLY
DEDICATED

CONTENTS

APPENDIX

LIST OF ILLUSTRATIONS

MAPS AND PLANS

PREFACE

THE period between the years 1890 and 1893 in Samoa was marked by civil war between the rival factions of Malietoa and Matafa, ending, as all the world knows, in the overthrow and deportation of the latter chief. A partisan feeling in the struggle, shared by me with Robert Louis Stevenson, my neighbour of Vailima, resulted in the extension of an intimacy with the Samoan people and their chiefs. It sprung, naturally enough, in the first place, from the interest I had always taken in their sports, and the assistance I was happy to afford them by distributing medicines in the outer districts during the epidemics of measles and influenza which unhappily carried off so many of the natives during these years. A keen interest in philology and kindred subjects (especially in connection with the Malayo-Polynesian peoples), dating from my college days and encouraged by the sympathetic counsels of the late Master of Balliol, could not well fail to take an active form under the stirring influence of the genial author of " A Footnote to History."

I entered fully into the romance of reef and palm, but a sense of work to be done banished effectually all thoughts of the *dolce far niente* so generally identified with the life of a settler in these isles of Eden. Deeming idleness a thing unrighteous, I spent three years in cultivating economic plants, mostly of the Eucalyptus order, for distribution amongst the natives. Supplies of seeds for this purpose were regularly sent me by the Forest Department of New South Wales, in return for which I consigned seed-packets of native trees and plants. Subsequently I disposed of my land to Stevenson, and on his advice, after election as a corresponding member of the Polynesian Society of New Zealand, I went further afield into Eastern Polynesia, where a somewhat lengthy stay in

Tahiti and the North and South Marquesas gave me a wider knowledge and a deeper interest in the customs, language and legends of the attractive people of these islands, now, alas ! fast disappearing.

Nor did my journeyings end here, for on my return to Sydney I met Louis Becke, the well-known writer of tales of the Pacific, who told me of an ancient island Venice shrouded in jungle, an enchanted region of archæology far away in the Sea of Small Islands, termed Micronesia by geographers. His theme was the story of a strange people scattered up and down the lonely atolls of the great Caroline archipelago, folk of a strange outlandish tongue, that promised rich results to the student of folk-lore and philology. It is of this people and this region that my story deals, and I must here say that even in this remote corner of the globe I found not virgin soil—a German had been there before me, an emissary of the firm of Godeffroy Bros. of Hamburg, by name J. S. Kubary. At the time I met him, he was engaged in collecting land-shells and specimens of birds (one species of ground-pigeon, a *Phlegœnas*, bears his name) ; and had already—in 1872—explored the mysterious island-city on the east coast of Ponape. To him I am indebted for the loan of his plan of the Metalanim ruins, of which I have availed myself, making a good many corrections in the names and a few in the charting of the island labyrinth, at the same time supplementing his account by the information given by the natives of the district and by an old American settler and his sons who accompanied me on my second and third visits to the spot. To many others, both native and European, I am deeply indebted for much valuable assistance, and their names occur more than once in the course of the story which I will not anticipate here.[1]

Before my first visit to Metalanim, Kubary promised to give me a full account later, so that I could have the

[1] Five interesting views of Yap Island have been very kindly supplied me by Admiral Cyprian Bridge, who visited these seas about 1884 in H.M.S. *Espiègle*.

satisfaction of working independently ; and on my return we had many interesting discussions together. Soon after my departure from Ponape in 1896, I received a letter at Yap telling me of Kubary's death, which occurred only two days after I had left, under very sad circumstances.

Those who would do work in Micronesian waters might well take example from the unobtrusive, painstaking work of this true man of science.

For many years in these remote lands he devoted a grand and tireless energy to clearing up problems which have troubled so many European scientists who, from an arm-chair in their studies at home, are sometimes inclined to settle offhand, with a few indifferent strokes of the pen, questions the weight of which they have only tested with a crooked finger. Only too often, those who have borne the burden on their shoulders are pushed aside into un-thanked oblivion. Those can sympathise best who have endured the scorching heats of the Line, the inclement rain-torrents of the wet season, fever and bad food, thirst and sleeplessness, the opposition of superstitious natives abroad and the indifference of men at home, such measure as the world metes out to the man who ventures to seek out new facts or new methods of arranging facts. Such men as Kubary during their life receive scant thanks, but their praise should be a grateful duty to all who honour pluck and enterprise. And though Kubary be no country-man of ours, Science knows no such narrow boundaries, such slender distinctions as race or birth-land, and bids us render honour to one of her most faithful servants whom the evil day found girt and harnessed to his task.

All honour to German scientists for their work in Pacific waters. And shall we, the English, sit by and dream whilst others are up and doing ?

F. W. C.

[Since these lines were in type Germany has taken over the Carolines for a sum of £800,000. It will be most interesting to see how she will develop the resources of these strange new lands, her latest acquisition.]

INTRODUCTION.

M R CHRISTIAN'S reason for asking me to prepare
an Introduction to his account of his experiences
and investigations in the Caroline Islands was, no doubt,
his knowledge of the fact that I happen to be one of the
few people who have visited those islands and who are at
this moment in England. It should be stated at once
that I fully understand how very slender a qualification
that is for undertaking the task which I have been
requested to perform. Indeed, so fully is this understood,
that a real reluctance to give any cause for being suspected
of a desire to pose as an authority on the subjects dealt
with by Mr Christian, was only overcome on its being
made apparent that a short preliminary discussion in
general terms, whilst it might not strengthen what he had
to say, would at the least not weaken it, although readers
will be likely to note the contrast between his prolonged
residence and deliberate inquiries in the places described
and my own more hurried visits and superficial observation. It is true that I have been to a large number of
South Sea Islands, and it follows, almost as a matter of
course, that the visit to each was a short one.

My service on, as we call it in the Navy, the Pacific
Station, dates back to 1855 ; and that on the Australian
Station—within the limits of which most of the South
Sea Islands lie—dates from 1859. On the latter station
I have served three times, and my most extended South
Sea cruises took place when I was a Captain in command
of one of H.M. ships, in the years 1882, 1883, and 1884.
Much of the water traversed was then imperfectly surveyed
or entirely unsurveyed ; the natives of many islands were
not friendly and had little knowledge of white men, and

the older " Labour Trade " was still being carried on. In
such circumstances a captain of a man-of-war had a great
deal too much to do to find any considerable amount of
time at his disposal to devote to subjects even as fascinating as the ethnology, the botany, or the zoology of the
archipelagos visited, had he, indeed, possessed the
requisite preliminary training. I paid two later visits
to the South Seas, when in command of the Australian
Station in 1895 and 1896. The cruise of the former year
embraced several different groups and many islands, some
of which were new to me. It was not possible, however,
to get as far as the Carolines, and therefore my knowledge
of that group is not nearly so recent as Mr Christian's.
I owe an apology to anyone who may read this for
dwelling in this way on what may seem personal matters,
but it is desirable that the reader should know the real
extent of the qualifications of the person who has con-
sented to address him.

Before leaving this subject altogether it may be
permissible to make a statement likely to have a wider
than a mere personal interest. During the last two cruises
mentioned the officers and men of the ship were received,
at every place at which we called, by the islanders—of
every stage of culture, from perfectly naked savagery to
Church membership—and by white men, when there were
any, with every demonstration of delight. Considering
that an important part of the duty of the squadron on the
station is to keep order in these out-of-the-way regions
and to engage in punitive expeditions against offending
tribes, it may be fairly claimed for the officers and men of
H.M. ships so employed during many years that such a
reception proves that they must have performed the arduous duties in question with a thoroughness and at the same
time a moderation in the highest degree creditable to
them. No apology is offered for making this statement
here. It is largely action such as has been just indicated
that has made it possible for travellers like Mr Christian

to move about many of the archipelagos of the Pacific Ocean with the freedom necessary to enable them to carry on their investigations. Moreover, as these parts of the world lie far beyond the " sphere of influence " of the war correspondent, nothing is known at home of the many displays of devotion and gallantry which have been the indispensable precursors of a state of affairs in which some of the fiercest savages in the world have become the trustworthy entertainers of peaceful men of science.

The friendly intercourse of naval officers and bluejackets with the islanders has been greatly assisted by the deep and wide-spread respect of the latter for the Queen. Her Majesty's name has been made known to many of them by the missionaries ; but I came across cases in which the knowledge must have been derived from others. On one of the Louisiades, where the people were so little used to white men fourteen years ago that they were frightened by the striking of a match, and put to flight by the report of a rifle, I found that the name of " Queen Victoreea " was quite familiar to them. To be recognised as one of Queen Victoreea's " white chiefs " was nearly always and everywhere to ensure a naval officer a friendly reception. Where the natives could make themselves intelligible to white visitors they frequently expressed warm regard and admiration for Her Majesty. They have an unfailing confidence in her desire to do them good. There was something inexpressively gratifying to an Englishman to notice this far-reaching effect of our Queen's beneficent character. In the Pacific it has been most advantageous to the Empire, as the native races generally are desirous of being brought under the sway of so kind and so just a monarch.

The reluctance, above alluded to, was, it must be owned, somewhat modified by a perception of the possibility, created by complying with Mr Christian's request, of inviting attention to the desirability, if not necessity, of investigations of the kind to which he has more particularly devoted himself. Paying visits, though short ones, to many islands, has at least the advantage of enabling the visitor to form an accurate estimate of the importance of studying that which, at any rate relatively to other things, has been studied but little, viz. the people. Few persons will be likely to dispute the assertion that far less attention has been paid to the manners, customs, language, institutions, and modes of thought of the inhabitants of the South Sea Islands than to the fauna, flora, and even the geology of their places of abode. The assertion holds good, though it may be objected that anthropological and ethnological observations were made by members of expeditions of discovery and exploration commanded by a Bougainville, a Cook, or a Wilkes. Passing observations, in great number and often of great value, were made, no doubt; but the trained students residing for long periods amongst the island people for the purpose of carrying out their investigations have been almost exclusively "naturalists" or geologists. We owe much of our knowledge of the south sea islanders themselves to missionaries; but their very calling put them out of sympathy with many native customs and institutions deserving of study; whilst the earlier missionaries, *i.e.* those most favoured by opportunity, were without the proper preliminary training.

There is ground for believing that men of science in Europe and America were alive to the desirability of obtaining more exact knowledge of the South Sea Island tribes and their ways. Their difficulty seems to have been to find a justification of the expense which the necessary investigations were likely to entail. If money were to be forthcoming, it must be for something that promised a return. Study of the botany, the zoology, or the mineralogy of Oceania might, indeed was expected to, result in the discovery of marketable commodities. Even now, as Mr Christian has probably found, it is well to combine, at least to a small extent, examination of the economic botany of an island with linguistic researches. Till lately, if not till this very moment, the general interest in the branches of science dealing with material was greater than in those which deal with man. The latter were, and perhaps still are, thought less worth attention by many of those who think about science at all. We may count with confidence upon greater interest being taken in the fortunes of an expedition to the Caroline Islands to prospect for gold or rubies, than in one to investigate the structure of the language or the history of the inhabitants ; and the greater interest in the former would not be confined to those who simply desire to add to their riches.

Yet a little reflection will suffice to make us doubt both the correctness and the durability of this attitude of mind. In the civilised world of to-day—which we may define as the world in which the men wear trousers and the women read novels—the number of pupils, irrespective of nationality, receiving a "general education," greatly exceeds the number of those who are being "specially" trained. The children of both sexes who are acquiring historical knowledge, though it be but a smattering, far outnumber those who are being taught "science," and still more those who are being instructed in any special branch of it. This means, in effect, the formation of a continuously reinforced body of readers in whom a preference for the perusal of narrative rather than "scientific" works has been implanted. The difference in the figures relating to demands for books on history, biography, and travel, and to demands for those on science—as shown in the reports of libraries—will furnish evidence corroborative of the above contention.

This preference, being in accordance with and representative of natural inclinations, promises to endure. We are really more desirous of knowing something about our fellow-men than about anything else. This justifies hesitation before accepting the conclusions of those who

assert that the British Empire will be maintained by the
establishment of " technical colleges " better than by
encouragement of the qualities which distinguished the
worthies who had a leading share in its formation. For a
long time to come there will be a more widely distributed
desire to read about Nelson or Clive than about volcanoes
or solar physics. This ought to be encouraging to men
who devote themselves to the study of the characteristics
of tribes in a world far removed from our own. These
students may hope for a larger and larger public. The
most influential section of that public may be respectfully
invited to note the advantages of which the studies in
question will make them the specially favoured recipients.
The section is composed of those who teach that widely
taught subject—history. In the South Seas they may
find producible living illustrations of the doctrines which
they occupy themselves in imparting to their pupils.
What a " cabinet of specimens " is to a professor of
mineralogy, what an " anatomical museum " is to a
professor of anatomy, the tribes of the South Sea Islands
may be to the professor of history, whether he teach from
a chair or by means of a printed book.

If only a small fraction of the time and intellectual
effort devoted to the investigation of obscure points in
the history of early Egypt, early Mesopotamia, early
Greece, or early Italy—or indeed of early Britain—had
been added to the little which has been devoted to South
Sea Island investigations of a similar kind, those points
would have been cleared up more easily. I will try to
support this opinion by evidence drawn from personal
experiences.

In one of the Marshall Islands there was a war, waged
for the recapture of a fugitive lady of rank. She and her
new consort were besieged by a force commanded, not by
a brother of her former spouse, but by her father. In that
warrior's camp was a grown-up daughter of the Micronesian
Helen. The latter's mature charms, like those of her

Argive prototype, were still powerful enough—so white observers thought—to furnish an excuse for hostilities as good as that made by the Trojan elders sitting on the tower by the Scæan gate. The chiefs on both sides were known to each other ; and between them there was a frequent interchange of compliments and abuse, such as passed between Tlepolemos and Sarpedon, or between Hector of the Glancing Helm and Diomedes. These were, however, merely accidental circumstances recalling incidents in a great poem.

What was of real historical interest was the mode in which the besiegers carried on the war. On the shore was drawn up a line of " hollow ships "—the great ocean-going canoes in which the fearless navigators of the Marshall group make long voyages. The besieging army, having disembarked, lay cantoned in rows of huts. The battlefield was the space between the cantonment and the beleaguered stronghold in which the runaway dame had taken refuge. The fleet was protected by a broad wall (τὸ ποιήσαντο νεῶν ὕπερ), and a trench which had been drawn round about. The belligerents were far from being mere savages. The leader of the besiegers was a chief of imposing stature, dignified manners, like all South Sea chiefs, and high intellectual gifts. Other chiefs were but little inferior to him. Whatever resemblance it may have borne to that which, perhaps, was waged for the destruction of Troy, this war reproduced scenes that must have been familiar, from personal observation or through tradition, to the composer of the Iliad. It therefore furnished a picture of a phase of life buried beneath many historical strata. It was like a fossil in a museum, to which the professor of geology sends the student who wishes to understand thoroughly the lecture just heard or the treatise just read.

In the Gilbert archipelago a little more than a dozen years ago the " Heroic Kingship " was in course of supersession by republican forms. In the more northern islands

of the group the king still existed ; in the others he had
disappeared.   In at least one island there was an am-
phictyony with every tendency to consolidate into a league
or federation.

In a second Marshall Island also there was a war.
White visitors on an errand of peace to one of the armies
—their object being at the first misunderstood—were
received by the whole force in battle array.   The warrior
in command took no part in, and indeed was not present
during, the subsequent negotiations.   It turned out on
inquiry that he was not a chief, but a commoner by birth,
whose valour and military skill had gained him the position of general.   The islanders, like the ancient Germans,
reges ex nobilitate, duces ex virtute sumunt.   This was
another proof that appointment to command on account
of personal ability rather than social rank was not—as
has been claimed somewhat pretentiously—an invention
of English radicals of the early Victorian period.   Ancient
German warriors and more modern South Sea islanders
at the same stage of culture metaphorically carried a
marshal's baton in their knapsacks long before even the
immortal principles of 1789 were heard of.

Acquaintance with several races of the South Seas will
tend to weaken the belief that certain institutions are
exclusively Aryan, as has been asserted—still less,
exclusively Teutonic.   *De minoribus rebus principes con-
sultant, de majoribus omnes*, though a concise, is an
accurate definition of the polity of more than one island
community.   The *comitatus* is known in the Pelew (Palao)
Islands.   There, it has peculiar features ; for instance, the
curious relations between the *comites* and the *hetaira* of
the chief, sanctioned by custom as long as the former
remain in the *cal-de-bekkel*.   Another practice attributed
to the ancient Germans — consecrated reservation of
particular areas—bears a strong likeness to the more
beneficent aspects of the *tàbu*, which is often adopted, on
the pretext of divine prohibition, to prevent unrestricted

access to fruit-bearing trees and cultivated plots. The traditional, perhaps historically warranted conception of the mediæval *Vehm-gericht*, as regards procedure, has a counterpart in the legalised regicide of the Pelew Islands. A secret tribunal condemns an unpopular king to death. A rude effigy of the doomed chief is carved on the bark of a particular tree. On seeing this—his courtiers eager to terminate the uncertainty as to the composition of the new household take care that he shall see it soon—the king learns his fate and, it is said, never tries to escape it. In the New Hebrides the *weregild* custom was, and in some parts still is, reproduced with considerable exactness. Fifteen years ago in southern New Guinea the unconscious imitation of the Corsican *vendetta* was, for all practical purposes, perfect.

The history of our own country might be elucidated by a variety of illustrations from the South Sea Islands. In many spots the descent of the inhabitants from immigrant sea-rovers is obvious. Estuaries, rivers, and creeks, are in the occupation of races quite distinct from the earlier residents who have been forced inland. If this does not exactly reproduce for us the conditions brought about by the successive expeditions of Hengest, of Ælle, and of Cerdic with their companions, it may, surely, be taken as illustrating what occurred in the more remote days when the Aryan Celts invaded the island in the occupation of primitive Euskarians. To have seen the settlements of certain tribes of the Pacific enables one to understand events of which we no more have written records than we have of the generation of the Permian fossils.

By observation of the islanders we may watch certain processes of great social and political importance. We may actually perceive the growth and evolution of classes, and even of ideas and principles. If anyone wants to see progress "from Status to Contract" in visible operation he should go to, say, Santa Cruz, which has just been brought under British administration. In half an ordinary lifetime it would be possible to note, as land, owing to the extension of trading settlements in the lowlands, became a marketable commodity, how chiefs of clans in some places can convert themselves into territorial magnates by the simple process of monopolising the *folkland*, or, if that name be objected to, the common property of the whole clan. It sharpens one's perception of the essential identity of human actions under similar conditions, when one sees in the Pacific also that the *ager publicus* tends towards concentration in the hands of patricians, and that amongst the commons the propriety of redistributing it rises, in time, to the rank of a political principle.

We can also observe how a missionary Church is received at first with wonder and submission by a population in a less forward state of culture ; how it grows powerful and, in comparison with even the foremost natives, wealthy ; how power and wealth breed a disposition to domineer ; and how a spirit of resistance to domineering methods arises and a belief in the justice and efficacy of secession is developed. There is little fanciful in discerning a parallel between contemporary conditions in the islands and those which, in this department of affairs, disclosed themselves in mediæval Europe. There have been moments when the white officials in remote archipelagoes must have thought that, after all, there was something to be said for Henry II.

It was not in the Congresses or Parliaments of the English-speaking nations that " stone-walling " or " obstruction " first originated. It was an established practice in the legislature of the Vaitupuans. Members of that body who were resolved not to allow their proposals to be " talked out " were provided with substantial wooden couches, on which they could take a nap and thus outstay the longest-winded orator or the most adroitly-arranged succession of obstructive motions. These couches, which had evidently been long in use, were shown to visitors sixteen years ago.

Several South Sea Island races are not now savage in any sense, except as to rarity of trousers and absence of novels, and never deserved that epithet in its sense of ferocious. There is no finer people on earth than the Tongans and the closely related and but slightly less vigorous Samoans. The physical beauty of both sexes —which attains its highest development amongst the Samoan women—is parallelled by their intellectual endowment. The grace of manner and general dignity of bearing, habitual with members of chiefly families, could not be surpassed in the most polished of European courts. The contrast in these respects between the natives of high birth and the proselytising and trading white men who come to " civilise " them cannot escape the notice of the least observant.

Where they have not been made the victims of deliberate and pertinacious corruption these people have shown a capacity for accepting our civilisation not inferior to that exhibited by the people who listened to the teaching of Augustine. The Tongans, till within the last year or two, showed that there was at least one constitutional monarchy that could prosper without a national debt. It does not require financial genius of a high order to enable you to discover that a young and inexperienced sovereign can be seduced easily into extravagant habits ; and—if you have the power of a great nation at your back and are sufficiently " detached " to have no scruples—though you may be but a tyro in finance, you can manage to convert private indebtedness into that of the nation and insist on liquidation in some form or other. The Tongans, it may be remarked, have a highly respectable political virtue not usually attributed to dark-skinned people by white men. They are as passionately attached to their independence as the Swiss or the Netherlanders ever were to theirs.

It is hoped that this rapid survey of South Sea affairs will at the least help to make it seem likely that they will prove interesting enough to justify efforts to widen our knowledge of them. One cannot help thinking how full and trustworthy the survey might have been had it been carried out, in a leisurely manner, by a trained expert instead of by a hurried observer with plenty of other and more urgent work on his hands. It may be admitted that to have been amongst the islanders, even the more savage of them, begets a liking for them. There is no unworthy prejudice in the longing that their good points may be made more generally known. To have been in the South Seas is apt to stimulate mental reaction against the complacent self-sufficiency of the modern view that the eighteenth century laudation of the " state of nature" was an unmitigated absurdity. There is much that is most attractive in the kindly communism of the island tribes, and not a little that is economically sound. When a civilised nation takes over the administration of some group of islands, there is ingratitude, as well as impolicy, in ignoring the fact that the institutions of the natives have provided the new government with a ready-made system of poor relief. The question of old age pensions had been settled by the islanders long before white men came amongst them. It would be interesting to be informed by authorities on economics where co-operative agriculture has reached a more efficient development than it has in some South Sea Islands. A general recognition of the true qualities of the people may ward off from them many ills. To even a callous heart there must be something shocking in the case of the gracious, kindly, and intelligent Samoans serving as the shuttle-cocks of rival gangs of money-makers in a hurry to grow rich. Belisarius begging for an *obolus* was not a more piteous spectacle than Malietoa Laupepa, with his seven hundred years of chiefly pedigree, accepting a dole of salted pork.

In that subject which Mr Christian has made his special study, viz. language, the Pacific Islands offer a fine field for investigation. The evolution of dialects, and, perhaps, of distinct languages, can be followed as we follow an

experiment in a laboratory.   On Mallicolo (Malekula) and
Espiritu Santo of the New Hebrides one could measure
the extent of the separation between adjacent but mutually
hostile villages by the varying pronunciation of personal
names which were common to all.

If we may regard the South Sea Islands as a museum
of living specimens to which students in many branches of
learning may resort in order to fortify their conclusions
and improve their knowledge, we must remember that it
is a museum which will not be open long.   The island
races are diminishing and, besides, are rapidly changing
under the influence of "civilisation."   The geology of
Oceania, whether examined now or a hundred years hence,
will yield the same results.   The greatest disaster that
can be caused by postponement is the disappointment of
someone with a theory who is in a hurry to test it.   Even
the fauna and the flora will have changed but little in a
century, and in easily discernible ways.   In a much
shorter time the people will have died out or have been
transformed into weak and ineffective copies of white
originals.   Therefore the student who wishes to do what
Mr Christian has done, and carry out his inquiries on the
spot, had better be quick about it.   The operation will
help to enlarge our knowledge of the natives and their
ways, and can hardly fail to benefit the Empire.

The formation of the British Empire in its wide
dominion over alien races was made possible by —
amongst others—two things.   The great men who were
the immediate agents of expansion possessed a high
capacity for understanding the native populations with
which they came in contact.   Amongst the British
people at home the trick of fussy and desultory inter-
ference with that of which they know nothing had not
developed into a serious malady.   The times are changed.
Nevertheless increased knowledge may counteract the
most menacing consequences of the disease.

There are a few particular points to which it may not

be impertinent to allude. I have ventured to form the opinion that the great Ponape and Kusaie ruins, explored by Mr Christian, are not those of buildings erected by the races at present inhabiting the islands. The opinion, I find, is not approved by persons of high authority. Whether the ancestors of the present Ponapeans or an earlier people built the great island Venice at Metalanim, it will not, I expect, be denied that the builders must have vastly out-numbered the existing population. The same may be said of every Pacific island on which prehistoric remains are found. Now, a tradition of a larger population in early times is very common in the South Seas ; and there is evidence beyond that supplied by the ruins to support it. That the native population is diminishing—equally under conditions of coddling and neglect—is certain. There is, however, nothing to show that the actual rate of decrease is greater than, or even as great as, that of former ages. Indeed it is reasonable to suppose that the natives had been moving rapidly towards extinction before the white man appeared on the scene. If the great ruins were the work of a pre-existing people it would strengthen the belief—which is quite tenable if they were not—that the dying-out is really independent of the white man's action. Consequently, we may console ourselves with the reflection that, however sorely we may have sinned against them, we are not responsible for the extinction of the island races of the Pacific.

It is impossible to think of the South Sea Islands without thinking of missionaries. They have played a great part there ; or, at any rate, have had the good fortune of telling the story of it themselves. For those who hold that it is a more sacred duty to evangelise some tens of thousands of islanders than some hundreds of thousands of dwellers in certain quarters of the great cities of the United Kingdom and the Australasian colonies, this must have been a comfort. We are often ready to assume that a work must be good because those who do it are men of

noble spirit and unselfish practice.   Intimacy with some
of the British missionaries of all the churches cannot fail
to raise one's estimate of one's fellow-men.   I have heard
many charges brought by laymen against missionaries, of
improper trading or impure life.   In not one single case
which I was able to investigate was there any truth in the
accusations.   I have *heard* of one bad case ; but the
accusers and judges in that were missionaries themselves.
Though the British missionaries of one sect will talk very
fully of the proceedings of those of another, I never heard
from any of them a single expression of jealousy or ill-
feeling.   On the contrary, they seemed to take a friendly
interest in each other's success.   All the same, any really
open-minded visitor to the islands will soon discover that
other white men who are too seldom remembered have
also exercised a beneficent influence amongst them.   The
civilisation of the islanders—Europeanisation would be
more accurate—has not been the work of the missionaries
alone.   The white trader has had no insignificant share
in it.

Those who believe that the " beach-comber," or the
copra-trader, of the South Seas is necessarily a scoundrel,
err grievously.   There is, proportionately to their numbers,
as much honesty, sobriety, and energy amongst the traders
as amongst any other body of business men.   They have
their black sheep, no doubt ; let the community which
has none throw at them the first stone !

Thursday Island is so often the starting place for
visitors to the South Seas that it cannot properly be
passed without mention.   I have occasionally found that
it is given—in my opinion most undeservedly—a bad
character.   It *has* a noisy quarter in which there is much
debauchery.   Anyone who expresses horror at this is invited to inspect certain waterside parts of Liverpool or
Antwerp before he formulates his indictment.   At one of
my visits to Thursday Island nearly all the residents were
good enough to accept an invitation to come on board the

flag-ship. What they thought of it I cannot say; I only know that their company gave me unalloyed pleasure. The Thursday Island community is, in my opinion, a most creditable one. The good Australian tradition of tolerating no lawlessness in newly formed and hastily populated settlements has been respected there as well as in many a mining " rush." Whilst nothing would induce me to cross a London Park after 10 p.m., I would readily walk from one end of Thursday Island to the other at any hour.

There is no need for me to dwell upon the romantic side of life in the South Seas. That side of it has been illustrated by such masters as Byron, Melville, R. L. Stevenson, most conspicuously, and Louis Becke.

I have now only to leave Mr Christian to tell his story. I apologise for having stood so long between him and his readers, and may add that I have discovered, not from information volunteered by him, that the whole cost of his expedition has been defrayed by himself; and that his only inducement has been a disinterested love of the studies to which he has devoted so much time and so much labour.

CYPRIAN A. G. BRIDGE.

LONDON, 21st March 1899.

GENERAL SKETCH OF THE CAROLINES

SPANISH MICRONESIA

SPANISH Micronesia, according to the treaty made with Germany in 1885, lies between the Equatorial line on the south and the eleventh northern parallel, and between 139° and 170° E. longitude.[1] The great island of New Guinea lies about 1000 miles to the southward. A long chain of 652 islands lie scattered over this wide stretch of sea, some 1400 miles in length. The inhabitants number some 50,000, a combination of the Black, the Brown, and the Yellow races. The Caroline archipelago contains thirty-six minor groups. We will take the more important of these one by one from west to east.

The Pelew group, lying on the western frontier of the Carolines, contains about two hundred islands, of which Bab-el-Thaob is the largest. The population of the Pelews is considerably over 3000. The language is the harshest and most impossible of all the Malayan dialects. The principal products are turtle-shell, copra or dried cocoanut kernel, and bêche-de-mer or dried sea-slugs. In the Chinese markets bêche-de-mer brings as much as £80 sterling per ton. Copra in European markets fetches about £25 per ton. It yields a capital oil, and the crushed residue furnishes a grand cattle-cake and is used as a basis for sweetmeats and confectionery.

Trouble is always going on between the various tribes, and a firm hand is needed to keep things in order. Captain Butron of the Spanish cruiser *Velasco* (lost in the late naval battle at Manilla), who visited the group in 1885, gives these natives a good name. Captain

[1] Since these lines were in type, Spanish Micronesia is no more.

17

O'Keefe, of Yap, who knows the Pelews very well, describes the people as regular pirates. In olden time there was great commercial activity in the Western Carolines. The Yap and Pelew natives used to go on long voyages of trading and conquest. The island of Babelthoab is rich in good timber, and produces all the tropical fruits. On the hillside are some interesting lines of ancient fortifications, which I hope to explore next winter.

Alligators, called *Gaiutsch* or *Aius*, are found in some of the creeks, and a peculiar kind of horned frog or *Cerastes* in the valleys of the interior ; this they call *Thagathaguk*. There are two kinds of snakes [*Bersoiok* and *Ngús*], some scorpions and centipedes. On the plateaus there is plenty of good pasture for horses and cattle. Goats are plentiful and very destructive to the breadfruit-trees ; they break into a plantation, gnaw the bark away in a circle, and then the tree dies, and so does the goat when he is caught ! There is no Spanish garrison or mission school or trading station in the Pelews. Nothing is done at all to show that these islands belong to Spain. A fringing reef, fifty-three miles long from north to south, surrounds the Pelews—a menace to navigation which has destroyed many a China-bound vessel. I have lately heard that the Spaniards are now determined to sell the Pelews, the Mariannes, and the Carolines to some foreign Power, but neither America, Great Britain, nor Japan need apply—and these the very nations best of all qualified for colonising these fierce and intractable islanders. In her business relations in Pacific islands Great Britain would do well to take heed of the saying of Horace, "*Tarde venientibus ossa*"—"Those who come late to dinner only get bones."[1]

Three hundred miles north-east of the Pelews lies Yap, surrounded by a coral reef thirty-five miles long and five broad. There are hardly any rivulets on the island, but inland are extensive swamps laid out in plantations of a

---

[1] Recent events have proved these words only too true.

water taro, the *Colocasia* of the Nile valley. The island
is full of relics of a vanished civilisation—embankments
and terraces, sites of ancient cultivation, and solid roads
neatly paved with regular stone blocks, ancient stone
platforms and graves, and enormous council lodges of
quaint design, with high gables and lofty carved pillars.
The ruins of ancient stone fish-weirs fill the lagoon between
the reef and the shore, making navigation a most difficult
matter, and calling forth many most unkind remarks from
trading skippers. The fruits of the soil are sweet potatoes,
yams, of which there is a great variety, taro, mammee
apples or papaw, pineapples, water-melons, custard-apples,
bananas, sugar-cane, breadfruit, and the tropical almond.
Copra, that is, cocoanut kernel chipped up, sun-dried, and
put into sacks, is largely exported, mostly through the
German traders, who have spent a great deal of money
and labour here for the last thirty years. A varnish nut
grows here which should give good results. The principal
timber tree is the *Voi*, with a leaf like that of a magnolia
and in the wood resembling mahogany. Tomil harbour
on the East coast is the chief port ; here is the European
settlement and a small garrison of Manilla soldiers, and the
Spanish governor of the Western Carolines resides here
with a few Spanish officers and officials. There are about
a dozen European traders, mostly Germans.

Yap has beautiful scenery ; the groves of bamboo,
croton, cocoanut and areca palms are magnificent.
Huge green and yellow tree-lizards, called *Galúf*, are
found in the bush, and the nights are brilliant with fire-
flies glittering in and out of the woods like showers of
golden sparks. There are very few birds, however, very
few cattle, and no horses on the island.

The Uluthi or Mackenzie group lies a little to the
northward of Yap. Mokomok or Arrowroot island is the
chief port and trading place, with a great trade in copra.
The natives have from ancient times been subject to Yap,
and they come down every February to pay their tribute.

They are peaceful and law-abiding, a great contrast to some of the people farther to the eastward. The next island of importance is Uleai. Raur is the trading depôt of this group, exporting great quantities of copra, pearl-shell, and bêche-de-mer. The language contains many traces of later Malayan, probably derived from trading vessels from Java, Timor, and Sumatra, and piratical praus from Borneo and the Sulus. All the central Caroline islanders have very similar traditions, customs, and language. In olden days they were great navigators, guiding their way fearlessly by a most accurate knowledge of the stars and ocean currents. When the Spaniards conquered the Mariannes about three hundred years ago, a great number of the Chamorro or natives of the soil fled to Uleai and Lamotrek to avoid forced conversion and slavery. I will give an instance of the great naval enterprise about the beginning of this century of the natives in this part of the Carolines. The Uleai folk and their neighbours used regularly to assemble at Lamotrek every February with eighteen or twenty great canoes. From thence they sailed to Guam, a distance of some five hundred miles, where they would stay until April or May and then return, fearing the southwest monsoon.

The two next Caroline groups, Hall and Enderby, are only to be visited with great precautions. The islands Pulo-Wat and Pulo-Suk are nothing better than pirate strongholds. It would be well for an English or American man-of-war to visit here, and warn the local chiefs against cutting off peaceful trading vessels in their lagoon. They have no respect at all for the red and yellow flag, for the Spanish have taken little or no notice of several murders committed here of late years. The next group is called Ruk, from the name of the highest basaltic island in the chain. It is also called Hogolu.[1] The group consists of

---

[1] The natives call Ruk " *Te-Fan*," " *The* Land," just as the Gilbert Islanders style their little sun-scorched coral atolls " *Te Aba*."
The island-name *Wap* or *Yap* in the Western Carolines has the same

about seventy islands of basalt and coral lying in the middle of a lagoon about one hundred and forty miles round.   There is a fine depth of water and good anchorage for vessels of large draft.   There is a great annual output of copra, mostly carried off to Europe in German or Norwegian barques.   Pearl-shell, turtle-shell, and bêche-de-mer are very abundant.   Here they make from the grated root of the wild ginger an orange-coloured cosmetic (*Taik*) in little cones, which are readily exchanged all over the Caroline group.   There are thirty Japanese traders in Hogolu lagoon, and a Hamburg trading firm sends many vessels every year to fill up with copra.   Figures are sometimes better than photographs, so for those interested in statistics I will say that the annual export of copra from the Caroline group averages four million pounds weight, of which Yap and Hogolu between them yield more than half.   Hogolu has a population of about ten thousand, composed of two distinct races.   The hill tribes are dark in colour and the people on the coast light reddish-brown.   There is generally some small civil war on hand, and the national game of head-hunting has interfered a great deal with business, for the Spanish let the islanders do just as they like.   The natives of Ruk and of the neighbouring group of the Mortlocks have a curious custom, observed also in the Visayas of the southern Philippines, among the ancient Incas of Peru, and the Polynesians of Easter island, of piercing the lower lobe of the ear, loading it with heavy ornaments and causing it to expand downwards to an enormous size. The Mortlocks consist of three groups, Lukunor, Satoan, and Etal, containing in all ninety-eight islands.   The population is about two thousand.   The Germans take

---

primitive meaning.   The element *Pon, Fan, Fal* or *Far* enters frequently into the names of Caroline Islands.   *Cf.* Ponatik, Fanadik, Faralap, Ponapei, Fanupei ;—and is cognate with Fijian Vanua, Malay Benua, and with Polynesian Fanua, Fenua, Honua, Whenua.   In Gaelic we find *Fonn* = earth : land, and in Sanskrit *Bonn* = id.

great pains to develop the copra industry here.   Of great interest to philologists is the existence of a pure Polynesian dialect upon two little island groups named Kap-en-Mail-ang and Nukuoro.   These lie to the south-east of the Mortlocks.   The language is an antique form, combining the phonesis of the Samoan and the Maori, spoken about three thousand miles away down in the South Pacific. I collected about five hundred words of the Nukuoro dialect.

The next group to the eastward is that of Ponape or Seniavin, with the neighbouring minor groups of Ant, Pakin, and Ngatik, of which more anon.   The islands in the Ponape lagoon are somewhat thinly populated, and serve mainly as fishing stations.   The islet of Mutakaloch, off the Metalanim coast, is remarkable for its cellular basalt formation ;   whilst near Kapara, which lies on the edge of the barrier reef on the south-west coast, is seen the pheno-menon of a spring of fresh water welling up through the coral.

Farther east from Ponape are the Mokil (or Duperrey), the Pingelap (or M'Caskill), and the Kusaie groups, the easternmost outpost of the Spanish dominions.   In con-clusion, I may express my opinion that England may one day have a great deal to do with the islands Kusaie and Ponape, the latter of which really deserves the name of the garden of Micronesia.   I may be pardoned for saying that our Government at home has of late years shown itself somewhat indifferent to events in the South Seas. The French and the Germans are pushing their interests in Pacific waters, whilst we stand still.   Even the Nor-wegians are busy there, and we look tamely on and do nothing.   Let us wake from this strange torpor like men of business and try what we can do.   Surely where French, Germans, and Norwegians can make money, we can make money too !

I will refer briefly to the principal explorers who have visited these waters.

On the 6th March, 1521, the illustrious navigator Magellan discovered the Mariannes to which he gave the name Ladrones ; from thence, he went on and discovered the Philippine group, and on the 27th April of the same year was murdered by the natives on the island of Mactan.

In 1526, Alonzo de Salazar discovered one of the islands of the Marshall group.

In 1528, Alvaro de Saavedra discovered the Uluthi or Mackenzie group, and took possession of them in the name of Spain. A little later he sailed into the wide lagoon of Hogolu, or Ruk, and in the September of the next year he found Ualan, or Kusaie. After him Villa-lobos and Legaspi, on their way to the Philippines from New Spain, made fresh discoveries in these waters, of which Yap was the most important.

In 1595, the famous sea-captain Quirós fell in with Ngatik, to the south of Ponape, which he called Los Valientes, from the warlike character of the natives he found there. In 1686, a small island to the south of the Mariannes was called Carolina, and from this little island the name became applied to the whole group. A series of expeditions of a religious character followed the Spanish discoveries in these seas. Attempts to introduce the Catholic faith on Sonsorol and the Enderby group, known as Los Martires, failed disastrously, ending in the death of the missionaries who conducted them, through the cowardice and incompetence of the captain who held temporal command. Other Spanish vessels, no doubt, on the course from Acapulco to the Philippines, may have fallen in with some of the Caroline Islands or been wrecked on some of the uncharted reefs. Of these we have no record save the grim story on the south coast of Ponape, of iron men who came up out of the sea and fought with the men of Kiti, until overwhelmed with sling-stones and spear-thrusts. A voyager of note in Micronesia was Kotzebue, who, with the famous Chamisso, poet, dramatist, and philologist, visited the Marshalls, the Mariannes, and a portion of the Carolines in 1815. After 1819, Lutke, Freycinet, Duperrey, and Dumont D'Urville, visited these regions. In 1839, an English man-of-war, the *Larne*, coasted around Ponape and entered Kiti harbour. A number of geographical observations and soundings were taken, upon which our present Admiralty chart is based. Most unfortunately, nearly all the native names have been cruelly mangled, and have become a meaningless jargon.

Ever since 1830 the island has been repeatedly visited by the New England and New Bedford whalers, who gave the natives little cause indeed to respect the white man. During the Civil War in America a Confederate cruiser, the *Shenandoah*, caught several of these northern craft in Chokach harbour, and burnt them to the water's edge. About 1850 the American Methodist Mission was established, and recent history may be summarised as follows :—

ABSTRACT OF HISTORY OF SPANISH OCCUPATION.

August 1885.—The gunboat *Iltis* raises the German flag at Yap. Excitement at Madrid. German Consulate assaulted. The matter referred to the Pope who pronounces in favour of Spain.

July 27, 1886.—Spanish flag raised at Ascension Bay in Ponape.

April 19, 1887.—Founding of the Colony of Santiago, and formal proclamation of Spanish rule at Ascension Bay.

April 24, 1887.—Founding of the Catholic Mission station in Kiti, followed by bickerings between the Methodist missionaries from Boston and the Capuchin priests.

June 16, 1887.—Mr Doane, the head of the Methodist Mission, deported to Manilla.

July 1, 1887.—Massacre of a detachment of Manilla soldiers under Ensign Martinez on the Island of Chokach, followed by a general native rising and the capture of the Spanish fort and the slaughter of Senor Posadillo, the Governor, and some seventy of the defenders.

October 31, 1887.—Arrival of punitive expedition. The new Governor, Senor Cadarso, proclaims a general amnesty.

1888 and 1889.—Interval of peace.

June 25, 1890.—Massacre of Lieut. Porras and his party of fifty-four soldiers employed on the military road at Oa on the east coast.

June 29, 1890.—Wreck of Mr J. C. Dewar's yacht, the *Nyanza*, on the reefs off the Mant Islands on the north coast.

September 1, 1890.—Arrival of relief expedition from Manilla under Colonel Gutierrez Soto.

September 12, 13, and 14, 1890.—Bombardment of the Metalanim coast. Landing of troops on Tomun. Burning of native houses and King Paul's residence destroyed. Abortive overland march of Spanish troops across the U highlands from the Colony and their return.

September 16, 1890.—Landing of Spanish at Tolopuel in Metalanim harbour. Colonel Soto killed.

September 19, 1890.—Attack upon Oa from the sea. The position brilliantly carried by the Spanish, but with severe loss. Death of Chaulik, one of the leading rebel chiefs of the League.

October 15, 1890.—Second desultory bombardment of the Metalanim coast by the *Ulloa*. Arrival of the American corvette *Alliance*, demanding compensation for the proposed expulsion of their missionaries, and obtaining 17,000 gold dollars, leaving on 2nd November, and conducting Mr Rand and his Methodist colleagues to the Island of Kusaie.

November 22 and 23, 1890.—Hard fighting at the
stockade of Ketam in the Metalanim district.
The position captured by the Spanish at the
sacrifice of a third of their force.

A trifling skirmish on the Chapalap River and a few
assassinations of stray Manilla soldiers wandering outside
the Colony, varied the monotony of affairs until the
arrival of Don Jose Pidal in 1894. His conciliatory
policy seemed successful, and the natives regretted his
departure in 1896. His successor, Don Miguel Velasco,
a distinguished naval officer, who it is to be feared perished
in the recently reported massacre, was popular alike
amongst Europeans and natives. The massacre was
doubtless caused by the imprisonment of Henry Nanapei
of Ronkiti, one of the principal chiefs, who held strong
American sympathies, and was head of the Protestant
Mission schools established in his district. Perhaps if the
Carolines are handed over to Germany, as Spain seems
disposed to do, we shall hear less of this *odium theologicum*
which elsewhere has proved such a firebrand to the world,
and here has brought about such lamentable waste of life
and treasure, and cruel humiliations to Spain.

LAGOON AND FORESHORE OF MILLE, MARSHALL ISLANDS

UCHENTAU, OUR CAMPING-PLACE IN METALANIM

PART I

CHAPTER I

SYDNEY TO HONG KONG

EMBARKING on the S.S. *Menmuir* we start from Sydney on a lovely evening, September 3rd, 1895, passing Seal Rocks above Newcastle, the bane of our ill-fated predecessor the *Catterthun*. A haze hung over the land for the weather had been very dry, and frequent bush-fires were torching up on our left. On the evening of September 5th we anchored in Moreton Bay to pick up some passengers from Brisbane. Next night we sighted Capricorn Light, and the 7th found us moored in a dense fog off the pilot station in Keppel Bay, where by and by we receive cargo from Rockhampton and a medley of Chinese passengers. We leave about noon and pass numerous barren islets that afternoon, and the morning of the 9th found us lying off Townsville. We raised Cape Grafton that afternoon, sighting Rocky Island about daylight, and anchoring off Cooktown about nine o'clock, where we took on board a cargo of *bêche-de-mer*.

Cooktown with her mangrove belt is left behind us. Several low islands lie to seaward, flat as the islets of Tonga or the Low Archipelago without their redeeming belt of graceful palms. The sea is calm as a mill-pond, and the sky heavy with smoke from the bush-fires raging along that desolate coast—the domain of savage hunting and fishing tribes which the white man has not yet ousted from their homes. But their turn will come by and by, and the surviving blacks will follow their predecessors as sure as the night the day.

Our dear old captain Hugh Craig is the life and soul

27

of our merry bachelor party. Day after day we creep northward, gliding over a glassy sea, our Lotus eaters' monotony only broken by sumptuous meals served by noiseless and discreet Celestials in airy attire. Evening after evening, many a noble rubber of whist is played out on deck with the Southern Cross and the myriad lamps of the sky gleaming overhead ; with the kindly breezes of starry-kirtled night playing softly round us, as with rhythmic beat of clanging machinery, the great boat marches on with a fiery trail of phosphorescent sparkles in her train.

On the evening of the ninth day out we anchor off the mouth of the famous Torres Straits, so as to steam through the jaws of the narrow and perilous Albany Pass with the morning light. At dawn a most picturesque scene unfolds itself. We are moving through a channel not above eighty yards wide, to right and to left we catch fleeting glimpses of pretty little sandy bays opening out here and there, backed by clumps of cocoanut palms, re-calling bits of scenery from the South Seas. On either side shelves and ledges of rock stand out in bold relief, while in the background stretches a wild bushland covered thickly with low scrub and dotted pillars of grass-tree. One picturesque foreland is covered with tall conical, not to say comical mounds, the mud-castles of the Termites or white ants. After a while the northern horizon is left clear, save for three or four small islands on the New Guinea side, but the great island itself lies too far off to view. We sight the residence of Mr J., an extensive landholder and J.P. of the district, a man of mark, and a stern man to the marauding savages who cluster round the lonely little settlement. This portion of Australia—all around the Gulf of Carpentaria—swarms with fierce and warlike blacks, tinged with a strong racial admixture from Malay pirates, trepang-gatherers, Papuan war-parties, and fleets of dugong fishers from South New Guinea, who have haunted these coasts for many a hundred years.

The seas hereabouts are famous for *bêche-de-mer* and pearl-shell, and Mr J. has several luggers in hand for this service, which is one of considerable adventure and hardship. The place is called Somerset, and was formerly the residence of the local magistrate appointed by the Government, who has now been removed to Thursday Island. The waterway round us simply bristles with hidden reefs and dangerous sandbanks. Later on we pass the four year old wreck of the *Volga*, a Newcastle collier of some 2000 tons, and soon after slip by the *Mecca* reefs (so called from the China steamer wrecked here thirteen years ago), and now Thursday Island and its mosquito fleet of pearling luggers and *bêche-de-mer* craft comes into sight as we round a curve and run alongside the William Fairbairn hulk, where we moor. Presently three or four shoreboats manned by Cingalese boatmen come alongside to take our party ashore.

The island is a barren sandy spot, and the township a miserable collection of tumbledown shanties and stores faced with shaky verandahs and roofed with corrugated iron, which with the fiery heat beating down overhead makes the interior a positive furnace, creating a hell-like heat and thirst, which many of the settlers appropriately quench with huge draughts of spirits that might have come out of Beelzebub's own private still. Here indeed is a wonderful mixture of races for poet, painter, or artist of an unhealthy turn of mind. Crapulous, unwashed white men with low foreheads and cunning shifty eyes, Cingalese, Malays, Papuans, Chinamen, Portuguese, African and Australian niggers, and half-castes of all sorts of lovely dissolving shades of white, dirty brown, sooty black and sickly yellow, pullulating together like vermin in the mud-honey of drink, opium, and filth, the paradise of the Australian larrikin and the type of native he influences. Picture the estimable Captain Randall in Stevenson's " Beach of Falesa," and you will get a notion of the white loafer of Thursday Island. A class of men

unreasonably large in number here, who must be a sad
annoyance to their sober and respectable neighbours. The
landscape is slightly redeemed by a few melancholy looking cocoanut palms and pandanus clumps, with here and
there a wilted and sickly pawpaw tree looking as if ashamed
of its surroundings. On every hand there are plenty of
vacant allotments covered with tall stalks of dried-up
vegetation awaiting a stray lucifer or spark from the pipe
of some careless wayfarer to break out into a glorious
conflagration of purifying flame, and make a bonfire of
this evil-smelling rookery. A few dull-eyed storekeepers
loll around on rickety benches grumbling at bad times,
and praying for some customer to come along, who when
he does come gets a taste of insolence for giving them the
trouble of getting up. Any remonstrance is answered by
a shower of invectives, which must keep the recording
angel very busy for the next few minutes. A tempting
curio-assortment lies arrayed in the windows of one shop
—but, alas, the shutters are down. The proprietor is
away " on the tangle," as a wild-eyed beach-comber passing by curtly informs us.

One of our party badly wanting a shave is rash enough
to approach a tumble-down barber's shop—one look at
the filthy interior, and the too sanguine customer flees in
horror. By-and-bye we come to a shop with heaps of
useful though not exactly ornamental household crockery
piled up in front. This is the " Hall of Arts," the title
set forth in bright blue letters on a green ground. By
the side of a broken window a flaring red-and-yellow
poster announces the production of a *Screaming Farce*—
a relic of a party of last month's strolling players. On
the hill overlooking the centre of the township are the
Barracks, wherein some fifty men of the Permanent Ar-
tillery are stationed—stalwart makers of roads, clearers of
bush, suppliers of water, and pioneers of civilisation generally, and preservers of law and order. Let us hope that
some years of Purgatory may be remitted them for doing

their duty amidst such unpleasant surroundings—and men say they perform it well. Lo! the dingy street is lighted up by a bright apparition of two neat little Japanese *musumés* patrolling in their national garb—a harmony in brown, blue and grey—under paper umbrellas, a pair of human busy bees from the hive, the other side of the jetty where lies the Japanese quarter. Now these Japanese have certainly established a solid foothold in Thursday Island. Possibly their nattiness, their thrift and superior business ability, account for the bitter hatred of a certain section of the white population towards them. Many of the settlers look upon them as dangerous rivals, and would gladly over-reach or terrorise these bright and energetic little people. But the resident is a firm and a just man, and a stern repressor of the lawless and rowdy element, and he does not fight alone. Therefore the dogs in the manger are allowed to growl and bark a little, but, when they take to biting, measures are taken to muzzle them.

We climbed the hill and lunched at an odd little hotel on top where there were a number of pet animals. After admiring a stuffed alligator fourteen feet long, and supplying the whisky-drinking baboon with sundry glasses of Scotch and Irish to his infinite relish, we descended and made our way back to the steamer. We found them hoisting on board quantities of sandal-wood brought down in some of the small schooners manned by crews of mixed nationality, which trade between Thursday Island and the southern districts of New Guinea.

The capture of a shovel-headed shark over nine feet in length caused some excitement. He was hoisted in over the side, and all but fell into the sheep pen, much to the dismay of the woolly bleaters, and his evil life was cut short by repeated slashes over the tail from the hatchet of the Chinese cook. We remained at our moorings overnight, and daybreak sent us ploughing across the Gulf of Carpentaria, with a smooth sea, a cloudless sky, and a pleasant breeze to waft us towards the magic East.

On the 15th we sighted New Year's Island and passed Cape Croker, anchoring off Cape Don for the night. Next day we passed Cape Keith, and sighted King's Table in the afternoon, reaching Port Darwin about two hours before sunset.

The town is situated on a plateau, reached by a series of steps leading up the hillside from the end of a long jetty which stretches out seaward about four hundred yards. At spring tide the rise is twenty-seven feet, which necessitates high and stout supports. The posts are suffering greatly from the attacks of the borer-worm, that pest of tropical seas. It may console mariners to know that the Board of Works is seriously contemplating the construction of a new wharf with solid iron cylinders. In twenty or thirty years the much-boasted innovation may be an accomplished fact. In the meantime sea-captains may grutch and grumble to their hearts' content.

The town consists of the usual cluster of four or five score houses, a distant vision of flat-topped roofs capped with the inevitable corrugated iron, shimmering like burnished copper in the glare of the evening sun. On a closer view, however, some of the houses of the better sort appear lying back in little gardens of their own, fronted by spacious verandahs with shades of split bamboo-cane, and embowered with masses of roses and climbing creepers, conspicuous amongst which are the rich purple leafy-petaled blossoms of the Bougainvillea and the blue and white bells of the convolvulus major. Here and there the eye rests pleasantly upon clumps of crotons, and masses of arum-lily and caladium. There is a Post Office lying back in a trim shrubbery; and two Banks, one of stone, one of wood, supply the monetary needs of the townsfolk. In company with Messrs Fœlsche and Holtze we drove out next day to visit the Botanical Gardens, which lie about three miles out of town a little way past Shell Bay, where a friendly tribe of neighbouring blacks are encamped. The former of our entertainers.

is the Police Magistrate of the district, who has contributed much interesting knowledge to scientific journals concerning the languages and customs of the native races of the Northern Territory. Mr Holtze is Curator of the Gardens, and is a great botanical enthusiast. On reaching the scene of his labours the first thing that strikes one is a grove of cocoanut palms only seven years old but showing vigorous growth. Clumps of feathery bamboo and sturdy bananas give a genuine South Sea Island aspect to the scene. There is quite a cosmopolitan gathering of palms. The prickly-palm of Queensland, the cabbage palm and the oil palm from Africa, the fan palm of the Marquesas, the areca palm of India and the Philippines, the date palm from Arabia and Egypt, are all here. Huge banyan trees tower around, spreading wide their aerial root-sprays, their tresses of small leaf nodding and whispering in the sway of the free ocean breezes. Strange shrubs and trees from the Moluccas confront us, the cinnamon, the Malay or jamboo apple, the jackfruit, the gardenia, the cycas and the freycinetia. The Australian flora is well represented. Here flourish the red gum, blue gum, spotted gum, stringy bark, lemon gum, black-butt, apple tree, sheoak, black wattle and golden wattle.

The site of the gardens was heavily timbered in former times and now green saplings are everywhere shooting up from the boles of the felled giants of the forest. I stayed to lunch at Holtze's invitation, and thus met two ardent cullers of herbs. Finally it was agreed that he should furnish me with a number of seed-packets and that I should make a collection of assorted Micronesian seeds, always giving economic trees and plants the preference. In return he promised me a number of North Australian curios and undertook to minutely tabulate and record the species and genera of plants raised from the aforesaid collection of seeds, which when they came to hand were to be sown and tended with special care. Then our talk turned upon the neighbouring tribes, and the new railway extension to Pine Creek. He told me of the Palmer Goldfield, of the Yellow Agony invading the Northern Territory, and discoursed learnedly on nuggets, faults, veins, signs, claims and codes of diggers' law, which failed to inspire me with golden dreams, though, for all I know or care, the reality may be hard at hand. He spoke of the lovely scenery on the creeks, and promised me first-rate sport in the way of alligator shooting, if I would only stay over two months. But even the tempting prospect of " Shikar " fails to draw me. " I hear the East a-calling " in Rudyard Kipling's phrase. What is this unaccountable glamour ? I ask—this intense fascination, ever drawing on that strange child of the ages the irrepressible youth of England, to explore new lands and court new adventures. Some such indefinable power holds us in its magic grip at some period of our lives— sometimes later, often earlier—and urges us forward and onward, and we go.

Despite the fierce tropical heat we spent two enjoyable days in Port Darwin—though I doubt whether the men at the winches enjoyed them. For, how the Menmuir manages to stow all the cargo she takes in at every port, must remain a dark mystery to landsmen for all time. Everybody, however, seems at peace with himself and the world at set of sun, and the evening whist on deck goes on with—I remember—a phenomenally uneven distribution of trumps and high cards, which left our veteran player nothing to lead from, little to lecture upon, and hardly a leg to stand on.

At last we are off—Australia sinking astern—our prow turned towards the golden Chersonese of the ancients, the fabled lands of the sea-robbers, the prahu and the poisoned creeze of spice and cinnamon, nutmeg and pineapple, the domain of the *Orang Laut*—those Phœnicians of Pacific waters. Four hundred and thirty miles ahead of us stretches the great island of Timor, on the southern horn of which lies Dilli, our port of destination, one of the last strongholds of senile Portugal, erstwhile the successful trading rival of the stubborn Dutchman in these far-off tropic seas. About fifty hours out, passing Nusa Besi (Iron Island) we sight the distant peaks of Timor melting into the soft summer haze of the dying day, and early next morning we are lying inside the reef abreast of the little town with the magnificent name. For *Dilli* is the Malayan form of *Delhi*, wondrous city of palaces, one of the numerous Sanskrit place-names which have come floating down into Malayan on untold waves of migration. And here follows a singular dilemma or rather trilemma, somewhat after the fashion of the triangular duel in Marryat's immortal " Midshipman Easy."

Our fellow-passenger, P. of Adelaide, has a number of samples of South Australian products, all excellent of their kind, to put upon the markets of the East. The question arises : How shall he set about in Timor ? The Portuguese Governor, so Captain Craig avers, doesn't know ten words of English, but knows a little French. The eager P. doesn't know a word of Portuguese, but from his schooldays preserves a sort of French that would be intelligible in Adelaide. There is an interpreter at Dilli, it is true, but his English is very limited. What is to be done ? Suddenly it occurs to me that where there are Portuguese, there will be some sort of ecclesiastic. All ecclesiastics understand Latin of a sort, even though it be that of Jerome or Augustine. Let us therefore have at them in good Ciceronian Latin, and expound unto the shepherds of the people the products of the magic land of South Australia.

So the very first night out, a most elaborate document is drawn up and duly set forth, describing the fertility of the great Provincia Australis, her groves of olives, yielding vats of yellowest oil, her cornfields white with nodding harvests of barley, wheat and rye, of African sorghum and the tasselled corn of America, telling of her vineyards crested with black and golden grape-clusters, and the generous liquor expressed therefrom, grateful alike to Cæsar and peasant, to Pope and to priest.

Mention is made of flocks and herds—innumerable as the finny droves of Ocean—that browse upon wide green pastures watered by mighty rivers; of the salted hindquarters of noble swine ("Terga porcorum salinata nobilium") and the flesh of goodly beeves and sheep, and delicious broth from their tails, encased in brazen pots where corruption cannot enter in nor the smell of decay mar their savour. "Pinguium caro bovum atque ovium intra vasa ahenea involuta. Neque deest jus caudarum, decoctio quædam maxime saporosa, ubi corruptio non potest intrare." (Ye ghosts of great Cæsar and Apicius, what think ye of this for hams, and the tinned meats and soups of commerce?) One suddenly-remembered tag from an Eton gradus helps us out of a difficult corner. It ran *Candiduli divina tomacula porci.* "*Heaven-flavoured sausages of whitish pork.*" This and Heaven knows what sad stuff beside, all reeled off in sonorous Latin, ridiculously pat and to the point, and may all the Cæsars, Christian saints, and Pagan heroes and poets downwards, forgive a stranger, and an Englishman, too, for misusing their mother tongue so damnably.

It was indeed quaint reading, left-handed and incongruous: and the thing came off, reader, the thing came off. We went ashore and looked up the Governor, who called in the Bishop of the diocese to give a churchman's opinion on a thesis that sorely taxed the Latinity of the lay mind. To see the good Bishop calmly and seriously reading off sentence after sentence, and halting here and there in mild doubt—then suddenly grasping the thing and translating it bit by bit into current Portuguese— cruelly tried our stoicism, as we sat by grave as judges but racked with inward laughter. When some corollary about woollen goods and hosiery was being sonorously read in some fearful dog-Latin, I felt I could not hold out much longer, and was seriously thinking of making a bolt for

the door, when the catalogue ended.   The Governor gave
a liberal order, which was promptly filled.   Up to present
date, however, I have never learned that my good old
friend or his firm ever recovered one farthing for the
goods supplied.   That's the worst of dealing with Portuguese.   They are a most unreliable lot.   It seems to
cause them no uneasiness whatsoever to incur an obliga-
tion which they know very well they have no funds to
meet.   It was just the same at Hong Kong the other day,
when one of the Sikh non-com.'s, who are great money-
lenders, summoned a Portuguese.   The defendant had
borrowed considerable sums, and, after losing the money
in gambling, calmly declined to pay, and somehow got off
scot-free!   The injured plaintiff took the matter pretty
coolly, remarking that he thought it rather hard to lend
out money and lose principal and interest too.   The
defaulter simply grinned provokingly, and said he didn't
care a straw.   And I don't suppose the Governor of Timor
cares either.   He has, doubtless, eaten the beef and biscuits, relished the wine and oil, and dismissed the vexatious
trifle of payment for ever from his memory.

During our visit we find that one of the tribes in the
neighbourhood has risen in revolt.   There has been a
skirmish in the bush ; the Portuguese have of course won
a glorious victory, but the enemy are unaccountably left
in possession of the field of battle, and a considerable
number of men and officers are laid up in hospital.   Our
good-natured Captain gave two or three of the poor little
widows of the fallen men a free passage up to Hong Kong,
en route for Macao—the sheet anchor of Portugal in the
China Seas.   In return for this service the Portuguese
some months later bestowed on our Captain Hugh an
elaborate decoration, which pleased the good old fellow
heartily.

The doctor and one of our party went off into the
interior on stout Timor ponies.   The rest of us strolled
aimlessly along the sea-front.   We meet a grimy little

boy parading around with a lemon-crested cockatoo. "How muchee?" says P. "No intendo. No savee," jerks out the urchin, and is gone down the road like a flash. We meet a man with a wizened-looking monkey, both looking as if life had used them badly. "How muchee?" once more demands the Inquisitor-General. "No savee," replies the terrified man, and clutching the poor little beast tight, turns and clears out for his life. We enter a shop and demand to see some goods. Again "No savee," sulky looks and muttered grumblings. Resisting with difficulty a strong desire to break somebody's head, we rally our forces, and enter a long thatched house by the roadside, where some natives are chewing betel-nut, with calabashes of sweet coconut toddy by their side for sale. Sorely smitten with thirst we attempt to deal. Again arises the eternal "No savee," and the idiots clear out, calabashes and all, as if the devil was at their heels. At last we meet one of the Portugese non-coms., whose company has been so roughly handled in the late action, and who explains the extraordinary behaviour of the people by suggesting that they take all English heretics for cannibals and fiends with tails like scorpions. Perhaps they really do.

Timor is very much like any high basaltic island in the Pacific—the beach fringed as usual with groves of coconut palms, with plenty of lemon hibiscus, pandanus, and native almond trees growing by the roadside. Its dense population is of mingled Malay and Negrito. The great extent and fertility of the island will in the near future render it a most attractive field for the botanist, the zoologist, and the philologist. Later on, in Macao, I was so fortunate as to receive from a worthy Jesuit Father a Portuguese vocabulary and grammar of the Teton dialect, which is a most bizarre and curious one, containing very many ancient word-forms akin to the Polynesian.

As I found out afterwards from further information carefully collected and sifted, Timor was anciently an important point in the migrations of the Malayan race, in whose calendar *Timor* is still preserved to denote the East Quarter, side by side with the more modern term *Masrak* (Arabic *Mashrik*).

The easternmost province of Yap is *Tomil.*

In the Sulu Archipelago the east is *Timol.*

In the Mariannes the northern quarter is *Timi.*

In the Pelews the southern quarter is *Dimis* and *Dimus.*

In the Pilam dialect of Eastern Formosa the west is *Timor.*

All variations of the ancient Malayan geographical name denote different points of the compass. So we may safely take Timor to have been one of the early homes of the Malayo-Polynesian, or, as some will have it, the Polynesian folk, ere they dispersed themselves wave upon wave, flotilla upon flotilla, on their long ocean wanderings.

After taking cargo aboard we leave the same evening and are soon past the south end of Kambing (Goat) Island. After leaving Sula Besi, Limbi and Banka behind, towards sunset on the 24th we fall in with the S.S. *Tsinan* going southward, threading our way the while through a multitude of carefully charted islands. A few days later we find ourselves skirting the west side of Mindoro. Every day now brings us nearer to our journey's end, and one lovely starlit evening we raise the well-known Peak, and a little later, amidst a host of shipping, great and small, we drop anchor a few hundred yards off the Praya or sea-front of the city of Victoria—the capital of Hong Kong. This and Singapore are the two keys to the gate of our commerce in the East, which the Pope or Czar, mighty though they be, shall never grasp, whilst British iron and gold and silver and steel shall last, and while British pluck and enterprise shall endure to hold fast the empire that Britain's sons have so greatly toiled to win.

CHAPTER II

HONG KONG TO MANILLA

IN these stirring days of travel all the English-speaking world, or nearly all, should know the city of Victoria —the threshold of the gorgeous East, worn by the countless feet of tourists on their nineteenth century pilgrimage in search of the strange and the rare. Victoria, the wondrous emporium of silks, teas, and curios, cunning bronze and silver work and quaint ceramics, ductile metal and fictile earth, obedient to the deft hand of the subtle Child of the Yellow Clay, teeming in his industrious millions. Time and space forbid me to describe at length the Lower Town with its steep narrow lanes and sky-scraping dwelling houses tenanted by untold thousands of the poorer Chinese, huddled together upon narrow noisome areas ; the solid and splendid buildings of the European merchants facing the craft-encumbered sea—the terraces and high white walls and domes of the Middle Town, the princely abodes of wealthy merchants. The Upper Town, high on the breezy hills, is reached by that engineering marvel, the Peak Railway, running up the steepest of inclines, through plantations of fir and larch and a hundred other woodland trees that clothe the gaunt hillside, the happy result of a grand Afforestation Scheme to fight the island fever that proved so deadly in the early years of British occupation. Below stretches a wonderful view of the native and foreign shipping in harbour, of the peninsula of Kowloon and its busy docks and stores across the water, and in the background the grey barren hills of China loom skyward. A week of wonders ashore, and I left by the *Menmuir* for Shanghai and Kobe, just to catch a passing glimpse of these two famous cities of the East, before setting out for Manilla and my yet far-off goal, the Carolines. I will set down here no thrice-told tale of places which have already been so well described by the omnivious and omnivorous tourist. Suffice it to say that I saw the sights of Shanghai, " did " the " Bubbling Well Road," and practised with great satisfaction on the magnificent cricket ground. My visit to Kobe, one of the Treaty Ports of Japan, was a most enviable experience. Here I met also with the greatest kindness and hospitality from the European residents.

The temples of Kyoto, the ancient capital of the Land of Niphon, where I stayed two days at the far-famed hostelry of Yaami, were a glory and a revelation to me. I wandered in the halls, cloisters, and gardens of Nishi-Hongwanji and her sister Buddhist shrine, and marvelled at the carvings of Hidoro Jingoro, the left-handed artist of cunning. I saw the Shinto sanctuary of Inari-Sama, the Fox-god and the guardian sentinels Ama-Inu and Koma-Inu, prototypes of our Lion and Unicorn, and heard the solemn chimes of the Temple bells ringing out in the midnight stillness.

I conversed with polite *samurai*, and traversed miles of street in rickety rickshas. I revelled in the island beauties gemming the Inland sea, and viewed marvelling the grimy procession of the basket-bearing damsels of Moji and Shimonoseki, passing like imps of Eblis, along our gangway with supplies of coal to help us southward.

Then back again for a brief space to the cheery life of Hong Kong with its cricket matches and dinner parties. Here I met several old London friends, amongst them the Hon. Stewart Lockhart, one of the most accomplished Chinese scholars in the East, who has since succeeded to the post of Colonial Secretary, for which his zeal and fine abilities had already marked him out. By his kind offices I received ample credentials from the Governor, Sir William Robinson, to the Spanish Governor-General of the Philippines, requesting him to direct his subordinates in the Eastern and Western Carolines to render me all possible assistance in my explorations. This stood me in good stead, and it is hardly anticipating matters to here very cordially thank the Spanish officials for the politeness and hospitality they always showed me during my travels in their possessions.

A fortnight after my return from Japan saw me off for Manilla *viâ* Amoy on a dark and drizzly evening, by the good steamer, *Esmeralda,* fighting her way through the tumbling seas in the teeth of a strong north-easter. Amoy— a great centre for the coolie traffic—is just like other large Chinese towns, laid out in the usual narrow and abominably filthy streets. An interesting local industry was seen in elaborate carvings in steatite or soap-stone. Of these I obtained some fine specimens at a moderate price. Down to Manilla we had rather a rough passage, which Captain Taylor, our genial skipper, managed none the less to enliven, and on the fifth night out I was glad enough to spy the lights of Manilla twinkling ahead through the gloom as we worked our way cautiously through the wide and shallow bay leading up to the capital of the island of Luzon. The population here, like the hill-tribes of the neighbouring island of Formosa, form the northernmost wave of migration from Indonesia and the Malay Archipelago, the teeming mother hive of the brown race, which occupies places so far apart as Madagascar and the myriad isles of the wide Pacific area.

Next morning we found ourselves anchored some little way out from the mouth of the Pasig River, which is so shallow a stream that even here vessels drawing above thirteen feet cannot enter. On our left lay the business suburb of Binondo, with its wharfs and counting-houses, with a number of small inter-island trading steamers and sailing vessels of every kind of rig drawn up alongside. We saw also numerous *Banka* or native craft (Javanese *Wang-Kang*) from which the South Sea Island canoe seems to have been named (*cf.* Polynesian dialects *Wanga*, *Waka*, *Vaka*, *Va'a*, and *Wa'a*). The Customs Officials were rather late aboard, and it was not until nearly sunset that I found myself ensconced bag and baggage in a comfortable upper room of the British Club-House in the suburb of Nagtahan, some three miles out of town. It lies overlooking a sharp elbow of the river, a substantial building embowered in palms and ornamental trees and shrubs, formerly the country residence of a Spanish official.

The next few days were spent in driving about the city and suburbs, and visiting the quaint Old Town and Fort across the river, with its massive walls, drawbridges, and weed-choked moats, looking for all the world like a bit out of the Middle Ages. I do not here propose to give a full account of all the architectural beauties of Manilla, interesting though they are. The churches are legion, the most conspicuous being the fine new one of San Sebastian, with a double spire, in the Quiapo quarter. In Tondo ward, that of St Niño, a conspicuous landmark ; and in Binondo, that of Santa Cruz. In Old Manilla, where monks and priests and friars do mostly congregate, are some magnificent edifices belonging to the great religious orders of St Domingo, St Augustino, and St Francisco. The Jesuit Cathedral of St Ignacio is a superb building within and without, and the chapel of the Capuchins— the poorest of the orders—is also worth seeing. Up to the date of the Filipino revolt and the American war, which almost marched side by side with it, the priestly orders possessed broad lands and ample revenues, and wielded enormous power over the indolent and superstitious races of the land. But since then the Wheel of Fortune has come round with a vengeance. To-day the men of the Black Robe are in sad straits as were ever the saints of old —threatened, plundered, beaten, tortured, burnt, impaled, crucified, and this by the very natives who a year or two ago were kneeling to them for a blessing, or imploring pardon and protection as from semi-divine beings.

But then these things were hidden from me, as I held my peace, looked and marvelled. In company with one or other of the Macleod brothers, heads of two important mercantile houses, I went through the bustling quarter of Binondo with its banks, offices, counting-houses, stores, timber yards, quays and wharfs. It is connected with the Old Town over the water by three bridges of stone and iron, the most important of which is the Puente D'España, over which all day long passes a continual stream of traffic. Down the middle of Binondo runs a fine street, the *Escolta*, traversed by a horse-tramway plying out to the districts of Tondo, Sempalok and Santa Misa. Along the Escolta lie the principal shops and cafés. Away to the left is artisans' quarter, full of odd little shops, stores and the bazaars owned by the Chinese and native half-breeds, of whom there are some seventy thousand in Manilla city and wards. Still further to the left lies the insanitary native quarter of Tondo, in early days the seat of an independent Kingling or Rajah, with a population of over seventy thousand, mostly of the poorer class. It is situated on low marshy ground, intersected by numerous canals half choked up with animal and vegetable refuse. Malarial fevers, small-pox and other zymotic diseases, as may well be imagined, are pretty common here. In fact the annual death-rate from these causes is terribly heavy. The parish is one enormous mass of palm-thatched dwellings, with walls and floorings of light cane, raised on a framework of wooden poles a few feet above the pools of stagnant water that day and night send up their exhalations. On Good Friday morning in 1895 one of these huts caught fire, and the conflagration, fanned by a strong breeze, marched two miles in the space of half-an-hour.

From Tondo a line of steam-trams runs to the village of Malabon some seven miles out, so lately a scene of battle and carnage, where are the go-downs and works of the Luzon Sugar-Refining Company. In time past Malabon was a centre of the tobacco industry, which has since been nearly strangled in the clutch of Government monopoly. A number of natives are still employed by a local firm in manufacturing the commoner classes of cigars, of which there is an enormous annual consumption. On the way to Malabon the tram-line runs through the village of May-payo, where there is a cock-pit keenly attended on Sundays and holidays by the local fancy. Parallel with this sporting rendezvous, a few hundred yards back through the palms and bamboos lies the village of Caloocan, the scene of the late furious engagement between the American forces and the Filipino rebels with their Igorrote allies, and the first station of the solitary railway of Luzon which, starting from the terminus at Tondo, runs through the Kandava marshes skirting the Pampanga border, and up to the port of Dagupan, the centre of a fertile rice and hemp-producing district. Taken all in all the scenery of the outskirts of Manilla is very rich and picturesque. There are rice-fields and clearings for growing bananas, taro and sweet potato, overshadowed by masses of Bolinao, areca, sago, and coconut palms, topes of mango and of native chestnut (*Dungun*), clumps of towering cane (*Kauaian* and *Boho*). Here the spreading umbrella-like leafage of the native almond (*Talisai*), there the yellow-wreathed glories of the graceful Cananga (*Ilangilang*). In between all nestle the frail cane and nipa huts of the natives, lying back half merged in the bowery wilderness.

Every day brought new sights and scenes, and regularly at sunset we used to visit the Luneta or Half-Moon Esplanade on the sea-side beyond the Old Fort, where crowds of citizens, rich and poor, stream out in the cool of the evening in every description of vehicle to enjoy the fresh sea-breeze, to hear the band play in the Kiosk, and to gossip and promenade up and down under the long flashing arc of electric lights. I saw the *Carabao* or native buffalo harnessed to uncouth waggons drawing timber, and watched a close-packed herd of these ugly beasts wallowing in their noonday bath of mud and water, nose to nose and horn to horn. I inspected factories of tobacco and hemp—the two great staple trades of Manilla—and examined the delicate fabrics of Jusi and Piña, a famous Philippine industry well known and valued in the marts of the East. I bought several *Panuelos*, specimens of the latter stuff, which is composed of the fibres of the pineapple leaf worked into an exquisite filmy tracery, resembling the finest Brussels lace, the designs on the border being taken from native trees, fruits and flowers.

I attended a grand *Fiesta* at Malate, interminable processions passing down the village street all day, the houses hung with gay banners, and after dark a glorious supper-party of the European residents followed by a brilliant fire-work display, and songs, music, cards and dancing, lasting well into the small hours. Some pleasant evenings were spent with the Spanish residents, whose hospitality fully bore out the old Castilian tradition. I took many country walks, and found the peasantry good-natured folk. Only it struck me as curious that the village children would always clear out at the sight of the *Castila*, by which name all Europeans alike are designated outside the Metropolis. Is it not a lively recollection of the early Spanish methods of conversion and conquest, which the milder rule of the present day has not yet succeeded in effacing ?

I spent one lovely morning in going through the Botanical Gardens near Malate, where I greatly admired the palms and ferns, as well as the rich flowers and foliage of ornamental shrubs and trees under cultivation. I succeeded in obtaining two monster packages of specimen seeds to forward to the energetic Curator of the Gardens at Port Darwin.

One Sunday Macleod and I indulged in a journey up the line to a big Pampanga village to view the national sport. They gave us the seat of honour above the cock-pit, whence we witnessed some sharp combats of warlike roosters before a large and excited audience of natives and half-castes who staked their money as freely and merrily as holiday makers at Epsom. Next evening we visited the European Opera House at the foot of the Calle del Iris, heard some interminable music and songs, and went away rather bored. At the native theatre in Sempalok we saw a drama in Tagala dialect, a highly comical perfor-mance, where a poor Christian knight of Manilla wooes the daughter of a " Moro " or Mahometan Rajah of the Sulu Islands, wins her, and carries her off with all her wealth after slaying her infidel father.

In company with a *mestizo* interpreter I entered several native markets, *Tiangui* or *Tianggi* (Mexican *Tianquiz*), taking down careful notes of all the odd fishes, fruits and vegetables, laid out for sale in the stalls.

The sight of my notebook and pencil so busily em-ployed aroused a deep suspicion amongst the simple-minded vendors of fish and buffalo-beef, shrimps and mussels, squid and sausages, taro and tomatos, onions and bananas, yams and garlic, cabbages and coconuts, sour toddy and medicinal barks. One and all they took me for a local official, genus *informer*, entering in his black book made-up complaints against the quality of their wares, in order to extort money on his own account out of their poor little profits. When assured of the real nature of my errand they marvelled, but being by nature pleasant people, they willingly gave me plenty of curious information.

I called on the British Consul, presented my letters from Hong Kong, and received the desired credentials from General Blanco to his subordinates in Yap and Ponape. Then I saw the head of the Capuchin Mission, to whom was entrusted the spiritual welfare of the wild Caroline islanders. He received me very kindly, and presented me with Spanish vocabularies of the Yap and Ponapean dialects. I secured further secular aid by engaging as general utility man and photographer in one, a quarter-caste from the Province of Pampanga, a quiet and docile fellow, but weak and unstable as water, who, little guessing what troubles lay before him in savage ands, recklessly " signed on " in a spirit of adventure.

Well, everything was in order at last for my departure. Two passages were taken on board the mail-steamer *Venus* of the Planet Line, for her bi-monthly trip to the distant outlying possessions of Yap, Guam and Ponape. She was to leave at noon on the Sunday (Dec. 17th), so I sent the lad on board overnight to take charge of the baggage. Next day at Nagtahan, sad to say, it was late when Willie Macleod and I arose. Hurriedly we got through our lunch and drove down in hot haste to the wharf at Binondo. Plenty of steam launches and small craft lying at the water side, but never a soul stirring to take us aboard ; and, to add to our perplexity, a distant warning whistle from the steamer lifting anchor down the Bay. In desperation we searched about, forcibly impressed two half-sober wharf loafers and a fuddled mestizo engineer out of one of the cafés, laid violent hands on a launch, and were away down the Bay as hard as steam would drive us. And none too soon. The *Venus* is slowly moving off. In reply to our frantic holloas and gestures, in the midst of which the excited engineer nearly falls overboard, the good-natured Spanish captain stops his vessel in her course, and she lies beating the water with reversed screw. A steam launch hissing shoreward nearly runs us down. In it was my Manilla man seated upon a whole pyramid of bags and boxes, his and mine, which, thinking for certain I had missed my passage, he was dutifully taking ashore. When he saw us his face fell like mercury before a storm. I roared to him to come along, and he meekly followed our craft to the gangway let down for us. Master and man climbed up, a thought taken aback at arriving in such dramatic fashion. Not a word of reproach from the Captain, only a little good-natured chaff. This forbearance of a choleric ocean potentate and a bit of a martinet reflects infinite credit on Spanish politeness.

The aforesaid Captain and the new Spanish Governor going out with us to the Mariannes were mightily amused when they heard of the impressed steam-launch driven by a strange engineer hauled head and shoulders out of a wine-shop. They also made merry over my Manilla lad. The poor creature, obedient to my orders, turned up early on Saturday evening to look after the luggage. Feeling a bit dull, he fell into talk with the ship's boys, and they filled his noddle with all sorts of horrible stories of cannibal " Carolinos," who, when he arrived at Ponape, would stick him full of javelins, and make a divining bowl of his skull. This wretched twaddle, and much more, Theodoro of course had taken for gospel, and all that Sunday morning had been peering wistfully over the side, longing to get ashore and have done with so perilous a service.

Towards sunset we got into livelier water, and once out of the St Bernadino Straits into the open sea, the vessel rolled a good deal. My poor photographic artist, refusing alike solid food and liquid consolation, betook himself to a nice gloomy corner, where, stretched on his mat wrapped in an ancient cloak, he lay dismally brooding on the ills that awaited him in heathen lands oversea. In a comfortable deck chair I made myself quite at home, attentively conning over some Spanish books of travel. On my departure friends in Manilla had thoughtfully presented me with hundreds of cigars. Hence a contented mind and holocaust unending.

CHAPTER III

IN a day or two we shook down into our places on
board. The ship was lighted with electricity and com-
fortably fitted up, the fare good, and there were plenty of
Manilla boys who attended well to all our wants. I took
a special liking to Señor Marina, the newly appointed
Governor of the Mariannes, who gave me some interesting
facts about the islands, in which he was going to maintain
law and order. Bound for the same port as myself is a
brusque Ponapean trader, Captain N., who does not always
appear to advantage, being taken alternately with fits of
gaiety during which he tells good stories, and bearish
moods in which it is hard to get a satisfactory word out
of him. Is this type peculiar to the Carolines? Another
source of amusement is the Captain's dog *Coco*, a grossly
fat, absurdly short-haired animal, with a hide the colour
of an old copper coin and the temper of the traditional
East Indian Nabob with a liver. The creature paces the
slippery decks, growling at every lurch of the vessel, and
snapping at the spray as it bursts up through the anchor
chains. When feeding he growls, when fasting he growls.
He was, however, left only one day without food, and this
piece of neglect brought the lad in charge of him a smart
taste of the rattan. The first and second engineers speak
English very well, as is generally the case with those on
the mail-service lines. Many of them, like my two ac-
quaintances came from the Pyrenean Provinces in the
north of Spain, and spent some years in the Engineering
School of Instruction in Liverpool. Naturally our con-

versation often turned on that philological puzzle, the Basque language.

At noon on the seventh day out, we raise the western-most isle of the long Caroline Archipelago—variously termed Yap, Guap or Wap—a low-lying strip of land rising in the middle into a round plateau looking down upon an exquisitely green belt of coconut palms, and recalling exactly my impressions on sighting Tongatabu on my first Pacific island voyage. Slipping cautiously through the narrow reef-passage we enter Tomil Harbour, with the islands of Tarrang and Ngingich hard by, and the little Spanish settlement of Santa Christina on the islands of Tapalau and Belolach joined by a causeway, right in front of us, and are soon beleaguered by a number of native canoes and shore boats. To my disappointment Captain O'Keefe, to whom I have a letter of introduction, and who is to act as my banker and general business agent in these waters, is away on one of his long cruises in the Pelews and Central Carolines ; but has left in charge as foreman and general agent a certain Joe Mitchell, with whom I have no difficulty in making all necessary arrangements. To Mr E. Oppenheim-Gerard in charge of the station of the Jaluit Gesellschaft on Ngingich or Dunnitch I also presented my credentials when he came on board. I found him a most interesting comrade with a fund of varied and curious information. He pressed me to come ashore to dinner at sunset, and stay overnight at his place ; so as the steamer did not leave till noon next day, I gladly accepted his invitation. Theodoro had plucked up spirit wonderfully at the sight of land and got camera and plates into working order, and we went ashore about sunset well pleased with the prospect of strange sights in a strange land. A jovial evening was spent and the night was well advanced when we retired. Captain N., on business thoughts intent, elected to stay overnight upon O'Keefe's island close by. How he fared I cannot tell.

Out of our table-talk I noted some peculiar facts about

the people of Yap, and their language, which appears to be a crabbed form of some ancient Asiatic tongue allied to the Dravidian coloured with a tint of Malay and Japanese, and crossed, or chequered, in a very remarkable way with unmistakable Polynesian words.

We are up bright and early, the man with the camera first of all.

The best photo he took was one of a group of natives with three women from the Fe-Bai or Lodge at Rul, with our kindly host a single splash of white in the background of seven ebony statues.

At the steamer's first whistle reluctantly we made our way on board, promising our kind host to look him up without fail on my way back from Ponape, which promise, it will be seen, I faithfully kept.   On my return to Yap I took many notes on the manners and customs of the natives—their antiquities, traditions and folklore, marine life, flora and geography—all of which I have reserved more appropriately for a later chapter ; our first glimpse of Yap being, as it were, a mere bird's-eye view, and as such I give it here.

We noticed that the people were very much darker than the light brown folk of Polynesia, and that their canoes were on a different model, running up high bow and stern with a peculiar fish-tail ornamentation fore and aft, and fitted with a wide and heavy outrigger that must stand them in good stead in long sea-going voyages.

Punctually at noon we are off, heading straight for Guam, which lies up some 400 miles to the N.E. towards the Bonins and Japan.   This track is followed by the mail-steamers in order to avoid the dangerous reefs which surround the imperfectly charted islets of the Central Carolines.

During our voyage from Yap, Senor Marina, who seemed very well up in the history of his new dominions, gave me the following facts: Discovered by Magellan in 1521 and Christianised about 1662, the islands of the

GROUP OF YAP NATIVES

Marianne or Ladrone group came under Spanish power. The present population is under ten thousand, of which more than two-thirds are located in Agaña, the metropolis and residence of the Governor. The native race are called Chamorros, and at the time of the Spanish conquests had reached some degree of civilisation and clan organisation, and had acquired no mean proficiency in agriculture and pottery-making.

What mightily stirred my curiosity was an account given me by the Governor of some interesting ruins in the group. For more minute information he referred me to a chapter in a Spanish historiette published lately in Manilla, of which I subjoin a partial free translation.

All over the Mariannes, in the seats of the native population, before their discovery by the white men, there exist certain pyramids and truncated cones, on the top of which are placed *semi-esferas*, *i.e.* half spherical bodies. These cones or pyramids on the island of Guahan do not exceed three feet in height, the diameter of the curious pieces on the tops being about two feet. Those seen on the island of Saipan near the village of Garapui on the west coast are somewhat larger and generally composed of stone. Amongst the natives these go by the name of *Houses of the Ancients*. They face each other in two parallel lines like a regular street. According to tradition the old inhabitants used to inter their dead in these houses or cairns. Many even of the present generation have a superstitious fear of touching the stones or cultivating the ground in their neighbourhood —a fear which is disappearing nowadays as shown by the fact that the Church of Tinian was partly constructed out of the ruins of one of these monuments. In 1887 a French naturalist, M. Alfred Marche, accompanied by the Spanish author referred to above and several Chamorro and Caroline natives, visited the site of some of the ruins on Tinian and Saipan. Those of the most imposing proportions are found on Tinian near the pueblo of Sinharon.

One of these monuments is styled *The House of Taga* and measures four and a half metres in height, and one and a quarter in diameter at the base. On the top, which runs up to ·75 of a metre in breadth, is placed a *semi-esfera* two and a half metres in diameter.

The monuments are twelve in number, arranged in a double row as those in Saipan. Seven are standing, but cyclones have levelled five with the ground, showing clearly that they have no solidity of foundation. The distance between each of them and its neighbour in line is about one and a half metres, and that between the rows about four. The material is ordinary rubble from the coral-reefs mixed with a great quantity of mortar made of burnt coral lime and sand. One of these curious pyramids still standing had on its top a large bowl about five feet in depth. This, according to tradition, was the grave of Taga's daughter and in it, sure enough, the explorers found some human bones ; but of these, unfortunately, no scientific measurements were recorded. This monument is at the end of the village and faces north-west.

Thus far the Spaniard, and it is much to be hoped that some English explorer will try his luck in turn and furnish our scientists at home with fuller information upon the origin, design, and distribution of these singular structures of an all but vanished people.

About sunset on Christmas eve, we sight the high table lands of Guam or Guahan. We draw in to a prospect of woods and green valleys, backed by steep cliffs and curiously shaped turreted masses of limestone rock, and finally drop anchor in Port Luis de Apra, about two miles off the little town, the water abruptly shoaling further inshore and blocked on every hand by coral-reefs. As there was nothing to be gained by going on shore long after dark, we deferred our landing till next morning. About nine o'clock a boat comes off, manned by a crew of natives under the command of the son of Joe Wilson, the pilot. We pulled in through the shallows marked out by a long

line of stakes.   Our way lay under the lee of Goat Island,
the scenery of which much resembles that of Mauke in the
Harvey Group.   It is composed of honeycombed water-
worn limestone of bluish grey tint, covered by a rich
green mantle of forest and low scrub.   The Thespesia,
the Cycas circinalis (*Fadan*), and the Pandanus grow
abundantly amongst the blocks and boulders, also the
handsome large-leaved tree, the Puka or Pukatea of
South Polynesia.

Landing at Port Louis next morning behold a strange
party setting forth for the interior in a strange vehicle,
drawn by a stranger beast of burden.   Captain N., his little
daughter, myself and the Manilla man, all perched behind
a red cow, who for evident reasons should have been
exempt, and who, under protest and the propulsion of a
small native boy armed with a switch sitting on her
shoulders, drags our clumsy old Noah's ark through the
ruts on a pair of wheels totally innocent of spokes and
each being of one solid circular piece like a table top,
hewn roughly out of Daok wood (*Callophyllum*).   From
Port Louis to Agaña is no very long journey, but it
seemed an age getting there, and when we did get there,
there wasn't very much to see.   A little township of some
six thousand souls, allowing a soul to each inhabitant, at
least as far as the Catholic priests will permit them to own
one.   The Chamorros, though akin to their neighbours
the Tagals and Pampangs of Luzon, whom the Spanish
military system has quartered on them in the form of
garrison, yet preserve some indefinable personality of
their own.   They are a pretty people, gentle, kindly, and
reasonably honest.   It is a pity so few of the old race
are left—less than ten thousand I believe, and they mostly
half-castes.   But the narrative of "Kotzubue's Voyages" has
given us one consolation.   In it Chamisso tells us clearly
of the emigration of the greater part of the Chamorros
into the Central Caroline area, whither the cruelty of petty
Spanish officials and the motherly solicitude of the In-

quisition with its gentle persuasive measures, dared not and dares not to this day follow them. Chamisso, poet, dramatist and philologist, has told us of *one* good, honest Spanish governor, and one alone, who really understood these Ladrone islanders. From results, we may guess what the others must have been, despite the furious denial of the Spanish historian. None of these things troubled Captain N., who all the while was thinking of nothing but dollars and cents, nor Theodoro either, poor creature, who did what he was told to do, when he would much rather have sat idle and slept. He did *not* sleep and he did *not* sit idle.

That afternoon I recollect to my infinite boredom, we interviewed a Japanese storekeeper, a Spanish padre, a Chamorro rice-farmer and a German trader, who barring a strong tendency to talk " shop," and nothing but " shop," seemed a decent fellow. He gave us a good Christmas dinner, and somehow our patient beast got us down to Port Louis that night about eleven. But it was hard lines on that cow. Thence on board and away next morning for another five days' tumbling and tossing, the wild winds whirring through our rigging as night and day we drone on and on into the south-east.

On the 1st January 1896, the *Venus* enters the harbour of Ascension, where the little white-walled Spanish Colony of Santiago lies, surrounded by a clearing on a slope by the waterside at the mouth of a wide creek, protected to the east and west by rude block-houses. I landed and presented my credentials to the Governor Don José Pidal, who scanned them and me narrowly, and appeared somewhat chagrined at an Englishman being unable to speak Spanish like a native of Castille, after only two months' study of that interesting tongue. However, we contrived to make our meaning tolerably clear to one another. It turns out from the Governor's account that the ruins lie in a district hostile to Europeans, the rulers of which are only kept in good humour by the receipt of monthly subsidies.   As late as six years ago they proved themselves treacherous and bloodthirsty to a degree.   He tells me that the natives are savages no better than heathen Moors or Ethiopians, and that sundry ignorant ·and self-willed bigots of the Methodist Mission from Boston have been all the while stirring them up against their lawful rulers to the great detriment of Spanish prestige, and the glory of the Catholic Church.   That extreme danger and much discomfort would accompany the quest, and that he himself should be much concerned at an English visitor under Spanish protection risking his life for so doubtful an advantage as photographing old stone walls, and excavating uninteresting relics.   Undeterred by this formidable picture, I still held firm to my purpose, and finally after much persuasion he yielded and gave his word under protest to do his best to assist me in my explorations.   And this promise I must say he kept most truly and honourably, once especially at a rather critical time, where a weaker man might have yielded to native craft and subtlety.

The interview over, and the required permission gained, with a light heart I introduced myself to the good Capuchin priests, Padres Saturnino and Augustino. I occupied all my spare time in studying a Spanish-Ponapean vocabulary and grammar, with which the head of their order had presented me in Manilla.

My late fellow passenger, Captain N., with whom I am lodging *pro tem.*, has once more turned gruff and snappish. He has plenty of hard work in hand, and is deeply immersed in business matters with his Madrid partner. The first few days hung somewhat heavy on my hands. The Manilla soldiery, who formed the garrison did not particularly interest me, though my photographer Theodoro fraternised with them readily enough.   But there were always a few natives from over the water, or from the coast districts, pottering around the store, who had picked up a little broken English.   Both the Governor and Captain N. advised me to wait until Henry Nanapei of Ronkiti came up from the South Coast, whom they declared to be the very man to help me to make a success of the undertaking.

One morning Captain N. expresses himself bluntly after the fashion of old trading skippers. " Ponape natives are a queer sort, but they aren't *bad* natives. They don't think much of killing a man. I know some of them down the east coast who'd like to have my head, sure enough, because I showed some Spanish men-of-war the way into one of their harbours in the last war. Go easy, my lad, go easy. They aren't like your quiet Tahiti and Samoa folk, but the real rough article and no mistake. You just remember that, and go easy with them, and you'll be all right. If you don't you'll get left, as sure as fate, as a good many others have been, that's all. So now you know what's what, and I can't stand here giving advice all day. It's none of my business after all. You stick to Nanapei and he'll see you through ; and the King of U is a good-natured cuss, drunk or sober. Old Lapen Paliker too is about as straight as they make them. Some of his people are sitting round outside now. You'd better go and yarn with them, and listen to a few of their lies. Just make friends with the old people first, give the girls some presents and the men a few sticks of tobacco, and you won't be able to get rid of the crowd. They'll talk with you all day, and want you to go and pay them a visit, and when they go home the story will go all round the island like a telephone, and maybe do you a lot of good. I'm busy. Now git ! " And I got.

I soon made friends with the Paliker natives and their headman, who entertained me most hospitably for a couple of days at the little hillside settlement just below Chokach. I also visited the Ichipau, or King of U, and the Wachai of Chokach, whose respective territories bounded the colony in the north-east and north-west. The two chiefs were a curious contrast to one another. The former is a very genial old gentleman, and

THE KING OF U AND FAMILY

a great admirer of English and Americans. He is neither
Protestant nor Catholic, and I am sorry to say I once
caught him using pages of a Missionary Bible for pipe-
lights. He joined in the native rising of 1887, was
deported to Manilla, tried for his life, acquitted, fêted, and
sent back safe home again. Since then he has rarely
known a sober moment. Every Sunday he appears in
the colony gorgeous in an orange-coloured kilt, a black
coat, and turkey-red shirt. Bottle under arm he marches,
offering a dram to every European he meets in the fulness
of his regal heart. The Spanish allow him about forty
dollars a month to keep him in good humour, and thus as
a rule he is able to pay his debts—a very rare thing in a
native, and from its rarity much esteemed. The photograph shows him seated in front of his house near Auak,
with the Likant or Queen, his children, and his faithful
yellow dog, *Clarita*, by his side. The Prince of Chokach
has a fancy for European garb. Like the King of U, he
also was in the rising of 1887, and draws the same monthly
salary. Unlike his brother monarch, he is a Catholic and
a teetotaler, hoards his money, and lets his debts run on.

A digression on the physical aspect and natural products of Ponape, the chief island of the eastern Carolines,
may enable the reader to picture our surroundings at
this time.

The area of the island of Ponape is some 340 square
miles. It is surrounded by a barrier reef (*paina*) enclosing
a lagoon (*nallam*) about a mile and a half in breadth, and
of varying depth, studded in all directions with detached
reefs (*mat*) and patches of live coral, the rapid growth of
which on the south and south-west coasts bids fair to
render navigation—except for the lightest canoes—an
impossible task. On the north coast, however, the lagoon
in many places is of considerable depth. In this lagoon
are scattered thirty-three islets, mostly low and of coralline
formation ; a few of them, however, are volcanic in origin.
The principal of these are Langar, Parram, and the

Mants on the north coast, Tapak and Aru on the north-east, and Mutok in the south.   The limestone islets are called Takai-mai or Light-blue Stone, and those of basalt formation Takai-tol or Black Stone.

Chokach has a remarkable scarp or precipice, the *Paip-Alap*, 937 feet in height, on the north side of it, where the columnar form of the basalt is very clearly defined. The glen below, tradition declares, was the quarry whence the early builders gathered the material for their wonder-ful works on the east coast, straight from the workshop of Nature.   Langar is the headquarters of a German trading firm.

The other islets are mere patches of sand and coral, overgrown with palm, pandanus and littoral shrubs, and visited occasionally by fishing parties.

The principal harbours are six in number: (1) *Ascension Bay* in the north, at the mouth of the Pillapenchakola River, on the south bank of which stands the little Spanish colony of Santiago, with the peaks of Kupuricha and Telemir towering some 2000 feet high in the background. To the south-west is the great scarp of Chokach, a notable landmark far out at sea.   (2) *Port Aru*, or *Oa*, on the U and Metalanim border, has a very narrow and tortuous entrance, and was the scene in 1890 of a brisk action, in which the Spaniards brilliantly carried the rebel defences from the sea.   (3) *Metalanim Harbour* on the east, over-looked by Mount Takaiu, or the Sugar-loaf Peak, in the neighbourhood of which are the celebrated ruins.   (4) *Port Mutok*, at the mouth of the Kiti river, with the peaks of Roi, Lukoila, and Wana in the background, with a remarkable obelisk-shaped rock, called by the native Chila-U, or the Adze-head, and by trading skippers, the " Sentry Box."   (5) *Ronkiti Harbour*, at the mouth of the river of the same name, which rises in the slopes of Mount Tolokom, the highest peak in the island, judged to be 2861 feet high.   (6) *Ponatik* or *Middle Harbour*, in South Metalanim.

The island is divided into five districts, U, Chokach, Not, Kiti, and Metalanim ; the two latter with a population of 1300 and 1500 respectively. The whole population is about 5000, living in Kanim or scattered open villages confined to the sea coast. They are Christianised, though some of them retain many of their old heathen practices. The north province of U is very mountainous, and some of the cliffs looking down upon the valleys show a very fine example of columnar basalt formation. The interior of the island is an almost impenetrable wilderness of densely wooded mountains and sierras, seamed with deep valleys, and ravines. The heavy annual rainfall sends down numerous torrents from the slopes of the mountains which form the central water-shed. A belt of swamp, covered by thick clumps of mangroves and other salt-water brush, surrounds the island. The mangrove belt at the mouth of the rivers is traversed by a network of shallow *tau*, or waterways, barely wide enough to allow a single canoe to pass. The scenery a little way up the stream is rich in beauty. The mangroves once pierced, one passes into a region of Nipa palm, tree-ferns, and tall trees interlacing overhead, hung with all manner of ferns, orchids, and creepers, the advance-guard of the hosts of the forest sweeping down upon the rich low levels. At a little higher elevation are found two varieties of the areca or betel-nut palm, which the Ponapeans, unlike the Malays and their Yap relations in the west, do not chew. Higher up still on the mountain slopes are found some valuable timber-trees (a full description of which as well as Ponapean economic shrubs and plants, will be found in the Appendix). Amongst the mountains there are some well-grassed table-lands admirably suited for the pasture of cattle. In the mountains behind Ronkiti is a lake swarming with huge eels. Other lakes doubtless exist, but unfortunately very little is known about the interior, of penetrating which the natives appear to have a superstitious dread.

The most productive copra districts are Kiti and

Chokach, and there is a considerable trade in fruit of the vegetable ivory palm.

The climate is hot and moist, tempered from October to May by the trade wind blowing fresh and clear out of the north-east. The rainy season sets in about June, lasting to the end of September. This is the time of light variable winds, with frequent calms, with occasional heavy thunderstorms and south-westerly gales. According to Dr Gulick's observations, the highest temperature marked in a period of three years was $31.7°$ Cent. (*i.e.* about $87°$ Fahr.), and the lowest $21°$ (about $70°$ Fahr.). The average temperature is $28.3°$ Cent. ($=$ about $81°$ Fahr.). The annual rainfall is somewhat heavy. In the year 1890, observations taken on the *Maria Molina* hulk in Ascension Bay gave 230 days in the year on which rain fell, and a total rainfall of some 36 inches.

CHAPTER IV

NALAP, AND PONAPEAN SUPERSTITIONS AND CHARACTER

SHORTLY after our visit to the Ichipau of U and his brother monarch of Chokach, we met Henry Nanapei on one of his visits to the Colony, who, on learning our needs, promptly agreed to place at our disposal the island of Nalap, just off the mouth of the Ronkiti River, on the south-west coast. Accordingly, after laying in various stores, and carefully stowing boxes, baggage, and photographic apparatus, we borrowed a big canoe and two natives of Not to sail her, and slipped down the coast past the great crag of Chokach, the hill ranges of Paliker, the valley of the Palang River, and the round hill-tops of Marau and Tomara. The lagoon in many places is filled with stacks of living coral shooting up to within four feet of the surface. Shoreward the thick line of mangroves marks the region of the salt marshes girdling Ponape like a great green ribbon. This, as already mentioned, is seamed by myriad narrow lanes or waterways just wide enough for a single canoe to pass. When Ponape is fully civilised there will be need to elect a special Minister of the waterways for the effectual clearing and widening of these precarious channels. For the canals are hardly navigable, and, worse still, from time to time, a vigorous gale of wind brings down some great forest tree across the passage, blocking the way to all craft until some one comes with an axe or crosscut saw and removes it.

We strike into the maze and pass swampy banks bordered by Nipa palms and tall forest trees, their boughs and trunks laden with drooping festoons of orchid, creeper, polypody, and lliana, and huge round, glossy green clumps of birds' nests firm-rooted in the fork where each sturdy branch springs out of the parent tree. A turn at length brings us in sight of the Ronkiti landing-place, called *Chakar-en-Yap*, *i.e.*, The Yapmen's heritage, and we know that our journey is over.

Nanapei took us over to see Nalap the same afternoon in his own boat. The islet lies out in the bay near the outer reef, some two miles off the mouth of the Ronkiti River, which waters a fertile valley of the same name, which Nanapei has planted with enormous numbers of coconut palms. We returned to the mainland that evening, and next morning bathed in the river, which near its mouth broadens out into a little lake, lively with the silvery arrows of darting fish, the palms fringing the banks mirrored to the life in the placid water. Here flits the kingfisher (*Kotar*) with a flash of sheeny blue. Fly catchers and honey-eaters chirrup in the tree-tops, and dragon-flies, gaudy with blue and brown, with red and orange, wheel and circle in the sleepy noontide. The whole valley is one great garden, sadly marshy in parts, but seemingly of a prodigious and inexhaustible fertility. A little dyking, ditching, and hedging would do no harm here. Sago-palms, bananas, mangoes, orange and lime trees, grow in the greatest magnificence. Great beds of wild ginger carpet the ground, sending up a pungent aromatic reek from their trodden leaves. Here and there peeps out from the green veil of forest a bit of rich russet thatch, a patch of yellow and brown house-wall of canes and reedgrass, occasional glimpses of native dwellings lying back in the shadow The valley is populous and the people industrious, for Nanapei has his folk well in hand. There is no lack of food in the land, for yams and taro are zealously cultivated. A giant species of Arum (*A. costatum*) is especially noticeable. The Caroline islanders call it *Pulak*, the Polynesians *Puraka* and *Kape* or *'Ape*. In the Philippines it is called *Gabe*. It has a very large tuber, but contains much acrid juice, only dispelled by long and careful cook-

ing, and is only eaten in times of famine.   There is quite
a mixture of nationalities in Ronkiti.   Men from Ruk and
the Mortlocks are easily discerned by the enormous size
of the lower lobe of their ears, unnaturally distended,
loaded down with shell-ornaments, as is the custom of
their race.   There are some Pingelap and Mokil men,
naïve, awkward, and stolid, but cheerful and harmless folk,
and there was a man from the remote islet of Nuku-Oro.
His name was Caspar, and Nanapei employed him as
carpenter and boat-builder—a very quiet, good fellow, who
was delighted at my being able to converse with him in
Samoan, to which the Nuku-Oro tongue bears an extraordinary resemblance.   At the mouth of the river is the
Chakar-en-Yap landing-place, where Nanapei has built a
substantial wharf, boathouse, and storehouse.   A steep
road runs up the hill-slope behind to the main settlement
on the plateau, where Nanapei has a pretty residence of the
bungalow type, with a lawn in front dotted with rose-
bushes and clumps of croton and scarlet hibiscus.

We stayed two or three days below by the waterside,
coming up hill for our meals, which were served either in
Nanapei's house or that of his mother Nalio close by.
Nalio, who has since unhappily died, was a lady of strong
character and intelligence.   She had a most kindly and
charitable nature, which very much endeared her throughout the tribes, and doubtless brought many powerful
local chiefs under the influence of her son.   When everything was ready, Nanapei sailed us over to Nalap.   The
house he placed at our disposal was roomy and comfortable, built of lumber, with all furniture complete, even
to tables and chairs.   There were two other households on the island.   The nearest to us was that of
Judas, the native teacher, his wife and their boy called
Chilon, a bright little fellow.   An old fisherman and
his wife, with a number of ugly yellow house-dogs,
lived away on the further seaward horn of the islet.
Close by Nalap was a tiny little patch or cay of sand

covered with mangroves and ironwood trees.   Here
an old Gilbert islander, Te Bako, "*the Shark*," and his
wife lived.   In his youth a notorious homicide, but converted in middle life, he was now passing a hale and
hearty old age, darkened by occasional fits of gloomy
repentance.   He said the ghosts of dead men wouldn't
let him sleep at night, and at all hours of the darkness,
storm or calm, one would see him out upon the reef with
torch and spear vehemently striving by hard toil to quell
both the devil within him and the devils that he declared
were ever mocking and gibing at him from without.   Fish
he brought us in plenty, and was always glad of a bit
of tobacco.   Biscuit he also accepted thankfully.   One
stormy night, seeing him pitiably drenched and chilled
through and through in the northerly gales, I offered him
a little rum.   This he refused, as a native rarely does,
giving me plainly to understand that in his youth he had
slain a relation in a drunken brawl.

"There was a feast in the Moniap (Council Lodge).
My head was hot with the *Karuoruo* (*sour toddy*).   Words
grew to a quarrel, and men fought.   In the morning my
brother (*i.e.* cousin) lay by me dead, and I was the man
who had slain him.   Bad is the strong liquor of Te-Aba
(the Gilbert Islands), but worse is the fiery water of
Te-Matang (the foreigner)."   And the old man was
quite right, for the drinking of coconut toddy has produced frightful consequences in the Gilberts and the
Marquesas.   Indeed the total extinction of the latter
islanders is now only a question of a decade.   The opium
of China, the rum and absinthe of the French, also work
their havoc there.   To these four grim foes add the
Chinese leprosy and the measles and phthisis of Europe,
which are pressing these hapless natives faster and faster
to extinction.   The Gilbert islanders will possibly just
scrape clear and make a new start.   But the Marquesan
race is doomed—a bright and amiable people sinking
down into lurid and smoky darkness.

Many a talk had Te Bako and I on the verandah by night, whilst the Manilla man was snoring. The old warrior would tell of inter-island wars and of the coming of the *Kaibuke,* "tree-mountains" or foreign ships. For my part I would tell him of the great wars in England and America, France and Germany, and of the little wars in the Pacific, Kamehamahas' conquest of the Sandwich Islands, of Mataafa in Samoa, Pomare in Tahiti, Thakombau in Fiji, Te Whiti and Tawhiao in New Zealand. And the more I told him of these things the more eagerly he listened, like all the natives I have ever met.

But my poor artist was another character altogether— pretentious child of an effete civilization. He dared to look down upon the magnificent old barbarian, who late in life was himself crushing out the inherited savagery of generations of fierce warriors and sea rovers. The Gilbert islander eyed the Manilla citizen askance, sized him up as a poor sort of creature, and despised him then and there. Theodoro for his part, as much as possible kept out of Te Bako's way, and always carried about with him a small revolver for fear of accidents! And this was the beginning of the terrors that his prophetic soul saw looming up before him on the steamer, that eventful Sunday of our start from Manilla Bay.

A term of serene and glorious weather succeeded. The days glided by filled up with excursions on the reef and in the lagoon, and occasionally to the mainland. My evenings, as a rule, were given up to the fascinating study of the Ponapean language and its curious idioms. Here I laid the groundwork of a Ponapean dictionary containing some four thousand words, since much elaborated and added to. The results obtained stood me in good stead during the rest of my stay on the island, upon which I found there were two dialects spoken by the tribes on the East and West coast respectively, mutually intelligible, but each with many words peculiar to its area, and a number of minor local variations, mostly vowel changes.

As an instance of the former, *Taip* is the East-coast word for the Pandanus, called *Kipar* on the Western side. The varying local names for the Morinda citrifolia—*Umpul, Wompul* and *Weipul*—show the vowel-changes. Not to detain the reader over the dry bones of philology, I will merely remark here that the Ponapean language is full of diphthongs, and that in grammar it seems to form a connecting link with the languages of Malaysia, with the somewhat complicated tongues of Melanesia, and the later and abraded forms of the Polynesian area. It has very many cognate words with those of the dialects of the Philippines and the Kayan and Dayak of Borneo. The simple root-words mostly consisting of one or two syllables are akin to those of the Indian hill-tribes, apparently belonging to the primitive Aryan substratum.[1] The letter-sounds *F* and *V* are conspicuously absent, their places filled respectively by *P*, which also does duty for *B*, and by *W*, agreeably to the precepts laid down by the father of Sam Weller. *H* is never heard, even in words cognate with Polynesian. *Cf.* Polynesian Hetau, Fetau, a Callophyllum.

Ponape,   Ichau id.
Polynesian,   Hetu, Fetu, a star.
Ponape,   Uchu id.
Polynesian,   Hoto, Foto, a barb ; prickle, sting.
Ponape,   Och, id.
Polynesian,   Hitu, Fitu, seven.
Ponape,   Ichu id.

(But Polynesian Hatu, Fatu, a stone ; we find Ponapean *Pat.*) where by analogy one would expect *Ach* or *Ech*.

The verbal roots are most elaborately modified by the addition of qualifying suffixes, which gives great flexibility

[1] This I know has been called in question, as well as the wider theory involved of the overflowing and infiltration of words cognate with Aryan roots into the Polynesian area. Yet after most careful and minute inquiry, I feel bound to range myself on the side of Fornander, Tregear, Percy Smith and the Rev. J. Fraser. Those interested further in the subject I may refer to my comparative Table of some 40,000 Micronesian and Indonesian words published shortly in the Journal of the Polynesian Society of New Zealand at Wellington.

and even elegance to a tongue which at first strikes one as rather harsh.

A common prefix to names of birds and fishes is *Li*, *i.e.* Woman.

It also occurs very frequently in compound words denoting qualities or actions held in light esteem.

Cf. Li-*kam*, a lie, *i.e. a woman's fault.*

Li-*ngarangar*, Fury, passion, *i.e. a woman's angry voice.*

Li-*porok*, Curiosity, *i.e. a woman's peering.*

Li-*mongin*, Conspiracy, *i.e. a woman's whispering.*

But Li-*mpok* denotes deep, sincere affection, *i.e. a woman's love.*

Li-*pilipil*, Favoritism, *i.e. a woman's choice.*

In Chinese we find the word for *woman* affixed to many uncomplimentary adjectives.

I pass rapidly over our life upon Nalap, somewhat uneventful, save that one evening we were nearly capsized on a shoal called the Horseheads, where two years ago one of the Kiti chiefs was upset, and lost an entire set of false teeth supplied him by a compassionate Spanish doctor in Ascension Bay. One little expedition of mine, however, is worth noting. Guided by Harry Beaumont, Nanapei's chief carpenter, I walked from Ronkiti through the woods to Annepein, through a picturesque but also sadly swampy district, stopping on the way to notice the Tumulus of Kona the Giant, whlch lies in a clearing dotted sparsely with wild pandanus trees, which give the name to the neighbouring settlement of Kipar. The mound or barrow is about ten feet in height, twenty in breadth, and about a quarter of a mile in length. It is considerably overgrown with a tangle of creepers and hibiscus.

The name *Kona* also occurs in Hawaiian and Peruvian as the name of a giant. The local tradition runs to the effect that a giant was buried here with his body on land, and his legs stretching seaward to the little islets of Kapara and Laiap, lying out near the edge of the lagoon. The Spanish historian Pereiro sets the mound down, and

I think correctly, as a construction for defence or a cemetery wherein they interred the dead after a great battle.
I had no implements for excavation handy, and soon afterwards the absorbing interest of exploring the Metalanim
ruins quite engrossed my attention.   But I mention the
Barrow of Kipar, hoping that the next explorer here will
come better provided, and that here also diligent excavations may bring to light many interesting relics of the
past.

We received a good many visits from time to time on
Nalap from the district chiefs, and saw a couple of whaling
vessels and one Honolulu trading schooner enter and
leave Ronkiti harbour, also a copra-laden vessel from
Nagasaki, with a Japanese crew and skipper.   We also
had an enjoyable two days' visit to our Paliker friends up
the coast, marred only by the discomfort on our journey
up, of missing the right landing-place in the twilight
amongst the dense mangrove thickets, and remaining
moored all night in utter darkness cooped up in our
narrow craft under a terrific tropical downpour.   Next
morning, chilled to the very bone, we struggled up to the
little hill settlement, where the warmth of our reception
speedily made us forget all our miseries.   A mighty feast
was prepared for us, there was Kava-making, there were
speeches and orations, and the proceedings closed with an
exposition of native dancing and singing.   The second
day was a repetition of the first, and after delighting our
good old host, the village headman, with a present of knives
and tobacco, we sailed back again to Nalap, where we
found the Spanish gunboat *Quiros* in harbour.   Nanapei
introduced me to her commander, Don Miguel Velasco,
who very kindly invited us all three to go down with him
to visit the Ant Islands, which lie about twelve miles off
the west coast.   They were colonised from Kiti as the
Pakin group, a little to the northward was from Chokach.
The Ant's are a cluster of thirteen small and two larger
islets, disposed in the usual horse-shoe formation, the prin-

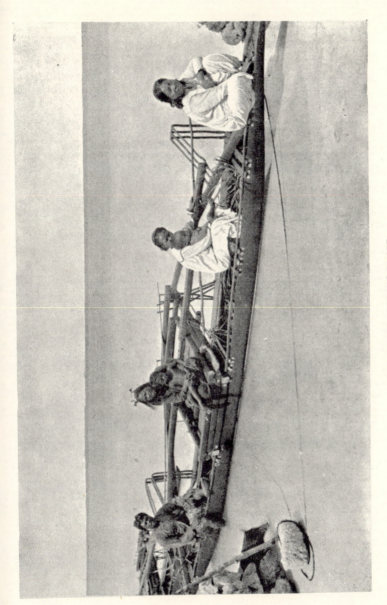

A PALIKER FISHING-CANOE

cipal entrance being the *Tau-en-iai* or Channel of Fire at the south end of Kalap, the largest, upon which live about thirty of the Kiti folk, engaged in collecting copra from the magnificent groves of cocoanuts that cover one and all of them. Here we stayed two days, taking soundings in the lagoon. I walked the length of Kalap and shot a number of green and grey doves. Theodoro took some views, amongst others, one of the coral-paved precinct of the Pako-Charaui or Sacred Shark, the Patron Spirit of Ant. In the background was a great native chestnut tree, with bundles of sugar cane and kava root, and some fishes' heads of no very recent date, hanging up in honour of the dread divinity. Then back to Nalap for a few days more study.

By this time I had formed an opinion upon native character, with its strangely mingled strength and weakness, which subsequent events rather tended to confirm. I here give it to the reader for what it is worth.

The character of the Ponapean, like that of the Caroline Islander in general, in whom so many different race-elements are merged, has some curious contradictions. He alternates fitful seasons of wonderful energy at work with long spells of incorrigible laziness. In supplying his simple needs he shows considerable ingenuity and resource. He is very superstitious, yet exceedingly practical in small matters. He has a good deal of the Malay stoicism and apathy, joined to great penetration and acuteness. His senses, like those of all half-civilised tribes, are very keen, and his powers of minute observation most remarkable. In many of his doings he exhibits a highly comical mixture of shrewdness and simplicity, of seriousness and buffoonery, of a light-hearted knavery tempered by a certain saving sense of rude justice—in short, a regular moral chamœleon. He is a capital mimic, something of a poet of the doggrel order, and very fond of dancing, feasting, and, of late years, of fiery alcoholic liquors. With strangers he is reserved and suspicious, and often shows a cross-grained reticence when questioned on the past history or traditions of his race, with which, I presume, he fancies strangers have no concern. As a rule he is fairly honest. Once lay his suspicions to rest and win his confidence, and he will prove himself a faithful friend and an excellent host, courteous and just in all his dealings, as I have very good cause to know. On the other hand, when dealing with his enemies he calls into play a talent for intrigue, lying, and chicanery that would delight a Machiavel. In his private life, he is unselfish, frugal, and economical, a man of careful small habits. Like all folk of Melanesian admixture, he is liable to fits of dangerous sullenness when he considers himself slighted in any way. He is inclined to be revengeful, and will bide his time patiently until his opportunity comes. Yet he is not implacable, and counts reconciliation a noble and a princely thing. There is a form of etiquette to be observed on these occasions—a present (*katom*) is made, an apology offered— a piece of sugar-cane accepted by the aggrieved party— honour is satisfied and the matter ends. The Ponapean is a stout warrior, a hardy and skilful navigator, fisherman, carpenter and boat-builder, but a very second-class planter and gardener. He is a kind father, but alas, according to western ideas, a stern and exacting husband. Many of the old men are skilled observers of the stars, the weather, the winds, and the prevailing currents. The Ponapean reveres old age, especially when coupled with wisdom or ability. The priest, counsellor, leech, diviner, and the culler of simples are held in high esteem. The generous and provident man is praised, the mean man and thief generally despised. Lack of filial piety or natural affection carries with it a lamentable stigma amongst them, and the curse of the ancestral spirits here and hereafter. It is much to be regretted that the Ponapean character has changed notably for the worse of late years. Many of the natives have grown thievish, churlish and disobliging : this more particularly with the Metalanim folk on the east coast who are the most difficult of all the tribesmen.

Their manner of life is simple and hardy. They go about in all weathers, rain or sunshine. Nowadays, greatly to the peril of their health, they have adopted European clothes. These they keep on their back whether wet or dry, which induces all manner of rheumatic and pulmonary ailments.

Their food consists generally of fish or shell-fish and a vegetable diet of yams, bananas, taro, and breadfruit. The forests yield pigeons and some smaller birds very good for food. On the occasion of a feast, pigs and fowls are added to the bill of fare. The flesh of the dog (*kiti*) is highly relished, especially on the east coast. Crabs, crayfish and freshwater prawns are also in request. The turtle is set apart for the chiefs alone. Eels, whether of the salt or fresh water they will not eat, and hold them in the greatest horror. The old name for eel is *Īt*—the modern *Kamichik* or the Dreadful One.

The special department of the women is the making of mats and shutters of reed-grass, the plaiting of baskets, and binding the leaves of the sago-palm into bundles for thatch. They make the leaf-girdles of the men, and compound the coconut-oil and fish-oil, and mix the cosmetic of turmeric, without which no Ponapean dandy's toilet is complete. They fetch water in calabashes, light the fires, build the stone ovens, prepare the food, and perform all the household duties. When required they cheerfully assist the men in their outdoor labours, and in time of war accompany their husbands and relations fearlessly into the battle.

Marriage.—The formality of marriage between young people is singular. The girl is brought into the house and sits down, whilst her future mother-in-law rubs coconut oil vigorously into her back and shoulders. This is called *Keieti* or *Anointing*. A garland of flowers is placed on her head and the ceremony is concluded by a feast. The marriage bond may be severed at any time at the consent of either party. The Ponapeans for the most part content themselves with a single wife, polygamy being the privilege only of the wealthy and powerful chiefs. Adultery is usually settled out of court by a sound thrashing of the offending wife and possibly a separation of the parties. Exchange of wives (*Peichipal*) between friends and relations, as in the Marquesas, is occasionally practised. The demi-monde class (*Raran*), like the *Niki-rau-roro* of the Gilbert Group, is tolerated in each district. Doubtless an heirloom of their Asiatic forefathers. The Sanskrit word *Lalana* has the very same meaning.

Adoption of children is universal and forms a complicated chain of relationships, an arrangement quite clear and simple to the native mind, but extremely puzzling to a European. Descent is traced through the mother—a custom tolerably common amongst the Oceanic races in general. Members of the same *Tipu* or clan cannot marry. A wife must be taken from one of the other divisions. The suitor serves for his wife in the house of his father-in-law elect, as Jacob did with Laban, and frequently has his pains for nothing. Men and women alike practise tatooing (*Inting*) on the arms and lower limbs. Unlike the Marquesan islanders they do not tatoo their faces. The women use a design taken from the interlacing of coconut fronds in their leaf baskets. Other designs are circles and eight-pointed stars and crosses; some of very bizarre form. The young men, to show their contempt for pain, are in the habit of inflicting knife-gashes and burning deep scars on their breasts and arms. A terrible ethnic mutilation is practised upon the young men on reaching marriageable age. It is called *Lekelek* and consists of the excision of one of the testicles—generally that on the right side. The Ichipau of Metalanim in a fit of religious mania, brooding over the threatened lake of fire and bethinking himself of a certain passage in St John, went even further than this.

Burial.—They bury their dead with great ceremony and solemn funeral orations. They are most unwilling to repeat the name of a dead ancestor—a very Melanesian trait. Consequently, I did not meet with in Ponape any elaborate family genealogies, like the ancient and carefully preserved oral records of the Marquesans and Maoris, and the kindred Polynesian races. Something of the sort may however exist.

The worship of the *Ani* or deified ancestors, coupled with a sort of zoolatry or totemism, is the backbone of the Ponapean faith.

Every village, every valley, hill or stream has its *genius loci*, every family its household god, every clan its presiding spirit, every tribe its tutelary deity. Thunder, lightning, rain, storm, wind, fishing, planting, war, festival, harvest, famine, birth, disease, death, all these events and phenomena have their supernatural patron or Master-spirit. The gloomy fancy of the Ponapean, peoples the swamp, the reef, the mountain, and the hanging woods of the inland wilderness with hosts of spirits, some beneficent, the greater part malignant. All these *Ani* are honoured under the guise of some special bird, fish, or tree in which they are supposed to reside, and with which they are identified. These they style their *Tan-waar*, literally *canoe, vehicle* or *medium* (like the *Vaa* or *Vaka* of the Polynesians, the *Huaca* or *Vaka* of the Peruvians). Thus the chestnut tree is the medium of the god of thunder, the blue starfish of the god of rain, the shark of the god of war, and the *Lukot* or native owl the emblem of the fairy Li-Ara-Katau, one of the local genii of the east coast.

In their mythology they have a submarine Paradise (*Pachet*), a place of perpetual feasting amongst lovely sights and sweet odours. They also have a subterranean Tartarus (*Pueliko*) of mire, cold and darkness, guarded by two grim female forms (Lichar and Licher), one holding a glittering sword, the other a blazing torch—a gloomy conception very much resembling the Yomi of Japan and the Yama of the early Vedas.

And now we made up our minds to fly at higher game, and dive into the mysteries of the Metalanim Ruins on the east coast.

CHAPTER V

FIRST AND SECOND VISITS TO THE RUINS
OF NAN-MATAL

EARLY in March 1896, we left Nalap in Nanapei's sailing-boat, our plans being to run up to the Spanish Colony in Ascension Bay to lay in a stock of European provisions and other necessaries, for neither stores nor groceries are found in Metalanim. After loading up to sail along the Ú. Coast to the north, and touch at two interesting islands, Mantapeiti and Mantapeîtak (Mant-to-leeward and Mant-to-windward), in the neighbourhood of which in 1887, Mr J. C. Dewar's fine yacht the *Nyanza* was cast away on the reefs, a total wreck.

After leaving the Mants we passed close by the islands of Tapak and Aru, upon the former of which are some ancient platforms and tetragonal enclosures of stonework. Thence we sailed down the east coast, and early in the morning came to the King's island of Tomun, or Tamuan, which lies a little inside the mouth of Metalanim Harbour. Here we found David Lumpoi, an English-speaking chief to whose care Nanapei commended us, and sailed home again. That very day a great festival was being holden under Mount Takai-U, the odd-looking sugarloaf hill at the head of the bay. Here King Paul with his nobles and commons around him, sat in state prepared to receive us. Our welcome was coldly ceremonious, and I instantly read distrust and dislike in the faces of the notables present. The king was a corpulent old man with a large broad head, and a massive square chin, his somewhat heavy features being of a Melanesian rather than Polynesian type. Looking into his shifty eyes I could see surly pride mingled with suspicion and vague uneasiness. The gruff old churl's countenance irresistibly recalled to me the description of the wicked island king in one of R. L. Stevenson's South Sea Ballads :—

" Fear was a worm in his heart, Fear darted his eyes
And he probed men's faces for treason and pondered their speech
    for lies."

The lodge was filled with smoke as a Highland cottage with peat-reek, whilst myriads of lively mosquitoes hovered up and down, in and out, seeking to flesh their suckers in the august assembly shrouded behind that fleecy veil. The interview was soon over. We obtained a sullen and grudging permission to explore the ruins, for which, how-ever, a fee of five dollars was demanded. For one of the Boston missionaries about 1880, foreseeing that on some later day Europeans might come here to explore, put into the head of the Metalanim chiefs to exact this toll, which the Spanish Governor had told us would certainly be enforced. I handed him over five Spanish dollars, which he eyed doubtfully, weighed, smelt and nipped between his teeth, to make sure I had not palmed off lead on him. With the remark, " Moni-n-Sepanich, moni chiuet,"— "Spanish money, bad money ; " he locked it up carefully in a box. Scenting, perhaps, further opportunities for imposition, and assuming an air of cordiality that sat but ill on him, he pressed us to stay. But I was firmly resolved to go before his majesty's dull brain had time to devise some new pretext for extortion. Therefore, as soon as we decently could, we departed, itching sorely from mosquito bites, half-choked, half-blinded, eyes and nostrils tingling sharply from the acrid smoke that filled every corner of the house. A portion of cooked and pre-served breadfruit, the latter in odour recalling a Stilton cheese some three years old, followed us down to the boat according to a hospitable native custom. With a stiff breeze behind us we stood across the bay. Just off

Tomun, David, who was steering, managed to run the craft upon a stack of coral rocks, staving in several planks and making an ugly hole in her bows, which we had some trouble in stopping. We put inshore awhile, and after repairing damages, loosed away south for Ponatik, catching our first glimpse of the famous ruins by our way.

We entered a wonder of tortuous alley-ways, a labyrinth of shallow canals, with shady vistas stretching away to the right and left, bordered on either side by dense walls of tropical leafage and the ever-present mangrove and salt-water brush, the vanguard of the hosts of the forest in their march seaward upon the rich belt of alluvial soil which the rivers of Ponape have washed down. Here and there grim masses of stonework peer out from behind the verdant screen, encrusted with lichen, and tufted with masses of fern waving from between the crevices in delicate feathery outlines. But we have little leisure to stay, the clouds are banking up ominously in the south. Mount Telemir is black with storm-wrack. "Onward" is the cry, and we push on in the fading light past foreland, sandspit and salt-marsh, down to Ponatik, where we land at the base of an enormous Tupap tree.

We found David's house all ready for us. Next day we looked round the settlement, in which there was nothing specially remarkable, save a singular abundance of *Parram* or Nipa-palm, which with the numerous coconut and sago-palms gave a pretty setting to the scene.

A couple of days later I visited the ruins accompanied by Keroun and Alek, two men of Ponatik, who were with difficulty induced to face the anger of the Ani or ancestral spirits and the tabu which enwraps the Lil-Charaui or Holy Places, and answers very much to the Luli so strictly observed by the natives of Timor. Passing the southern barricade of stones, we turned into the ghostly labyrinth of this city of the waters, and straightway the merriment of our guides was hushed, and conversation died down to whispers.

A NATIVE OF LOT

We were bound for Uchentau, where a little native house had been set apart for our temporary camp. We arrived about nightfall, and as there was no particular use in exploring ruins by torchlight, we reserved our energies for the morning.

Next day broke clear and bright, the canoe was manned, and away we started. As we shoot round a sharp bend on the right after five minutes' paddling, a strange and wonderful sight greets our eyes. We are close in to Nan-Tauach (*the Place of Lofty Walls*), the most remarkable of all the Metalanim ruins. The water-front is faced with a terrace built of massive basalt blocks about seven feet wide, standing out more than six feet above the shallow waterway. Above us we see a striking example of immensely solid Cyclopean stone-work frowning down upon the waterway, a mighty wall formed of basaltic prisms laid alternately lengthwise and crosswise after the fashion of a *chock and log* fence, or, as masons would style it, *Headers and Stretchers*. Our guides smile indulgently, as they assist me and my Manilla photographer up the sides of the great wharf, for it is now low tide in the streets of this strange water-town. On a brimming high-tide, landing is an easier matter. We were soon at work tearing down creepers and lianas, and letting in the light of the sun upon the mighty black masses.

The left side of the great gateway yawning overhead is about twenty-five feet in height and the right some thirty feet, overshadowed and all but hidden from view by the dense leafage of a huge Ikoik tree, which we had not the heart to demolish for its extreme beauty—a wonder of deep emerald-green heart-shaped leaves, thickly studded with tassels of scarlet trumpet-shaped flowers, bright as the bloom of coral or flame tree.

Here in olden times the outer wall must have been uniformly of considerably greater height, but has now in several places fallen into lamentable ruin, whether from

earthquake, typhoon, vandal hands, or the wear and tear
of long, long ages.   Somewhat similar in character would
be the semi-Indian ruins of Java, and the Cyclopean
structures of Ake, and Chichen-Itza in Yucatan.   A
series of huge rude steps brings us into a spacious courtyard, strewn with fragments of fallen pillars, encircling
a second terraced enclosure with a projecting frieze or
cornice of somewhat Japanese type.   The measurement
of the outer enclosure, as we afterwards roughly ascer-
tained, was some 185 feet by 115 feet, the average thickness of the outer wall 15 feet, height varying from 20 to
nearly 40 feet.   The space within can only be entered
by the great gateway in the middle of the western face,
and by a small ruinous portal in the north-west corner.
The inner terraced enclosure forms a second conforming
parallelogram of some 85 feet by 75 feet; average thickness of wall, 8 feet; height of walls, 15 to 18 feet.
In the centre of a rudely-paved court lies the great central
vault or treasure chamber, identified with the name of
an ancient monarch known as Chau-te-reul or Chau-
te-Leur, probably a dynastic title like that of Pharaoh
or Ptolemy in ancient Egypt.   (*N.B.*—*Chau* was the
ancient Ponape word denoting, (*a*) the sun (*b*) a king.
The latter signification tallies with the Rotuma *Sau*,
a king, and the Polynesian *Hau* and *Au*, a king, chief.)
The plan of the enclosure facing this page shows three
other of these vaults, the double line of terraces built
up of basalt and limestone blocks, and the several
courtyards separated off by low intersecting lines of
wall.   In this connection Kubary remarks, and I think
very truly, " A certain irregularity in the whole building, as in the differing height and breadth of individual terraces, betokens a variety of builders, following
one another, and knowing how to give expression to their
respective ideas."

Over the camp fire that night the Spanish doctor's historiette again is eagerly studied.   Let us hear what the good

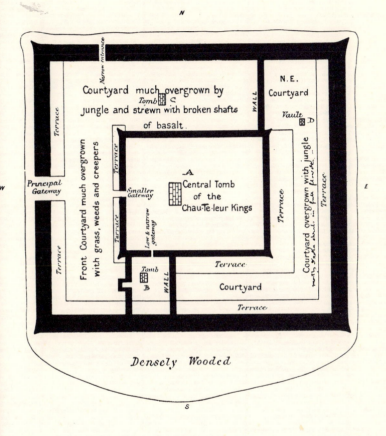

N

W   E

Narrow entrance

Courtyard much overgrown by
Tomb C
jungle and strewn with broken shafts
of basalt.

N.E.
Courtyard

Vault D

Terrace

Front Courtyard much overgrown
with grass, weeds and creepers

Terrace

Courtyard overgrown with jungle

Smaller
Gateway

A
Central Tomb
of the
Chau-Te-leur Kings

Terrace

Low & narrow
gateway

Terrace

Tomb B

WALL

Terrace

Courtyard

Terrace

*Principal
Gateway*

Terrace

WALL

Densely Wooded

S

Scale 1 inch to 40 feet

Plan of the double parallelogram enclosed by the walls of Nan Tauach,
in the district of Nan Matal, tribe of Metalanim, East coast of Ponape.

doctor, Pereiro Cabeza, who in 1890 nearly lost his life in battle near these same ruins, has to say. " Between the discovery of Ponape in 1595 and modern times the island must have been re-visited by the Spanish. In 1886 a *derrotero Inglese* or map-making Englishman (name not specified) noticed them as follows : " Around the harbour of Metalanim there are some interesting ruins whose origin is involved in the greatest obscurity. The oldest inhabitant can tell nothing about them, and has no tradition as to their history. Doubtless there existed here a fortified town inhabited by a folk of superior civilisation. Some of the stones are about ten feet in length and worked into six faces, no doubt brought from some civilised country, for they have no stones like them in the island. The whole settlement appears to be a series of fortified houses, and various artificial caves have been discovered inside the fortifications."

Without anticipating the narrative, or pausing here to seriously criticise Dr Cabeza's view (which Kubary clearly shows to be untenable) that these structures were the work of pirates or early Spanish voyagers, it may be worth while here to remark :—

1. The old inhabitants do retain certain traditions about the origin of these ruins, but will not tell everybody, least of all a mere passing traveller. They would regard it as casting " pearls before swine." The Englishman of 1886 evidently does not know what native reticence means. The Ponapean tradition told me by the Au of Marau is sufficiently explicit. Two brothers, *Ani-Aramach*, God-men or Heroes, named Olo-chipa and Olo-chopa, coming from the direction of Chokach, built the breakwater of Nan-Moluchai and the island city it shuts in. By their magic spells one by one the great masses of stone flew through the air like birds, settling down into their appointed place. These two names of curious assonance are cognate with those of the Tahitian Demigods *Oro-tetefa* and *Uru-tetefa*, the traditional founders of that remarkable brother-

hood the *Areoi*, which before the introduction of Christianity wielded so grim and tremendous an influence throughout the whole of the Society group.

2. The doctor speaks of "stones worked into six faces." The stones, as a matter of fact, are polygonal or multi-angular, some five, some eight-sided. Many are certainly six-sided, but by no means uniformly so. Here comes in the interesting question of the early use in Micronesia of iron or copper tools, which is fully discussed in the chapter upon Ponapean tools and implements. It is enough here to say that I saw no marks of cutting or graving tools on the stonework, neither did Kubary. I do not say they may not exist, but we certainly saw none. The native Ponapean axe of Tridacna shell, excellent as is the edge it takes, would be far too brittle to chisel such hard and massive blocks into shape. A geologist would immediately declare them to be unhewn slabs of basalt of natural prismatic formation.

N.B.—Dr Wichmann of Leipzig says they are akin to the basalt of the Siebengebirge.

3. " No stones like them in the island." If the Englishman of 1886, and the Spaniard who quotes him, had had time or opportunity to inquire further, they would have found that on Chokach Island, below the Paip-Alap or Great Cliff on the north-west coast, and away up one of the mountain glens of Ú, on the north coast, are the two places whence all this enormous quantity of basalt was brought down. The landing stage at Auak in Ú, and some remarkable sacred enclosures on Tapak Island near the Mants, are built of the same stone. Moreover, as we sitting by our camp-fire already know very well, similar remains occur on Tauak Islet off the Paliker coast. Subsequently we fell in with others at Nantamarui, Lang Takai, Ponial and Pona Ul, on the Kiti and Metalanim borders, and at Chap-en-Takai, an ancient fort and holy place crowning one of the hills above Marau on the Kiti coast. In the same district similar

ruins are reported in the hill-settlement of Chalapuk near the head-waters of the Ronkiti River.

Kubary with his usual keen and minute observation remarks : " The oblique inward slope of the upper basalt layers seems to suggest that the stones were brought here by means of an inclined plane." Such a system, in the absence of powerful cranes and other machinery, certainly seems to me very feasible. In my mind's eye I viewed an even slope of felled tree trunks copiously sluiced with coconut oil, to avoid friction, up which the great blocks would be hauled, one relay of workmen above pulling upon long and thick cables of coir fibre or cinnet and supplementary ropes of green hibiscus bark, another relay below with solid staves and handspikes by turns pushing the huge mass upwards and resting with their poles set against and below it to prevent it slipping back.

Kubary adds that the blocks of basalt were rafted down from the Not district on the north coast. This tallies exactly with what Nanchau of Mutok and the Au of Marau told me, and with the singular phenomenon I observed in the shallower portions of the lagoon : the presence of numberless broken fragments and sometimes pillars of basalt lying upon the coral bottom. To my inquiry of my boatman what brought them there the answer was always the same—*Takai-tol poputi nan chet-uech, o ari,*—" *When a bit of black stone falls into salt water it grows, and that's all about it.*"

The tale of how we fared amongst the fortified houses and artificial caves shall supplement the account of the mysterious map-making Englishman of the Spanish chronicler.

As far as we could gather, then and subsequently, in olden time Ponape (in the West Carolines *Fanu-Pei,* the Land of the *Pei* or Holy Places), then much more populous than now, was united under the rule of the Chau-te-Leur line of kings like the Tui-Tongas of Tonga-tabu. The last of the dynasty met his death facing a barbaric horde from the Pali-Air, the barren lands of the south, probably some portion of New Guinea or the Melanesian Islands, led by a fierce and terrible warrior, Icho-Kalakal, Kubary's Idzi-Kolkol. Swarms of savage invaders poured in upon the peaceful settlers, and almost completely destroyed the ancient civilisation after an obstinate resistance, in which numbers were slain on both sides; the king himself, in his flight, being drowned in the Chapalap River at the head of Metalanim Harbour. The pitying Ani or gods changed him into a blue river fish, the *Kital*, which the Metalanim folk to this very day refuse to eat. And the conqueror Icho-Kalakal ruled the land, and in process of time died and was buried on Pei-Kap (one story says *Nan-Pulok*, and another *Peitok*). He became the War-God of Metalanim, and remains a dreaded spectre to this very day.

It is an interesting fact that two of the principal septs or clans on Ponape, the *Tip-en-Uai* or Foreign Folk and the *Tip-en-Panamai* or People from *Panamai*, trace their descent from Icho-Kalakal—Panamai being the name of the land from which the invasion came. Possibly the island of *Panapa* (Ocean Island), or one of the Gilbert or Line Islands may be designated, where we find a mingled Polynesian and Melanesian population. Other interesting facts in this connection are :—

1. The presence of an elaborate chief's language in Ponapean, some words of which are pure Polynesian and others later Malay.[1] [*Cf.*—*Lima* is the hand of a chief, *Pa* that of a commoner. *Kumikum* a chief's beard, *Alich* a subject's beard. *Chilani* a chief's eye, *Macha* the eye of a subject. *Achang* tooth of chief, *Ngi* tooth of common man.] In Malay *Kumi* is a moustache, and in Javanese *Alis* is the eyebrow.

[1] To my mind this is proof positive of the coming in of a conquering race forming a ruling aristocracy, like William the Conqueror's Normans amongst the Saxons, or Strongbow and his brother barons amongst the Irish of a later day. And this conclusion, indeed, is amply borne out by the Ponapean tradition of Icho-Kalakal and his invasion from the lands of the south.

S.E. INNER ANGLE IN REAR OF GREAT CENTRAL VAULT

SHOWING DENSE GROWTH OF HIBISCUS, CREEPERS AND BETAL-PEPPER VINES,
WITH TRUNK OF CHATAK TREE IN FOREGROUND

2. A wonderful similarity in root-words between Pona-pean and the language of the Gilbert group and the dialect of Efate in the New Hebrides and that of Mota in the Banks group.

3. The presence of Ponapean place-names in the Melanesian area.

4. The occurrence of stone buildings like those of Nan-Matal, but on a smaller scale, sketched and described by the Rev. R. H. Codrington at Gaua upon Santa Maria, one of the Banks group.

The result of our first visit was to give us some idea of the lie of the land. Clearly, in my opinion, the place was a town built out of the water by a sea-faring race, not as Hale has pronounced it, a land city which has sunk. In this I find Kubary and Dr Gulick agree with me. Darwin and Dana, however, hold Ponape as an instance of the subsidence of an island within the sunk plane. We took a few photographs, and managed to scratch up a few beads in the central vault, which, of course, only whetted our appetite for more. So we went back to Ponatik to engage more labour, and the morning after our return an old American settler in the neighbourhood, J. Kehoe, called on me and volunteered to give his help in exploring the ruins, where he had himself often been before. So we arranged a second expedition, and left on March 14th. Our party consisted of J. Kehoe, Theodoro, Nanit, a native of Kiti, Keroun and myself. Arriving at Nan-Tauach by way of Uchentau about noon, we set about our excavations in the main vault (A). We all took turns with the digging and worked till sunset, turning out heaps more bracelets and shell beads, some of the latter thick and some of very delicate make. We returned muddy, grimy and weary, with marvellous appetites for beef and biscuit, and lay down longing for the morrow. Next day we were hard at work again with increasing good fortune, for several mag-nificent shell-axes or Patkul rewarded our efforts. Then we went in for a new sort of toil, hewing and hacking away, making tremendous gaps in the jungle which envelopes the precinct within and without, climbing around on the walls heedless of tottering slabs, tearing away long festoons of creeper and great clumps of weed and fern, close-rooted in the crevices of the mighty structure. The patient man with the camera clicks off view after view of the massive walls sullenly frowning down upon the assailants, who have rent their way through the mazy wilderness and lifted the veil of clinging greenery and let in the light of day upon these halls of Eblis. A jovial party surrounds the blazing hearth that night, all but Keroun, who sits apart fitfully muttering to himself, a prey to supernatural terror, and a horror of unseen horrors.

March 16.—Next morning we visited Pan-Katara and cleared the angle, and measured the height of the wall, which turned out to be 27 feet. With difficulty we forced our way through the jungle into the paved enclosure in the heart of the island, where in olden times the king used to sit with his priests and nobles round him, drinking the *choko* or kava in solemn state. Keroun flatly declined to accompany us, and remained with the canoe on the canalside in a state of great nervousness. The afternoon was devoted to a second onslaught on the bush and creepers. The inner courtyard and surrounding terraces of Nan-Tauach were cleared of undergrowth, together with portions of the walls of the inner enclosure and the inner and outer angles at the corner of the great wall facing south. These operations put the finishing touch to Keroun's dismay, who repeatedly declared the precinct to be haunted. " The eyes of the spirits are watching everything you do," said the obstinate old donkey. " They will not hurt you because you are a white man, but they will punish *us*. I cannot sleep at night; I am very much afraid, and I should like to go home."

March 17th was spent in digging in chambers A and B with moderate results. I returned with my party to Ponatik in the afternoon, leaving the exploration of the

PONAPEAN PATTERNS CARVED IN *KARARA* WOOD

pits, the taking of more elaborate measurements, and photographing of the north side for next excursion. We were busy sorting and washing curios till late that night, and during the whole of next day. The people of the settlement still continued sullen and stupid, and left us strictly alone. Keroun thought to make a brilliant move by suddenly demanding double pay, but looked very blank when calmly informed that in future his salary was to be *reduced* in proportion to his services.

Next morning (March 19th) Alek came in with some ornamental dance-paddles, and a collection of square tablets of native woods which he had carved into beautiful patterns, and stained in red, black, white and yellow, using native dyes.

That afternoon I went over through the woods with Keroun to Nantiati, and attended a Kava festival at the waterside. I met Joe Kehoe there, and went home with him to Nantamarui in the evening in order to discuss our plan of exploration quietly together, not caring to take the selfish, sullen Lot or Ponatik natives into my confidence.

When I returned to Ponatik next morning I found that Chau-Tapa, a native preacher from Aru, whose church name was Obadiah, had, on Nanapei's recommendation, come to look after our spiritual welfare, and at the same time earn a few honest dollars by teaching me some key-words in the dialect of the Mortlock group, where his missionary labours had long engaged him. A few years previously his white superiors had transferred him to Aru, viewing with alarm his devotion to the bottle, and several sad lapses from grace, in which certain fair young female converts were equally blameworthy. He amused us mightily with his comical ways and glib Biblical quotations, and on the least provocation would put up an extempore prayer with all the unction of a Salvation Army captain. I don't know how far he deceived himself, but I know he never deceived me, for I had seen plenty of that kind of native before in Tonga and Samoa, especially Tonga. Obadiah really was a curious study. He was the oddest mixture of shrewdness, fanaticism, and fatuous self-complacency that I should say the Boston Mission ever turned out. He was avaricious yet benevolent, covetous as a Jew, yet, strange to say, liberal. What his left hand grabbed, his right would disperse again in largesse. Nobody ever visited his place at Aru and left hungry. For the rest, he was a diplomatist of the species *trimmer*. His air was grand and consequential, and last, but not least, he dearly loved strong liquors. All that day he took great pains to teach me the rudiments of Mortlock, by no means refusing a glass or two of red wine in between whiles. He descanted earnestly as a monk upon fasting and vigils. Yet he supped heartily at sundown upon beef, pork, yam, ship-biscuit and baked dog, and I am sure his potations of Vino Tinto must have given a rosy tinge to his dreams that night.

Next morning (March 21st) our guide Joe came over, and we made final arrangements for a third expedition to start on the next day but one.

CHAPTER VI

THIRD VISIT TO THE RUINS

AFTER paying off Obadiah, who was further gladdened at the gift of an old black coat and trousers,— "*Him broke behind*" critically murmured the recipient ;— on the morning of the 23rd we started from Lot, forming quite a respectable party. Keroun, it is true, yielding to spectral terrors had begged earnestly to/be left out this time. Two men from Lot who volunteered for five dollars a day have been politely sent about their business. Alek, too, is away on the service of the king, who, instead of making roads and plantations, has a mania for building churches and private mansions all over the Metalanim district. Our party consisted of Joe and his two stalwart sons, Lewis and Warren, a fine young fellow from the Kiti border called Nanit, and a smart little boy called Chétan. The Manilla man with his camera came too, but he was never quite at his ease. That very afternoon we set to digging by turns in the central vault. This delving carries a peculiar charm with it. One never knows what may turn up next. The prospect of a reward for every undamaged bracelet or shell-axe proves a famous incitement, even the apathetic Manilla man turning to and scratching away at the mould like an old hen at a rubbish heap. We continued next morning, and held on with unabated vigour until noon. Then we counted up our treasures and thus reads the tally :—

A quart of circular rose-pink beads, worn down by rubbing from the Spondylus strombus and Conus shells varying generally in diameter from the size of a shilling to a three-penny bit, some being very minute and delicate in design.

They answer exactly to the *Wampum* or shell-bead-money of the North American Indians, who use them for ornamenting pouches, mocassins and girdles.

Some were circular (*Pul*), others rectangular (*Pake*), used strung in regular rows for adorning the primitive girdles woven from banana-fibre. Some were very much abraded and others decidedly bleached in hue as though they had been buried a very long time. Beads exactly similar in design have recently been discovered in the ruins of Mitla in Central America. The shell-discs found in Nan-Tauach are more elegantly ground and finished than those in the other graves, a circumstance which induces Kubary to believe Nan-Tauach to be a later structure. This, I may add, is the opinion also of some of the older Ponapeans, my informants.

Eighty pearl-shell shanks of fish-hooks in a more or less perfect condition, exactly resembling those used all over Polynesia before the coming of the white man. The hook itself was generally of bone, but we found some fragments of pearl-shell which were clearly relics of the barb.

Five ancient *Patkul* or shell-axes of sizes varying from $2\frac{1}{2}$ feet to 6 inches.

Five unbroken carved shell-bracelets of elegant design (*Luou-en-Matup*), so called from the district of Matup to the north of Metalanim harbour, the seat of this industry in olden time—just as Icklingham in East Anglia was noted for the manufacture of ancient British flint implements.

A dozen antique needles of shell used for sewing together the leaves of the Kipar or Pandanus to make the *I* or mat-sails for their canoes. Others who have seen them declare them to be shell-ornaments strung in rows and worn round the neck, curving outwards like a necklace of whale's teeth.

Thirty or forty large circular shells, bored through the centres and worn as a pendant ornament on the breast.

We also turned up a vast number of fragments of bone, portions of skulls and bits of shell-bracelets, a couple of

GREAT CENTRAL VAULT, NAN-TAUACH

small shell gouges, a piece of iron resembling a spear-head, and a smoke-coloured fragment of vitreous appearance, that Kubary and others since have pronounced to be obsidian or volcanic glass, the *Itztli* of the ancient Mexicans.

The underground chamber A from which we took these relics lies in the centre of the inner precinct facing the great gateway. It is about 8 feet in depth, roofed in by six enormous blocks or slabs of basalt. The floor consists of loose coral and soft vegetable mould thickly matted with the roots of a breadfruit tree which has sprung up just behind the structure, and which, by a vigorous root-growth, is gradually displacing the blocks from their old position. The side nearest the entrance is threatening to sink into ruins at no very far-off date. In fact no little caution was needed on this side during our digging operations to avoid a disastrous collapse of masonry. J. S. Kubary, when photographing the ruins about twelve years ago, used this very vault as a dark-room for developing his negatives, all unconscious of the treasures under his feet. My photograph of this tomb, taken on Expedition No. 2, represents our shifty workman Keroun, and gives a very fair idea of the size of the basalt blocks forming the roof. A tangle of grasses and creeper carpets the precinct ; amongst them a poison-weed like a Wistaria, the bruised roots of which, tied in bundles, native fishermen dabble in the water of the surf-pools at low tide, to which they impart a milky tinge and stupify the fish. The Ponapeans call it *Up*, the Malays *Tuba*. All around are springing up saplings of Oramai, a broad leafed shrub, a species of Ramie (Kleinhovia), the bark of which is used for making nets and fish-lines. In the middle of the court we saw several fine Ixora trees in flower, possibly the same as those observed by Mr Le Hunt in 1885, who happily describes them as a scarlet waterfall of blossom. The afternoon of March 25th was spent in clearing the walls of the inner precinct, and taking various photographs. Just beyond the cross-wall at the back of vault B we saw a long basalt slab curved into a shallow crescent and balanced on two projecting shafts of masonry on the inner side of the southwest wall. When tapped it gave a clear ringing sound, and was probably used for an alarum or for a sort of bell in sacred ceremonies. We found just such another subsequently in Nanapei's settlement of Ronkiti. I brought it home and it is now in the British Museum.

On March 25th we visited the island of Nakap, and photographed the reef and ruins of an old sea-wall, with *Na* in the distance, and King Paul's canoe in the Nach or Lodge. After Nakap we landed on the breakwater of *Nan-Moluchai* at considerable risk, for the approach is dangerous even in calm weather from the heavy swell. Out in the lagoon off the harbour-mouth the magnitude of the task of the early builders impressed us deeply. For three miles down to the south one can descry here and there the massive sea-walls showing out through the mangrove clumps which girdle the islets of Karrian, Likop, Lemankau, Mant, Kapinet, Panui and Pon-Kaim, the last of the seaward series, which make up the outer line serving as a breakwater against the deep sea roaring at the doors, yet interrupted at intervals, and forming a re-entering angle between Karrian and Nan-Moluchai.

On Nan-Moluchai are the relics of another walled sanctuary, and in this lonely and surf-beaten spot an old castaway Frenchman spent his failing years. A pile of enormous stones block the entrance to the re-entering angle, at the head of which is Pein-Aring Island. They lie half submerged here in deep water. The photograph shows our American guide's eldest son sitting thereon, with a breaker just curling over ready to fall.

There are over fifty walled islets in the parallax which, together with the intersecting canals, occupies some eleven square miles.

It may be well here to take some of the island names

BREAKWATER AT NAN-MOLUCHAI

and explain them, giving at the same time any interesting points attaching to them, for some of them throw light on the early history of the place. The meaning of a few of these antiquated names is apparently lost altogether, but by the aid of an old man of the district much of the difficulty was overcome.

The phonesis of the names and their spelling has been revised, and the correct native renderings given instead of the bewildering and meaningless jargon into which even Kubary has fallen in the otherwise valuable sketch-plan which, with his permission, I have adopted as the ground-work of the present chart. With the aid of Joe Kehoe and his sons, and the minute and careful scrutiny of some old tribesmen familiar with the locality, we managed to advance Kubary's industrious work another stage forward towards completeness.

The name *Nan-Tauach* or *Nan-Tauas* means the *Place of Loftiness* or *High Walls*. (*Tauach—cf.* the Philippine *Taas*, high, and Hindustani *Taj* or *Tej*.) [Kubary calls it *Nan-Tauacz*, and Mr C. F. Wood, in the account of his visit, *Nan-Towass*.]

Chap-on-Nach means the *Land of the Council-Lodge* or *Club-House*.

The name *Nan-Moluchai* is variously given as *Nan-molu-chai*, *the place to cease from paddling*—an ironical designation for one of the most dangerous landing-places on the coast, or *Nan-moluch-ai*, *the place of the cinder heaps*, *i.e.* those left from the cooking fires of the host of workmen who assisted the demi-gods Olosipa and Olosopa in the construction of the mighty breakwater and the walled islets which occupy the space within.

Na means a ridge of rock. (*Cf. Nana*, a cordillera or mountain chain.)

Na-Kap means *New Na*, an islet of later origin.

Pal-akap means *New Sanctuary* or *New Chamber*. With the Ponapean *Pal*, a temple or chamber, compare Sanskrit *Pal*, a tent, habitation ; Pelew *Blai*, a house ; Yap *Pal*, a house set apart for the women ; and Malayan *Balai*, a hall ; Polynesian *Hale, Fale, Fare*, a house, dwelling.

Pei-kap = New Pavement or *New Enclosure.* On the east side of Pei-kap is the turtle-stone of Icho-Kalakal (*cf.* p. 96), and a long narrowish slab called the *Uanit-en-Tare*, or shield of Tare.

Lemenkau or *Lamenkau = Deep blue water off the edge.* There is another Lamenkau in the Banks group in Melanesia.

Panui, at the southern angle, may be a Polynesian word, and = *big wall.* More probably, however, it means " under the *Wi* or Barringtonia trees.

Peitak = Up to windward. The rumoured burial-place of the great warrior Icho-Kalakal, *i.e. Prince Wonderful*, progenitor of the famous Tip-en Panamai clan, who led the invasion from the south which blotted out the civilisation of the Chau-te-Leur dynasty.

Chau-Icho = King and Prince ; also name of a small district on the south coast near Marau.

Pan-ilel = the place where you have to steer—a most appropriate designation of the maze of shallows, choked up with water-weed and salt-water brush. Near Pan-ilel is a huge block lying under the masonry at the canal-side with two other masses supporting it, called *Uanit-en-Chau-te-Leur*, the shield of Chau-te-Leur.

In the waterway close by is the Tikitik of stone known as the Head of Laponga, a famous wizard of old mentioned in Ponapean folklore in a quaint tale entitled " The Naming of the Birds," " Ka-atanakipa-n-Men-pir-akan."

The name Laponga recalls the Lampongs, a tribe of Sumatra, distinguished among its less civilised neighbours by the possession of *Untang-untang*, or hieroglyphic records of ancient law (*Cf.* Ponapean *Inting* to write). This fact may have spread the use of the word *Lampong* as a generic term for wizard in these parts of the Malayan area.

The islet of *Pulak* gets its designation from some fine specimens of the timber tree of that name which over-

THE HAUNTED ISLAND OF PAN-KATARA

INNER ANGLE OF GREAT OUTER WALL, NAN-TAUACH

shadow it, and similarly a neighbouring islet is named *Pan-Tipop, i.e. Under the Tipop* or *Tupap,* from a huge umbrella tree (the Pacific almond) which grows at its north angle.

Pan-Katara, the haunted island, which our guide persists in styling *Pan-Gothra* (Kubary calls it *Nan-Gutra*), " the place of proclamation," or, " sending forth of messengers." A native gloss is *Pach-en-Kaon* or the House of Government, denoting a metropolis or capital. This precinct, from all accounts, was anciently the seat of government and solemn feasts of king, priests and nobles. The solitary inhabitant is the white goat in the picture, who, tired of the society of ghosts and shadows, came down bleating his welcome, anxious to meet with honest flesh and blood once more. We see him browsing upon the green leaves and shoots of the masses of shrub and creeper we tossed into the canal below. There is another Pankatara amongst the ruins of Chap-en-Takai across the Kiti border, and yet another on Ngatik or Raven's Island, some thirty miles away on the west coast of Ponape.

Kubary made an elaborate plan of Pankatara and of the neighbouring island of Itet in connection with the ancient ceremonies observed there. His description of these is very graphic and I quote it here.

The Dziamarous (*Chaumaro*) *i.e.* High Priests of the district of Metalanim had their chief temples in Nanmatal, and on the Island of Nangutra, where once a year, in the end of May or beginning of June, they met together and celebrated the feast of the " Arbungelap." All the natives of the district repair for this purpose to Kuffiner, a place in the Bay of Metalanim.[1] All canoes made ready during the past year are launched on this day to be consecrated, only the vessel destined for the Divinity remains suspended in

---

[1] The wives of the chiefs were not present, as the men of the lower classes are forbidden on pain of death to see them.

the king's house. After having begun the celebration at Kuffiner with religious dances and kava drinking, the whole crowd adjourns to Nangutra with singing and boat-racing, where the king plants his spear by a long stone visible to this day by the entrance. The lower classes range themselves in the space marked off to the left, the chiefs however and the Dziamarous place themselves round the Kava stone before the god's house in the middle space. On the right side food is heaped as an offering for the god or spirit. Then kava is pounded and the first cup, as is customary to this day, offered to the god, and the two next to his two priests. No one may enter the temple except the king's two magicians, Nangleim (*Nallaim*) and Manabus (*Manapuch*). After the kava offering, they adjourn to the Island Itet, where the gigantic deified Conger-Eel[1] lives within a wall five feet high and four feet thick. On a huge stone a turtle[2] is killed, and its entrails laid on a paved space in the Eel's house.

I give here an independent native version of Kubary's tale of the Itet monster.

In the reign of King Chau-te-Leur, a huge lizard (Kieil alap amen) came swimming into the great harbour and took up its quarters on the island of Pan-Katara, other-wise called Pangothra. Taking him for an *Ani* or tute-lary genius, they brought him baskets of fruit and savoury messes of cooked yams and bananas to conciliate the favour of their spectral-looking visitor (man likamichik aman). As might well be expected, vegetable diet did not content him, and there was soon a disappearance of some of the basket-bearers, which the chiefs, after losing some of their most industrious slaves, considered a mean act of ingratitude. So the big lizard was proclaimed a public enemy and a cannibal fiend, and the warriors of

---

[1] I did not myself hear of this Conger-eel, but I did hear of a pet alligator which was kept in Nan-Matal and fed as a sacred animal.

[2] This probably represents a human sacrifice. In the same way in New Zealand, *Ika* or *Ngohi*, a fish, is used to denote a human victim.

KING PAUL'S BIG CANOE, IN THE LODGE AT NAKAP

the tribe went forth to battle with the monster. But he came forward very angry, seized some of the boldest in his iron jaws, and crunched them up in pitiable fashion. They belaboured him industriously on every side, but their spears and shell axes failed to make impression upon his thick skin, whilst pebbles and sling-stones glanced off him harmless as raindrops. So at last since the lizard would not run away, of course the Metalanim braves had to. Finally subtlety triumphed where numbers and valour availed nothing. It was suggested to slay a fat hog, cut him open, and after stuffing him full with pounded Up root, to leave him roasting over a great fire blazing in the basement of the Nach or Council Lodge. All the sides of the Nach were to be walled up with logs and driftwood, save one opening big enough for the monster to crawl through—attracted to his last meal by the far-reaching scent of the crackling pork. When their foe was fairly stupefied with the working of the narcotic drug, the opening was to be quickly filled up and the building set in a blaze. Such was the fate of this solitary alligator, no doubt washed out to sea on driftwood from one of the great rivers of New Guinea, or drifted away through the Straits of Gilolo by the ocean currents. He crawled right into the trap set for him, devoured the cooked pig, felt very drowsy and went off into deep sleep, to wake up finding himself lapped shrivelling in a merciless furnace of flame, with his triumphant enemies shouting and dancing round his funeral pyre.

Pon-Kaim is the southernmost and last of the parallax, as its name "*On the Angle*" or *Corner*, sufficiently indicates. There another great line of partially submerged blocks, remnants of an ancient dyke, with a narrow passage in the centre, closes in this strange island-city.[1] In the absence of written annals, a careful examination of

---

[1] Nan-Matal contains in all some fifty of these curious artificial islets and encloses an area of some 11 square miles.

local names sometimes gives us useful little bits of history. As an instance of how geographical names embody an historical fact, take such names of cities as New York, New Orleans, Newcastle, and Carthage (Kiriath or Karth-Hadeschah, *i.e.* New Sanctuary). Thus even in lonely little Ponape History repeats herself.

That evening Joe Kehoe is in high spirits over his good luck. "Happy as a clam at high water," as he poetically phrases it. He gives many old-time reminiscences—one tale really characteristic of the times, the people and the place. The reader will pardon the digression, for his account is an independent version (1) of a crude minor paragraph on current events in a Boston missionary journal ; (2) of Mr J. C. Dewar's account of the wreck of his yacht the *Nyanza* off the Mant Islands in 1889 ; and (3) of the historiette of Don Cabeza Pereiro, medico of the first column in the Spanish attack on the rebel stronghold of Oa in the same year. We shall see how these four independent accounts tally.

Joe Kehoe's story concerned a Portuguese negro half-caste named *Christiano* (no connection of the author's), a deserter from the whaler *Helen Mar*, who settled in Ponape some twelve years ago in the fearless old beach-combing fashion, and roved about at his own sweet will like Stevenson's Tahitian hero *Rahero*, who "as an ' aito ' wandered the land, delighting maids with his tongue, smiting men with his hand." This negro Don Juan certainly did bear the marks of some twenty knife-wounds, gained in these adventures. The Spanish chronicler mentions him acting as a guide to their first column in the morning march from Oa, through the ravines of Machikau, towards the eastern front of the stockade of Ketam (where that same evening they met with a disastrous repulse). The account runs :—
" Cristiano, a negro of Cabo Verde, a Portuguese subject, led the way, a man of herculean strength and proved valour, whom the natives held in dread. His three Caroline wives accompanied him, one of whom, Li-Kanot, in

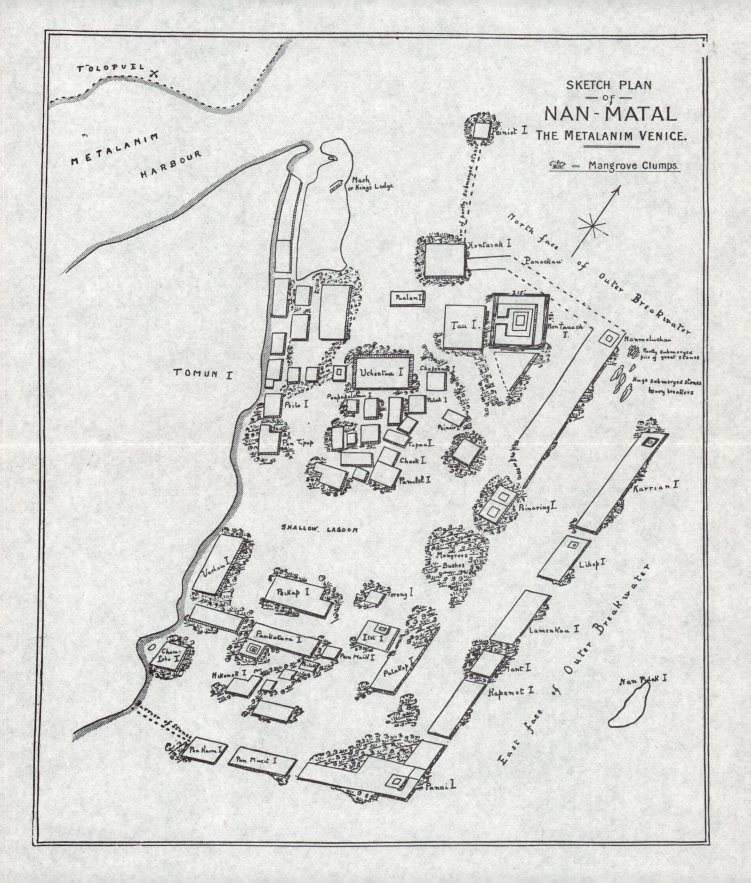

SKETCH PLAN
—OF—
NAN-MATAL
THE METALANIM VENICE.

🌿 = Mangrove Clumps.

T'OLOPUEL X

METALANIM HARBOUR

Mach or Kings Lodge

Einiot I

North face of Outer Breakwater

Kontarak I

Panackau

Pualan I

215

Tau I.

Nan Tauach I.

Nanmoluchau

Partly submerged pile of great stones

Huge submerged stones heavy breakers

TOMUN I

Uchentau I

Chabonos I

Poupokaloma I

Peilo I

Palak I

Peinot I

Pan Tipop

Tapou I

Chack I

Pamlol I

Peinaring I

Karrian I

SHALLOW LAGOON

Vachou I

Mangrove Bushes

Likop I

Peikap I

Torong I

Lamenkau I

Pankatara I

Itet I

Mant I

Chau-Leho I

Pan Maitl I

Palakot I

Nikonok I

Aiou

Kapenot I

Nan Pulak I

line of stones

Pan Karn I

Pan Mueit I

Panui I

East face of Outer Breakwater

the firing which presently began from a body of natives in ambush, was disabled by a bullet in the knee" (for which she still enjoys a small monthly pension).

Compare with this, the terse and uncomplimentary notice given of him, sent from Ponape by one of Mr Doane's co-religionists, and published in a Boston paper. " We have had great trouble here lately from a black Portuguese, banished some time ago from Manilla for some enormous crimes. He has sought the favour of the Spaniards, asserting that in time of need he supplied the late governor (Don Isidoro Posadillo) with food. This atoned in their eyes for many huge sins, and he is allowed to roam up and down the island doing Satan's work most completely. But we fear him not."

Mr Dewar's account tells feelingly of the stranding of his vessel on the reefs of the North Coast and the rascality of a certain Portuguese settler of Ú, who, when left in charge assisted various natives to plunder the wreck. Now the aforesaid negro Christian, who seems on the whole to have been a good-natured, honest old soul, gave evidence which led to the conviction of some of the delinquents, and their subsequent detention in irons on the hulk *Maria Molina*.

If missionaries mean that giving up Church members who are thieves and wreckers to justice is doing Satan's work, I confess they appear to me to have singular ideas of right and wrong. I should counsel them to teach their congregations industry, and, if possible, sturdier notions of honesty. And Joe Kehoe's account, as might be expected, ends by the cowardly assassination of the negro witness by one of the convicted wreckers—called Chaulik. This scoundrel, who had vowed revenge, by a lying message enticed him to an island called Mang off the Paliker coast, laid wait in the bush by the landing place, and shot him through the head at short range ; then darting from ambush, hewed to pieces his expiring victim, whom he was not man enough to encounter fairly hand to hand.

Joe Kehoe the same evening told us of a curious large

flat stone on the Chapalap River called Takai-nin-Talang. It stands near Ketam where the Spanish met with such a warm reception in 1892. It has prints of a man's feet in the stone, and on its face weapons carved in outline, which from his description mightily resemble the Japanese Katana or curved swords. He gave us further edifying anecdotes; amongst others, one of his meeting a boat-load of missionaries on the Matup flats near Metalanim Harbour, whilst he was taking a cargo of kava down to a Fijian trading schooner lying in port. "Oh, for shame, Mr Kehoe," rose their reproachful chorus. "Why have you got your boat loaded with that nasty root?" To which impertinence Joe answered like a man, and thus he took up his parable. "See here, and don't make no mistake. You won't use it yourself, more fools you! You won't let natives use it or sell it. Haven't you got sense to see this is the only way to get quit of it out of the country. You make me tired."

On the next day, March 26th, we continued our clearing operations and took more photographs of portions of the wall at various angles, and explored the underground chambers C and D, which, to our disappointment, yielded only scanty results. C is about fourteen feet deep and extremely narrow. Joe Kehoe, being of slender though wiry build, was lowered with a lantern to assist him in his labours. He turned over a lot of soil, but only got a few beads, fragments of shell bracelets, and mouldering bones. Just as we are finishing chamber D with a like result, a native arrives in some excitement to tell us that a steamer is coming into the great harbour, a rare occurrence, for prudent skippers nowadays give the place a wide berth. She turns out to be the *Quiros*, on one of her cruises round the island. Her kind-hearted commander, Don Miguel Velasco, has put into this uninviting port on the chance of conciliating King Paul, and at the same time rendering any possible assistance to our expedition. That very afternoon I sent Nanit and Chétan on board

SOUTH SIDE OF INNER ENCLOSURE, NAN-TAUACH

JOE KEHOE, OUR GUIDE, IN FOREGROUND

with a letter to the Captain and his Lieutenant Don
Lorenzo Moya, inviting them next day to visit the scene
of our operations and witness the clearing of the east and
north sides of the great outer wall, and the photographing
of further portions of the stone-work. By and by the boys
came back with a courteous letter from Don Miguel accepting the invitation, and asking me to come on board
to dinner that evening. Joe preferred to stay with
Theodoro and Nanit and keep watch and ward, but his
two sons and Chetan willingly came along. Once in the
broken water by the entrance to the great harbour, we find
navigation in our small canoe a very different business from
paddling along the still backwaters of Nan-Matal. The
wild white horses are cresting the seas outside the harbour
mouth to eastward ; inside there is a very heavy ground-
swell, the rollers sweeping in one after another, and huge
masses of green water toss us skyward like a plaything.
Then down again into the deeps we sink, with the spume
hissing and tingling in our ears, and another great wall
forming up behind us in the gathering dusk. Just off
Tolopuel there is a submerged stack of rocks over which,
even in calm weather, comb great shoal-water breakers.
Our little steersman from Kiti, not knowing the dangers
of this part of the coast, takes us right into the heart of
the foaming welter, and the next quarter of an hour is
lively indeed. But the lights of the *Quiros*—welcome
beacon—are shining out ahead in the deepening gloom.
Our canoe, though small, is solid, and we dash our paddles
in with a will, and after some narrow escapes from upsetting
win our way slowly into calmer water, and think ourselves
fortunate to be there.

We met with a warm welcome on the *Quiros*, but
noticed with misgiving certain sinister-looking fellows—
strangers to us—on the deck ; spies of King Paul, sent
under the mask of friendship to take note of the vessel,
her fittings and stores, and to repeat every word uttered
which might give information of Spanish plans. When

they saw us their countenances fell, and they were soon paddling ashore—their plans for the time defeated—from which I augur a sleepless night for suspicious King Paul and trouble brewing for us in the near future. We received cordial congratulations on our success, and after spending a pleasant evening rowed back, passing under lee of Tomun and reaching Uchentau about midnight, by a new route altogether, through an uncharted portion of the amazing labyrinth—a thorough clearing and exploration of which would entail the labours of a small party for several months.

March 27th.—As agreed, the first and second lieutenants, with two Manilla sailors, turned up at Uchentau about nine o'clock in the morning. This was their first visit to the ruins, and the sight of the great gateway and the high walls peeping out of the masses of jungle, keenly excited their wonder and admiration. We showed them the central vault, and pointed out the peculiar Japanese-looking frieze or cornice running along on the top of the inner line of wall. We then viewed the portion near tomb C, where the inner wall is in a ruinous condition, and the court strewn with broken shafts and pillars of toppled masonry, taking our visitors round the courtyard, which by this time had been cleared of its jungle by vigorous knife and axe work.

With the assistance of the two Manilla sailors we fell to work once again to bring more of the masonry into view, and more photographs were taken of the south-west and north-east angles. Clearing as we went, we made a complete circuit of the Place of the Lofty Walls, as the Ponapeans term the precinct. Every foot of the island is covered with almost impenetrable forest and jungle. On three sides the walls face directly on the waterway, on the south there is a belt of vegetation which we had no time to explore. Standing on the south-east angle, where the wall is nearly forty feet in height, one looks down on a green abyss of nodding woodland, with never a glimpse of

N.E. INNER ANGLE OF INNER COURT, NAN-TAUACH

N.E. ANGLE OF OUTER WALL, NAN-TAUACH

the network of canals rippling beneath the screen. In clearing this angle on the inner side we found the stone-work less regular than on the outer face, where these astonishing blocks lie alternately sidewise and crosswise on a plane of the greatest nicety. Effect from the out-side was clearly the aim of the builders. The north-east angle is occupied by an enormous *Aio* or Banyan tree, firm-rooted in the solid masonry, over which it towers full fifty feet, buttressed with its long root-sprays, and thrust-ing bunches of thread-like root-fibres into every crevice. As they swell these exercise a constant and gradually increasing force, wrenching asunder the blocks from their resting-places. When a high wind blows through the tree-tops the continuous swaying and rocking movement racks the structure through and through in every joint and key-stone. These mighty forces, working slowly but surely, must sooner or later bring the wall down in ruins.

The picture of our group excellently shows up the pro-portions of the masonry, with its tasselling of birds'-nest and polypody fern, and the mighty Incubus, king of the forest, perched above firm-rooted, shaking his myriad branches in the breeze. After resting awhile we hewed our way along the north terrace, finally coming out upon the canal which bounds the west side. Our photograph [1] of the north-west angle gives a happy impression of the style of masonry at this junction, the two walls running up high and bluff like the bows of a Japanese junk, from which model they were possibly designed. The figure in the foreground is that of the Spanish first lieutenant, bestriding a projecting shaft of the stone-work that shoots out like a bowsprit over the canal below. Beneath stretches a belt of young coco-palms of recent growth, their reddish stems just merging into green.

In order to take the bearings of the place properly, our visitors kindly promised me the use of the cruiser's compass next day, and as it was now getting near sunset,

[1] Journal of Royal Geographical Society, February 1899, p. 122, *q.v.*

insisted on my taking a couple of boys and going on board with them to dinner. Not content with this, on our return they supplied us with various articles from the ship's stores to reinforce our scanty commons. We retired to rest, taking no thought for the morrow, and well contented with the day's work done. But whilst we were sleeping mischief was brewing.

March 28*th*.—Early next morning a canoe glides up manned by five of King Paul's braves, evil-looking vagabonds, bearing a request from that monarch for the two white-faces and the Manilla dog (Kiti-en-Manila)—(poor Theodoro!)—to present themselves, and give account of their nefarious doings. It turns out that King Paul is filled with rage at the coming of the *Quiros* into port, and suspects some deep design of the Spaniards. His superstitious terrors have been awakened by tales from stray fishermen, who, passing through the waterways of Nan-Matal, were startled to view the havoc wrought in the shrouding jungle by our axes and knives. At first they thought the devils of the wood and air had done this thing, but a closer inspection revealed human agency. It seems that they had a tradition that the spirits of the slaughtered Builders had entered into the trees that have sprung up where the great battle was fought. Mr C. F. Wood mentions the same superstition shown during his visit to Metalanim, and Mr H. O. Forbes tells of a similar experience of his in one of the Uma-Luli or sacred groves in the interior of Timor. His Majesty has also heard of our find, which he interprets as a hoard of hidden gold or silver. This appeals to his ingrained avarice, and he wants *his* share. Theodoro, with a small revolver, slips out of the house and takes to his heels into the bush. The little boy Chétan also makes good his escape—steals somebody's fishing canoe and flees for his life down the coast, and never looks behind him till across the Kiti border. Wondering what rod in pickle lies ready for us, we are conducted to Tomun where King Paul and

S.W. SHOULDER OF INNER LINE OF WALL ENCLOSING THE KING'S VAULT

NANIT AND LEWIS KEHOE IN FOREGROUND

two or three of his chiefs await us. Amongst them I saw my Ponatik landlord, Mr David Lumpoi, who seemed very ill at ease. The angry old monarch turned to us and rated us sharply for our unhallowed work which he bade us cease once and for all, and leave the district that very day on pain of being treated as enemies to the tribe. As the Roman philosopher said to Julius Cæsar, " It is ill arguing with a man who commands ten legions."

Nevertheless, observing that David was not giving full effect to my answers, I took up my parable, regardless of etiquette, addressing the irate monarch in a few straightforward sentences in the local dialect to this effect :— (1) That we had made a contract and expected him, having received payment before hand, to keep his side of it. (2) That we had done no harm to the masonry, and had dug up no gold or silver as he supposed. (3) That since our coming in the tribe we had behaved peacefully and defrauded no man. (4) That as he desired us to go, go we should, but at our own convenience, not his. (5) That we would make him a by-word amongst the tribes for his broken faith. Finally I told him that if he meditated any treachery that an English man-of-war might call in one day and ask inconvenient questions. To these observations he made no reply for a while, scanning me earnestly, seemingly puzzled and at a loss what to make of it. At length he grunted out sulkily that he didn't like white men, and that his people didn't either, and was dismissing us with further threats and warnings, which, to his infinite wonder, I treated very lightly. " Tell your king there," said I, in the current Ponapean, to a chief close by, " that I will return in a year or two and bring with me a party of Irishmen with picks and spades and lamps and muskets, and we will dig where we please. By and by you will understand white men better." The king took my jesting remarks, which may come true some day after all, in earnest. We parted gravely and ceremoniously. And this was the last I saw of that puissant monarch the Ichipau of Metalanim. We made our way back to Uchentau, and consoled poor Theodoro whom we found in a very dismal frame of mind. But he brightened up about mid-day when a boat of armed Manilla sailors came ashore from the *Quiros* with the promised compass. We soon turned to and established the bearings of Nan-Tauach, made certain measurements, which hitherto we had left undone, and the man with the camera took shots until nearly the last plate of his stock was used. We took a farewell pull around the canals—our crew gazing with wonder at the relics of a past civilisation that greeted them at every bend.

Presently we gathered from our escort that overnight a present of bright-coloured poisonous fish had been sent on board from King Paul. The cook or one of the forecastle hands, happening to taste a portion, was seized with violent pains to which he almost succumbed. Treachery, without doubt, is in the air.

Between Kontaiak and Panachau it appears that we are not the only folk out on the water this day. Two other boat-loads of sailors and marines, on shore leave, are rowing up and down the waterway in an aimless sort of fashion. One or two native canoes are also going about under colour of fishing, but doubtless in reality sent out to observe and report upon the movements of these un-authorised bodies of strangers invading the precinct. Quite possibly many more of King Paul's spies lie hidden in the bush, burning to make a dash upon the unconscious liberty men. For the sight of a Manilla man to a native of these parts is like a red rag to a bull. Fortunately, however, nothing of the kind happens.

Our Manilla men land us at Uchentau and return to the ship, taking off some curios as a present to the captain, also a note informing him of the interruption of our opera-tions in the district, begging him to report the facts at headquarters, and strongly advising him to run no risks by giving his men leave to go ashore in the present state

RELICS OF OLD SEA-WALL. NAKAP ISLAND

of affairs. And the same afternoon we started for Lot, where for the next two or three days we had ample work in hand, sorting and washing curios, with Theodoro industriously developing plates with his mysterious and evil-smelling chemicals. Curious natives dropped in from time to time sniffing the strange odours, which they plainly told us in the jargon of their kind savoured strongly of *Rakim*, or demoniac powers and the Lake of Fire and Brimstone—*Lé-en-Kichiniai*, the mainstay of their charitable creed. After a day or two our landlord arrived and promptly demanded double the original rent agreed upon, clamouring loudly for instant pay. His ruse absolutely failed, and we elected to leave his inhospitable roof and move further down the coast towards the Kiti border.

A good opportunity for departure was given us by the arrival of a Tahitian trader, Ruiz, with his sailing-boat, engaged in collecting copra and ivory nuts along the coast. He readily agreed to take us off, and to land me at Joe Kehoe's place at Nantamarui, and take the Manilla man and the curios over to his own place in Kiti. So we paid our small debts in Ponatik after a deal of palaver with Keroun — mercenary old rogue — who demanded five dollars for the loan of a kettle, three for a fowl, and ten more for a dozen wild yams he had supplied. He frightened the Manilla man into tears with his loud talk and bluster until I flung him a dollar and a few sticks of tobacco in full quittance, and as he was still dissatisfied, forcibly thrust him off the verandah. David, for his part, agreed to meet us up in the Colony a little later on, and there receive a full settlement of the rent due to him. I may here remark that when we met a fortnight later this Ponapean Shylock caused us great annoyance by his extortionate demands. He behaved in a most insolent manner before the Spanish Governor, who, though plainly unwilling to disoblige a chief of influence in so turbulent a district, could not in justice allow him to make such unheard-of overcharges. For he kept on demanding double pay, utterly repudiating his own written and signed agreement when shown him, and putting forward yet further frivolous and unreasonable claims. Finally, Master David, after a stern reprimand from the Governor and a sharp rebuke from Nanapei, who acted as mediator, received his just payment with the sour phiz of a cabman accepting his exact fare, and amidst the undisguised contempt of the Kiti and Paliker natives in town sailed away home again, still grumbling.

To resume. We embarked and dropped down with the afternoon tide to Nantamarui, where I landed at Joe's to stay a few days with the good old fellow. During this visit I examined a curious pile of stone-work about three hundred yards in the rear of his house, and added still further to my long list of rare and curious dialect words, Mrs Kehoe (*Litak-en-Nā*), a most kindly old lady, lending most zealous and effectual aid. We also indulged in a deal of speculation as to the origin and history of the engineering marvel we had so lately quitted, and I may here quote in conclusion Kubary's able summing-up of the whole matter, which to me seems amply borne out both by native tradition and inherent probability, not to mention the result I was fortunate enough to obtain on the spot. In his conclusions I heartily concur.

1. *The stone buildings of Nanmatal were erected by a race preceding the present inhabitants of Ponape.* For tradition declares that the last king of the primitive race, the Dziautoloa (*i.e.* Chau-te-leur), lived on the island of Nangutra. He himself resided in the stone-town, whilst the people lived on the chief island and had to support the ruler. One day a stranger of the name of Idzikolkol landed on the little island of Nan-Pulok. He came from the Ant or Andema Islands, lying about ten nautical miles west of Ponape, and fearing that Nanmatal was too thickly populated, he thought it advisable to go back again. A new landing followed in Metalanim, and being informed by a woman of the military weakness of the Dziautoloa,

A PONATIC CHIEF

HOLDING A CARVED DANCING PADDLE, WITH A PILE OF IVORY NUTS BESIDE HIM

THE BEACH AT LOT

RUIZ SURROUNDED WITH BUNCHES OF *KARRAT* OR GIANT PLANTAINS

he was fortunate enough to drive the king back upon the chief island, and even to kill him. This Idzikolkol was the founder of the customs which endure to this day, and the Idzipaus of Metalanim are his successors.

2. *The builders of Nanmatal belonged to the black race and the Ponapeans are a mixed race.*

The proof lies in the following. At the excavation of the three vaults of Nan Tauacz, and the till then undisturbed graves of Nanmorlosaj (*i.e.* Nan-moluchai) and Lukoporin, Kubary found amongst the human bones four calvaria—skull-tops—which clearly showed that the heads were dolichocephalous, or corresponded with a middle form between long and short skulls.[1] The difference between one of these disinterred skulls and those of the present race, is :—

Disinterred skull : length 181 millimetres, breadth 127 mm. [cephalic index 70·2], facial angle unknown.

Native skull of to-day : length 170 mm., breadth 135½ mm. [cephalic index 79·7], facial angle 76° 30′.

3. *The ruins of Ponape afford no proof of the sinking of the island, on the contrary they unmistakably show that they are the remains of a water-building.*

4. *The four-fold aspect deprives of all support the theory that the ruins are the remains of fortifications built by Spanish pirates.* The discovery of a Spanish cannon in the year 1839 by H.M.S. *Larne* proves nothing, beyond confirming the rumour of the wreck of a great ship on Ant Island long before the rediscovery of the Seniavin Islands by Admiral Lütke in 1828 ; probably one of the cannons lying on the shore was taken from thence to Roan Kitti (*i.e.* Ronkiti).

[1] A skull measured by Dr Cabeza Pereiro from Ponapé had a length of 184 mm. and a breadth of 140, which gives a cephalic index of 76·1. Four other Micronesian crania from the neighbouring group of the Mariannes had respectively cephalic indices of 76·55, 73·31, 71·27, and 70·98, giving a mean of 73·66.

CHAPTER VII

VISIT TO CEMETERY OF THE CHOKALAI OR LITTLE PEOPLE, PONAUL AND LANG TAKAI, AND RETURN FROM METALANIM TO KITI AND COLONY

ON hearing from my kind old host of some curious ruins on a hill-side in the back country, I determined to explore them. Theodoro, my photographer, it will be remembered having finished all his plates, much to his satisfaction had been despatched across the border to the Catholic settlement of King Rocha at Aleniang—to perform his chemical operations in peace, and there abide collecting and labelling botanical specimens until he received further instructions. Accordingly one fine morning Joe Kehoe, his eldest son Lewis, and myself are trudging sturdily up the hill-ridge behind Nantamarui over a rough, steep and intricate trail—I will not call it pathway —thickly carpeted with the convolvuluses *Yol* and *Chenchel*. The weeds underfoot treacherously hide from our view numerous slippery boulders and fragments of shivered basalt. By and by the labyrinth gets worse than ever, and for several hundred yards we have to fight our way on, hewing right and left with our eighteen-inch knives, climbing over fallen trunks of great forest trees and ducking under low natural archways of *Kalau* or hibiscus. As by degrees we worked our way nearer to the region of tall forest trees the underwood became less dense. On our right lies a green valley planted with taro, bananas, and breadfruit, with a full-fed brook singing down through it in its zigzag course beneath the mellow shadows. To our left stretches a steep mountain-slope, along whose slippery sides we scramble, picking our way cautiously amongst

Note.—A portion of this chapter is from a paper read by the author before the Royal Geographical Society, December 12th, 1898.

gnarled roots and spreading buttresses of the ficoids *Nin* and *Aio*—the lesser and greater Banyan trees. Scattered at our feet like little bright-blue olives, lie the berries of the *Chatak* or *Elæocarpus*, dear to the fruit-pigeons, the grey-dove (*Murroi*), the green-doves (*Kinuet* and *Kingking*), and the violet-brown ground pigeon (*Paluch*). These Elæocarpi grow often to over 100 feet in height. Finally passing one of the buttressed kings of the forest we suddenly came upon a low breastwork of stones enclosing the object of our search, which turned out to be a cemetery in the shape of an irregular or broken parallelogram, as can be seen from the sketch plan. Six graves were found in the lower enclosure and three on a platform raised five feet above the level of the ground. All were little vaults not exceeding four or four and a half feet in length—roofed in with massive slabs of basalt—the graves of the *Chokalai*, Kichin-Aramach or Little Folk, woodland elves, answering to our own pucks and pixies, to the Trolds, Cobolds, and Dwarfs of the Teutonic peoples, and to the *Patupaiarehe* of the Maoris. Ethnologists would style them dwarf Negritos. These, according to Ponapean tradition, were the little dwarfish folk who dwelt in the land before the coming of the *Kona* and *Li-ot*, the giants and the cannibals. The two latter terms probably represent respectively the Malayo-Polynesian settlers and the Melanesians from the south. The speech of the dwarfs, it is said, was a chattering and a gibber as that of bats. They were dark of skin and flat-nosed (*Timpak*). They are believed still to haunt the dark recesses of the forest, and to be very malignant and revengeful. I was told that one man who came to this haunted dell to plant kava was caught up and spirited away by the revengeful goblins, and his lifeless body was found days afterwards stretched upon a great flat rock by the seashore off Nantiati Point. A curious fact concerning this primitive race was supplied me by the Au of Marau shortly before leaving Ponape. The people at the mouth of the Palang River near the

Chokach and Kiti border are said to have been descended from the *Chokalai*, who it seems were not everywhere exterminated by the Malayo-Polynesian conquerors. The Au's description runs thus. " In the speech of the Palang folk is a most foolish undercurrent of chatter ; they are shorter in stature, and their skins darker than their neighbours ; their noses are flat and they are known throughout the tribes as *Macha-en-Paikop* or the *Paikop-faces*. Now the Paikop is the most ill-favoured of fishes, with wide goggle-eyes, and a face as flat as a dish."

Unluckily I had no opportunity of visiting the Palang folk, who are said to be thieving and treacherous. There seems no reason why the tale of the Au should not be true, and that we have here overlapped and all but exterminated the survivors of the Negrito race who made these curious little graves. Be it remarked that in Ponape, the Marquesas, and many other islands, the natives have a dread of venturing too far into the interior—their sensitive fancies filling the mountain jungle with deadly lurking influences and the arrows of fairy foes—doubtless a recollection of early struggles of the Malayan races in Indonesia and their own islands with the dwarf aborigines of the mountain and the bush.

The name of the dell is Ponial, *i.e.* " Over the pathway," so called because the mountain slope overhangs an old trail leading down to Nantamarui, over which we have with such difficulty won our way. The wild pandanus (*Matal* or *Taip*) shoots up everywhere around the cemetery, waving her sword-shaped blades, triply fluted and edged with fine rows of prickles, and the *Hibiscus tiliaceus* weaves her intricate labyrinth of shoots ; branches and roots spreading in, out, above, around and below. The *Talik-en-Wal*, or climbing hartstongue fern, twines thick around the stems of infant forest trees in this grand nursery of Nature. The small round yellow fruits of the Nin and the blue oblong fruits of the Elœocarpus lie sprinkled amongst greenest cushions of moss and the

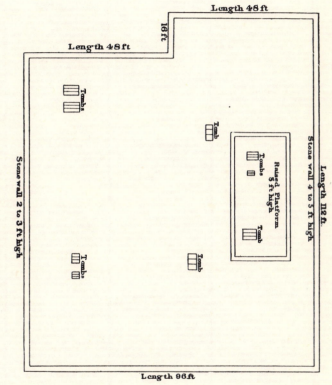

GRAVES OF THE "LITTLE PEOPLE"

Length 48 ft

Length 48 ft

16 ft

Length 112 ft.

Stone wall 4 to 5 ft. high

Stone wall 2 to 3 ft. high

Length 96 ft

Tombs

Tomb

Tombs

Raised Platform 5 ft. high

Tomb

Tombs

Tomb

fibrous roots of the bush-ferns, which in thick wavy clumps flourish under the shadow of great forest trees. We set to work at our excavations. After clearing away the luxuriant undergrowth, we cautiously removed the basalt slabs at the top of each little vault, and found in the red soil within an abundant deposit of blue mould promising good results. In the first few minutes a very diminutive stone gouge was turned up and a stone knife. No other results rewarded our efforts, save a few pieces of mouldering bone. All the rest with the great lapse of time in a damp and hot climate have literally melted away like sugar. A fresh proof of the great antiquity of this burial place is the fact that not one single red or white shell-bead was brought to light in any of the seven graves opened, although in the central vault of Nan-Tauach we had found a very large number. The form of the cemetery is an irregular or broken parallelogram, as will be seen from the accompanying sketch. The upper portion of the cemetery was occupied by a raised platform of basalt blocks five feet in height. Upon this were three vaults overgrown by a tremendously thick awning of the ever troublesome Hibiscus. The graves on the upper platform gave no better return, yielding only a few pieces of mouldering and unsubstantial bone to our most careful search ; whereupon Lewis shrewdly remarked that the Chokalai must have been either very stupid people who wouldn't work, or very poor and barbarous wretches not to have any treasures to bury.

Whilst making our measurements and excavations, we came across several skink lizards rather large in size, called *Kieil* by the natives, who hold them in a holy horror. During our work we were bothered by the attentions of numerous minute bush or sand-flies (the *Em-en-wal*), which, however, are not nearly so troublesome as their cousins of sun-scorched Nukuhiva in the North Marquesas. Towards sunset we departed, leaving the dell to the fairies whose solitude we had so rudely disturbed. A second journey next day proved equally fruitless as regards relics, resulting only in the clearing away of a huge quantity of brushwood, which the teeming life of the bush by this time has certainly replaced in ten-fold luxuriance, to cover up the sleeping-place of these departed folk once more from the face of man.

The evening of our second visit to the Valley of the Dwarfs, my host told me of another ancient burying-place on one of the hills to the north-west of our valley.   So next day, armed with a whale-spade and a bundle of digging sticks, we struggled up the steep hill-side over the most primitive of pathways.   A quarter of an hour's sharp climb brings us into a dense thicket crowning the summit of the bluff.   A few areca palms are in evidence.   From the tree trunks the Freycinetia droops her narrow sword-shaped leaves, and the long green tongues of the Bird's-nest fern are waving in their ærial circles, and the plumes and crests of many another knight of the forest army glance and glimmer in the cool dark silence.   Restful to the eye are the mellow harmonies of green melting into one another on every hand like the notes of a mighty anthem.   Masses of wild ginger (*Ong-en-Pele*) carpet the ground below, dappled with the shadows of boughs see-sawing overhead in the deep fresh draught of the trades.   The air is filled with the aromatic fragrance of their crushed leaves, as we patiently win our way onwards.   Under the shadow of lofty forest trees flourishes many a clump of lowlier shrub of the woodland, the Ixora with its gorgeous cascade of yellow-centred umbels, and the minute starry blossoms of the *Ka-n-Mant*, a firm-grained yellow-wood shrub, and the knotted stems and powdery catkins of the sombre Kava plant.   These and many another, some ornamental, very many medicinal, each with its picturesque native name, associated with some quaint legend or fancy.   Ever and anon comes down through the aisles of the woodland a waft of fragrance from the *Matakel*, the flower of some remote tree-pandanus, distilling its subtle and delicate exhalation rich as incense-cloud, all as though some old god of the forest were breathing down a benediction upon the weary sons of men.

Working our way through the wilderness we came upon a double parallelogram of stone-work, the outer wall on the east side measuring 115 feet in length, and the south side 75. The average thickness of the wall was 6 feet, the height about 5 feet. It was built up of rough blocks of stone of varying sizes, the largest being 4 feet in length by 3 in thickness. The inner conforming parallelogram of wall measured 35 feet on the east side and 30 feet on the south, and was about 4 feet in height. In this last enclosure were two platforms of stone facing one another, doubtless the tombs of two heroes of ancient date. These we cleared of loose stones and excavated superficially. Nothing, however, but a few fragments of bones and bits of shell ornament rewarded our labours. Perhaps the next comer with more time and better implements may be more fortunate. In any case it will not be labour lost. There are many more such stone enclosures (*Lil-charaui*) upon Ponape, especially upon the island of Tapak, a little south-east of the Mant Islands, off the coast of Ú, near the Nallam-en-Pokoloch deeps, before you come to Aru on the Metalanim border. It is for future explorers to make them give up their secrets, and for the skilful artist to set down upon his magic canvas some of the wonderfully beautiful woodland scenes and effects which I have striven feebly to depict in words. Neither must they, nor indeed can they, pass over indifferently these relics of a gray antiquity, venerable as dolmen, kistvaen, or kjoekkenmödding—the work of a vanished people who, Titan-like, have stumbled down into the darkness of a mysterious doom.

A few days after our excursion to Pona-Ul we visited the remains of an ancient native fortress near the summit of a hill to the eastward. We reached the place after a tedious hour's climb, tramping along winding slippery paths and over boulders and masses of fallen rock, making our way upward through the shadow of hanging woods. We passed the foundations of some old houses and two or three clearings in the lonely mountain wilderness where bananas were growing, and at last, high up on the slope of another steep hill, its rugged sides carpeted with the large round leaves and white and sulphur bells of the mountain convolvulus, we find ourselves confronted with a forbidding-looking wall of loose stones, up which we scramble on to a rude terrace, with another high and compact mass of stone-work looking down upon us. Yam creepers have everywhere forced their way up through the stones, their long twining stems furnished with a bristling array of small black prickles. These possibly the relics of an old plantation in the neighbourhood, which when there was no one left to tend it any longer, was swallowed up once more by the envious bush.

We climbed gingerly up the slippery face of the masonry and found ourselves standing on a flat level terrace on top of the pile which is some 15 feet above the circling ring of stone-work below. The length of the terrace facing seaward is 48 feet, and its width 20 feet. Tradition declares that many years ago the Noch or chief of the Nantamarui and Nantiati districts built this stronghold and reared a great Lodge on top of the platform, which looks very much like one of the Mexican teocalli or truncated pyramids. As he failed to pay *nopue* or tribute, the king of Metalanim assailed him in his mountain stronghold, but on two or three occasions was hurled back with great loss. Despairing to take the fort by storm, the besiegers had resort to subtlety, and drew off their forces. Some while after news came up from the valley of the Chapalap River that civil war had broken out and that a favourite cousin or brother of his own was in danger. The fearless defender of this mountain fastness determined to take his best warriors with him and go down to the aid of his hard-pressed relative. When he reached the village with his succour, the very people he came to help, who were in the plot all along, turned on their bewildered visitor and massacred him and his whole following. Another party stormed Lang-Takai, killing old men, women and children who had been left behind. Only two or three of the women were spared from the butchery, and were added to the seraglio of the conqueror, and their descendants are in Metalanim to this very day.

Another tale of blood will further illustrate the martial side of Ponapean character.

Nearly one hundred years ago there was war between the tribes of Kiti on the south-west and Metalanim on the east, and many were the men of might who were slain on both sides. Now it fell out that there was a mighty festival holden on the southern slopes of Mount Wana, near the settlement of Aleniang. A Metalanim war-party came softly up the *tau* through the marshes and stole upon the settlement. The Nach was filled with feasting and the noise of revel, when in burst the enemy and slew and slew till they were weary and—behold the weakness of mighty men—sat them down to drink and boast and make merry, for a strong delusion was leading them to doom. For the conquered were no cowards, and some of them that fled turned again and took counsel together. One crept back and from his hiding-place saw the foes drinking in the lodge and heard the insults of their triumph songs. He returned and told his comrades, and wrath and desire for revenge quenched their fear. Through the woods they sent to Annepein for succour, and the dwellers on the banks of Palikalau armed and came over. Some of the people of the Ichipau were sleeping, and more were drunk and helpless, when the Children of the White Bird broke in upon them like a raging sea. And the scent of more than kava greeted the hovering crowds of Spirit-shapes (*Ani*) in that reeking temple of slaughter. Hence the proverb to this day :

" Many came unbidden, but all came to stay." Thus the Children of Kiti held their own and more, taking five lives for every two. And the hearts of the "Stammerers"[1] turned cold and for many months there was peace in the lands of Wana.

During the revolt of 1890 and the Spanish bombardment of Metalanim that followed, Lang-Takai was the fastness whither King Paul determined to send the old men, women and children of the tribe for safety if the hated white men gained the upper hand.

A fine view of the island and harbour of Mutok, the Tenedos of Lütke, was obtained from the level terrace above. The island resembled in shape an artist's soft hat with its broad brim and deep depression in centre. Far to the westward stretches away the line of mangroves and salt water brush bordering the fertile lowlands of Kiti. In the distance are Nálap and Kápara and several smaller islets, which the natives declare are broken portions of a once extensive mainland. Further off yet, a long low blue line on the horizon, lie the Ánt Atolls, quaintly styled in the maps, by an obvious error, " *And-ema* " or " *Ant-over-There.*" On the slopes below flourishes a forest world full of rich promise to the botanist, if any should hereafter visit these remote regions. Here and there a clearing devoted to the culture of the coconut, the banana, the plantain, the taro, the breadfruit and the yam, all of which bear names cognate with their equivalents in the Polynesian dialects. Below, the hanging woods sweep lower and lower, merging into the tract of marshy land overgrown with mangrove clumps encircling Ponape. In middle distance the varying green and blue waters of the still lagoon, the outer edge of the reef crested with the white heads of the eternal breakers. Beyond, the deep blue Pacific studded with myriad islets, far, far out of ken

---

[1] The Metalanim folk speak a curious crabbed and antiquated dialect, much ridiculed by their critical neighbours of Kiti as " *Nannamanam* " or jargon.

beyond the sunset, where many a liquid unharvested acre stretches on and onward to the gates of Gilolo Sunda, and San Bernardino, whence for ages and ages the swarming populations of Asia have been pouring out through Indonesia, all too small for their teeming myriads, to spread themselves further eastward and southward, launching out their bold keels upon a great waste of unknown waters, wider than those known to Greek, Phœacian, Viking or Phœnician.

A pleasant week soon passed. But alas! I could no longer remain in this most hospitable corner of an inhospitable province. For it was high time to be gone across the border into the friendly territory of King Rocha of Kiti.

For that most Christian monarch, old King Paul, for whom one day a halter surely waits, has passed the word from parish to parish down his coast line, breathing out dire threats upon all or any of his subjects who should venture to receive, entertain, or in any way aid me. To my kind old host he despatched one of his myrmidons with an insulting message and a most vengeful letter, to the effect that his coconut palms were in danger of being chopped down, his pigs slaughtered, his effects plundered, and his home burned over his head if he dared any longer harbour the *macha puotapuot karialar*, the *accursed white man*, as the old rascal rudely styled me.

Well, there was no help for it. Nantamarui, if I stayed, was plainly under ban. A nice place for an industrious settler, who may, at a despot's whim, have his live stock destroyed, and all his improvements swept into instant ruin. So, with many expressions of regard, I took leave of Joe and his kindly helpmate, their little girls Aroline and Adeline, and their stalwart sons Lewis and Warren, who paddled me across the bay and up to Aleniang, on the Kiti River, where my Manilla man, in charge of the curios, was staying with our friend the Tahitian trader. Here I put up for a few days, rambling about the beautiful and picturesque district of Mount Wana, and receiving much kindness from the people of the valley, their king Rocha, and the chiefs of Tiati, Roi, and Mutok, across the bay.

All of these rendered me great assistance in my work by pointing out places of interest, and calling up many a tradition from the memories of some of the older natives, mere whispers of the olden time echoing fainter and fainter year by year down the long corridor of the ages, destined all too soon, if they find no speedy chronicler, to merge into the eternal silence. Whilst I sat conferring with the chiefs in the Council-Lodge, the Manilla man was scouring hill and dale with an attendant posse of small boys busy in collecting seeds and fruits, of which every evening they brought home good spoil, and the packets given me to fill for the Port Darwin Gardens were soon crammed to bursting point. Fearlessly the Camera-man ranges in the friendly valleys. No longer he quakes at the thought of sharp-shooters hidden in every thicket. No longer he pictures grim forms lurking in ambush behind every boulder, axe and knife in hand, to split his skull or crop his nose and ears. Nevertheless, by-and-bye, he would fain be gone, and I let him go. Longingly he bethinks him of the fascinating follies of Manilla, the cock-pit, the theatre, the languid gallantries of the Parian and the Luneta, and the attractive, but not always winning hazards of Panguingui and Chapdik, dear to the Tagal and Chinese gambler. Or he is home-sick for the pleasant woods and lowlands of Pampanga, and his *mal de pays* is stronger than his fears of *mal de mer*.

And thus Theodoro's term of work drew to an end. Our host's sailing-boat conveyed us to the colony where we stowed the curios and made our preparations—he to go, and I to stay. A few days later the mail-steamer came into port; and, in a brand new suit of clothes and with a cheerful countenance, laden with commissions and borrowed coin from all sides, the worthy artist went on board. And here my comrade vanishes out of the story. But not quite out of men's memory. For some of his creditors in the garrison I left awaiting his return to Ponape with the most lively interest and anxiety. But, alas, so unjust is man to his fellow-man! He cometh not along. News was brought me a little while ago of his end. It was in keeping with his life. It seems that he returned to Manilla, joined the rebellion that had just then broken out, and was taken prisoner in a skirmish. A court-martial was held, and one fine morning the Spanish shot him on the water-front with a batch of his fellow-rebels. And that was the last of the poor creature.

And here ends the story of my first four months in Ponape.

PART II

CHAPTER VIII

PONAPE: DRESS, INDUSTRIES, AND MANUFACTURES

THE various excursions in and around Ponape described in the First Part had rendered familiar to me much of the inner life and outward fashions of the natives both on the east and west coast. Before detailing any further adventures, I will now give a carefully-considered description of the domestic economy of the Ponapeans, their weapons and dwellings.

The dress of the men worn at work was a narrow girdle (*Uaiuai-loi*, in Yap *Guai*), about a foot in breadth and some four feet in length, exactly the same as formerly worn in Japan, made of the woven fibre or baste of the banana or of the Nin tree, often dyed yellow from the juice of the Morinda citrifolia. It goes once round the waist, down between the thighs, and is tucked in behind at the back, so as to leave a piece depending like a tail. (It is the *Hume* of the Marquesas, the *Malo* or *Malomalo* of Hawaii, Samoa and Fiji, the *Maro* of Tahiti, Mangareva and New Zealand, and the *Palpal* of the Mortlock Islands.) The dress worn on occasions of festival or after work was the *Kol* (that of a chief in the language of ceremony was called *Mol*) or native kilt, composed of the split filaments of young coconut leaflets (the pinnæ of the branch) steamed in the oven, steeped a day in water under heavy stones, scraped with cockle-shells to remove the green vegetable matter. These also were often dyed bright yellow with turmeric, or with the juice of the bark of the Morinda citrifolia or Flame Tree. A new *Kol* is a pretty sight, but exposure to the sun quickly makes the bright hues fade out. Sometimes with the cockle-shell each frond would be carefully pinched, crimped, and creased into wavy lines, the work of the old women. This was a *Kol-Ikoch*. The working dress was called *Likau-mal* or *Likau-en-tuka*, and their regular dress for festivals or leisure *Kapuot* or *Kapot*. The chiefs and men of note in the community used to wear belts of banana fibre (*Tor, Tur*), elaborately woven out of banana fibre on which was strung rows of pink, white and grey shell beads. Curiously enough, in Hebrew *Tur* denotes a *row of jewels*. These were of two designs and varying sizes, one resembling in shape the Maori *hei-tikis* or rectangular pendants of greenstone called *Pake* or *Puake* —the other round, which they call *Pul*. For a common man to put on the belt of a chief was a serious offence in Ponape as in Hawaii, in which latter country the penalty was death : *cf.* the old distich—" Ina hume ke kanakai ko ke alii malo, e make noia." " If a common man bind on a chief's girdle, he shall die for it." Carved and plain shell-bracelets were also the fashion styled *Luou-en-Matup* from the place of their manufacture. A wise woman named *Kamai* is said to have invented them. The same word is applied to a ring of turtle-shell as far as Yap, fourteen hundred miles to the westward. (Possibly the word is the *Lio* or *Liko* of Polynesia, and denotes a hoop or circle.) Ear-rings of turtle-shell (*Kichin-pot*) were sometimes worn, but the Ponapeans of the present generation do not pull down and distort the lower lobe of the ear as do the Mortlock Islanders, and as the primitive people on Easter Island did, who were destroyed by a Polynesian invasion under Hotu-Matua, and styled by their conquerors the *Taringa-Roroa* or Long Ears. A similar custom prevailed amongst the early Bisayas in the Southern Philippines, and the Spanish chroniclers of the Conquest of Peru remark upon it as a fashion of the early Inca nobles.

The dress of the women of Ponape was called *Li-kau* or *Li-kau-tei* (*Kau*, clothing ; Polynesian *Ahu* or *Kahu*), a wide deep girdle depending as far as the knees, woven from the bark of the *Nin*—a common forest tree of the ficoid order. Native cloth made from the Paper Mulberry bark (Broussonettia)—the *tapa* or *siapo* or *Ngatu* of Polynesia does not appear to have been known to the Ponapeans. Necklaces of shells and flowers were much in use, likewise garlands of the fragrant Gardenia and Cananga odorata. Wreaths of polypody fern and various aromatic herbs and grasses were greatly in favour. Dancers, male and female, were fond of wearing fillets of banana leaf, dracæna (*Ting*) and coconut leaflets. These last they would wind round their fingers, so that the tips projected above the knuckles. These, as they quivered in their hands, produced a rattling, whirring effect in the choruses, and were styled *Anichinich*.

Their hats were made of pandanus leaf, helmet-fashion, with projecting peak—used by fishermen on the reef— called on Ponape *Li-chorrop*, on Kusaie *Surafraf*, on Yap, (where they assume the umbrella shape as worn by Chinese coolies and fishermen) *Ruatch*. Of late years the people of Pingelap and Kusaie have become famous for their clever workmanship in plaiting broad low sailors' hats on the European design.

MATERIALS. The raw material for their textile operations were (1) the inner fibre of the banana—the *Basho-fu* of the Japanese; (2) the bark of the Nin tree used in making a coarse sort of native cloth; (3) the bark of the Kalau (*Kala-hau*), the *Fau* or *Hau* of the Polynesians. The Ponapean name means the *Au* from which *Kal* or string is made. It is the *Gili-fau* of the Mortlock Islanders, whose dialect has preserved so many South Polynesian forms. Strips of the bark of this tree whilst fresh are as tenacious as the green withes with which Samson was bound. This handy makeshift is called *Tip-en-kalau*. It is a valuable substitute for string, and when split fine is used for making nets. The fourth indispensable material is the *Tipanit* or coconut fibre, obtained after sinking the husks a few days in the sand about high water mark. Each

tiny strand is laboriously twisted end on end between the
deft fingers and thumbs of the old men, until a surprisingly
strong cord or rope is formed—the thickness varying according to the patience of the operator.   This is the far-
famed cinnet cord so extensively used in Pacific waters for
lashing cross-beams and posts into place in house-building,
and in canoe-making as a substitute for nails in keeping
the framework and delicate cross-pieces of the outrigger in
place.   This material the Ponapeans call variously *Puel*
and *Kichin-mot.*

TRAPS AND CAGES.   The natives used to be very
adept in constructing all manner of traps and snares out
of the pliant strips of hibiscus.   The nooses they used in
snaring birds and wild pigs.   These they called *Letip* or
Litip, which being interpreted means a *woman's deceit.*
Other kinds of traps they called *Katikatia-mau*, a word
which in plain English signifies *a good device.*   Nowadays
this name is admiringly applied to those elegant instruments of torture sold by the traders known as gins or
tooth-traps for the capture of the rat and the *mus ridiculus*,
with whom the native is at endless feud.   The primitive
rat-trap was made of slips of reedgrass or fine cane, and
the central ribs of coconut leaflets formed the *Kachik* or
spring.   The bait consisted of a lump of odorous *Mar*
or fermented breadfruit, whilst a heavy piece of rock was
laid so as to fall upon and crush the intruder directly the
spring was touched.   In Yap they call this trap *Bildil.*
Now and then, but rarely, there is to be seen a cage
(*Pachapach* or *U*) made of slips of hibiscus wood cunningly
joined together, in which sits a disconsolate-looking bird.
The modern Ponapean, whatever his ancestors of a remoter
day did, does not trouble his head much about taming
birds—a pretty trait, by the way, in the character of his
southern cousin the Samoan.   However, one may see
sometimes in a Ponapean hut a ridiculously tame blue
heron (*Kaualik*), or a pretty black and white sea-bird
called *Chik*—children's pets.   Their matter-of-fact elders,

knowing the trouble in times of scarcity of filling hungry mouths, are hardly likely to let childish sentiment interfere with the just claims of the larder.

FISH HOOKS AND FISHING.   The name *Kách* denotes the hook of wood or bone, (in Kusaie *Kou*), the body of it mother-of-pearl (*pai*), the glitter of which attracts the fish like the bright metal spinner used in trolling for pike in the English meres and the lakes of Scotland and Switzerland.   The metal fish-hooks of varying size which the traders have introduced are greatly in request.   The Ponapean is a most keen fisherman.   One skilled in this art is always assured of a goodly alliance in marriage, to which his resourcefulness as a food-provider entitles him.[1]

For bait they use bits of squid or cuttle-fish (*Kich*), or else the bodies of hapless hermit-crabs (*Umpa*) torn from their snail-shell homes.   They frequently use bundles of *Up* root for stupefying fish in the pools.   When crushed up and dabbled in the water these roots exude a milky juice of a most powerful narcotic property, and the fish soon are floating about helpless.   The larger Murænas or sea-eels are the last to succumb, and finally writhe upwards out of the deeper and remoter holes in a stupid and comatose condition.

NETS.   *Uk* is the generic term for nets.   They are made as a rule of strips of bark from the Hibiscus tree, or of the *Oramai*, a species of Ramie.

Uk-alap.—Large stake-net or seine-net used for catching turtle and big fish, some twenty fathoms long by five in depth.

Uk-e-tik.—A small seine-net.

Chakichak.—A small casting net used for fishing on the edge of the reef just above the deep water.

Naik.—A hand-net, with a bow-shaped rim.   Used for scooping up fish driven down a narrow pass or ditch in the coral reef.

Lukuk, Lukouk.—A hand-net used for catching small fish.

---

[1] The verb *Lait* or *Lalait* means "to go a-fishing."   *Cf.* Malay, *Laut*, the sea ; Orang-*laut*, a pirate.

NANAUA, NEPHEW OF KING ROCHA OF KITI, SEATED ON HIS *PARROR*, OR CARPET OF CEREMONY

Liem.—A bag-net used at openings of weir or passage at the beginning of ebb-tides, generally four days after full moon.

Macha (Polynesian *Mata*) is the word used for the *Mesh* of the net.

A fish-pen or weir of stone is called *Mae*, one of cane or reeds *Ilu*.

In Yap *Thagal* is a cane-weir; *Aech* or *Etch*, a stone weir; *Maot*, a fish-pond.

HOUSEHOLD IMPLEMENTS, &C.   Ponapeans style them all *Kapua-kai*.

MATS.   *Loch* is the mat of the country.   It has a peculiar Japanese-like design and is sewn together, not plaited, and made of the leaves of a species of pandanus (*Kipar*), which answers to the *Raufara* of Tahiti, the *Rau-ara* of Rarotonga, and the *Lauhala* of Hawaii.   Length generally about seven feet, breadth about five.   The Paliker district is noted for its manufacture of these mats, which cost from six to eight Spanish dollars apiece.   The *Loch* of a great tribal chief is called *Parror* in the language of ceremony.

(2) *Li-rrop* or Woman's *Rrop*, is the name applied to mats of foreign make and pattern, such as those from Pingelap, Strong's Island, and the Marshall Islands— many of them very ornamental in design.   The name itself seems to be a foreign word (*Cf.* Yap *Tsop*, *Trop*; Gilbert Islands *Roba* Pingelap; *Rop*).   *Cf.* Maori *Repa* a coarse mat.

(3) *Teinai* are coarse mats plaited from coconut leaves. The article and its name alike borrowed from the Gilbert group, as also the rough baskets of the same material known as *Onoto*.

(4) *Kie, Kiei.*—Sleeping mats made of finely-woven pandanus.   Derived from the Mortlocks.   *Cf.* Polynesian *Kiekie*, a species of pandanus used as a textile fabric; and Kusaian *Kiaki*, a mat.

MOSQUITO SCREEN.   *Tei-'amu-ché.*—The *tau namu* of

Nuku-Oro, and the *Tai-namu* of the south-west Pacific. The Ponapean mosquito screen, before the introduction of gauze and linen, is said to have been composed of a cloth made out of the bark of the *Nin* tree. The Paper Mulberry, from which the *tapa, kapa, siapo*, or native cloth of south-west Polynesia is made, is not used for this purpose in Ponape, although it does occur sparsely.

PILLOW. *Ulul, Ulunga.*—The *Alunga* of south-west Polynesia—either made of bamboo, or a log of wood— a length of the trunk of a tree-fern or pandanus tree, for the Ponapeans are a hardy vigorous folk, and care not over much for soft lying and sumptuous fare.

BASKETS. *Kiam.*—A long flat basket or tray plaited roughly of coconut fronds split down the middle and interlaced in a diamond fashion. (Upon Kusaie *Kuam*).

Kopo.—A circular basket of varying depth made of the same material.

Kop-en-lait.—A fisherman's basket, somewhat larger than the above.

Onoto.—A large coarsely-plaited fish-basket, a Gilbert Island word.

Paikini.—Some thirty or forty of the above *Kiam* or flat trays fastened together, end on end, so as to form one long tray. This is heaped with food, and carried in solemn procession by about twenty men in the festivals celebrated in honour of a plenteous season. It is laid down on the grass, and a band of men approach with shell axes on their shoulders, with which they sever the strips of *Kalau* bark which bind the component *kiam* together. Then the food is apportioned, the *choko* or kava is brewed, the ancestral spirits are invoked, and the people fall to serious business tooth and nail.

FAN. *Ta-n-ir, i.e. Thing for fanning.*—A fan made of pandanus or coconut leaves. Those intended for fanning up the embers are clumsy in make, but those designed for personal use are much more neat in finish, and resemble the Marquesan very closely.

Et (Maori *Kete*, Samoan and Tahitian *Ete*).—A netted bag of Nin or Kalau fibre.

COMBS.   *Rotam* or *Rokom*.—Like those of Yap made out of the wood of the *Koto* or white mangrove, and of similar design.   Now scarcely ever seen, and the name is now applied to the gutta-percha, celluloid and tortoise-shell combs supplied by the ever-active trader.

For BOTTLES they use the hollowed circular fruits of the *Pulel*, *Pelak*, and *Ichak* plants, which belong to the Calabash family.   The gourds are strung together by fives and sixes with cinnet.   They use the large ones for storing drinking-water, the smaller for the various scented oils, in which native fancy so strongly delights.

COOKING UTENSILS.   In Ponapean *Tal* (Ngatik *Thal*), denotes a wooden dish, platter, and even a coconut cup. It is the old Indian word *Thal*, *Thaliya*, *Chaliya*, and is doubtless a survival from some remote era of crockery-ware in Southern or Central Asia.   *Chapi* is another name given in Ponape to vessels of wood of a circular shape.   The latter word occurs in the Mortlock *Sepei*, Marshall Islands *Chebi*, Gilbert Islands *Tabo*, Pelews *Theb*.   In the Mari-annes *Tape* denotes an earthen pot, the Yap equivalent being *Thab*, *Thib* or *Tib*, *cf.* Hebrew *Saph*, a bowl.   The occurrence of this common word over so wide an area, points unmistakably to the gradual substitution of wooden for earthen vessels in Micronesia, owing to the industry of pottery-making falling into abeyance in certain spots where no suitable clay or kaolin was available.   It is rather astonishing to see the art of pottery-making lost in a good-sized and well-settled island like Ponape, and retained in a small spot like Yap.   A curious fact, illustrating the same lost industry, was pointed out by the Rev. Lawes of Port Moresby in British New Guinea, in the preface to his useful vocabulary of the Motu dialect, in which the word *Tunua*, which in south-west and east Polynesian means *to cook by broiling or roasting*, is used in a special sense for the *baking of pottery*.   The white man's iron-pot is supplanting everywhere the earthen vessels of Micronesia, where the primitive industry is yet preserved, The *ainpot* is to be found in most Ponapean households and embraces a variety of uses, being alternately used for making huge brews of black tea, and boiling quantities of yam and coconut milk, the result being frequently a weird blending of different flavours on the palate of the European who drops in by chance to *pot-luck*.

The *Um*, or earth-oven, where the raw food is steamed (*cf.* Motu *Amu*, the *Umu* of south-west Pacific lands), has too often been described by travellers to need detailed notice here.   Cooking underground is the general mode in Ponape, although fish are frequently broiled on the glowing embers of dried coconut shells, their favourite fuel.   An important kitchen utensil is known as a *Kachak*.   It is an oval, flat-bottomed trough of *Tong* or *Chatak* wood, pointed at both ends like the bows of a boat, used like the *Umete* or *Kumete* of South Polynesia for concocting various toothsome masses of pounded yam, taro, bananas, plantains, or bread-fruit, mixed with coconut milk and salt water in varying proportions.   In Ponape a whale-boat is actually called *Waar-en-kachak*, from its sharp fore and aft build.

Their carving (*Chap*, *Alal*), was very ornamental, confined almost wholly to the bows and sides of their canoes and the blades of their dancing-paddles.   I saw no carved pillars in their houses, as in Yap, neither did I notice any carven bowls or maces as in Samoa and the Marquesas.   Specimens of the chequer and chevron designs from Metalanim may be seen from the originals now in the British Museum.[1]   The Ponapeans use a needle of human bone for tattooing the elaborate designs on arms, thighs, and legs.   This they call *Kai*, the operation *Inting* (Sulu *Indan*).

No well-ordered establishment is complete without a

---

[1] *Vide* photos facing p. 86.

A PONAPEAN CANOE

CARVED DANCING-PADDLES FROM METALANIM DISTRICT

husking-stick (*Ak*), (called in Samoan *O'a,* and in Tongan *Oka*), used for tearing off the fibrous outer envelope of the coconuts. It is a stout stake of mangrove-wood, pointed at both ends, and driven into the ground at an angle of about 95 degrees.

The same useful wood is used as a digging or planting stick like the *Oka* of the Hawaiians, and the *Koa* of the Aztecs in Mexico. Cut a little longer they make capital poles for punting canoes along in the shallower portions of the lagoon. These the Ponapeans used to call *Lata* (Hindu *Latha*), or *Parrak*. Where the *Ak* is found, the *Pelik* or scraper is seldom far off.

LOOM. The Ponapeans in olden times had a sort of loom resembling the *Puas* of their neighbours of Kusaie, with which they wove the fibre of the banana and the bark of the Nin tree into the *Uaiuai-lol* or narrow girdles, or iuto the *Li-kau,* or woman's petticoat. This machine, now long out of use, they called *Tantar* (Hindustani *Tant : Tantra* id). The verbs describing the process in Ponapean are *Tilpori, Toro* and *Ka-tantaki*).

Native houses often get dusty, so the industrious house-wife always has two or three brooms in hand for sweeping out the rubbish and keeping the mats clean and neat. These brooms are called *Kap-en-nok* or Bundles of *Nok*—the central ribs of coconut leaflets.

In the house of any person of distinction there will generally be found a huge sea-chest (*Kopa*) or at all events a small camphor wood box (*Kokon*), in which the islanders love to secrete their possessions.

If a native be given to carpentering pursuits, one may possibly see a cross-cut saw (*Racharach*) hung up carefully out of harm's way, or a grindstone (*Ú*) standing sentinel in the courtyard amongst the pigs and chickens.

The boat-builder greatly prefers the modern gimlet of steel (*me-n-kapurropur*), *i.e.* " the thing that whirls round " to the primitive borer of his forefathers made out of a long sharp-pointed Murex shell. It was formerly used for

piercing boards and planks in canoe and house-building.
The word for a hammer or mallet is *Chuk* or *Kangar*; a
wedge or nail is *Pach*.   In olden times holes were bored
and cinnet fastenings used, or wooden trenails or bolts, in
the absence of the nails lately introduced by traders.
These they now call *Kichin-mata* or bits of iron.

Another thing necessary in household industry was the
Tikak—a bone or shell needle used for sewing together
the layers of *Och* or Ivory palm-leaf for thatch, and joining
the leaves of the pandanus into the form of *Loch* or sleeping mats.   They were also used in making the ancient *I* or
mat-sails out of the *pit* or pandanus leaves, which had
undergone a preliminary steaming in the earth-oven.   The
roll of pandanus leaf for fashioning the sleeping mats was
called *Chal-en-pitipit*, also *Tanepit*.   For making the native
belts of banana fibre with their garnishing of pink and white
shell-beads, the Ponapean housewives used a fine tortoise-
shell hackle (*Mera*) for combing out the rough material—
the inner portion of the banana suckers.   These belts from
their scarcity are much esteemed by the present Ponapean,
and he will not part with them under ten dollars apiece.

The ready wit of the Ponapean is sufficient to supply
his simple needs.   Nature has been bountiful, and he has
proved himself of no mean adaptive powers in dealing with
economic plants and the various resources of the lagoon
and reef in providing himself food, shelter and clothing.
This will be apparent as one by one we will examine his
household implements, his tools, his devices for procuring
food by sea and land, his instruments of music, and his
weapons of war.

AXES AND KNIVES.   The Ponape words for axe and
knife are doubly interesting historically.   They indicate a
reversion through long isolation to the primitive stone or
shell age ; moreover, they inversely show the early influence of an active Malay element radiating throughout the
extensive Caroline Archipelago.   Writing clearly was not
the only art lost by these Ocean tribes during their long

isolation. And by examining these words we can easily infer how these two things came about, though the dates of the early migrations and forays are almost hopeless in the lack of proper chronological data and the snapping of traditional links in the process of untold generations.

Now the general term in Ponapean for instruments of the axe, adze or hatchet type is *Chila* (in Kiti they are called *Ki*, and in the Metalanim district *Patkul*). From their polished marble-like appearance some have taken their material for white jade-stone, but J. S. Kubary has clearly shown them to be pieces of the central shaft of the *Tridacna Gigas* or Giant Clam worn down into that form by long and careful rubbing. In our excavations in the central vault of Nan-Tauach, we settled the question beyond dispute, for we dug up a number of these implements both in the rough and the smooth.[1] They are now getting somewhat scarce on the island, ousted from use by the introduction of steel adzes, American axes and tomahawks, through the ever increasing competition of traders. (The new introduction they call *Chila-pangapang*.)

In early days they used to cut down trees with these primitive instruments, with the aid of fire. One charred layer chipped off, fire would be applied again—a somewhat tedious process. At great festivals the grandees used to sit in state with their adzes crooked over their shoulders for the same reason that a European wears a Court sword,—*de rigueur*.

The *Matau* was a shell-gouge used for hollowing out canoes, with its handle spliced along the back. In Samoa it is called by the very same name. A small adze was known as *Maluak*, and resembles the first, only smaller.

The word *Chila* is the Motu *Ila*. It is one of the primitive Asiatic words which any minute observer cannot help noticing in the wide Pacific area. It appears in the Sanskrit *Shila : Shil*—a stone, and in the Latin—*Silex*—flint. In the language of the Garo tribesmen in India

---

[1] Some of these are now in the British Museum.

Sil means iron.   The root *Sil*, in the sense of piercing or cutting is, according to Isaac Taylor, of frequent occurrence in the Ural-Altaic tongues.

On the other hand the Metalanim word for "knife" *kápit* takes us into times when early Malayan or Sulu pirate-voyagers landed with creeze and sword (*cf.* Bismarck Archipelago *Kaput*, iron ; Philippines *Kampit*, short sword ; Philippine and Sulu *Kampilan*, a sword) with which they doubtless made an exceedingly striking impression upon the ill-armed aborigines.   At the beginning of this century, before the traders brought machetes and 18-inch and 2-foot knives, the Ponapeans made their *kapit* of split bamboo.   Those of shell were called *Lopuk*.   These they used for slicing up fish or bread-fruit, as do the Yap people to this day, who call these latter *Yar-ni-matsif*, or cutting things of shell.   (In Central and Western Carolines a shell-knife is called *Char* and *Yar* (*cf.* Southern Philippines (Pangasinan) *Yoro*, a knife).   The Metalanim folk use the old name *Kapit* for the new article, but the people of Kiti and Not have adopted the English word.   *Naip* they call them, not *cuchillo* as one might expect.   Characteristic is this preference for English words instead of Spanish.

Now there are two other highly significant names of Malayan derivation running through these 1400 miles in the Sea of the Little Islands.   Iron is called *Mata* in Ponape, and *Marra* in the Marshall Islands.   *Masra*, *Mossa*, and *Wessa* in Kusaie.   In the two next groups, the Mortlocks and Ruk, we find the form *Wasai* and *Wasi*, *Asi.*   A little southward and westward we find it reappear in Nuku-Oro and Kap-en-Marangi as *Wasei.*   In Yap it is *Wasai.*   In German New Guinea it occurs as *Bassi.* The Malay word is *Basi* or *Besi*.   *Badja, Wadja*, steel, of which the above are doubtless slightly differentiated forms.   Finnic *Was* or *As* ; Caucasian *Asa* and *Vasa*, iron.   Magyar *Vas*, iron.   Sanskrit *Asi*, iron, bronze, copper, a sword.   Latin *Æs*.

N.B.—In the language of the Tinneh group in North America we find the words *Pesh, Pash, Mash,* and *Bash,* denoting *knife.*

N.B.—Another very peculiar word for *Iron* is found in the Mariannes or Ladrones in the north-west, and in Uleai and neighbouring islands in the West and Central Carolines. Marianne, LULIK, LULUG, Iron. Uleai, Uluthi, and Satanal, *Lulu,* id.

Cf. Sanskrit *Lohi, Lauh* and *Lauk,* iron, steel, and Ahom LIK; Khamtis, LEK; Lao, LEK; Siamese, LIK. In Ponapean we find a root LUK, LAK, or LEK, with the signification of *cutting.* Philological experts must give us a satisfactory reason for the above coincidences, and tell us plainly *how* these words came into the Caroline area, and also, whether Ahom, Khamti, Lao, and Siamese borrowed the word from the Sanskrit, or whether the Sanskrit-speaking folk borrowed the word from their neighbours. And from which of these did the Caroline Islanders receive it?

It stands to reason, that as the basaltic or coral lands of the Pacific produce no iron, steel is unobtainable. It may be presumed that some of the early settlers in the Carolines brought with them a stock of iron or steel weapons, or wrested them from stray pirates of a ·later day. When these rusted away or got broken, and could not be replaced, the traditional name would in all probability remain, and the natives under stress of necessity, would fall back upon the handiest materials available to supply their place. Those who live on low coral islets would find the shaft of the Tridacna (*Kima* or *Pachu*) a shell very abundant on their reefs, a convenient substitute. Those who inhabited high basaltic lands, as Tahiti or the Marquesas (on the first of which the water is always deep over her coral reefs, and the latter has no reefs at all) would fall back on the black basalt stone to fashion their cutting instruments. Samoa and Fiji have done the same. In those islands the blackstone axes were common enough before the advent of the curio hunter. They can still be picked up sometimes on the mountain-tops or on the sites of deserted villages. In Ponape I met with no axes of blackstone, the reason probably being that the shell was easier to work than the basalt, which does not so readily shape into flakes with keen cutting edges.

The other Malay word is *Parang*, which in the Central Carolines is used both for knife and iron. In Malayan vocabularies it is given with the meaning of a bill-hook or short sword, and its survival in these remote lands appears to indicate a lively and deep-seated apprehension of " *the noble white weapon* " wielded by the piratical hands of these Vikings of the Pacific Seas.

WEAPONS. *Pai*, a sling (Yap *Gol*) *Pai-uet*, a sling-stone, the favourite missile-weapon of the Ponapeans before the introduction of fire-arms by the New Bedford and New England whalers. The sling was plaited out of strips of Hibiscus bark, or else out of the cinnet-fibre or that of the Nin-tree bark. Amongst the Ponapeans, there is no more favourite passage in the Old Testament than the famous duel of David and Goliath, the translation of which is particularly spirited and happy in the missionary vernacular. The incidents of the encounter are peculiarly in accord with native fashion in every way, and the name David (*Tepit*) is very common amongst the Protestant folk on the south-west coast.

The BOW is called *Kachik-en-katiu*, literally, " make-shoot-of-Katiu-wood " ; the arrow *Katiu-en-kachik*, a weapon not much in favour on the Polynesian and Micronesian area. It is more of a Melanesian weapon. In the Gilberts it is called *Bana*, in the Marshall Islands *Li-ban*, i.e. the *Ban* or bow of a woman, regarded as a woman's or child's weapon. In Polynesia known as *Fana*, and in the Melanesian area as *Vana, Van, Bana*, and *Fan*. The Malayan form is *Panah* (in Sanskrit, *Ban* or *Van* is an arrow, and *Panach* is a bow-string). It may

PILUNG ADOLOL, A CHIEF OF RÚL

be worth mentioning that in ancient Hawaii the bow was used by lads, old men, and women for the noble sport of shooting at rats—a sad come-down for the weapon which won Merry England such high renown.   The Ponapeans say the bow was used by the *Chokalai* or dwarf aborigines. The bow was made of *Katiu* or Ixora wood, the bow-string of the bark of the Hibiscus, the arrows of Hibiscus wood, or slips of Alek or reed-grass, tipped with the spine of the sting-ray.   Nowadays it is entirely out of use.

The CLUB was occasionally used.   It was known as *Lep-en-tuka* or *Chup-en-tuka* ; by the Mortlock Islanders as *Sop-en-ura*.   Also called in Ponape *Chup-en-pok*.   The word *Chup* is evidently the Indian *Chob*, which denotes the same weapon amongst the Hindu peasantry.   According-ing to Nanchau of Mutok (*Tenedos*) stone clubs called *Permachapang* were used.   Of these I found no traces either at *Chapen-takai* or *Nan-Matal*, neither did I see during my stay on the island any of the elaborately carved war-clubs or maces noted in the Marquesas, Fiji, Samoan and Tongan Groups.

SPEARS were the favourite weapon in hand to hand conflict.   They were called *Katiu* from a species of Ixora of that name.   Its straight-growing stems were used by the natives for fashioning their spears and javelins.   The *Ak* or Mangrove also was much used for making spear-shafts.   They were pointed with the sting of the Ray (*Likant-en-kap*).   In the Mortlocks the spear is known as *Uak* or *Silak*, in Ruk *Anek*, Pulawat *Lil*, in the Central Carolines as *Tillak*, *Tallak*, *Dilok* and *Thilak*.   In the Marshalls *Mori*, *Marre* or *Marri*.   In the Philippines it appears in the Tagala *Tulag* or *Tolak*—a war-spear (the Favorlang of Formosa has *Roddok* and *Biloagh*, a spear, *Silek*, a knife).   In Metalanim a wooden dagger is called *Tillako*, in Yap *Muruguil*.

The most formidable of all the Caroline spears were those of Yap fashioned out of the wood of the *Bû* or Areca palm, and manufactured chiefly in the district of

Madolai. They were often nearly twelve feet in length, pronged and barbed on either side in the cruellest fashion so as to inflict a most terrible wound. The prowess of the men of Yap with this redoubtable weapon earned for them a very extensive dominion in the Central Carolines, and indeed up to Ponape, which some of their more distant forays seem actually to have reached.

MUSICAL INSTRUMENTS AND DANCES. Like all islanders they are very fond of music. Any up-to-date trading skipper with a cargo of banjos and accordions would sell them off in double-quick time. The *Chaui* (Fijian *Davui*) or shell-trumpet—the *Pu* of the South Polynesians, is used as a signal of war or assembly like the *Atabal* of the ancient Mexicans. Close by the pointed end of the shell a circular hole is bored. The sound travels a long way up hill and down valley, and I firmly believe that between village and village is a regular code of signal-calls almost as effective as our telephone. Some of these, " CHAUI," are of very large size and are often picked up amongst the foundations of old houses.

The native flute is called *Chup-en-ro* or *Chup-en-parri*. It is made of a piece of *Ro* or reed-grass or of *parri* or bamboo. It is not quite a foot in length—closed at one end by a stopper of leaves and pierced with six holes up to the mouthpiece. It is not a nose-flute like the *Tosarri* of Formosa or the *Fango-fango* of Samoa, or that of the Sakais of the Malay Peninsula.

The native drum is called *Aip*—the old name *Peu* or *Pau* (the *Pahu* of Tahiti). One I saw in Paliker, now in the British Museum, is about five feet in height and made of the wood of the *Tupuk*. It is shaped exactly like a huge erect dice-box like the drums of the Jekri in West Africa, Niger territory. It was covered with the skin of the Sting-Ray and beaten with a stick of Hibiscus wood on occasions of festival. The Spanish chronicler Pereiro describes a smaller sort which he saw in Not district which

he calls *Piki-piki*, evidently from mistaking the meaning
and application of the word *Pikir* which is a verb meaning
to beat a drum—not, I think, denoting the drum itself.
This one, he says, was about three feet high and covered
with fish-bladders which they collect fresh on the day of the
festival—he describes it as adorned with square markings
and painted with various colours, especially red and black.
When the feast is over they take away the skins and get
others, for they are easily burst and need constant renewal.
It may be observed that the Ponapeans are very fond of
the accordion and of the modern Jews' harp which they
call *Kachang, i.e. make sound.* It seems that they had a
sort of Jews' harp of their own like the Samoan *Utete*, but
the modern ones have ousted the ancient article.

DANCES. There are two kinds—one peculiar to the
men called *Kalek*, the *Purek* of the Mortlock Islanders,
the *Sorosoro* or *Talisa* of Kusaie, and the *Dalisia* of
South-East Formosa, on the Favorlang River—danced
standing ; and another of men and women together, like
the *Siva* of the Samoans performed sitting (*Uen* or *Wen*)
with graceful wavings of hand, wrist and arm. The
elaborate dancing-masks of the Solomon Islands and
New Hebrideans are not found here. The dancers are
always in *Kapot*—holiday dress, anointed with fish or
coconut-oil—the men in bright yellow *Kol* or kilts, their
heads garlanded with flowers or chaplets of green fern,
their necks and arms copiously hung with festoons of
fresh coconut leaflets and on the fingers of each hand
a sort of ring with bunches of *Nok* or ribs of coconut
leaflets bristling out. These, in shaking, produce a sort
of harmonious rustling. Some of the choruses have a
fine deep sonorous chime like those of the Marquesan
Islanders. Many of the dances are anything but decorous
in character. It is said that a number of the words used
in the chants both in Yap and Ponape are different
altogether from the spoken language. Certainly some
specimens of Ponapean songs written down by Kaneke

and Chaulik on Paniau were hopelessly unintelligible to me although I could both read and converse in the vernacular Ponapean with considerable ease and fluency. It would seem that many Sagas of the acts of legendary heroes would have come in from the Marshall Islands and from Yap, and thus would be of great historical interest in tracing ancient connections and the gradual or accidental fusions of different Micronesian races. It is here that the Phonograph or Graphophone as well as the Camera comes to the aid of the ethnologist. Once get the exact sounds recorded on the wax cylinder, and the task of the philologist becomes tenfold easier. *Melakaka* is the word for the song or dramatical composition of a priest or chief, and is therefore very happily adopted by the missionaries to denote the *Psalms* of David and the Song of Solomon. (*Cf.* the Hawaiian word *Mele*—a song, and the Pelew word *Moloik*—dancing and singing.)

During the burial of any person of note was intoned a funeral dirge, wake or Threnody called *Tarak*. It is said to be very solemn, weird and impressive.

Ponapean houses are, as a rule, well and solidly constructed upon platforms four or five feet in height, built up of broken pieces of basalt. and sometimes limestone blocks. The walls composed of shutters (*Tet* or *Tat*) made of bundles of reed-grass or cane about the thickness of one's little finger, laid side by side with the greatest neatness and regularity, and bound together in rows with the ever-useful cinnet-fibre. The thatch is composed of tightly packed bundles of leaf of the *Och*, the vegetable Ivory or Sago Palm called by the Spanish *Palma de marfil*. The doors (*Uanim*) are often very narrow, and it is quite a trouble to squeeze oneself in. The floor within is covered with a planking of boards, or else with numerous flat shutters of reed-grass, which are also called *Tat* or *Tet*. (Compare Hindustani *Tatti*—a shutter of reed or cane of a similar design.) The pillars that bear up the

PONAPEAN HOUSE. DISTRICT OF U, NORTH COAST

house are made of *Katar* or tree-fern, of bread-fruit wood, or that of one of the useful timber trees with which the island abound. The rafters are of the sturdy *Ak* or mangrove branches (Polynesian *Oka*). The height of the central roof-tree varies from fifteen to twenty feet in houses of moderate size.

The cook-house, called *Parra* or *Par* (Polynesian Fare, Fale, a house ; in Ponapean there is no F, P takes its place), was an unpretentious building of mangrove stakes and thatch, situated a little to the rear of the premises.

The *Nach* or Council Lodge was a lofty, wide, long and spacious building with a raised platform, at the end of which there was often a room for the sleeping place of the Chief and his family, railed off by shutters of cane sometimes called *Pel* or *Ueip* ; the partition is called *Mech-en-tet*. On this raised platform, about six feet in height (*Lempantam* or *Leppantam*), ascended by a rude ladder (*Kantake*), sat the chiefs and distinguished men. Along both sides within the Lodge ran a wooden terrace or platform, with reed-grass or cane flooring, where the women and children and those of lower estate sat. In the open space below were several huge flat slightly concave basalt stones, upon which the Chakau, Choko, or Kava root was pounded. From the presence of these flat basalt stones the lodges are sometimes called *Im-en-takai* or Houses of the *Takai* or Stones. Very often a boathouse on the edge of a creek or by the seashore is used as a *Nach*, as in the case of the *Horau-Nanui* of Nuku-Oro.

The *Nach* is open at the lower end. Above the entrance some slight protection against the wind and rain is afforded by the Lolo or cross-thatching that can be easily increased in case of bad weather. I may add that I saw no carved posts in these houses, as I afterwards remarked in Yap. It seems strange the omission here of a custom so universal in the Polynesian and Melanesian area.

CHAPTER IX

VISIT TO MOKIL, PINGELAP AND KUSAIE[1]

ON May 2nd, 1896, just after the departure of the mail steamer for Manilla, there arrived in Ascension Bay a little **trading-schooner**, the *Tulengkun*, belonging to Captain M., an American subject, who offered me a passage by her to Kusaie, his headquarters. Taking advantage of the opportunity of her return trip, arrangements were speedily concluded, and on a miserable Saturday afternoon we ran from the Langar anchorage in a raw chilly drizzle, which later on increased into a regular downpour. The wind comes off shore in occasional puffs, and the vessel rolls considerably on the long heavy swell, clearing the harbour mouth just before sunset. However, an hour or two after midnight a steady breeze comes along, and daybreak finds us plunging through white-crested seas with the great cliff of Chokach and the cloud-capped peak of Kupuricha fast sinking astern. A dull and wearisome Sunday drags along. The first stage of our journey is only one hundred miles, and we sight the blurred outline of Mokil on Monday at sunset, just before a huge inky curtain of cloud closes down, rudely blotting it out and bringing a hissing white squall. Early next morning the sky was clear and bright, and we were lying close up to the island, and by-and-bye we ran inshore.

Mokil, otherwise called Duperrey from the French navigator of that name, is properly a group of three low islands—Urak, Manton and Kálap—lying close together

---

[1] A portion of the narrative below appeared in the *Hong Kong Telegraph* early in the following year.

in a lagoon of no great extent.   Manton is rounded in outline like a boomerang or horse-shoe ; Urak and Kálap are longer in stretch, and crescent-shaped.   Kálap and Manton are inhabited, the former containing the main settlement surrounded with yam and taro patches, and embowered in palms and hibiscus (*Pá*), screw-pine and Barringtonia.   Urak is one wild palm-grove, full of pigs and wild fowl, and is often visited from the main settlement.   A pretty feature hereabouts at half-tide are the numerous primrose, mauve and sulphur-tinted bits of coral studding the bottom, with bright yellow fishes, six or eight inches long, darting in and out of these submarine rockeries, like flashes of living gold.   The natives call them *Tapurapur*.   Gorgeous star-fish of a bright Prussian blue (*Sukunap*) [called On Kusaie, *Si-keniaf*] lie around.   With the Ponapeans the creature is connected with the Rain God, and lifting it out of the water is said to be invariably followed by heavy showers of rain.   Between Manton and Urak a narrow boat-passage leads up to Kálap beach, across a strip of flat reef almost dry at low tides, studded with numerous masses of honeycombed limestone rock. Close here are two large blocks.   Tradition says the *Ani* or demi-gods, in the form of a pair of frigate-birds, brought them from the eastward.   These were the mythical ancestors of the Mokil islanders.

The nearest of the Ralik chain is only about one hundred and fifty miles from Mokil.   The Mokil folk, who number some two hundred, probably have a strong Marshall Island admixture like their Pingelap neighbours. Many of their words are akin to those in Ralik, and some again are an obsolete form of Ponapean, but nowadays the modern Ponapean is everywhere spoken, introduced by the American missionaries and native teachers.   The natives are Christianised ; coconut toddy is tabooed, and all use of intoxicating liquors and tobacco strictly forbidden.   They make capital sailors, for which calling a certain cheery hardihood peculiarly fits them, but on land, like all Pacific islanders, their zeal is occasionally dashed by fits of laziness. A steady aversion to settled labour ashore has left many a promising contract half completed. It is so with all the brown races—it is otherwise with the black or yellow—but this roving nature, impatient of control, engendered by numberless predatory raids, and long sea-rovings in the olden days, is the true heritage of the Malayan. These bold navigators, as any up-to-date philological chart will show, swept out wave upon wave through Gilolo Straits, conquering and blending in various proportions with the agricultural black races which had preceded them. This is clearly proved by the frequent occurrence of Malay and Sanskritoid root-words along the north coast of New Guinea and down to Port Moresby, where the Motu dialect is spoken. Let the doubting reader only glance at the long list of Caroline root-words in the Comparative Table soon to be published by the Polynesian Society of New Zealand, and then doubt any more if he can.

It is to the black races therefore that we are to look for supply of plantation labour, and to the brown people for sailors. Each will then follow his ancestral bent to the great saving of time and temper of the long-suffering trader, and of his colleague, that irascible and leather-lunged potentate, the trading skipper.

The King, or Icho of Mokil, lives on Kálap, and is a bland old gentleman, but, like nearly all converted natives, has a keen eye for business. The chief trader on the island is John Higgins, a capital boat-builder and carpenter. He was the son of a Massachusetts man, afterwards murdered upon Pingelap by a Gilbert islander from Arorai. He leads as quiet and industrious a life as any Norfolk or Pitcairn island settler, and bids fair to end his days as a patriarch of the old Pacific school.

One would fancy that the traders in these parts must needs put up with a woeful number of bad debts, the competition in trade moving in the old vicious circle.

Still the shiftless credit system goes on, the native now
and again paying a trifle on account, after alternate bully-
ing and cajolery.   Very often the native reserves to himself the right of repudiating his debts altogether, and when
he does receive a little money, of going straight across to
the rival store, and paying ready cash for goods to the
frenzied excitement of his creditors.   On the other hand,
when the trader gets a little ahead of the native, as sometimes happens between seller and buyer in the best
regulated communities, the voice of the Spanish law
thunders forth : " How dare you rob the poor innocent
native ? " ignoring the fact that the noble savage is every
bit as versed in deception and trickery as his white
brother, whom if he fails to strike at the first venture, he
will surely bring down at the second, place, time and
opportunity, and lack of honest interpreters being all in
his favour.   Who else could say to his white creditor :
"*If you will not lend me money how can I ever pay ?* "

There is no lack of fowls and ducks on Kalap, but only
a few little pigs are allowed here, for fear of the ravages the
big ones would surely commit amongst the taro and banana
patches.   There is no supply of running water, but there
is a heavy annual rainfall, which the natives make the
most of by digging numerous shallow pits and wells
(Kallip).   A species of jack-fruit (Mai-mat) is cultivated.
When mature, the wood develops a firm reddish grain,
and is much prized by local carpenters for housebuilding.
The palm-groves yield an abundant supply of green drinking nuts, and much copra is made from the kernels of the
older ones called *Pen* (*cf.* Samoan *Penu*, Gilbert Islands
Ben).   The lagoon teems with fine fish, the most esteemed
of which are a species of mullet, the bonito and the flying
fish.   The Mokil canoes are built of seasoned bread-fruit
wood, fitted with a long, solid, and heavy outrigger, curving boldly upwards bow and stern, recalling somewhat the
Yap canoes, without, however, the curious fish-tail ornamentation on the figure-heads.   Their *Yi* or sails, like the

old-fashioned ones of Ponape, are wide and triangular, formed of parallel rows of pandanus leaves neatly sewn together.   The usual littoral shrubs common on low coral islands flourish here, amongst them two medicinal in quality, the Ramak and Sisin (known in Ponape as the Inot and Titin).   Giant screw-pines (*P. edulis*), with their quaint leaf whorls, their huge orange-red fruit like exaggerated pine apples, and long sword-shaped, prickly-edged leaves, fringe the shore, and the air is filled with the subtle perfume of the delicate white blossoms of the tree-gardenia (*Pur*).

After a stroll in the woods, a bathe in one of the water holes, and a hearty meal of fried flying fish and taro, it is time to leave.   Towards evening, with a good load of copra, and some of the Urak porkers and seven or eight native passengers on board, we set sail for Pingelap, which lies some sixty miles away to the southward.   Next day nothing but dismal and dirty weather and heavy seas.   A powerful odour of copra permeates the ship from stem to stern, which must be extremely delicious to those who are accustomed to it.   Everything is hot, damp, muggy, and uncomfortable.   Hosts of cockroaches are on the war-path below, and up above there is a dank drizzle, hardly a breath of wind stirring, and the great cradle of the deep is rocking us to and fro in something more than a motherly fashion.   So the long dreary afternoon wears itself slowly away.

Late in the evening of Thursday, May 7th, after a steady struggle with a strong north-west current, which future navigators in these waters should allow for, we catch a glimpse of the lights of the Pingelap canoe-parties fishing out on the reef.   Next morning early we are anchored near the beach, and numerous folk have already boarded us, clamouring for an extended credit system, and excited like very children at the prospect of fingering and handling, and perhaps even purchasing, the much-coveted foreign goods.   Voices, a regular Babel, are raised, some in solemn argument and serious questioning, some rippling into light jests, chaff and repartee, some melting into those coaxing, pleading and wheedling accents wherewith the native so often reaches the soft spot in the white trader's heart.   However, business is somehow concluded at last. Some natives make small payments, some pay liberally in promises and compliments which sometimes pass current in Micronesia as elsewhere, whilst some again are refused credit altogether, and away they troop into their canoes and go ashore evidently in high feather.   After a while I went ashore in the ship's boat, pencil and note-book in hand, as beseems a seeker after strange things, arousing the curiosity of the worthy folk on the beach, who for naïve and rustic stolidity and ludicrous ignorance are the very Bœotians of the Pacific.   The following rough notes were taken.   The group consists, like Mokil, of three low coral islands lying close together, named respectively Pingelap, Taka, and Chikuru styled on the charts *Tugulu*.   The population a little over 1000 ; pretty dense considering the meagre area, but compare with this the island of Tapitouea in the Gilbert Group which is one huge village.   The natives of Pingelap form a sort of ethnic link between the Ponape and Mokil type.   Their language is a harsh and antiquated dialect of Ponapean with a sprinkle of Marshall Island words.   As in Mokil, however, the new missionary Ponapean, introduced in the lesson books and New Testament translations and songs, is fast ousting the old language, and this is a living instance of the instability of Pacific Island tongues.   So fast one stratum of population overlaps another —" *Velut unda supervenit undam.*"   Most of the inhabitants here live on the main central island, which is neatly laid out in shady walks and avenues, skirting trim and well-kept plantations of bananas and various sorts of taro.   Plenty of arrowroot is found in the bush.   The beach is thickly lined by rows of small boathouses backed by quite an imposing array of native huts.   I saw numbers of canoes drawn up on the beach, running up very high at bow and stern, and still more were scattered in the offing, for the Pingelap folk are sturdy and energetic fishermen. The approach was picturesque, the grey coral reef rising up like a great sea-wall out of the deep blue water. The bottom is seamed with profound cracks and fissures, the lurking places of great fishes and giant crustacea and squid. Orange and scarlet patches of coral light up the wavy masses of oarweed, tangle and sea-fan, and many a quaint and gorgeous zoophyte spreads its delicate tentacles in the current in odd nooks and corners. Numerous grey and white sea-birds skim the surface in middle distance, following the shoals of fish " *Un en mom* " in their course, and now and then a white or blue heron wings his way heavily overhead. (The former they call *Kara*, the latter *Nankilap*.) The coconut groves are very productive, and in profusion are found two varieties of jack-fruit (" *Mai-pa* " and " *Mai-si* ") one with slightly, the other deeply, serrated leaves. The sea swarms with fish, and there are plenty of pigs and fowls. The numbers of bright healthy young children playing about the landing-place gave a very pleasant and encouraging testimony of the vigour and vitality of the race—a quality now, alas! growing rarer and rarer amongst South Sea island peoples. Quantities of fishing nets were seen hanging up on every side. From the frequent sheds and cooking-houses on the waterside were rising grateful aromas of baked pigs and roasting fish. In a trice we were conducted to a cool shady spot, mats were spread out, green coconuts husked, and a savoury repast was soon smoking before us. Later on we visit Tomas, the native teacher, and duly admire the pretty little native church and schoolhouse with its palm-thatch and burnt coral walls. Tomas' sleek and contented appearance irresistibly recalls the merry old Scottish distich :—

> " O the monks of Melrose made gude kail
> On Fridays when they fasted
> And wanted neither beef nor ale
> As long as their neighbour's lasted."

Heaps of coconuts and baskets of cooked food were lying on the ground outside—forming the *Mairong* or church offering to which every good member of the congregation is expected to contribute.   Then I visited the alleys and neatly paved pathways of Michor, the main settlement, bordered by gardens and taro patches on every side.   Hereabouts are some groves of bread-fruit carefully cultivated, not only for the fruit, but for its timber, which, when it gets old and seasoned, has a fine reddish-brown tint.   They use it for boat building and as posts and rafters for their houses.   They also split it fine to make their lattice or shutters, as the reed-grass, common enough in Kusaie, Ponape and the Mortlocks is not found here. The name they give these shutters in this part of the Carolines is *tat* or *tet.*   Compare the Hindustani *tat* or *tatti*, a term widely used, as all Anglo-Indians well know, for delicately woven shutters of cane which keep out the mid-day dust and heat.

When we got on board a host of natives followed us, headed by the Icho or King with his Queen and interpreter, and plenty of hats (*Sorap*) and mats (*Rop*) for sale —both cunningly woven of the leaf of the Pandanus in which manufacture they are very skilful.   His Majesty after begging in a naïve fashion for a Turkey-red shirt, refused the offer of a cigar as a bad example to the church members.   Quoth his majesty to me : " You my friend. You see Pikitoria (Victoria *sic*).   He one big chief—Pictoria he talk.   You speak Pingelap man he good."   This same worthy chief and his colleague of Mokil some little while ago when guests on board the gunboat *Quiros*, proved a source of great amusement to their Spanish hosts by their very free and unconventional table manners, helping themselves to double handfuls of food from the nearest dishes, in utter disregard of knives and forks, to the dismay of the poor steward who gazed on them with eyes wide open with horror.   When the King of Pingelap saw and smelt a large dish of curry, his eyes glistened.   When it came within reach he eagerly scooped up a double handful and without more ado supped it up.

Reluctantly taking leave of our new Arcadian friends, we hoisted sail the same evening and left our anchorage on our 140 miles' sail down to Kusaie. Continual calms and light baffling winds checked our way, and several heavy rain squalls burst over us. Towards sundown on Saturday the 9th, after a spell of miserable weather, the clouds lifted a little and disclosed the sharp and angular outline of Kusaie standing out clearly defined under a pall of inky blackness, the tops of the mountains hidden in bank upon bank of cloud-haze and smoky wreaths of teeming vapour. Anon the curtain descends anew, a fresh violent squall comes down, and we fly scudding over the heaving seas, rolling and pitching, like a Deal or Sandgate lugger in the chops of the English Channel.

I had nearly forgotten to remark that the Pingelap men though dull and heavy in temperament, are exceedingly nervous withal—a rare thing amongst Caroline Islanders. A trifling operation such as the removal of a splinter will make a strong able-bodied man faint. The same is related of the people of Nuku-Oro and Kap-in-Mailang further south. They are said to be easily subject to hypnotic suggestion, a fact which recalls the peculiar disorder called *Lata* mentioned by Swettenham as common in the Malay Peninsula, and called *Malimali* in the Philippines. Pingelap used to be a favourite recruiting place with whaling captains plying northward, who found the men docile and hardworking, and better able than many other islanders to stand the cold of the Arctic regions.

Late at night we pass the twinkling lights of the missionary settlement of Mout, high up on the hill-slopes, flashing out a greeting as it were through the dense gloom. In the early morning, May 10th, we are off Coquille, and make a long tack to double the North-East Point. On rounding the promontory, the island of Lele with its spacious harbour of Chabrol on the far side, comes in sight.   Hereabouts a powerful current runs, setting to the eastward, which any future navigators will do well to remember, giving the point a pretty wide berth to avoid stranding amongst the breakers on a dangerous coast.   The main island reminds one somewhat of Rarotonga, with the bizarre features a little softened down. The altitude of Fulaet, the highest peak, is about the same, some 2300 feet.   In the middle are two needle-shaped peaks set close together.   A belt of rich low land surrounds verdant hill-slopes thickly clothed with forest up to the summit.   Here and there one spies scattered native houses lying back amongst groves of pandanus and palm.   We have passed lonely little Star Harbour, and are skirting the coast-line dotted with the straggling huts of Puia, the Gilbert Islanders' settlement.   And so we sailed along, each foreland opening up fresh beauties in the landscape.   From off the entrance to Chabrol or Lele Harbour the main island looks almost divided in two by the deep inlet.   Close at hand stretches a flat-topped mountain, like that of Vatu Vara in the Fijis, resembling in shape a fashionable tall silk hat with a broad low brim running round it.   Side on to us on the right is the outer edge of Lele.   Beyond the mainland looms up, rising into several peaks and ranges, opening out into rich vistas of valley and emerald woodland, with snow-white birds circling and wheeling in the far tree-tops. The swell is heavy, and there falls a spell of light variable breezes.   About two hundred yards off under our lee beam, heavy rollers are dashing upon the reef, sending up jets and clouds and sheets of finest spray that fill the middle distance with a misty haze.   Slowly we approach the land, the passage at its narrowest point being only about three-quarters of a cable broad, hardly giving fair room to tack in should a sudden white squall sweep down from the mountain gorges above.   Just as we entered the passage a chicken flew overboard and was left behind rising and falling on the swell astern. By order of the captain the boat was lowered, however, and the hapless fowl rescued from one liquid grave, only to appear a little later in another—to wit, a savoury soup.

This same harbour of Lele in days past was a great rendezvous for the New Bedford and New England whaleships. There the famous " Bully " Hayes, the modern Buccaneer, played fine pranks after losing his beautiful vessel on the reefs, half frightening the lives out of the peaceful Kusaians by landing a number of fierce and warlike Ocean and Gilbert Islanders, who brewed huge quantities of coconut-toddy, and set the whole place in a ferment with their carousals and mad orgies. Night after night they kept it up, alternately drinking and fighting. Murdered men's bodies were picked up on the beach every morning, and the poor natives of Lele fled in terror of their lives. Hayes at last brought the crazy mutineers back to their senses and meditated settling on the island, when, greatly to the American missionaries' relief, a barque came in from Honolulu with the intelligence that a British man-of-war was coming up fast in search of that very dreadful sinner and reprobate, the aforesaid Hayes. But what became of the redoubtable captain of many resources is matter for another and a longer yarn. We are now close up to the settlement with the King's new lumber and shingle house standing forward prominently amongst many humbler abodes, under the shade of a noble Callophyllum tree. Right in front of us lies Captain M.'s dwelling, his storehouse and copra shed flanked by white-walled outhouses. Seaward extends the wharf built up sturdily of blocks and lumps of coral and basalt fragments, with a topping of black and white pebbles and sea-shells. There we anchored about ten o'clock.

Numbers of natives are passing and repassing on the road beyond, for it is Sunday and church time is nigh, and defaulters rnn the risk of censure. Everybody seemed

LANDING-PLACE NEAR THE KING'S HOUSE, LELE HARBOUR

greatly interested in our arrival, and many thronged the landing-place to welcome us on shore. The men were neatly dressed in European garb, the women in loose graceful gowns. Most of them wore flowers in their hair, and for head-gear broad low hats of Pandanus-leaf trimmed with tasteful ribbons of banana fibre, in tinting which delicate fibre they excel. Pink, white and red roses, crimson hibiscus and the amber and purple tassels of the Barringtonia flower, form so many bright touches in a pretty picture of rich and subdued tones of colour happily blended. Thus we landed on the shore of Kusaie. How befel the King's hospitality, the visit to the good missionaries at Mout, and the exploration of the ruins, must be told in the next chapter.

CHAPTER X

STAY ON LELE

SOON after landing on Lele we went up to see the King or "Tokosā-Teleusar," who speaks very good English which he learned from the American whalers he made many long voyages with in his youth, even visiting the town of Grimsby.

On July 26th, 1890, Mr J. C. Dewar, in his yacht the *Nyanza*, visited Lele, and was favourably impressed with the island.

The King bade us heartily welcome, and introduced us to his wife and household, who seemed thoroughly pleasant people, and made one feel quite at home from the very first. The afternoon passed rapidly away in conversation, the King apparently taking a lively interest in the proposed exploration of the ruins on his island, and promising, without any hesitation, his hearty aid and co-operation— a different character from the sour old fanatic of Metalanim. He placed his house immediately at my disposal, and promptly sent his dependants to search the larder, and levy hasty contributions amongst the villagers in case anything be lacking. A dismal cackling presently announces the demise of sundry chickens. Whilst these preparations were going forward we paid a visit to Li-kiak-sa, the aged native teacher of the district, a keen, alert, wiry old man, with an indefinable air of mingled wisdom, shrewdness and benevolence, of whom we shall hear more anon. He owns a small islet planted thickly with sweet potatoes, of which he is a keen cultivator and consumer. He did not appear to deserve the harsh criticisms passed upon him in Louis Beck's logbook and in Mr Dewar's account of his cruise—

both of whom style him a cheating, canting and self-righteous rascal. Similar unfavourable first impressions are common enough in tales of travel, which a more extended experience of a stay, one likes to fancy, would dispel in good time, or at least qualify. Then we visited the other end of the village to call upon Kevas, the intelligent school-teacher, named after Caiaphas, the High Priest, of evil fame. We persuaded him and Li-kiak-sa to share our evening meal, and ere long roast fowl, fried fish, eggs, turtle, and taro were disappearing with fearful rapidity. Our dessert consisted of a mixture of taro, yam, coconut cream and ripe bananas mashed up together into a pudding, and steamed in leaves underground. The two holy men refused wine and beer, contenting themselves with drinking huge mugs of scalding black tea, sweetened with table-spoonfuls of brown sugar. Soon after the meal was ended Li-kiak-sa left, and Kevas remained behind. Kevas had compiled a small English-Kusaian list of words which he undertook to go through with me on the morrow, with some school-books and a native New Testament in the vernacular. Finally, for a moderate remuneration, he agreed to give me two long lessons in the language every day, the evening lesson lasting regularly from seven to eleven. That night and the whole of the next day we worked steadily, as an uninterrupted downpour of rain forbade any outdoor excursions. The following extract from my diary shows the occasional thorns in the explorer's path. "Monday, May 11th.—Touch of low fever contracted in the Ponape marshes. Symptoms—headache, dizziness, loss of appetite and bearing down pains in the back, with general disinclination for exertion Weather miserable, no chance of going outdoors."

My instructor turned up punctually to time, and by and by most of the principal words in use are carefully noted down; then a little light began to break in upon this peculiar dialect. The grammatical system and the numerals and many of the rootwords I soon saw resembled the Ponapean. There were many Marshall Island words also. The strong original consonant and vowel sounds alike are curiously twisted in pronunciation by the Kusaians. But for a detailed treatment I must refer to my comparative table which the Polynesian Society of New Zealand are now publishing.

Mr Dewar's description of Kusaie has a humour of its own. " The island of Kusaie is a great Protestant missionary stronghold, and the people appear to be painfully good. They none of them dared to drink or smoke, and when I offered the local trader a newspaper, he piously replied that he never read anything but the Bible. Notwithstanding all these fine professions, the missionaries have not succeeded in inducing the King to stop his grog and tobacco, if he can get a chance of enjoying himself in this manner in secret." It describes Captain M. to a hair, and the good King Teleusar to the very life.

Curiously enough, there seems a paucity of local traditions. The name of the island itself seems to be pretty well known from one end of the Carolines to the other. The Ponapeans call it *Koto*, and declare the Ivory Palm and the Kava plant were introduced on their island by Kusaian visitors. The Mortlock and Ruk islanders, more in the centre of the great archipelago, call it *Kosiu* and *Kotiu* respectively, whilst in Yap, the farthest west of all the Carolines, they denominate it *Kuthiu* or *Kuziu*.[1] The resemblance to the great southern island of Japan, Kiu-siu, is too remarkable to pass idly over. The name of Kusaie is generally applied to the mainland across the bay, otherwise called Ualan. The little island of Lela or Lele (from a word meaning " permission ") was no doubt settled by a band of Japanese, either from a wrecked junk, or equally likely from one of the early trading vessels, which, according to a Japanese merchant, used in ancient times to make long voyages to the south and east, before the Emperor

[1] The name probably reappears far to the S.E. as *'Atiu* in the Cook or Harvey group. *Cf.* also Maori *Kotiu* the N.W. wind.

To-Kogunsama interdicted distant trading expeditions about the year 1640. Nagasaki, according to these traditions, used to be the great emporium of trade with the Marai-jin or Malays a thousand years ago. The Caroline archipelago and the isles of the Pacific were known under the name of Nan-Yo. As to the possibility of chance additions to the population by shipwreck, witness the case of the drifting ashore of a Japanese junk in 1885 on Uchai in the north of the Marshall group, resulting in the massacre of a portion of the crew and the plundering of the vessel. The natives of Lele themselves attribute the building of the great Cyclopean walls (in Kusaian *Pot Falat*), enclosures and canals that thickly stud their island, to a dominant foreign race who arrived in vessels (Wak-palang) from the north-west, and who raised these forts as defences against their neighbours on the mainland, whom they put to tribute, imposing upon them, when visiting Lele as vassals of the Tokosa, the humiliation of doing obeisance by crouching down low and of never raising their voices above a whisper in addressing him. It may here be observed that the Ponapeans have a tradition that Icho-Kalakal, who commanded the great invasion from the South, called at Kusaie and the Ant Islands on his way up from Panamai. The stones, massive blocks and shafts of prismatic basalt, were brought, the natives say, from South Harbour on rafts and floats. The ruins on Lele are not so elaborately constructed as those of Metalanim, but they have a rude and massive grandeur of their own. Like the Ponapeans, these people for working wood (not stone) used axes and adzes (*tola*) of excellent make, laboriously ground and polished down from the great central piece of the *Tridacna-gigas* or great Kima-Cockle shell. The specimens received from Li-kiak-sa are exceedingly white, and smooth as polished marble, with fine cutting edges. In length they measure from six to nine or ten inches, by two or two and a half inches in breadth.

Many of the words in Kusian resemble Malay-Polynesian

words far to the westward, and there is also a slight Melanesian admixture.   There are also some Marshall Island words, *Lo* the Hibiscus, *Iter* the Callophyllum, *Nukunuk* clothes.   They use long delicate tapering paddles of *Pana* or Thespesia wood, like those of the Sonsorol islanders. They make fairly good sailors, and appear to be of a peaceful, obedient and easy-going nature.   Their chief manufactures are pandanus-leaf hats, which they plait with as much skill as the Pingelap natives.   From the same invaluable fabric they make ornamental baskets of pretty design, and light delicate sleeping mats of fine texture (Kiaka).   But the most interesting industry of all is their weaving of fine belts and ribbons, called *Tol*, from that soft and delicate textile, the banana fibre, recalling the early national Japanese garb of *Yu* or *Bashofu* made of the same material, imported from the Ryu-Kiu or Lew-Chew group.   In making these, a loom or primitive weaving machine is used very similar in model, I am told, to that seen in some of the less advanced villages in the interior of Japan, where the restive demon of machinery has not yet wholly ousted hand manufacture.   This machine goes under the name of *Puas*, *cf. Pisa*, the loom used in the Bencoolen district of Sumatra.   The patterns are quaint and graceful, and the grouping of the tints carefully considered and worked out to the avoidance of harsh, crude, or conflicting colours.   A rich blue tint is obtained from the juice of the trunks of young banana-suckers, the wild turmeric root or the Morinda Citrifolia juice supplies the shades of yellow, black tints are obtained from burnt candle-nuts (Aleurites), and a rich reddish brown is prepared from the scraped and pounded bark of the mangrove roots.   Other gradations of hue they get by carefully boiling in small quantities of water pieces of gaudy cotton fabrics, which their innate good taste rejects as an eyesore. No doubt their æsthetic taste is due to a remote Japanese ancestry or some admixture of a high Malayan type.   For a more particular description of these fabrics *vide* Appendix.

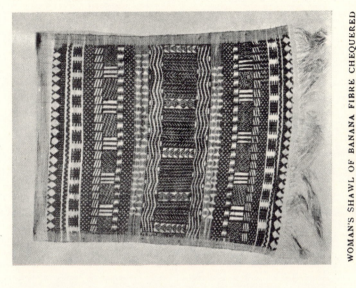

WOMAN'S SHAWL OF BANANA FIBRE CHEQUERED
SALMON-PINK, BLACK, BROWN AND WHITE

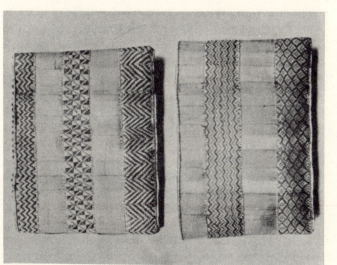
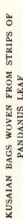

KUSAIAN BAGS WOVEN FROM STRIPS OF
PANDANUS LEAF

Products : — Coconut oil (*Kaki-fusas*), Copra (*Kaki*), Pearlshell (*Fai*), and Beche-de-mer (*Moet* or *Penipen*).

A fine clear morning at last. The King suggested an excursion along the coast to see something of the country, and visit the settlement and schoolhouse of the Boston Mission, offering to accompany me part of the way, but when pressed to introduce me to the missionaries he excused himself, saying that he was not very well pleased with them, and considered that they were unfairly usurping the power which properly belonged to him alone, but declining at the same time to more expressly state the grounds of his grievance. " However," said he, " I will tell a boy to sail along the coast in my canoe and catch us up early in the afternoon at the Gilbert islanders' settlement, so that you will easily get to Mout by nightfall." Accordingly we started on our walk, cautiously wading the narrow channel between Lele and the mainland. We hailed in passing the venerable Li-kiak-sa hard at work on his little island of Yenei weeding and digging amongst his sweet potato beds. He is devising traps and snares for the rats which have evidently been very busy amongst his cherished tubers. " The Kosso Kisrik (*i.e.* rats) won't leave me a potato soon," ruefully grumbles the poor old gentleman, as he turns with a sigh to his interrupted labours. " I wish I had a good big *Kosso Kuchik* to catch them." (*Kosso Kuchik* is the Kusaian name for Grimalkin, called by the Malays *Pusang* or *Kuching*.) The King promised him a fine yellow Tom on the first opportunity, and we left the holy man somewhat comforted, delving and grubbing away with an energy astonishing for a man of his years. We trudged along some three miles of glittering white sandy beach backed by the usual thickets of Barringtonia and Pandanus and coco palms, halting every now and then to admire the black and white sea-snakes (*Kafelála*) basking on the warm sand at the bottom of the shallow waters. We managed to secure one of them by hooking him suddenly out of the bay with a crooked stick, and stowed him away in a bottle to join the scorpions, centipedes, lizards and kindred horrors in their alcohol bath. By-and-bye the boy Mok-Lal was seen coming along with the canoe. He took us on board, and we skimmed before the wind along the shallow lagoon which is now gradually filling, for the tide is on the turn. We soon reached the village [1] of Puia and its shady palm-groves. A venerable old guide directed me inland through the salt marshes to a picturesque waterfall, the scene of the ending of one of those romantic friendships common in island history. Two young chiefs defeated in battle, too proud to seek safety in flight, ended their lives together by casting themselves from the precipice to be crushed upon the rocks that surround the boiling pool below.

Sixty feet sheer the clear current purls down a black runnel of shiny water-worn basaltic rock, edged by tufts of mosses and fern, lichen and weed sprouting greenly out of myriad cracks and crannies. A peculiar black-shelled mollusc (*Neritina*) is found adhering to the stones, resembling those found in the mountain streams of the Marquesas. Below, the stream irrigates a native hazel-copse, and abruptly burrowing loses itself in a sandy subsoil of marshland, the haunt of the *Op*, a fierce and monstrous red and blue crab with stout claws a cubit long, the Birgus latro or Robber crab of the naturalists. It climbs the trunks of the coco palms, bites off the clusters of ripe nuts, tears off the tough and fibrous outer husks with its powerful nippers, and devours the kernel, to the consequent shortage of copra and the indignation of the planter.

Wending our tortuous way through the swamps, we come out on firmer ground. By-and-bye, pushing out of a thick spinney, we emerged upon a piece of abruptly rising ground. This surmounted, we saw before us a deep yawning chasm in the hillside towering above us. As we neared the entrance to the cavern, a doleful gibbering

---

[1] In Kusaie a village is *Tili*, in Ponape *Tel*.

assaulted our ears, like the twittering of uneasy spirits in torment. Stumbling over heaps of pebbles and detritus, we gained the gloomy portal. Our eyes, gradually accustomed to the dim light, made out swarms of fluttering small bats, *Kalekaf* (the *Peapea* of Samoa, *Emballonura* Sp.), like swallows on wing, darting hither and thither around the arched dome overhead, and ever and anon brushing in headlong panic against the intruders. Untold generations of these creatures have piled up strata upon strata of the finest guano on the cavern floor—a grand business coup for the next trading-skipper who may find himself disappointed in the Chincha or Malden Island deposits, which bid fair to pan out one of these days. Right at our feet stretches an inky pool of Cimmerian blackness, doubtless stretching far back into the shadowy recesses of the mountain. A few pistol shots fired at random amidst the gloom awoke sharp reverberating echoes and set the winged vermin circling and shrilly screeching overhead.

On returning, we found that the king had gone as far as he intended. A piece of tobacco and a sea-biscuit amply satisfied my guide, and leaving the king to his walk overland, I embarked with the faithful Mok-Lal rather late in the afternoon. The tide was fast running out, and before long it became clear that we should have hard work to make Mout before midnight, if at all. To crown all, Mok-Lal, after much vigorous pantomime with an accompanying symphony of wonderful double vowels and treble consonants, took us flying into a tiny cove where ten or twelve crazy huts, and say a dozen starveling folk and a few lean yellow dogs represent a native settlement. Certain of a kindly welcome, but sorely suspecting fleas in these squalid habitations, I besought Mok-Lal not to rashly pledge us to stay overnight. Whilst in dire suspense, lo! a welcome sight. The *Tulengkun*, which I know is bound for Mout, as her captain had told me the day before, appears round the next promontory. The opportunity was too good to be lost. A word to Mok-Lal, and two sturdy paddlers volunteered ; the frail canoe was launched and over the reef we went into the tumbling surf. Fortunately it was not much after half-tide, and there was just a chance to clear the outer line of breakers.   After some very exciting moments and hairbreadth escapes, dodging the heavier rollers by a miracle, we are out in the open sea and presently, sound in limb but with dripping garments, I clambered on board the barque.   The ancient cricket-bag, sorely the worse for wear with stress of rain, sun and salt water, was passed up over the side ; Mok-Lal and the boys taking a long compass round to the harbour mouth.   They will not risk the breakers again—not they.   The *Enuts* (ancestral spirits) won't work miracles twice running.   We duly recognised their pluck and skill, and once more the *Tulengkun* is put before the wind.   The sun goes down on the reddening waters, and the shadows of evening darken upon peak and cape, shore and valley.   We barely strike the narrow reef-passage of desolate Star Harbour in the fast-failing light. Once within, however, we speedily glide up the inlet, mooring, after various tackings and fillings, close to a steep bank where a full-flowing river joins the salt water.   The cause of these breaks in the barrier reef in the line of valleys where a river flows into the sea, is familiar to all those who chart out coral-formations in Pacific waters.   A current of fresh or even brackish water means death to the myriads of busy little cellular zoophytes who pile up their rocky barriers against the inroads of ocean.   Only in the noble rich salt water can these wonderful builders pursue their labours.

We found the place almost bare of inhabitants, for it is only visited from time to time by fishing or copra-cutting parties.   An old man directed us to a tumble-down building with a crazy verandah, formerly a trader's store, where, surrounded by tame cats and dogs, we hunted up some tinned food, biscuit and breadfruit, and made ourselves comfortable for the night.   Next morning bright and early

the ship's boat was speeding me over the drowsy lagoon,
its still deep waters barely yet a-sparkle. The pearl-grey
of the eastern sky is melting into a shimmer of pink and
gold and bronze. To our left wave the feathery plumes
of the graceful palms, softly stirring into life at the breath
of the morning breeze—acre upon acre of woodland—
flecked with broad irregular patches of shadow shrinking in
the amber light of early dawn. Light and delicate airs laden
with subtle fragrance float down from ferny dells above
steeped in the glistening dewlight of the young day. Up
comes the sun chasing the truant shadows one by one out
of their hiding places on slope and valley, and everything
is quickening into life. The forest is all astir with a
rumour of birds. The *sus*, a tiny redbreasted honey-eater,
flits cheeping amongst the creamy clusters of palm-bloom,
and the coo of the wood-pigeon echoes through glade
and thicket where, with no tell-tale plumage, she perches
hidden though close at hand. All too soon our journey
is over, and entering a little sandy cove we run alongside
the wharf built of coral fragments, and, climbing the
winding stairway hewn in the hillside, find ourselves in the
little settlement which forms quite a township—the headquarters of the mission after its expulsion from Ponape.
Like Cæsar's Gaul it lies in three parts. Each of these
centres round its schoolhouse. The first establishment is
allotted to the education of youths and boys from the
Marshall Islands, in which archipelago the Germans, under
certain restrictions, have granted the missionaries leave to
establish stations for their propaganda. Dr Rife is in
charge. The second, under Dr Channon, is for the instruction of Gilbert Island boys ; and the third, highest up on
the mountain side, is occupied by the girls' school, where
a mixed bevy of Gilbert and Marshall Island lasses live
under the ægis of the ladies of the mission, one of whom,
Miss Palmer, was in charge of the establishment on the
east coast of Ponape at Oa, the scene of the massacre of
Lieut. Porras and his working party in 1890. Drs Rife

and Channon, with true American hospitality, soon have refreshment at hand which the heat of the day imperatively calls for. By and by the *Tulengkun* turns up in the bay, having waited for the turn of the tide. Captain M. and the two doctors are soon deep in business talk. I left them and sought a comfortable cane lounge, prying deep amongst Marshall and Gilbert Island root-words, with a sufficiency of green drinking-nuts at my side to counteract the dryness of my labours. A little after noon we were expected to dinner with Miss Palmer and her colleague at the girls' school. Captain M. was too busy to turn up and a little grumpy into the bargain, so Dr Channon took me up the hill instead, and introduced me in due form to the ladies. After doing justice to an excellent meal, the rights and wrongs of the 1890 business in Ponape were once more raked up from oblivion. Native merits and demerits were freely touched upon. Miss Palmer is a bright and sensible little woman with a deep interest in her work, which she declares is fairly successful, though now and then rather trying to the patience. However willing and docile, the savage convert will hark back at times to the crude notions of his forefathers, and deceit appears ingrained in them. Hence a strange moral obliquity leads them into the most needlessly crooked paths. Horace, when he speaks of driving out Nature with a pitchfork only to see her return in greater force than ever, doubtless had tried the experiment on some surly barbarian, and found him all unimproved by his gentle admonitions. The outward change for the better, however, to give the missionaries their due, amongst the *Gilbert* Islanders has been remarkable. They have always been the vindictive and ferocious of all South Sea Islanders, and under the careful instruction of sundry white miscreants had taken high honours in the school of piracy, cutting off unfortunate trading craft by diabolical treachery, plundering, and scuttling or burning the craft and cutting the throats of every soul on board. These playful pursuits would sometimes give way to a game at civil war. This kindly folk would vary the programme of murder, rapine, infanticide, and the wiping out of some unpopular village or other at stated intervals, by consuming huge quantities of coconut-toddy (*Karuoruo*) at their village festivals. These merry meetings invariably terminated in a fierce free-fight, where men and women joined in the mêlée with ironwood clubs and wooden swords, thickly studded with sharks' teeth, with which they inflicted ghastly lacerations.

Nowadays these noble savages are altered in some ways greatly for the better. They don't kill helpless infants any more. They don't cut off trading vessels—though possibly a vision of English *Kaipukes* or men-of-war has tended somewhat to this laudable change of purpose. They go to church, in European garb; the men wear shirts and blue trousers, some wear black coats, and the women tawdry Manchester goods, and for fear of breaking the Sabbath by mistake, they abstain accurately and impartially from every sort and condition of work week in week out—except under stress of actual hunger. They like money very well, but liquor and tobacco still better. They are told they mustn't smoke and musn't drink, so of course they do it on the quiet the first chance they get. There is a certain bluntness amounting almost to churlishness in the Gilbert Islander that distinguishes him from his politer brethren, the Tahitian and Samoan. This and the complacency and self-righteousness of the native convert does not particularly endear him at first sight to the European visitor. The Pacific Islander in a word is passing through a transition period. He has left behind him many of the vices of his forefathers, but at the same time the savage virtues—bravery, hardihood, self-help, and honesty in his dealings with his neighbour—are also flickering out of him. His individuality is lost and he has become a Christian of the colourless humdrum order, full of goody-goody texts and Scriptural references

—a harmless fellow enough, but scarcely as interesting to the student of human nature as his barbarian ancestors. The duplicity and sly reticence of the savage is unchanged in him, and ever and anon the old natural man peeps out to gambol in most unorthodox cantrips. Unstable as water and at first sight without any real depth of character, he is as shrewd a hand at a bargain as any chapel-going grocer who sands his sugar. Anecdotes to the above effect whiled away the afternoon as we strolled about the little settlement. The students, some one hundred and forty in all, appeared on their very best behaviour, perfect models of that meek deportment which the supple natives, like schoolboys and monkeys, know well how to put on and off like a glove. Altogether the community wore an air of quiet prosperity and contentment. The boys are taught various useful trades, such as carpentry and joinery, and the girls are instructed in the use of the needle and all manner of housewifely duties. It is a miniature copy of the Kamehameha School for native boys and girls at Kalihi, a suburb of Honolulu, and doubtless the native in time will be the gainer for the gradual formation of settled habits of industry.

Of the kindly and hospitable people in charge of the Mission Station of course there can be but one opinion. They believe genuinely in their work, and devote themselves with single-hearted zeal to what seems an unpromising and thankless task. With those who frankly differ from them in their ways or methods they can argue without bitterness or lack of charity, as all seekers after truth should surely do.

At sunset we went down to Dr Channon's pretty little house to a spread of native and imported dainties, and a most interesting evening's talk ensued. My host proves an exceedingly well informed and liberal-minded specimen of the professional man of brain and action that Yale, Harvard, Princeton, and their sister universities are turning out year after year to enrich Young America. By and by

we pay a visit to the class-rooms and converse a while
with the boys, most of whom understand English—of the
parrot order, one must confess.   Then the talk runs on
musty antiquities and certain singular native customs with
which the reader shall not be bored at present.   The lads
gave a sample of their powers as choristers, singing various hymns pitched in a doleful key—keeping capital time
the while.   The reader will perhaps be surprised to learn
that part-singing has been a popular institution amongst
Pacific island races from time immemorial.   Then home
and to bed, and up with the calling of the fowls—" *Lan
mon kakla* "—as the islanders phrase it.

A pleasant breeze was ruffling the waters of the
bay, and the *Tulengkun* straining at her moorings.
With a hearty farewell to our friends on shore, we
pushed off and boarded her, and in some twenty
minutes were slipping merrily through the water on
our twelve miles' run to Lele.   The hill-slopes of
Mout are soon left astern.   Range after range of
mountain and valley glide past us and the sun is high
in heaven, looking straight down on the reef, when we
round our last headland and work our way slowly into
the home wharf through the rollers washing into the
narrow harbour, all shimmering in the soft and golden
haze.   The mid-day meal at Capt. M.'s despatched, the
Tokosa and I take a long woodland walk, sauntering
slowly through the palm-groves and fairy glades in the
waning afternoon which ushers in my last night in Lele.

The sun sinks—a wheel of ruby flame—amidst a
wonder of flaky cloud-wrack, lit up with tenderest hues
of pearl, emerald and amethyst, undreamt of by artists
of sober northern climes, who reck not of Nature's prodi-
gality in sounds and sights to these her favoured children
of the tropics.   From the domain of the on-creeping host
of shadows, from the dim and cool recesses of darkening
woodland, trills the chirp of myriad cicalas.   The placid
waters of the harbour here and there dimple in the grow-

ing twilight with swirling rings to the splashing of leaping fish. One by one in the gathering dusk cooking-fires gleam out like lamplight all around the bay from the scattered native huts lying back in the fringing belt of palm and pandanus. Side by side brushing through a tangle of trailing creeper, we make for the Tokosa's house, where I am to pass the night. The king has agreed to show me the ruins next morning without fail. Li-kiak-Sa has parted with three beautiful shell-axes (*tola*), some baskets and mats, and a quantity of the dainty native sashes of woven and dyed banana-fibre. In the king's household, for the last two or three days, the fair maidens Kenie, Kusue and Notue, have been hard at work producing specimens of their delicate fabric—gifts for their guest to take away to his bleak northern home. The worthy old deacon Kevas turned up, and we put in four hours' solid work up to midnight mastering the intricacies of the Kusaian tongue ; and the good old man handed me over several crude Kusaian translations from the New Testament as a parting gift. He had worked very conscientiously, never shirking a difficulty, but explaining everything within his power. The king, also, who speaks English correctly and even elegantly, has proved a valuable assistant. Since the visit of the *Coquille* nobody has apparently taken trouble to collect any facts about these interesting islanders, and now it is indeed high time, and only *just* not too late. It is a sad pity that the language of Kusaie, with all its elaborate grammatical inflection, and quaint post-positions so suggestive of Japanese influence, seems likely ere long to be classed with the dead languages of the earth. For the population is not over four hundred, all told, and the island is one vast garden capable of supporting with ease twenty times that number. But the health and vigour of the folk have been sapped by terrible diseases introduced by the brutal and lawless crews of visiting whalers whom Dr Rife, from some heart-rending medical experience, with perfect justice denounces as the

vilest miscreants, the enemies of God and man. Any un-
prejudiced reader of history—of the voyages of Cook and
Roggenwein and other early navigators—must needs admit
the truth of these awful facts. Little cause indeed have
Pacific Islanders to bless the greater part of their white
brethren. There was true historical foresight in the prediction of the Tahitian sage 'Avira.

> " Ua haere te fau
>   E mou te fa'arero,
>   E nao te ta'ata."

> " The leaves are falling on the sand,
>   The sea shall swallow coral strand,
>   Our folk shall vanish from the land."

On the following day (May 15th) we were early astir,
for Capt. M., who was rather in an irritable mood, had
solemnly vowed to wait for neither of us after four o'clock.
The king, to my great delight, is coming up to Ponape to
pay his respects to the Spanish governor, Sr. Pidal—a
precise but not unkindly old gentleman of Spain, who,
after a successful and popular administration, is returning
home to Madrid. We borrowed the *Tulengkun's* compass,
and the Tokosa and I, with pencil, note-book, and bush-
knife in hand, set out on our exploration. A boy came
with us, carrying a knife and a six-foot pole, carefully
graduated from a carpenter's foot-rule.

To reach it we had to skirt the remains of some Cyclopean walls built of enormous rough basalt blocks rudely
fitted together, immensely old, but now falling into ruins, in
the neighbourhood of the king's house, and Captain M.'s,
which we have already viewed. The latter, yielding to a
Vandal instinct, has dismantled those nearest to his
house, using the huge blocks as a groundwork for his neat
new wharf, caring little what became of the ancient structure. Leaving these behind us our way lies some three
hundred yards inland, along a narrow muddy lane shut in
by fern-fringed walls some five feet high, where we catch our
first glimpse of the great outer wall of the principal enclosure

" *Pot Falat.*"   The masonry is composed of basalt blocks and prisms of varying shape, many enormous in bulk but clumsy in disposal.   In careful and minute adjustment they are inferior to the structures of Metalanim or Java, but doubtless the work of a kindred race of builders labouring under less favourable conditions.   Looking at their solid outlines, seamed and furrowed with the rain and sun of untold generations, one cannot help marvelling at the ingenuity and skill of these primitive engineers in moving, lifting and poising such huge and unwieldy masses of rock into their present position, where these mighty structures, shadowed by great forest trees, stand defying Time's changing seasons and the fury of tropic elements.   Why in distant little spots of the Pacific do we find the like engineering marvels ?—sites held as sacred, guarded by shadowy traditions of mighty kings, magic builders and giant folk of old.   Ponape has her *Tikitik-en-ani* or Teraphim of stone, has her sanctuaries of Nan-Tauach and Pankatara, and her *Lil-charaui* or sacred precincts ; Tobi, her massive platforms topped by stone images of her *Yari*, or ancient heroes, gazing out upon the deep ; Hawaii, her demon - temples (*Heiau*). The Marquesan has his holy places (*Meae*) and his *Tiki*, giant images hewn out of black basalt ; the Tahitian his *Marae* and *Ahu-rai*, sepulchral monuments of ancient kings. The Easter Islander his giant long-eared statues of black stone with crowns of red-brown Tufa on their heads, his lofty platforms, stone houses, and wooden tablets inscribed with mysterious hieroglyphics.

The key, doubtless, is to be found in human ambition, which reveals itself even amongst the fragments of a forgotten folk occupying these little spots in a waste of waters.   These remains, insignificant as they appear beside the works of Mycerinus, Cheops, Apda-martu, Sargon, and Nebuchadnezzar, may yet serve to show what eloquent sermons dumb stones may preach ; what stories they tell us of the generations of man vanishing

"Pot Falat" Ruins

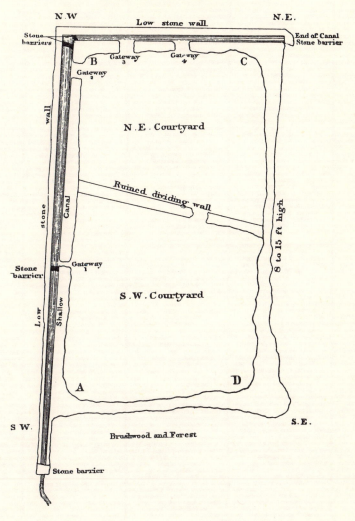

N.W.   Low stone wall   N.E.

Stone barriers

End of Canal
Stone barrier

B   Gateway 3   Gateway 4   C

Gateway 2

wall

N.E. Courtyard

stone

Canal

Ruined dividing wall

8 to 15 ft high

Stone barrier

Gateway 1

Low

Shallow

S.W. Courtyard

A   D

S.W.   S.E.

Brushwood and Forest

Stone barrier

one by one into dim immensity, ephemeral as the leaves
of the forest fluttering down year after year to their dust.

But time is passing, and the tide will not tarry for us
either, and briskly we set to work on our measurements,
hewing our way through the jungle, splashing into muddy
puddles, and tearing a path through the tough ground
creepers which conceal many a slippery stone.

The enclosure forms a parallelogram, the side between
the western and northern angles measuring 194 feet, and
that between the eastern and northern 110 feet. Cutting
a path on the south-west side, where the masonry lies piled
up in vast ruinous heaps overgrown with a maze of hibiscus,
we started operations at the western angle, moving along
the north-west side.

The following are some of the measurements :—

The height of the wall, at the west angle, is 25 feet.
At the foot of the wall, facing north-west, runs a shallow
canal. At a distance of 72 feet along the canal-side is a
modern barrier of small stones built to keep out high tides
—the height of the channel above sea-level being very
trifling. Doubtless this canal, like the others, of which
there are abundant remains on Lele, was constructed for
the purpose of rafting up these huge blocks of stone from
the beach whither they were brought from South Harbour,
where Nature, as in Ponape, has further indulged her
spoilt children by providing natural pillars ready cast in
her furnaces underground, crystallised out into hexagonal
prisms ready for the workman's hand. The geologist will
recall the Giant's Causeway, the rocks of the southern
promontory of Tasmania, and the organ-pipe formation on
Staffa and Iona, as illustrative of this phenomenon elsewhere. Just beyond the aforesaid barrier is a gateway
7 feet in breadth. The height of the wall here is 16 feet.
Great fragments of shivered basalt that have toppled
down from time to time strew the rocky floor below.
From this cause the wall varies considerably in height.
About 40 feet along from the gateway a massive slab of

basalt stands out among its smaller brethren, length, 9 feet 6 inches ; depth, 2 feet 4 inches ; breadth, 3 feet 6 inches.

The breadth of the canal is 9 feet. Here the wall is 15 feet thick. 50 feet beyond this point we reach a second portal 15 feet wide. 10 feet beyond this is the northern angle occupied by a huge banyan-tree, which seems obstinately bent on the destruction of the masonry, with its myriads of clinging roots digging into every crevice and hollow of the stonework in the exasperating manner known to every botanist familiar with the tricks of ficoid plants. These root-fibres develop into high aerial buttresses. Whenever a strong wind comes, as for instance during the N.E. trades, there is a tremendous strain on the masonry. This is not the only destructive factor, for the continual expansion of the roots tends more and more to throw these gigantic masses of stone out of position— an accident which these primitive engineers could hardly have anticipated. Fire and water these structures could resist for untold ages—sub-aerial denudation for them would have no terrors, but the capillary forces of nature are stronger than even these old foes. Thus the irony of Nature loves to set at nought human endeavour. How simple a method of disruption is the swelling of milky sap in clinging root-tendrils that would once have yielded to a penknife. But from the days of Aristotle downwards, ὕλη was ever a disturbing element.

The height of the wall at the northern angle is 26 feet (*vide* frontispiece). The face is thickly overgrown with masses of hartstongue and Asplenium fern (called *Fwa* and *Malaklak*). Dense weeds and trailing creepers occupy every available crevice, and forest trees in every stage of development are springing up above and behind.

At the northern angle there is a massive pentagonal corner-stone measuring 9 feet in length, 3 feet 6 inches in breadth, and 3 feet in depth.

The branch canal running along this (the north-east)

side is 4 feet in breadth, bordered by a wall built up of rubble 5 feet high.

25 feet along from the north angle is a gateway (No. 3) about 5 feet wide. The thickness of the main wall is here 15 feet. 20 feet further on is a fourth gateway, and 50 feet beyond we reach the eastern angle, where there is a remarkable octagonal corner-stone 3 feet 6 inches across, 3 feet 10 inches in depth, and 6 feet 2 inches in length.

The height of the wall at the east angle is 20 feet. Progress along the south-east side we found very difficult, and we had to form a passage through a dense labyrinth of hibiscus. The walls are much dilapidated on this side, varying in height from 8 to 15 feet. In many cases they have collapsed into mere heaps.

There is little of interest in the interior at first sight. A ruined wall divides the interior into two courtyards, both considerably overgrown with straggling coco-palms, banyans, Ixoras and jackfruit trees. There is also a bushy undergrowth of scrub and a network of running vines.

At last we reach the south angle, where the wall is seen at its greatest height (30 feet).

Here some massive pieces of rock are let into the masonry.

The dimensions of one six-faced corner-stone let into the wall about 20 feet from the ground were found to be : length, 10 feet ; depth, 4 feet ; breadth across face, 2 feet 6 inches.

The foundations of the wall at the south angle are three roundish masses of basalt piled together. The lowest measures 6 feet in length, 4 feet in depth, and 3 feet in thickness.

Here our survey concluded, much to my regret. There was no time to make any excavations which might have brought to light, as in the ruins of Metalanim, some interesting specimens of native weapons, beads and shell-bracelets. Any future visitor, however, who is ambitious of making excavations around or within the *Pot Falat* need have no anxiety that King Teleusar will behave as badly as his brother monarch of Ponape. Doubtless a thorough exploration of the little island lasting several weeks would reveal many other curious relics of the past. The interior is somewhat hilly and very thickly overgrown with brushwood and forest. Most of the south-east and south-west portion of Lele, like the south coast of Tongatabu, is a tract of lowland patiently and laboriously reclaimed in olden time from the sea. A network of canals—very much out of repair—intersects this portion, many of these partially filled or banked up by the natives in modern times to keep the tides from turning their taro-patches and cleared lands into a salt swamp. The remains of immensely solid walls in the neighbourhood of Captain M.'s store and the king's house along the beach, are no doubt like the *Pot Falat*, relics of an elaborate system of fortification, the product of large numbers of native workmen toiling under the orders of an intelligent minority of a superior race who had a practical knowledge of engineering. A mixed expedition of intrusive and conquering Malays and Japanese would probably account for the phenomena ; and, as said before, the natives have a dim tradition of foreigners coming in strange vessels out of the north, settling on Lele and putting the chiefs of Ualan, the main island, across the bay to tribute.

The natives seem to attach no special sanctity to these structures. Though possibly the work of a kindred race, the ruins of Lele are far rougher and ruder in design than those of the east coast of Ponape. It may be, however, that on Ponape, a much larger island, there were more workmen and better material for the work.

And thus we took leave of these labours of Titans. We sailed that evening, touching at Pingelap and Mokil on our return journey, and anchoring in Ascension Bay after a tedious and uneventful voyage of ten days, a succession of calms alternating with heavy rain-squalls.

PART III

CHAPTER XI

RETURN TO COLONY; TO MUTOK AND PANIAU

THE day after the *Tulengkun* came in I visited the
Spanish Governor, who listened with much interest
to the account of my doings. I then went over to Langar, and spent three days with Captain Weilbacher, where
I had some interesting talks with the Lap or Headman
of Langar, and with some of our old friends from Paliker,
who are loyal customers of the German firm. I also met
some natives from Ngatik or Raven's Island, some thirty
miles away to the south-west, who had come up on one
of their rare visits. They are the descendants of an
American negro castaway, who, with his native wife and
children and a few relations and servants from Kiti, landed
on the islet about forty years ago. Strange to say, during that short period of isolation they have actually developed a new and peculiar dialect of their own, broadening
the softer vowels and substituting TH or F for the original
T sound in the parent Ponapean.

I spent a day botanising amongst the hill-slopes of Not
and in the ferny dells of Kamar, and another on a visit to
Kubary at Mpompo, and collected many seeds of economic
trees and plants from the densely-wooded district around
the big waterfall.

A day or two afterwards I met Nanapei again in the
Colony. He seemed rather *distrait*, and told me that
things were going badly on the East coast; that influenza
had broken out and carried off many of the people, for
which King Paul, who was in a very bad humour, held
me and the Manilla man to blame. I was advised not to

visit Metalanim until Nanapei had smoothed matters over, and to content myself for the present amongst the tribes on the south and south-west coast, who would welcome me gladly.   With Nanapei was a young relation named Chaulik, an amiable lad with the manners of an Eton boy and the kindliness of a Tahitian chief.   We were soon firm friends.   At Nanapei's suggestion Chaulik invited me down to his uncle Nanchau's island of Mutok on the south coast, to which I paid a couple of flying visits, the latter lasting from June 8th to 23rd.

I visited King Rocha, and explored the beautiful valley below Mount Wana, through which the Kiti river flows.

I found Nanchau a fine old host.   The King of Kiti and his people were most friendly, and the good Catholic padre of the Aleniang mission station showed me great kindness.   One day I had a glorious little climb to the top of one of the two round masses of wooded hill which, separated by a deep chine, stand out upon Mutok like humps upon a camel.   I was accompanied by a bright young lady named Eta, who made a capital guide, and showed a remarkable knowledge of plant and tree-names. She took considerable interest, somewhat tempered with awe, in my grammar and dictionary-making, and in a spirit of true camaraderie tendered me valuable and very unselfish assistance afterwards amongst her kinsfolk by stirring up the most intelligent of them to tell me what they knew of the gods and heroes of the olden time.

Accordingly one fine morning succeeding a stormy night we wait till the sun is high over the coconuts, and start climbing up the runnel of a watercourse, working our way through a maze of roots and branches which overhang the steep and stony trail.   We wrestle with treacherous creepers, and scale fallen trunks of trees lying scattered over the hillside.   A brief but violent shower of rain suddenly patters down and as suddenly ceases, leaving the bush all a-drip and steaming in the noonday heat.   At length we struggle up to the dividing ridge, where a clump of sago-palms in varying stages of growth looks down through hanging woods upon the calm bay below. At their roots a little spring bubbles up fresh and clear from the basalt, amongst masses of greenest leafage and the erect rose-tinted flower-spikes of the Aulong or wild ginger.

Pursuing a track along the western hill-slope we plunge into thickets of prickly wild pandanus. With many a scratch we emerge, hot with much hewing, into an open space with a platform of stones in the centre, the foundation of some old native house. This hill is called *Tol-o-Puel* (Anglicé *Mud or Clay Hill*). The landward one, where sundry wild goats do roam, is called *Tol-en-Takai* or Stony Hill, and fully deserves its name. A few wild pigs and some jungle-fowl inhabit the recesses of the bush, and all the day long the covert is alive with the notes of green and grey doves. The usual forest-trees of the basaltic uplands are found here. The banyan *Aio*, the ficoid *Nin*, the Elœocarpus *Chatak*, the wild nutmeg *Karara*, the graceful ash-leaved *Marachau*, and many another tree that never grew in European woods. Unseen cicalas fill the tree-tops with their shrill chorus, and up from the mangrove-belt below floats the harsh croak of the *Kaualik* or blue heron, fishing in the reef-pools and paddling around the logs and tree trunks rotting in the ooze and mud. Around us the rustle of thickets and a rumour of small life. To seaward the shining waters of the lagoon, its blue tints merging into green, and the thin grey line of the outer reef fringed with creaming breakers. Over all, rising and falling in deep and changeless cadence, floats their echo. Like Stevenson in Apemama, " I heard the pulse of the besieging sea," sound sweet to the ears of those who dwell in the little sea-girt lands.

These and other excursions I made, and day by day felt myself more in the people's confidence. And so before long, the bêche-de-mer season being nigh, Nanchau and his kinsfolk of Mutok, some fifteen souls in all, determined

M

to establish a fishing-station upon the little island of
Paniau, out upon the barrier-reef, near the harbour
mouth. I was to go up to the Colony in their boat
to get my mails due by the steamer on the 25th, and
take in a store of European provisions, medicines, and
all things needful for a lengthy stay ; then to return
and spend several months with them, collecting shells,
and viewing the strange fishes and forms of marine life,
for which study they declared the spot unequalled. And
so indeed it proved, and most loyal was the help they
gave me. Accordingly I went up to Ascension Bay and
received my long-looked-for letters from home and elsewhere, some thirty in all, and came back again with all
arrangements made, and the boat well loaded up with
stores of biscuit and beef, tea and sugar, tobacco and
kerosene, matches, and knives, and an axe or two.
And in two or three days we all crossed the bay in an
odd little fleet consisting of five canoes, a flat-bottomed
punt, and a sailing-boat ; the latter rather the worse for
wear after frequent collisions with the coral-rocks in the
shallows. The following somewhat minute description
of a stroll round my new island-home will give some
idea of the scenery of the islets lying in the lagoon
off the Ponapean coast, and indeed of the character of a
Pacific atoll-island in general. And maybe the reader
will follow me in thought to a spot, which I would
gladly have him visit in body, far, far out of the
track of tourist and artist, and likely to remain so for
many a long day.

Starting from the end pointing shorewards where our huts
and drying-houses are established, one comes upon a fine
crescent bend of silver-white sand stretching along some two
hundred yards, the high water mark of the tides indicated
by little ridges of driftwood, sea-weed, and floating seeds
washed up by the ocean currents. Immediately above
tide-mark is a belt of coarse, creeping grass, mingled
with a tangle of yellow veitchling (*Keiwalu*), and a

large purplish-flowered creeper (*Ipomea* sp.) (the *fuefue* of Samoa), which bind the sandy soil together with their matted roots.   The *Nkau*, a medicinal weed of rapid growth, with yellow flowers resembling a single Michael-mas daisy, occupies much space in the interior.   At the edge of our settlement are some fine pandanus trees, but-tressed with high and solid aerial roots, laden with huge orange-red fruit, looking like glorified pine-apples.

And now, strolling onwards, we come to the prettiest thing in the island, a magnificent nursery of young coconut palms, leaf and stem just passing from their early light-red tint into harmonies of light and dark green, as Nature, the great chemist, is quickening into action the chlorophyll within them.   In the young fronds the pinnæ or leaflets are set firmly and evenly together, and do not present the ragged and wind-worn outline of their elder brethren, which flutter crisping in the trade-wind overhead.   Turning a little way into the bush, piles of husk and fallen nuts in all their stages lie around.   The sprouting nut, called *Par* by the Pona-peans, is filled with a soft spongy mass, which has taken the place of the solid kernel, and is highly valued when roasted.   In the previous stage, *i.e.* when the nut is *below par* and the kernel has reached its maximum hardness and thickness, it is called *Mangach*, and then is ready to be cut out and dried for copra.

Upon Paniau there is, or rather was, a thriving colony of *Ump* or robber crabs (*Birgus latro*), levying contribu-tions on the coconuts.   Upon these the native proprietors look with an evil eye on account of the nuts they destroy. Once, at King Rocha's entreaty, we organised a regular battue.   The boys in camp lived on dressed crab for a whole week after.   This, however, by the way.

Coming out on to the beach again, it is rather inter-esting to turn over and examine the drifts of weed and jetsam.   Stems of reed-grass and bamboo, bits of dry hibiscus wood, the long-seeded rhizomes of the mangrove,

the round, black, scaly nuts of the sago or ivory palm,
and the fluted fruits of the Nipa or swamp-palm, the
seeds of Pulok, Waingal, Marrap-en-chet, and Kamau;
the first named polygonal, the second round and flattish,
the third long, slender and keeled, and the last of just the
size and wrinkled shape of a walnut taken out of its shell.
Specimens of seeds of the common littoral shrubs are
washed up in great numbers.   Guppy, in his book on
the Solomon Islands, has some very interesting passages
on the flotation and drifting of seeds on the ocean currents, and the consequent wide distribution of certain
littoral trees in the Pacific area.

The drifts of deadwood, sea-weed, and decayed fruits
and nuts, show how ingeniously Nature contrives to build
up a suitable soil for the seeds surviving their ocean journey.
Numbers of hermit crabs (*Umpa*) and some small brown
lizards (*Lamuar*) are very busy amongst the rubbish.
Many of the hermit-crabs are crawling around ensconced in
the prettily-mottled green and brown shells of a sea-snail.
The tenant adopts a house according to his colour—for
the occupiers of these first-mentioned dwellings have a
dull green body with red markings, others again have
sky-blue antennæ, and their claws speckled with rich
blue and gold.   One very large blue and red Cænobita
of allied species we found had wedged his body into an
ancient coconut, the top of which had been broken in.

Looking out into the lagoon from the crescent sand-
beach as the tide ebbs, one remarks some curiously shaped
limestone rocks, about forty in number, studding the flats,
most of them much worn away at the base, and locking
like flowers on a stalk.   Captain Wilson, of the ill-fated
Antelope, noticed many of these formations in the Pelews
in 1783.   He calls them "*Flower-pot islets*," from their
narrow bases and bulging tops.   These are often crowned
with a bristle of small littoral shrubs, which flourish in the
scanty soil, the resort of the sea birds *Parrat* and *Kake*,
the latter of which deposits its eggs here in the tuffets of

grass, sea-pink and parsley fern, being too lazy to build a proper nest.

At low tide the flats are dotted with shallow pools and thin sheets of salt water, where the *Chila*, *Pachu*, and *Pacho*, species of Tridacna or Clam, open up their valves to bask all pink and purple in the sunlight. Here are also found several sorts of oysters, oblong, circular and hammer-shaped, and a great abundance of other mollusca and small crustacea. Portions of the reef lie bare, seamed with long cracks, in which lurk fishes innumerable of the Leather-Jacket or of the Chœtodon type. The coral floor of the pools is thickly pitted with little circular holes, the abode of the Murænas or grey sea-eels, which at the rising of the tide are seen darting about actively, gorging themselves with the small fry who issue from their hiding places in endless shoals at the first stirring of the waters. Leaving the beach, we pass inland once more along a shady pathway running through the coconut groves which lead past the two water-holes supplying our little colony with water for bathing and washing. Our drinking water, by the way, comes from a spring on Mutok, which we fetch over twice a week in calabashes, bottles and a couple of big earthen vessels, designed for storing biscuit, but which make capital water-pots.

This path is a dividing line marking off the land of my hosts, Nalik and Nanchau, from that of the King of Kiti to whom belongs all the seaward end. The water holes are just in the centre of the island, and here there is some rich soil. King Rocha has planted a number of jackfruit and breadfruit trees which are doing well. There is also plenty of Giant Taro, and the Tacca or native arrowroot grows abundantly. Beyond this the seaward end of the island is occupied by a dense grove of Wi or Barringtonia, where the *Parrat*, a brownish-grey sea-bird, has established a regular rookery, which in the night season when the moon is bright is continually astir, or was, before squab-pie became a standing dish amongst us. The

Barringtonia is a very handsome tree, with creamy white and pink tassels of deciduous blossom and long broad leaves, with an elegant sheaf of ruby-hued leaflets shooting out in their midst.   The yellow-wooded Morinda Citrifolia, which the Ponapeans call *Weipul* or Flame-Tree, is abundantly in evidence, also the *Kiti* or Cerbera. Struggling through the undergrowth we make our way toward the end facing the outer reef, which the tides have left high and dry.   The *Konuk* or Betel-pepper climbs like ivy over the trunks of the coconut palms, where spirals of Polypody and great tufts of *Talik* or Birds'-nest Fern are also found growing—the long broad leaves of the latter being much in use for plates.   Large bundles of them are also collected to serve as a dry foundation for the sleeping mats at night.

On the coconut trunks also are seen growing tufts of Parsley Fern, the *Ulunga-n-Kieil* or Black Lizard's Pillow of the Ponapeans.   The seaward end of Paniau reached, about half way between high water mark and the edge of the great outer barrier reef, runs a remarkably deep natural ditch, trench, or crevasse, in the coral limestone, which they call the *Warrawar*, where on certain dark nights at high tide we used to fish by torch-light.   All the back of the reef is thickly strewn with coral fragments, ruinous alike to shoes and feet.   The little narrow strip of beach on which we stand is overshadowed with a fringe of *Pena* and *Ikoik* trees.   Here the palms stop short, for the dense masses of Barringtonia have ousted them.   From this point on, our way lies over beds of honeycombed limestone rock, studded with rough knobs and bristling with points and edges of a razor-like keenness.   The inland path on this side is narrow, dark and tortuous.   At the foot of the thick-growing Barringtonias, the ground is covered with chunks and slabs of broken coral of all shapes and sizes, liable to turn underfoot when stepped on, and to inflict unmerciful raps on shin and ankle.   Under the tree-roots lurks the ever-watchful Birgus in his burrow on

a couch of coconut husk, gloating over his unholy spoils.
To seaward one at all events has the satisfaction of seeing
one's way.   These cruelly sharp coral ridges are appropriately called by the natives *Racharach*, a word which also
denotes the teeth of a saw.   Close to the end of the *Warrawar* are two pools about four to five feet in depth, into
which a number of fish used to find their way at high
tides.   At low water a judicious use of the narcotic *Up*
root on several occasions stocked our larder well.   About
this point the Barringtonia gives place to the *Inot* and
Titin, two medicinal trees common on all the island
beaches.   A little further on stretches our chief fish-
pond, closed in with a stout stone dam to seaward, and
often yielding us good sport with net and spear.   All
this rugged side of the island is strewn with driftwood,
from whence we draw a welcome and never-failing supply
of fuel to keep our bêche-de-mer-curing operations vigorously going.   The fish-pond passed, we find ourselves at
the back of the settlement from which we started, with
the camel-backed outline of Mutok and the distant peak
of Mount Wana showing up to our left, and in the
fore-ground the little sandbank of Tekera separated from
us by a narrow channel, a mere ridge of broken coral,
crowned with the graceful and feathery foliage of the
Ngi or Ironwood.   The reader will gather some notion
of the beauties of lagoon and reef lying around us, from
the subjoined description of one of our frequent trips to
this charmed region of lovely and ever-varying scenes.

As the canoe shoots over the edge of the great coral
barrier that looms up through the water like a mighty
sea-wall sloping down into the deeps, the voyager for
a moment feels a novel sensation, like that of looking
over a giddy precipice.   The landward reef edging bristles
with a thousand graceful forms of branching coral and
a marvel of submarine algæ ; a true garden of the Nereides
laid out in gay parterres of oarweed and sea-fan, picked
out with scintillating patches of sea-moss of intense

electric blue. Nature here deals in odd and whimsical contradictions. Sponges like corals flourish beside corals like sponges. On the sandy bottom inshore bask herds of sea-cucumbers (*Holothuria*), black, brown, red, green, and speckled, stretching out their wavy tassels of tentacle to engulf the tiny sea-eels or other small fry. Great bright ultramarine five-fingered starfishes lie spread out below, fearless of snatching fingers, for the Ponapeans firmly believe that the lifting of one of these creatures out of water will be followed by a heavy downpour of rain. All around, on the shelves below the reef edge, out of crevices in the living rock, sponges are growing in vivid rows and clusters. Sponges grey, sponges green, sponges scarlet as geranium flower, sponges yellow as marigolds, parti-coloured sponges chequered dark blue and black, sponges soft and sponges horny—a goodly sight for any but a Turkey merchant. For the traders say the homeliest-looking alone are of commercial value, and these are only found in any number on the Paliker coast some fifteen miles up. Solemn blue herons stalk round the flats. The distant cry of the *Káke* or white gull and the screech of his grey cousin the *Parrat*, hawking hither and thither out to sea, shrills fitfully on the ear—whilst ever and anon comes the rhythmical boom of ocean's ceaseless thunder rolling on the outer reef and reverberating through the hollow caverns in the honeycombed lime-stone below ; dens where grim and giant poulps and crustacea lurk in the pale green light glimmering deep down below the combing line of surf; where priceless orange-cowries stud the debris of the ocean floor like crocuses, living out their little lives, far from the reach of conchologist, and shadowed under the ægis of Nature's mightiest forces.

Light airs are stirring. The bracing scent of the reef comes off in frequent whiffs, brisk, eager odours of fucus, sea-tangle, and things marine, rich in ozone and iodine, with a sickly phosphoric aftertang from heaps of dead and decaying coral. To seaward the air is thick with motes of spray, and over Ant Atoll in the west ominous banks of cloud are forming up. Mid-heaven as yet is clear, and the sun shines out serenely. But the camel-backed outline of Mutok over the bay seems close at hand, and a languor of damp heat hangs heavy over all. Nature is awaiting her Titanic shower-bath that the coming squall will surely bring. At each dip of the paddle, forms of beauty, unlimned, undreamt of by artist, flash under our keel below the shimmering ripples. Forms of liquid ruby and topaz, strange living shapes, fiery, crystalline, translucent, amethystine, opalescent, iridescent. Landward we turn, and straightway the tender dissolving hues of the coral and its accompanying dream of colour-miracle are fading out into soberer tints, as the water runs shallower. Memories of good Canon Kingsley's "Westward Ho!" float back, the yearning dreamy fancies of Frank Leigh's gentle spirit ripe for its passing. "Qualis Natura formatrix si talis formata." "How fair must be Nature the Former if her forms are so fair."

We pass over large round table-topped corals of greenish or yellowish brown—each a miniature coral atoll in itself, depressed like a plate in the centre, with raised edges crested by the lip-lipping of the light ripples brimming around their furrowed rims. Brownish masses of disintegrating coral and dull fragments of limestone rock strew the sandy bottom, from which the fierce solar heat which has been storing here all the sultry noontide is radiating upward. Now is the time for a hot salt-water bath for those who prize the luxury, but beware! Bathers with fresh cuts or unhealed scratches will suffer a fiery penance.

ASHORE! is the word. The squall is coming droning up from the westward. Hastily we haul our craft high up on the sand and dive into the friendly shelter of a palm hut, whilst overhead patter thicker and thicker the rain-drops, heralds of the coming storm.

CHAPTER XII

FEAST IN MUTOK, KAVA-MAKING, NAMING OF BIRDS, AND MAKING OF FISH OIL

ONE day, Chaulik's birthday I think, Nanchau made arrangements with some of the Wana chiefs to hold a feast on his island of Mutok, so as to give me the opportunity of getting some further historical facts from the old men. On the appointed day, therefore, we all went across the bay, leaving a couple of old women behind to look after the fires in the curing sheds. Our company was not very numerous, for two of the largest Kiti whale-boats had gone up the week before to the Colony along with King Rocha to see the Spanish Governor. However, some of the oldest and most influential chiefs of Roi and Tiati had remained, and came over with a great store of fruits and roots. A fatted hog, a goat, and some fowls were promptly slain and consigned to the earth-oven. Chau-Wana, our principal guest, having expressed a wish to eat dog, poor little Pilot, the house-cur, who insisted on coming from Paniau with us in the boat, is straight-way doomed to death, the sentence being ruthlessly carried out by three strokes of a heavy club in the hands of young Master Warren Kehoe. Pilot's funeral oration was of the briefest—" Pilot no good," says Chaulik, " him no fight, no catch pig, ugly little dog, very cross all time. Before, him steal meat ; now we eat him, son of a gun." And eaten he was every bit, sure enough, to the great satis-faction of Chau-Wana and the old men. I contented myself with a lump of goat's flesh and a piece of lean pork, in lieu of a hind leg of the canine victim and a huge mass of the pig's fat proffered with ceremony in a lordly dish. There

were plenty of yams boiled and baked, breadfruits plain
and preserved, plantains and bananas roasted and raw,
cooked tubers of taro, and cakes of arrowroot and coconut
cream, with a dessert of roasted sprouting nuts. There was
also corned beef and ship's biscuit, and a plentiful brew
of tea and preserved milk. But for fear the meal should
take on too much of the appearance of a Sunday-school
picnic, a small demijohn of red wine was broached, and
subsequently plenty of kava-root was brought in and
pounded solemnly. Occupying the post of honour, with
Nalik and Nanchau on my left and Chau-Wana on my
right, I did my best to enliven the company with a
running fire of chaff. A toast to Queen Wikitolia, her
ships at sea and her soldiers on land, produced great
enthusiasm, but I really fear we forgot to remember the
Spaniards. Which was ungrateful. However, things went
merrily enough. Rising to the humour of the situation,
I bestowed the title upon Chau-Wana of the " King of
Hearts "—a monarch with whom the Ponapeans, thanks
to card-playing American skippers, are perfectly familiar.

It was good to see these solemn and sententious folk
unbending into mirth with such good grace, sinking all
private grievances as cleverly as Christians at a public
dinner, or rival politicians at a private one. The lips of
the silent were unsealed, the shy took heart of grace, the
sulky grew affable, and dull men waxed witty. Songs
and lively tales went round, and aged men, the last to
find their tongues, kept me busy scribbling. Offers of
service assaulted my hearing on every hand. " I can show
you all the good fishing spots," cries one. " And I know
the names and virtues (*manaman*) of every plant and
tree on the hills," says another. " My uncle has a pretty
daughter," cuts in a frivolous third. " I can tell you star
names, and I can bring you stone axe-heads," declares a
fourth putting in *his* say. In a flash I nail him to his
word. " Listen, boys," said I, " old shell-axes lying underground will neither clothe nor feed you, nor will they

yield you the black tobacco you like so much. Set to then, I pray you, and dig up these axes, fear not the spirits of folk dead and gone. Behold, he that brings me an old axe of shell shall receive a new axe of steel."

A speech that next day brought me five of them. In the dark night cheerily rang out songs in chorus until the sober moon swam up over the tree-tops. The King of Hearts at last rose with tottering legs to take his leave, and was tenderly escorted down to the wharf, and put on board his canoe. "It is strange, indeed," quoth he, "how stiff my old legs get when the dews of night are falling. Twenty years ago it was not so." The guests disperse with cordial adieus, and another pleasant merrymaking has rolled away with the kava that inspired it far into the *Ewig-keit* of mortal things.

The effects of kava have been noticed ; now for the moving cause.

The plant from which this national beverage is made is pretty well known to the public from the description given in several South Sea books of travel. It is one of the Piperaceœ, with the pendulous flower-catkins of its kind, broad, deep-green, veined leaves, and spotted stalks knotted at regular intervals like those of the bamboo. It is the *Chakau* or *Choko* of Ponape, the *Seka* of Kusaie, the *Namoluk* of the New Hebrides, the *Yangona* of Fiji, and the *Kava* or *Ava* of the south-western Polynesians. Botanists term it the Piper Methysticum or Intoxicating Pepper. The modes of preparation are various. In Samoa, by the chewing of the Aualuma or bevy of village girls. In Tonga, Fiji and Ponape, by pounding between flat stones. In Samoa, however, nowadays, the ruminating process so horrifying to English readers and certain over-squeamish early voyagers has given place in the civilised districts to grating. It is styled the *nasty root* and the *accursed liquor* by certain good and worthy missionaries whose convictions are sometimes sturdier than their charity. The symptoms, however, which follow an overdose of kava by no means coincide with the accepted notions of intoxication. The head remains perfectly clear, but the legs sometimes suffer a sort of temporary paralysis. This, however, as with tea, coffee and alcohol, is only the punishment which, under a wise law of Nature, the abuse or excessive use of any of her precious elixirs bears with it. *Abusus non tollit usum.*

There is a closely allied species widely distributed, which the Yap people variously call *Langil, Thlangil* or *Gabui,* the Marianne folk *Pupul-en-aniti,* the Marquesans *Kavakava-atua,* the Samoans *Ava-ava-aitu,* and the Tahitians *Avaava-atua.* This is the plant whose leaves supply the wrapper of the fruit of the betel or areca palm, extensively used as a chew in the Malayan area, of which Yap and the Mariannes are the outposts. Strangely enough Yap, where kava drinking is not, has kept the old Polynesian word in a recognisable form ; whereas in Ponape and Kusaie, where there are two varieties of areca palm (*Katai* and *Kotop*) growing in great plenty in the highlands, betel-nut chewing is not in vogue, and kava drinking is. Yet the Ponapeans and Kusaians have lost or tabued the old Polynesian word, and adopted one which, to say the least of it, offers a curious resemblance to the Japanese *Saka* or *Sake,* which in that tongue denotes strong liquor in general, and a weak rice-spirit in particular. Unfortunately I had not the chance of visiting the basaltic islands in the great lagoon of Hogolu or Ruk, where I am told both the kava and the areca palm grow. I might thus have determined once and for all whether *these* Caroline natives are kava drinkers or betel-nut chewers.

It seems highly probable that kava drinking was a logical development of betel-nut chewing ; the betel-nut kernel itself, even when mixed with the *chunam* or lime, being a somewhat inert substance. Doubtless the natives, who are great botanists, and, up to a certain point, most logical and analytic observers, very early saw that it was in the kava plant leaf that the pleasing qualities of the national *quid* lay embosomed. If the leaf was good, doubtless the root was better. Perhaps some scientific Curtius flung himself into the gulf or rather gulp, with a thirst for knowledge and the reward of knowledge; or else some slave was called in and set to work upon portions of the root or a decoction of the same, probably not without some protest from within. The slave would presently fall into a blessed swound, and wake up next day bright and refreshed, with a dim remembrance of blissful dreams, coloured of course by his own personality, and interpreted in accordance with his peculiar capacity for decorative lying. On all-fours with this are their curious traditions about the origin of the kava, one of which declares that *Cherri-chou-lang*, or the Little Angel from Heaven, in pity for mankind and their woes, dropped a piece down to earth from the Celestial board; and the other telling us how a mighty magician of old raked up the wondrous root with his *Irar* or magic staff, and made his memory blessed.

The ceremony of kava making, already referred to twice or thrice, is as follows. The *Nach* or Council-Lodge is the scene of operations. On the raised platform above, the king or principal district-chief used to sit with the *Chaumaro* or high priests on his left hand, their long hair all ashine with *üchor* or scented oil, dressed in their *mol* or kilts of split coconut-filaments dyed orange with the juice of the Morinda, ceremonially styled the *Kiri-kei*. The lesser chiefs and commons sat around at a respectful distance. On the ground below were ranged several roundish pieces of basaltic stone resembling broad shallow plates. Around these squatted the kava makers, their stone pestles swaying and ringing in sonorous rhythm as they pounded up the pieces of tough root into mere masses of trash. The root, be it observed, is neither dried in the sun as in south-western Polynesia, nor carefully washed with water. The latter ceremony, they say, spoils the flavour and weakens the strength.

By and by the *Ani* or ancestral spirits are supposed to be present, with Icho-Lumpoi and Nan-ul-lap, the demon lords of the festive hall. Water is poured in, and the first cupful is squeezed out from the strainer of Kalau fibres. Taking the cup in his hand, the chief of the Chaumaro, not without blinking and shivering and other signs of demoniac possession, mutters a charm for the spirits to take their place, sips a little from the cup, and pours out a drink-offering to the invisible guests. Then the bowl is offered to the king. It is customary for the recipient to stand off and keep declining the draught for a minute or two, a peculiar ceremony never omitted. At one of *our* dinner-parties it would certainly sorely mortify a good old British butler, and probably lead him to take the unfortunate guest at his word. To seize the proffered cup and forthwith drain it to the dregs would be considered by Ponapeans the act of a hopeless churl. Again, the drinker never swallows more than about half the contents, unlike the Samoans, who finish the bowl in one long pull. One night I sprang a Samoan custom on the people of Chau-Icho in Kiti which rather tickled the assembly. In Atua on Eastern Upolu, where they often drink the kava made from green and immature roots, the Samoans put two or three small red chili-peppers into the strainer along with the pounded root. The Ponapeans thought it a strange innovation, but as usual curiosity carried the day, and no less than six of the pungent fruits were slipped into the strainer, and a venerable patriarch, ugly as traditional sin, eagerly stretched out his hand for the first taste. The effect was instantaneous. The little red pepper-pods had indeed made their presence felt.

"Too muchee hot—makum feel down here all same fire," gasped out the poor old gentleman, beating the air around him, arms flapping hard to catch his breath, tears streaming from his eyes, and his face screwed all on one side like a turbot's at the first taste of that potent brew. The paroxysm once past, he soon forgot his woes in a stick of black tobacco. Every man then took a little of the stuff, but with more caution, amongst them the Teacher of New Things, who with unmoved countenance supped up a good half-pint. Then there ran around the lodge a low murmuring hum of " Akai! Akari! See what it is, brethren, to cross the great sea." " Lo, the white man is even as one of us," quoth another ancient. And *then* the world went right merrily.

Now, with regard to the kava, which has found such an army of detractors, one mistaken impression shall here be dispelled. Travellers in Pacific waters have declared that the kava resembles soap-suds in taste ; but that must be only the dulness of their spiritual perceptions. Now this is a base libel on a noble root. The aroma is that of mingled ginger and nutmeg, with a soupçon of black pepper, and an undefinable waft of the fragrance of green tea running through it. If people *will* drink more than three large cupfuls, as even Ponapeans sometimes do, they have only themselves to thank if, as the classic Glabrio says, one leg struggles south while the other is marching due north. If, again, the white trader insists on mixing good kava and bad gin, he has simply to face the consequences. But this gives the Prohibitionists no right to rail against a valuable medicine, of whose best and innermost qualities they are presumably ignorant. The members of Catholic orders do not often make so silly a mistake. Beer, whisky and wine, or other alcoholic compounds, are strictly to be avoided on these occasions as incompatible with what Lloyd Osbourne defines as the true kava frame of mind. If these simple and useful instructions are disregarded, as the writer has no doubt they will be, the innocent kava root cannot be held answerable. Into the hands of the doctors I commend it. They may blend it as they will, but let it not fall into the clutches of Exeter Hall.

To the thoughtless reveller, the kava-bowl is in itself an end, to the philosopher a means of catching at some floating thread of tradition to weave into the fabric of his theme, be it folk-lore, history, or ethnology. To the expansive influence of those social gatherings I am indebted for many curious legends, and this is one of them.

Laponga was a High Priest of old in Metalanim. It was he who sat at the left hand of the first Chau-te-Leur king; it was he who first tasted the kava, and he who uttered the first *uinani* or magic spell invoking the presence of Nan-Ul-Lap, chief of the Ani or local genii, who love to be honoured when the feast and the dances are the order of the day in the Great Lodge. The second man in the land, the keeper of the king's conscience, as it were his father-confessor, he sat in the Place of Council; his unshorn locks streaming below his girdle after the manner of his ancient caste, crowned with the yellowing leaves of the Dracæna, his *Patkul* or shell-axe crooked obliquely over his shoulder, and his carved *Irar* or magic staff laid close at hand; in his fingers a bundle of leaves of *Alek*, the native reed-grass traditionally used in casting lots. Such was the wizard, and such his estate. And he was wise beyond the wisdom of all men, but his love for his fellows tallied not therewith. For his heart was cold, and he ever delighted in mischief and ill pleasantries, and would wander at times over the land in all manner of strange animal shapes working his evil will. In one of his freaks in the form of a *Lukot* or native owl, he took to wife one of the Likat-en-ual or nymphs of the forest. Numerous was their progeny, and the hanging woods of the lofty island were filled with beings endowed with human utterance, who could change from bird into human form at will. In process of time, as mortal men are wont, Laponga grew weary of his fairy queen, and would have taken to wife a high-born lady of the Court. The children of the forest knew of it, and it came to pass that whenever the great magician took his walks abroad the woods re-

sounded with the cry "*Ipa, Ipa*," which being translated
signifieth "*Papa, Papa*." In great wrath at this interruption of his meditations the great man turned, like the
bald-headed prophet of another tale, and with a solemn
imprecation took away from them human utterance and
shape for ever, and left them birds.

Then in a twinkling a strange Babel broke out in the
forest glades. The injured children ceased not calling
out upon their unnatural parent, each as his peculiar vocal
organs gave him utterance. The *Kaualik* or blue heron
croaked out "*Ko*," "*Kau*," "*Kau*," the doves, after their
kind, murmured "*Murrorroi*," "*Kin-uet-uet*," and "*Kingking*," and the brown parrakeet broke out into inarticulate
chirpings "*Cherrerretret*"; the small sea-bird with black and
white tail feathers could only scream out hoarsely "*Che-
a-a-ok*." The other birds could utter nothing but doleful
and woeful screeches. Some went away into the deep
bush and let themselves out in very spite as tenements
(*ta-n-waar*) to the wood-demons there, and still delight at
times to afflict human settlements with their ill-omened
voices pouring forth songs of impending death and doom
in the stillness of the night. The blue heron went out on
the salt marshes and the edges of the reef, where he stalks
about to-day in mournful dignity picking up little fish and
crabs. All day long the *Murroi* or grey dove wails for her
lost voice in the woods, like Philomel of Grecian legend ;
the *Cherret* twitters round the coco-blossoms, whilst the
Kulu or sandpiper, with his elder brother the *Chakir*, wail
dismally over the sandy flats, the shingle, and the coral
limestone. But one small bird, more persistent than its
fellows, pursued Laponga on his way and so deafened
him with its angry twittering that growing weary he
turned about and loosed a fresh curse upon the head of
his hapless offspring. Thus ran Laponga's imprecation :—

"May your head turn round and round when man
casts a stone at you, that you may fall at their feet from
very dizziness, and men shall bake you in the oven for

their meat. This, I say, whenever the hungry wanderer does as I do now————." With these words he chased away the wretched fowl with showers of pebbles.

And so it happens to this day with the generations of little brown birds in the inland bush, that whenever one throws a stone in their direction, whether he hit or miss, down they come fluttering to the ground, helpless and paralysed. And the name of the bird is *Li-ma'aliel-en-takai* or *Miss-giddy-at-stones*.

And Laponga's miracles held men's minds in awe, for he did many notable deeds. The record of his sorceries and of the manifold knaveries he wrought, is it not set down in the lost book of the annals of the Kings of Metalanim ? After Laponga's death, from which his arts could not protect him, his head was changed into stone, and lies unto this day right in the middle of the water-way between the islets of Pan-ilel and Tapau. The tale must be true, for there is the very stone. And well we know it, for we collided sharply with it one low tide, and all but caved in the bows of our canoe ; keeping the Manilla man busy enough for some minutes alternately bailing, and praying to the saints, until we beached her and fixed up the leak.

Nanchau and I paddle, a day or two after the kava party, over to Mutok from Paniau to view the labours of three old ladies left in charge of the house on the beach, who were engaged in making fish-oil. With this strong-scented product of native industry the Ponapean islander loves to smear himself on state occasions. The process begins by breaking up a quantity of full-grown coconuts and scraping down their kernels.

The instrument used is a billet of wood, over which the native throws his leg to keep it steady. It is fitted with a wedge-shaped piece of metal, toothed like a hackle at the broad end. A segment of nut is pressed against these teeth, and a rapid twirling motion in the hands brings off shavings fine as feathers.

It is in this way that the *Ungitete* is produced. It

is then put into a *Kachak* or low oblong vessel of reddish-brown wood like a whale-boat pointed at both ends. Next a number of strings of dried fish-heads are lowered from the ceiling, where they have been mouldering for weeks amongst clouds of flies and mosquitoes in order to ripen into prime condition. The names of the kinds of fishes most in request for this use are Pakach, Toik, Tomarak, Mak, and Wakap—names as sweet in sound as in savour. Without any sign of disrelish, these ghastly relics are one by one carefully chewed up by these venerable dames, and then ejected into the vessel of coconut scrapings. They sit solemnly ruminating, placid as cows chewing the cud in meadow, and the gruesome mass of disintegrated fish-heads steadily grows and grows.

When the arduous task of mastication is over, the whole nasty mess is submitted to a squeezing and kneading process, in order that the scraped nut and broken fish may unite their fullest virtues, and the stuff is taken outside to be put in the sun for a few days before the resulting oil is pressed out into small calabashes or glass bottles, where it is stored ready for use. It goes without saying that numerous hungry dogs, fowls, and cats watch all these proceedings with the deep interest of a starving man viewing a Lord Mayor's banquet. But not one fragment of savoury stock-fish, not one silvery flake of coconut ever reaches those watering mouths. The workers keep watch like witches round their gruesome brew. For the fish-oil of Kiti, like the mats of Chokach and the sponges of Paliker, and the yams of Metalanim, is far too precious a local product to be lightly lost.

CHAPTER XIII

PANIAU TO COLONY

JUST about this time, I remember, King Rocha came over to see us, and formally took off a tabu that had been laid on the coconuts on the island. On this occasion we organised an attack on the coconut-crabs, digging them out of their burrows and slaying numbers. A few days after we went down coast to a great feast given by Nanchau-Rerren at Annepein-Paliet.

Towards the middle of September the stock of biscuit and canned food began to run short in camp. The marine creatures preserved in spirits, after a prolonged spell of hot and damp weather, called earnestly for a fresh supply of alcohol. Therefore, Chaulik, Kaneke, his cousin Nanchom and I, on a beautiful starlit evening (September 20), determined to run up to the Colony for a few days' change of scene to obtain the sorely-needed supplies, and pay our respects to the Governor. We launched a canoe, and soon found ourselves across close inshore to Nantamarui. Cautiously poling over the flats and through the narrow channels in the salt-water brush, we reached Nantiati just as the moon rose over a wild and picturesque scene, lighting up league upon league of hill and valley, and a filagree network of twining creeper, the forest-line trending downwards till lost in the dark and eerie zone of mangroves which rustle around us, dipping their long forked root-sprays into the muddy water like the claws of famished spectres groping for their prey. A wild half-light is stirring amidst a world of flickering shadows.

We land at the little cluster of huts by the waterway where an old ex-whaler dwells, a native of Tahiti, whom destiny has wafted into these remote northern waters. We had an hour to wait for the rising of the tide, so telling the boys to snatch what brief repose they might, I took a stroll outside with the old fellow to examine a pile of enormous basalt slabs like a heap of colossal ninepins shadowing the still canal in the silvery moonlight. The most striking prism of all measures twelve feet in length. It has six sides or faces each measuring three feet. One end seems to have been rudely chipped into the semblance of a human head. I thought at first I should actually make out the features, but alas, my fancy was not lively enough. Another ponderous mass almost as long is resting by the water-side on top of two rugged blocks, for all the world like a giant club. It recalls the huge fragment topping the pile of half-submerged blocks near the Nan-Moluchai breakwater.

I could find no local tradition to explain who laid these great masses of stone in place. Less fortunate than Sarung Sakti and Lidah Pait, the magic artificers of the Passumah monoliths in Sumatra, these early engineers have passed away and their very names are lost.

At sea again, about midnight, we found ourselves off Mal Island, the abode of an old Metalanim chief called Nanapei, no relation of the chief of Ronkiti. The chief of Mal has some years past vowed a deadly vengeance on the head of a Captain N., the trader in Ascension Bay, of which that astute gentleman is perfectly well aware. Indeed he told me on board the *Venus* how mortally he had offended the Metalanim insurgents by piloting the Spanish cruisers of a punitive expedition into Oa Harbour in 1886.

The reader will remember that some months previously old King Absolute had strictly forbidden me to explore or even visit these parts again. Therefore we were re-visiting these spots at some degree of personal risk.

We are once more in the heart of Nan-Matal, threading the labyrinth of narrow canals intersecting the rows of walled islets of the water-town. We pass Peikap, Chaok, Tapau, and Nan-Pulok, catching stray glimpses of massive masonry looming up dark and imposing behind the waving screen of jungle, a vivid contrast of shifting lights and shadows. All is as fair as a dream, all as unreal. Even the cicalas are still. A deep hush, broken only by the bark of some distant watch-dog, the sough of the night-wind amongst the sedges, and the lapping of the bubbling waters under our keel plough-ing on through the gloomy solitudes, the theatre of a vanished civilisation. We have passed the mouth of the great harbour ; the islet of Mutakaloch, with its cellular basalt formation is left behind. Under full sail we double the headland of Aru, and are slipping merrily across a broad bight with the unsurveyed wilderness of the Ú highlands and the peak of Kupuricha looking down upon us. Just as the dawn breaks we find our-selves amongst wide stretching beds of Olot or sea-grass in very shoal water, close to our journey's end, off the dominions of Lap-en-Not, with the tide running rapidly out. Whilst wading in the shallows, pushing our boat ahead over the flats, we caught sight of several black and white sea-snakes coiled up in the weeds. After several unsuccessful attempts one was hooked on board, and after a stout resistance slipped into the alcohol bottle.

As soon as we managed to struggle clear of the shoals we put across to Langar, a favourite port of call on these expeditions. Our kind and hospitable friend Captain Weilbacher receives us with the usual cordiality of Germans trading in these waters. Ahmed, the Malay cook, is sent out to dig "*Inchang*," a species of blue and white crayfish, of a flavour yet unknown to London epicures, and found on the mud-flats at low tide. Poor Ahmed is in the wars. He has taken to himself a Not wife ; she is not very beautiful and she is not by any means an agreeable spouse, but forcibly asserts her inde-pendence and treats her meek and all but uncomplaining lord and master as a nonentity. A true Ponapean virago, when angry she would vigorously pull at his straight and bristly crop of hair. The single native women were hugely tickled to find so determined a champion of Woman's Rights amongst them, and rare sport they promised themselves when *their* turn came.

The mid-day meal ended, we launched out and were soon over in Santiago. We first visited the principal store, our base of supplies. Having duly collogued with Captain N. and various priests and officers there assembled, we marched up hill to pay our respects to the Governor, who seemed glad to see us again. The new medical officer of the station appeared, and proceeded to ask some questions upon the botany of the various districts. Without delay I reported numerous cases of influenza and low fever in the Kiti and Metalanim districts. As I expected, the kind-hearted medico promptly offered to put up useful medicines which I was to distribute on my return, which of course I readily agreed to do. He also promised me as much alcohol as he could afford, and agreeing to meet him at lunch next day, I went across that evening to Kubary's house at Mpompo, near the waterfall. Three days soon pass by, the boys working wonderfully well in packing up and securely stowing away the curios ready for my long sea voyage back to civilisation *viâ* Yap. For my stay is drawing to a close. Yet my Ponapean friends, in true native fashion—careful to put any untoward idea or thought aside—seem hardly to realise it.

On the morning of the 26th, Chaulik, dreading the wrath of his uncle Nanchau, and bethinking him of the short rations in Paniau, strongly urges our return. Therefore, after several short delays, we set sail from the Colony. The canoe was already fairly well laden, but some fateful fancy seized Kaneke that he would like to get a cross-cut saw out of the earnings which he, like a prudent lad, had been carefully saving up for the last two months. Nothing would serve us but to visit the German branch store at Chau-inting, close by the headland of Not. So the little craft, what with this and that article declared indispensable, is loaded down to the very gunwale. Meanwhile the sun is westering more and more. Loosing thence we pass Langar, Parram, and the two Mants. Tapak is well behind us, and we are skimming along under full sail, the canoe running very deep in the water, with a man on the outrigger to keep her steady. Suddenly, without a note of warning, a gust of wind sweeps down from the distant mountain gorges. Mast and sail collapse, the canoe turns turtle, and we find ourselves soused in some fifty feet of water in the Nalam-en-Pokoloch pool, the deepest hole along the coast, and reputed to be the lurking-place of sharks and sea-monsters innumerable. We discover ourselves in a tight position, two miles off a scantily-inhabited foreshore, with no fishing canoes anywhere to lend us aid, and the short twilight fast fading away. When we right the canoe she is hopelessly waterlogged, and all but sinking. Pushing her before us we swim on, and on, and on in the gathering gloom, each man expecting every moment to find the sharks nuzzling at his toes, or the icy grip of some monster cuttle-fish's tentacles closing round his ankles. Here and there the darkling waters around and below us flash with the luminous body of some swiftly-circling denizen of the deep, but if sharks they be, they pass us by unnoticed. Kaneke unselfishly begs me to climb on to the outrigger and leave to him and his two comrades all the hard work and hidden dangers from below, and is quite vexed when his offer is rejected. And such is the patience and perseverance of my brave boys that at last we reach one of those isolated stacks of coral, reaching up to three or four feet of the surface in certain places in the wide lagoon. Here, after a brief rest, we make shift to bail our craft empty of water, and find that our losses are not so great after all as far as provisions are concerned. Some of the tinned meats are gone, an umbrella has floated off into the darkness, and alas! saddest loss of all, Kaneke's long-desired cross-cut saw has gone down into the depths beyond reach or ken of diver. "Never mind," says the cheery Chaulik, who has a mangled text of scripture for every emergency, "cast your *lead* upon the waters and you shall find it after many days." A little later on, when Nanchom is bewailing the soaking of our store of biscuit by the salt water, Chaulik is not wanting to the occasion, and again proffers consolation. "It's all right. Man shall not live by bread alone." Laying in the paddles with a will, the draggled party with undamped spirits ploughs along steadily, mast and sail safely stowed for fear of going faster and faring worse. Late at night we draw in towards the north side of Aru Island, which lies just on the borders of Ú and Metalanim. Opetaia (*Obadiah*) lives here in the bosom of his family, the same comical old native teacher who, it will be remembered, paid me a visit in my dearly-hired house at Lot, some four months before. We were received with all the attention usually extended to unfortunate mariners; dry clothes were supplied us, and after a good supper and some hot grog, which Obadiah and his son eagerly shared with us, we made ourselves extremely comfortable. After looking at some Mortlock curios, which our host pressed upon us in unwonted exhilaration, we fell asleep.

The next morning is Sunday, no Obadiah visible. He has gone ashore early to attend his devotions. As the day wears on a boy comes off shore in a canoe with his face all one broad grin, with the news that the Machikau church-folk on the mainland are scrimmaging together like demons, and breaking each other's heads in the liveliest fashion. We do *not* put into Machikau, having had our fill of excitement for the present, and bidding farewell to our hosts, pursue our way, heartily devoting the contending parties to the fate of the Kilkenny cats. By and by, when we find a couple of bottles of spirits missing—laid

in strictly for medical purposes—grievous suspicions fall
on Obadiah and his fellow-deacons. With the hopes of
clearing up this question we put in at Matup, a little
further down the coast, the residence of the *Nôch*, the next
Metalanim chieftain in rank to King Paul, or heir-presump-
tive to that monarch's slippery throne, for this religious
maniac has no children and no prospect of any.

It had been told me that the *Nôch* held Europeans in
disfavour, and myself in particular ill-will from the recent
outbreak of influenza in the tribe, which many of the folk
took for the outpouring of the wrath of Icho-Kalakal and
the " *Ani* " at the letting in of the light of day on their
time-honoured sanctuary. Therefore I thought it would
be as well to pay a visit frankly, interview him, and gain
his confidence.

We go straight up to the Council Lodge, and are kept
waiting some while for the chief. His eldest son, however, a bright little boy of about seven or eight, climbs on
my knee in most friendly fashion. By and by in comes
the *Nôch* with a beaming countenance. Some trick of
Fortune has evidently turned in our favour.

Cordially shaking hands he unburdens his mind after
the following manner in a dialect abounding in double
and treble consonants. For the benefit of those unversed
in primitive and analytic languages I will give the naïve
literal translation sentence by sentence, together with the
conventional English expressions.

Well, white man.	Hail ! O white-face.
You've surprised King Paul and his folk this time with a vengeance.	*Their* honourable intellects and the little minds of *their* flock will now soon be tangled up like a ball of string.
They've just sent me word along shore	Swift the words have come to me shouted from mouth to mouth along villages on the coast,

That you have been making Obadiah the deacon and other church members very vilely drunk.

That you have made strong drink to trickle down the throat of the peoples' shepherd Obadiah, and the throats of the men of heaven, and their minds are changed to those of swine.

Moreover, there has been a free fight in church.

And the *Pel-charaui* (*i.e.* sacred precinct) has been even as a field of battle.

All the teachers and the congregation vow that the King shall know it.
The King will be pretty wild about it.
But the cream of the joke is
Obadiah entered the church tipsy.
Service was nearly over, another man was in the pulpit.

The shepherds and the heaven-destined flock say, *They* shall be told.
Their wrath will smoke like an oven when it is opened.
One thing make laugh, make laugh very much :
Obadiah he come in, he walk this way, that way, see-saw.
Obadiah come very late; one man go upstairs—talk, talk, talk—preach, preach, preach—teach, teach, teach.

Obadiah interrupted him repeatedly with insulting questions.

Obadiah he break him talk—all time ask him what his father, what his mother—all same fool.

And kept continually grumbling that he could preach a better sermon himself.

All time he go " *Ngar, Ngar, Ngar,*" all same woman, and he say " *He* no preach good. Me preach very good."

Says the preacher in possession : " Turn him out."

Words floated down from the lips of the eloquent man above : " Help that rude fellow to go forth."

And to weary the reader no more with pidgin English,

DEACON OBADIAH OF ARU

the congregation was in an uproar, each party manfully upholding their favourite. Knives were brought into play, and blood flowed freely from some ugly gashes, as each man pitched into his neighbour. It was the counterpart of the famous fray in the loft described in the " Pickwick Papers," in which the Rev. Mr Stiggins took such a vehement and unexpected part. Obadiah suffered the fate of Stiggins after a most obstinate resistance, and was consigned to a cool and dark apartment to meditate in seclusion on his sins and his bruises.

The *Nôch* is much amused when we detail our experiences at Aru, but advises us in future not to rely too much on the saintly professions of church members. " I'm one myself," says he, " but I think the Old Man at Tomun goes too far in his notions. For instance," he continues, " when a man wishes to marry a wife he has to work three weeks for the King before he gets permission, and has to pay the teacher who marries him a good stiff sum. There are more churches than plantations in the tribe, and there are no end of worrisome little laws and restrictions. You mustn't go out for a sail on Sunday, you mustn't drink wine, even in moderation, you mustn't smoke, you mustn't do a good many other things you would like to do, and all for the sake of an old man who grumbles all day long and never gives a civil word to anybody.

" The King doesn't like white men at all, and he and David Lumpoi are trying to set the tribe against you, and, of course, his people have to do what he tells them. The white men haven't always used us well, and, not knowing you, we thought you were like the rest of them. Lately, however, some of my men who have met you at different times told me of the interest you take in collecting our old stories, and in bottling lizards, spiders, and such like. Such work does us no harm, and gives the boys and girls a chance of earning money honestly. Therefore, my people and I in thinking ill of you were in the wrong. Now you and I understand each other, and I shall treat you as a friend and guest. I am very pleased to see the young chiefs who are with you, and have no doubt they are helping you well in your work. When you go home you will tell the *Chaumaro Akan*, or wise men of Britain, that Ponape people are not all cannibals and pirates or wild men of the woods, but have white hearts though their skins are dark."

Whilst this somewhat lengthy conversation is going on dinner is being got ready. In good time the ovens are opened, and we are soon deep amongst the yams and taro of Matup. The *Nóch* drinks Spanish wine with great zest but strict moderation, as becomes a gentleman and a chief. With oriental hospitality he pressed us to stay a day or two, but bethinking us of our people on Paniau eking out their scanty commons and impatiently looking for our return, we determined to push on, and dropped down coast with the tide that very afternoon. We are running merrily across the roughish waters of Middle Harbour, with the quaint sugar-loaf peak of *Takai-Ú* shooting up before us, and are slipping past the island of Tomun where the king has his *Tanipatch* or regal dwelling. Not without anxiety we view the rapid approach of a boat manned by five of Paul Ichipau's myrmidons, pulling their very hardest in chase. We lower sail and let them come alongside. It turns out that they have orders to carry us bound into the presence of King Paul for the appalling crime of sailing on a Sunday. But we are four to their five, and three of us are Kiti men, a tribe which has given Metalanim some very hard knocks in time past. So their summons to surrender being greeted with derision, and seeing us resolute on self-defence paddle in hand, they turned peacefully back, receiving meekly some highly uncomplimentary messages to their worshipful ruler. We do not loiter about here for fear of the rascals swarming out on us in superior force, but holding on our way, once more enter the labyrinth of Nan-Matal with lively anticipations of possible rifle-shots singing out of the dense masses of greenery on every side. We pass Uchentau and leave a message for Alek, my cunning carver in native woods, and on past the walled islets of Peikap, Pan-Katara, and Nikonok, and last of all Pon-Kaim, which lies on the extreme end of the *Kaim* or inner angle of the great enclosure. Here the bottom of the waterway is strewn with basalt blocks, some of great size, and some caution is needful in picking our way past and over these rocky barriers. Finally emerging from this wonderful system of walled islets we pass over the shallow flats below the little hill settlement of Leak, and work our way down to the sand-spit of Pikanekit where twenty or thirty friendly natives are domiciled under a worthy old chief named *Echekaia* (Hezekiah). At this place we are to pick up Kaneke's wife Lilian and her baby boy who are down here on a visit. A very stormy night comes on, and we are glad to break our voyage. Next morning dawns raw and dismal. The temperature has fallen, the sky is black with tempest, the palm trees are bending and swaying in the stream of a lively gale, and sending down their nuts rolling and rebounding like balls on the sward. A thick grey veil blurs the distant hill-slopes, the brook at the door is in freshet, and a streaming downpour of rain is pattering on a drenched and draggled creation. A huge iron pot, the relic of some calling whaler, is on the fire, wherein a mixture of fowl and rice and floury yam is seething away merrily. After breakfast the weather shows no sign of clearing up, and the gale, if anything, blows a thought harder. So we determine to push on— dividing our party into two canoes for fear of a second accident—for the sea is rough and the cases heavy. The good old chief supplies us with a second canoe, on which Nanaua, with Hezekiah's little boy and myself embark. The larger craft, with most of the cargo, carries Kaneke, Chaulik, Nanchom, Lilian and baby. The result proves the wisdom of our plans. Both canoes, after some narrow escapes of upsetting, after much rude buffeting from wind

and wave, ultimately reach their destination.   A pig pur-
chased from Hezekiah shows a wild and untamed nature
in repeated attacks on Nanaua's legs in canoe No. 2, until
quieted with an axe-handle.

Our friends on the little green island, with its row of
curing-houses and huts, are anxiously looking for us, and
help us to haul the canoes high on the sandy beach.
Plenty reigns once more in camp.   Our small woes and
discomforts are all forgotten, a tot of grog is served out
to all hands, dry clothes are put on, and we sit down to
a much-needed supper of clam soup, baked fish, Irish
stew, yams, biscuits and preserved fruits, washed down at
stated intervals from a goodly demijohn of rough Vino
Tinto.   Amidst clouds of tobacco, Nature's boon to weary
voyagers, plans are discussed and projects put in order.

Next morning, September 29th, as we rise up refreshed
from our mats, the sun is shining from a clear blue sky ;
the tide is out and there is glorious sport with Up, with
spear and basket amongst the reef pools, and the stock of
bottled fishes grows larger and larger, to say nothing of
untold basketfuls of live shells, mostly Cyprœas, buried in
tins under the sand at high-water mark for the tide to do
the work of washing them clean and free from all traces
of their former occupants.   Besides gathering shells, I had
plenty to do on the mainland, to which I paid several
further visits, and took care to distribute the medicines
with which the good Spanish doctor had so kindly furnished me, and so two more busy weeks soon rolled by.

CHAPTER XIV

FROM PANIAU TO MARAU

THE time of my departure now drawing near Nanchau suggests that we go down the coast for a day or two to visit the settlement of Marau, where an old chief lives, the *Au* or headman of the sub-district, who will tell us something about the old traditions, and will besides take us into the interior to show us some remarkable ruins of an old fort called Chap-en-Takai, which is situated on a tableland among the mountain-slopes behind the settlement. So taking a couple of natives with us we launch our canoe one fine forenoon, and with a lively breeze are soon slipping past Roch Island, the station of Nanchau-Rerren of Annepein, who had lately entertained us at a solemn feast. Between Roch and Laiap we pass a bed of bright yellow sponges (*Paia*) showing up on a shelf about four feet down on the edge of a detached reef. We hold on our way, keeping out of the shallows as much as we can. The rapid growth of the coralline formations bids fair to speedily fill up the whole lagoon between the outer reef and the shore. It requires considerable local knowledge to pick out the *tau* or deepwater passages in this labyrinth of shoals. A little below Laiap we meet Chaulik and his wife coming up from Ronkiti bringing news from Nanapei that the mail steamer is expected on the 19th instead of the 24th, and advising us not to make our departure too late. The breeze holds, and by and by we are off the mouth of the Ronkiti River close to the islet of Tolotik (Little Hill). Of course, as usual, we find ourselves stranded amongst the shallows, and have to get out the four of us and shoulder her across, gingerly picking

our way over numerous beds of prickly corals, with which
the detached reefs in the lagoon are thickly studded.   To
the south-west Ant Atoll stands out in a long blue line.
Before us is a wide stretch of lagoon, down which we glide,
every now and then fending her off the stacks of coral which
rise within a foot or two of the surface of these variable
depths.   We catch stray glimpses of brilliant sponges and
corals, quaint medusæ and zoophytes, and of gorgeous
fish playing in and out of these submarine forests.   We
pass three little islands to seaward, lying close to the
barrier reef—the central one, distinguished by a few palm-
trees springing out of it, is tenanted by one old fisherman.
Close to Kapara is seen a rather unusual sight—a spring
of fresh water bubbling up through the reef—a boon to
thirsty fishing parties.   A similar phenomenon occurs near
Nei-Afu on Vavau in the Tonga group.   In front of us the
hazy blue rounded outline of Tomara is backed by the
long wooded promontory into which the Paliker country
runs.   With the slowly-rising tide we find ourselves off
the flats of Marau, amongst beds of seagrass, with a
curious round bald mountain showing up in the background.   Wading along with our craft in tow we pick up
on our leisurely way a number of cockles and a spider-
crab of surpassing ugliness.   We have to traverse a considerable stretch of thick black mud, taking us up to the
knees at every step—by no means an uncommon thing
in the approach to a Ponapean settlement.   At last we
reach firm ground, and are glad to take a bath in a clear,
shallow pool, into which the rivulet watering the settlement is dammed as it pours into the salt marshes.   About
two hundred yards climb inland stands the house of the
Au, built on a high terrace of basalt blocks, some of considerable bulk, resembling greatly the dwellings of the
Marquesan islanders standing out upon their solid *paepaes*
or platforms of stone.

A little higher, and the inland wilderness with its thick
tangle of forest, scrub, weeds and climbing vines, shuts in

the little village. The clearing below is occupied by banana and breadfruit trees and clumps of giant taro, a tiny portion wrested from the all-prevailing jungle by the patient labour of man. Around the house, Kava plants are flourishing with their speckled stems, broad, dark-green leaves, dangling catkins and spreading branches, the stalks bulging out every four or five inches into knotty joints. Masses of black rock lie scattered around carpeted with the little veined leaves of betel-pepper vines, climbing and clinging like ivy at home. A profusion of fern and plants of the wild ginger kind add a fresh setting of verdure and freshness to the woodland picture.

The good old man receives us with great cordiality, for he has always been interested in the ancient history and folk-lore of his people. Future voyagers in Pacific waters should clearly understand that it is the *old* generation not the *new* who give their minds to these things. The new for the most part are in a transition state. They are neither good heathens nor earnest Christians. In this connection, and upon such a quest, one fine old heathen who really knows something that the white man hasn't taught him is worth a dozen paltering mediocrities who have forgotten their own history and swamped their identity ; whose only ideas are to ape their white teachers in snuffling Bible texts and grabbing dollars to buy cheap Manchester goods and white men's luxuries, which they really do not need at all.

The afternoon is far advanced. In the growing dusk, under the influence of coffee and tobacco, the Au, whom we have not hurried, but left to take his own time, starts in first with personal reminiscences, harking back by and by to things of ancient date. He tells us how, many years ago, the supreme power over the four tribes of the island was held by Chokach, until a Palang chief, appropriately named *Chou-pei-achach* (Man-fight-know-how), roused the people from their apathy. Kiti then began to be an independent power and the obstinate rival of her neighbour Metalanim. Some while after, on the north side, a portion of the Chokach folk broke away, forming the independent fifth tribe of Not, which seems to occupy in Ponapean politics the same place as the little republic of San Marino in those of Italy.

Passing on to more ancient history and folk-lore, he told us of the arrival of a large castaway canoe from the south on the Paliker coast, with eight chiefs on board, who settled in the country. Their sounding titles were: Man-chai, Chiri-n-rok, Man-in-nok, Chinchich, Pairer, Roki, Machan and Chei-aki.

A brief account of an ancient voyage of discovery I give here, in which some may see evidence of a real historical fact.

" Two brethren went northward from Ponape to seek new lands, sailing many days in a big canoe. At length they saw the midnight sky red with a great blaze of fire as if of a million torches. In terror they turned and got them back to their own land again." Another account says that the elder brother perished, and that the *Kotar* or kingfisher bird saved the younger, and carried him on his back home again. Have we here a reference to the great volcano of Kilauca of Hawaii in eruption? An ancient Raiatean tradition records a very similar phenomenon which scared away a party of Tahitian navigators. The Marquesan islanders, whose ancestors were certainly mingled with the Ponapeans, have a legend agreeing thereto :—

> "Great mountain ranges, mountains of Havaii,
>   Havaii, where the red flaming fire springs up."

> "Aue mouna, mouna o Havaii,
>   Havaii tupu ai te ahi veavea."

Or, again, is the scene of the midnight sky on fire in one of the northern Ladrone islands, where many active volcanoes are always in play? Some again may contend that the

explorers penetrated into the zone, where the fiery lances
of the Aurora Borealis or Northern lights are visible
darting across the heavens. In any case the story illus-
trates the energy of early Caroline island navigators in
this great waste of waters.

We seek our rest early that night, for time presses, and
we must be stirring at dawn if the proposed exploration
of the ruins on the hill-top is to be a success. The morning turns out fine, and after hastily partaking of coffee
and biscuit we set forth on our winding path up the
mountain slopes, picking our way over stocks and stones,
hewing down all branches and boughs obstructing the
trail, burrowing through dense thickets of hibiscus, ever
and anon stooping down to collect come of the curious
flat spiral land-shells with which the ground is strewn,
called *Chepei-en-kamotal* or " the washing bowl of the
earth-worm." On we splash through shallow mountain
streams, scaring up half-wild hogs wallowing in the rich
black mud of the wayside pools—threading still shady
glens, but ever going upward and upward. At last we
pause awhile amongst a grove of sago-palms and mountain plantains in a swampy little dell, watered by a briskly
flowing stream. By the side of the water lies a long
tapering slab of basalt rudely worked into the form of a
shark. It is some fifteen feet in length. A sharp three-
cornered ridge runs along the centre of the back ; the
dorsal fins are decidedly in evidence, and the tail distinctly indicated. The head is left pretty well to the
imagination. This is one of the rude *Tikitik-en-ani* or
images found here and there in Ponape, and dedicated to presiding genii or guardian spirits of a community or family. (Compare Maori and Marquesan
Tiki and *Tikitiki*, an image.) This and Laponga's head
were the only ones I saw, but I have no doubt that there
are many more of them; and that the unconverted folk, as
well as many of the church members, have hidden them
away in odd nooks and corners, where they can secretly

have recourse to them at will in time of need.   Such a thing is quite in accordance with Ponapean character, and really very natural.   For the cult of old gods dies very hard indeed all the world over.   But the night of ignorance is passing, as the gathering sunlight of science chases one by one lingering superstitions like shadows from their lurking-places.   It may be observed that the sharks *Pako* and *Tanipa* are held in great awe by the Ponapeans. The cult of the shark is, or was, strong on the Ant Islands, where there is a special holy place dedicated to that divinity.

An hour's more climbing brings us to the edge of the tableland close under the old fort, the scene of a great battle a century ago between the King of Kiti and Chau-Kicha, the chief of Wana, who besieged the king in his stronghold and captured it, slaying him and many of his chiefs and warriors.   The enclosure forms a nearly complete square, bulging out at the north-western angle.

The northern end along the Takiririn road was defended by a row of palisades, for which system of fortification the *Ak* or mangrove supplies excellent materials. These *estacadas de mangle* gave the Spanish considerable trouble to carry during the eventful two days' fighting on the 22nd and 23rd of November, 1890, before the strongly fortified post of Ketam.   At Ketam these were eleven feet high, in length six hundred and eighty yards, and a foot in thickness.   The positions of Chap-en-Takai and Ketam are laid out pretty much on the same pattern, the Ponapeans in ancient and modern times being no mean proficients in fortification and the art of war.

Proceeding along the south - east line of wall about thirty paces, we came to a wide breach, through which, tradition declares, the troops of Chau-Kicha, repulsed on other sides, finally broke their way in.   Doubtless some excavations made hereabouts would bring to light many interesting relics such as *permachapang*, or stone clubs,

like the "*mere*" of the Maori, war-axes made out of
the centre shaft of the great Kima-cockle, and head
ornaments and necklaces of shell resembling the North
American Indian "*wampum*," with which these warriors
profusely adorned themselves on going into battle. The
name of the architect who built these walls is given as
Lumpoi-en-Chapal.

Passing along the Takiririn road we visited the site
of the old village at the north-western end. Close by
the site of the ill-fated King of Kiti's house we saw a
high raised platform called *Mol-en-Nanamareki*, where,
during the siege, the king with his councillor and war-
chief *Kaeka* used to sit in solemn council. Some of the
blocks of basalt composing the platform were near four
feet thick. The site of the king's house was occupied
by modern cook-houses newly thatched with sago-palm
leaves. Everywhere round were marks of recent cultivation, showing a practical and thrifty proprietor. There
were groves of breadfruit-trees and well-weeded rows of
plantains. Kava cuttings had been planted and were
thriving vigorously. Yam-vines were trained everywhere
along the tree-trunks, many of their leafy festoons turning
yellow and brown, a sign that the coveted tuber is ready
for digging. From the north-west corner at C, there
is a fine view of the broad pronged outline of the Ants,
and the three long islets of Pakin a little to the right.
Here we took our frugal noonday meal of cold cooked
breadfruit washed down with a few drinking-nuts. This
concluded, the Au and Nanchau suddenly find their
memories, and blossom out into a wealth of fairy tales
as fast as one can write them down.

Just where we were sitting, the King of Kiti and his
choicest warriors made their last stand. But the name
of this Ponapean Priam has gone down unchronicled into
the dust and shadow. On the north-west and south-east
sides of the fort the walls were either built much higher
or have been left in much better preservation. Some of

the blocks let into the masonry measure a yard across the face, a yard in depth and four feet in length. The height of the walls varies from six feet to twelve or fourteen. Yet even here destruction has been busy, the ground in front being strewn with fragments which have from time to time toppled down. To judge from the size of some of these fallen masses, the walls must once have stood considerably higher. The greatest height is found on the south-east side which faces a thickly wooded slope of a hill-spur running down steeply towards the sea. Here we remarked a high watch-tower (*Im-ruk-en-chilepa*), so this side appears to have been particularly well guarded against the approach of stealthy foemen through the dense jungle stretching below.

The interior of the fort is thickly occupied by a bewildering growth of tall grasses, ferns, creepers, weeds, and flowering shrubs, amongst which the handsome red and yellow spikes of the Katiu (*Ixora*), the broad white bells of the morning glory, and the brilliant blue petals of a rough-leaved shrub called Mateu, are most conspicuous.

Our survey done we strike inland from the north-east corner, where our guide promises to show us some further remains. Presently we come upon an old stone platform (*Lempantam*) embowered amongst a mass of wild ginger plants. On it lies a broad and flattish piece of basalt, shaped like a long dish, deeply hollowed out in the centre, wherein in olden times the Kava or Chakau root was pounded up to make the national beverage for the king and his court. This one bears the ceremonial name of *Pel-en-Mau* (which either means Sacred to Good Purpose, or The Pleasant House). The everyday name of such implements is *Pat-alap* or *Big Stone*. (*Cf.* Sanskrit *Path, Pattar, Pattal*—a stone; Malay and Melanesian *Batu*, and Philippine *Bato*—a stone; Polynesian *Hatu, Whatu, Fatu, Atu*—a stone.

Close here, about the year 1882, a small bronze cannon was discovered and taken away by a party of explorers

from the *Larne*, which circumstance may give some colour
to the *ipse dixit* of the Spanish, who insist that the ruins
on Ponape were the work of buccaneers or early navigators of their nation. The people of this very district of
Kiti have a tradition of a body of iron men who landed
on the island, and though assailed in superior force, long
defended themselves, and proved invulnerable against the
axes, clubs, darts, and slingstones. At last the natives
destroyed them by stabbing them through eye to brain
with their long lances. This reminds one of the tale told
in Herodotus of the brazen men whom an oracle pre-
dicted should come out of the sea to help Psammitichus to
his promised kingdom of Egypt. Doubtless some of the
light armed Egyptians tried the same experiment with
success against Psammitichus' mail-clad Carians. From
the Kiti tradition we may safely infer the destruction of a
landing party of men in mail from a vessel or vessels of
some early navigator in these seas.

A little further on and we come upon five round stones
(*Pai-n-uet*, lucky pebbles) shaped like cannon balls, lying
side by side in a hollow. " I see the eggs and the nest,"
said I to the Au, in the figurative way natives like, " but
where are the birds that laid them? Do you think they
would miss one if I took it?" The old man cackles
feebly, but assuming a serious tone: " The birds," says
he, "are nearer than you think." He declares that the
air is full of viewless eyes of spirits viewing us, and that
serious results would follow meddling with the stones,
which, it appears, are used now and then for some sort of
divination. This place is called *Itet*, and the precinct
Pan-Katara, and a pile or stack of masonry close at hand
Nan-Tauach, three names borrowed from the holy places
of *Nan-Matal* over the Metalanim border. Do we not
see here history repeating itself as usual? Kiti is jealous
of the shrines of her hated rival Metalanim, and founds
for herself a hallowed place of pilgrimage and worship
under the sanctifying denominations of old traditional

landmarks, the very names of which carry with them some degree of indefinable prestige.   The rival shrines of Bethel and Jerusalem, and the divided papacy of Rome and Avignon, are distinct cases in point in parallel history.

The precinct called Pan-Katara, unlike its weird and desolate prototype of Metalanim, is bordered with patches of the Kava plant, and shadowed by some fine Kangit trees. *Nan-Tauach* is a pile of masonry built up of the usual basalt blocks. It measures ten feet in height, thirty feet in length, and thirty in breadth, densely overgrown with brushwood. Formerly it was a very sacred spot. In the middle on top are two holes eight feet in depth, the graves of the ill-fated King of Kiti and his marshal Kaeka, who were interred here after the great battle in which they fell. The masonry is built up after the style of its Metalanim namesake; but as often happens with imitations, the work is on a smaller scale and the workmanship lacks finish. Upon the island of Ngatik (Ravens Isle), some thirty miles away down to the west, is another Pankatara—a rude stack of stones—partly thrown down of late by the vandal hands of native converts.

Some years ago the flat stones covering these pits were removed by searchers for the *moni uaitata* or red money, *i.e.* gold. Some lunatic or other, presumably as a practical joke, had been putting in circulation all manner of cock-and-bull stories about hidden treasure. Nothing, however, but a few mouldering bones rewarded their search. Probably if they had found money they would not have paid their debts. Nan-Tauach proves to be our guide's trump card, and we wend our weary way homeward. Going down is worse than coming up, but we fight our way on through trackless mazes of *Kalau*, over fallen trunks of trees, and through mud-puddles and stone-paved torrent beds, till patience well nigh wears herself out. Late in the afternoon we limp into a little clearing, weary, bedraggled, and mud-daubed—a sorry spectacle for saints and sinners.   Not so, however, to a mirthful company of some forty persons there collected.   An important cere- mony—the building of a council-lodge—has just been concluded for the day, and another equally important— the feeding of the hungry clan who have toiled fasting during all the fiery tropical sunshine—is just going to begin.   The sewers of palm-leaf thatch, the plaiters of house-mats, the hewers of wood, the stone-workers, and the carpenters and joiners, are knocking off work.   The deft fingers of the shutter-weavers are ceasing, gathering the stalks of slender cane and reed-grass into neat bundles for the morrow's task.

A vast pile of native food lies hard by ; plenty for all and to spare, for native hospitality does not do things by halves.   To be styled niggard, or one who grudges meat to his neighbour, is to suffer nearly the uttermost taunt in the Ponapean vocabulary, and, indeed, in the Pacific lands in general.

Pending the distribution of the food we converse with the young chief for whom the house is being built, whose pleasant open countenance prepossesses one directly in his favour.

The folk here rarely stir abroad, and view with the deepest interest the advent of a white visitor from the wondrous island, rich in ships and sailors, far across the seas, dim rumours of whose teeming cities and their wealth have reached even this little spot.   The greatest respect is shown us.   The feelings of a courteous host overcome the inborn curiosity of our new friend, who is really anxious to be asking questions, but refrains for fear of being troublesome from pure natural politeness.   How- ever, we are soon chatting away as if we had known each other for years, discussing all manner of social and political questions, and, as it were, making an exchange of our experiences.   Tales of the wars in Europe, and deadly modern engines of war, particularly rivet his attention.   In return he deals with the history of his own people, not with authority as the *Au*, but modestly as an inquiring student (what south-western Polynesians call " a child of the Red House "). He shows great surprise at the close resemblance of Samoan, Tahitian and Marquesan numerals, and other key words to those in his native tongue ; and is fairly amazed when shown over what enormous stretches of ocean these families of a kindred race lie scattered. When told of that great statesman Sir George Grey's magnificent dream of the federation of all the Isles of the Pacific under the British flag, he was greatly moved, and declared his opinion in no doubtful fashion. " It is indeed well," says he, " one family, one flag. The sea-girt lands will hold together like one household, the people will plant the ground and gather the fruits in security, and war will vanish as the night at sunrise."

I have dwelt somewhat at length on this conversation, because it is an excellent sample of many others held with friendly chiefs throughout the five tribes. It redounds greatly to the honour of our nation, the confidence and goodwill so widely established in the Carolines and elsewhere by the whisper of that *open sesamé* name of " English." As I heard an old Cornish friend say of the Samoan, " *They know who's kind to them.*"

It is now time for the portioning out of the food. Saturday here, as in Samoa and other islands, is the day for cooking quantities of food to last over till Monday. It is no working-man's half holiday, but often a day of hard, honest work. A very active old man, and two or three young fellows with him, pounce upon the heap, and in a trice fish out four large baskets filled with baked yams, fermented breadfruit (*mar*), and cooked plantains. These, together with a baked sucking pig, he and his acolytes lay before the chief as his share. The merry old gentleman then hastens, or rather dances, back, skipping about vigorously, showering around him plenteous jokes and japes. It seems to be expected of him,

and every jest is honoured with hearty laughter. Without
delay, up comes the English visitor's portion. A haunch
and shoulder of roast pork, a large baked breadfruit,
a remarkably fine green drinking coconut, a cooked
sprouting nut—a dainty much relished by the Ponapeans
—and a package of *Itiit* for dessert, a sweetmeat made
of scraped yam and coconut-cream, twisted up into a
dracæna leaf, and baked together into a cake in the
earth-oven. Looking round, one is struck with the
colour-note of red and yellow running through the
buzzing assembly. Most of the young bucks (*Pon-
machu*) are dressed in bright orange-yellow kilts with
scarlet woollen borders. The same hues appear here and
there amongst the gowns of the women folk, who look
like a bed of tulips in full bloom. Altogether the scene
recalls the brightly-coloured Sunday-school illustrations
of patriarchal times, to which illusion the noble Semitic
profiles of many of the company lend some emphasis.
Many of the workmen have by their side long, slightly
curved knives, which give quite a warlike touch to the
picture. By and by two young men come down the
hill bearing a large newly uprooted Kava-plant between
them. The ever-ready knives are brought into play, and
the top branches quickly lopped off. The stems are
pruned of leaves, cut into yard - lengths, and tied in
bundles for planting. The sharp edge of a cockle
is used in the pruning. Numbers of the shells lie
strewn about, showing a large annual consumption
of this leathery bivalve. The assembly now breaks
up, streaming downhill to the Lodge by the water
side, where the Kava root is being prepared with
pestle and mortar; and the modulated ringing of the
stones, like hammer on anvil, is pealing up cheerfully
through the greenwood. The chief, who is dead lame
from a fearful abscess in the ankle, is carried down on the
shoulders of the merry old gentleman. Amidst polite
greetings we enter the Lodge, where ten or twelve

men, whose faces are new to me, are sitting.   Four
are busily engaged pounding Kava on the ground
below.   We ascend the platform, and are warmly wel-
comed by one of the strangers, who turns out to be the
brother of our excellent old friend, Chau-Wana of Mount
Roi, with whom we have spent sundry merry meetings.
Here again it is borne in upon us how well it is for a
traveller in these parts to be backed by a substantial
introduction from a chief of recognised status—the older
the better.   The visitors will be sure of a cordial reception,
the cloak of suspicion and reserve with which every native
wraps himself in self-defence will be thrown off, and a
little geniality will do all the rest.   In due time the
aromatic national beverage is ceremoniously handed
round, pipes are lit, and our hosts wax communicative
on the subject of seasons, constellations, guiding stars,
and early navigation, cheerfully adding their quota to
the notes already in hand.   The entertainment winds
up with some fine war-songs roaring out in a deep,
sonorous chime, resembling in cadence and intonation
the songs of my old friends the Marquesan islanders, who
in many another striking way show a decided relationship
with the Ponapeans.   At length we take our departure,
and soon arrive home, pushing through dripping woods in
a heavy rainstorm, which has come down on us out of the
stormy north.

Supper awaits us, and with sharpened appetites we are
sitting down to despatch it, when two young men arrive
in a small canoe from the island of Mang, up by the
Paliker coast, to announce to the *Au* that a chief lady,
a near relation of his, is lying at the point of death,
and earnestly begging him to come to her side.   Our poor
old host, evidently in great distress, with many apologies
for having to leave us, hastily takes his departure, refusing
all refreshment, and leaving us in charge of his wife,
whose kindly solicitude for our comfort seems to outweigh
her own private griefs.   Immediately after his leaving,

a thick, black squall comes humming over the waters, with a fresh tremendous downpour of rain. With sympathy we picture the old man toiling on in a little canoe through the mirk of the night in that howling welter of winds and waters, to obey the sacred duty of kinship and family affection which calls him, aged, infirm, and fasting, to face the bitter elements. Indeed, some of our people at home who talk of virtue and duty as if they had invented them, might well be instructed by the example of the unselfish *Au*.

Under the circumstances, unwilling to intrude upon their griefs, and to burden their hospitality further, we decide to leave. The heart of our kind entertainer's wife is gladdened with the present of a bundle of strong tobacco, a black silk handkerchief, and a fine Sheffield blade, stamped with the magic words " *Made in Germany.*"

The sky is heavily overcast, threatening rain, and faithfully it keeps its promise. We arrive at Paniau after an unpleasant morning's voyage, and forthwith engage in busy preparations for getting the shells and other curios ready packed for the mail. Two trying days follow. We pursue our outdoor work under the discomfort of a ceaseless downpour and a chilling wind, disinterring frail upon frail of evil-smelling shells from their sandy burrows, and carefully cleaning and packing them in wisps of grass to prevent breakage. All join cheerfully in the work, and at last the monotonous task is ended by the ready co-operation of deft and willing hands.

The last day but one of my stay on Paniau, we made up a little party to go ashore at Tiati and say goodbye to our friend Chau-Wana and his household, who had treated us so kindly. In the afternoon Nanchau, Eta and I, climbed Chila-U, the " Adze-head Rock," from which we had a fine view of Mutok Harbour and the richly-forested lowlands. In the evening the Tiati folk gave a feast, and many people from the outer districts came in with little presents and with kindly expressions of goodwill to their honoured guest and comrade about to cross the great water.

Cheerless and grey broke the day of my departure, the bay ruffled with gusts and squalls of wind and sheets of driving rain. If ever I saw unfeigned sorrow and regret upon human face I saw it in those of my *panainai*, compánions and friends of many a pleasant expedition. Our leave - taking was affecting.   Poor old Nanchau and his wife quite broke down, and some of the others were very little better.   I had hardly looked for such strong sympathy and feeling in the stern, rugged, and seemingly apathetic Caroline island character.   But it was even so, and I shall think of them all my life the better for it.   It was hard to go, and getting ready was sad work, but it was over at last.

As I clambered on board the heavily - laden sailing boat which had done such good service, and as I turned and looked back, the western sun broke through the clouds and threw a feeble watery ray upon the pensive and sad-faced knot of men and women clustered on the little white beach, backed by a waving belt of wind-swept palms.

CHAPTER XV

PANIAU TO COLONY, THENCE TO GUAM AND YAP

THE little green island sinks astern, and we run down the Kiti coast in the early afternoon, putting in at night-fall at Ronkiti to say goodbye to Nanapei, who just then was in great trouble owing to the illness of Nalio, his mother, who died a few days after. About midnight came a high tide, upon which we passed out over the sand and mud-banks, and the morning found us rocking in a dead calm in the lagoon off Tauak Island. Later on a breeze sprang up and brought us up towards the Paip-Alap or Great Cliff of Chokach.

We sighted a large vessel ahead. By the smoky trail behind her on the sea-line we made her out to be the *Correo*, or *Mail*, steaming out of the north down upon Ascension Bay, whereupon we row along with a will, for we know she only stays a night in port, and we have still much work to do. We pass the islet of Tolotik or " Little Hill," steering carefully clear of numerous blocks of honeycombed limestone that stud the boat passage. To the right of us towers the Paip-Alap, a sheer bluff nearly a thousand feet in height above dense hanging woods on a little promontory where, shaded by a huge *Tupap* or Umbrella Tree, lives the Nallaim or High Priest of Chokach, an aged patriarch and very wise, who knows the names of kings and heroes of old and the ceremonies due to the ancient gods of the land—himself one of the last of the old generation, whom alas! I have left uninterviewed, and now perhaps shall never meet at all. A little further on lies the *Tanipach* or abode of the *Wachai*,

and the modest little Catholic chapel nestling under waving woods. Yet further, and we sight the *Nach* and the
dwelling of the Nanekin, scene of the massacre of Ensign
Martinez and his party in 1887. Above us are opening
out the peaks and ridges at the back of Chokach's great
seaward scarp, but the north-west horn of the island which
shuts out the Colony from our view is not yet passed.

This day the sides of the great precipice show out
wondrously in the rays of the rising sun. The cliff-
face shows a strongly-marked formation of columnar
basalt, like that of the Giant's Causeway and the South
Cape of Tasmania. Right under the great pile, one
views in the solid rock stripes and veinings of umber
and slaty-grey with vivid velvety black splashes of rich
volcanic soil, washed and filtered down from the highlands
above. The effect is further diversified by ledges of
shimmering herbage where flying seeds of grass or weed
or fern have lodged. On the summit, far, far above
our heads, wave clumps of pandanus, and the native
gardenia, flinging out their feathery outline against the
sky, firm-rooted on the verge of the dizzy gulf of air.

As the north-west side of the island opens up to us
broadside on, we catch sight of another rocky and
precipitous mass, similar in shape but smaller, and
topped by a peak like an obelisk ; and on the further
side overlooking the Tau-Mokata boat-passage which
divides Chokach from the mainland, a third wall of
basalt looks down on the swamps and their shadowing
maze of mangroves. In the middle of the island is a
great break or cleft, a regular *chine*, through which a
narrow path, leading across the island, runs over the
dividing saddle of mountain amidst dense groves
chequered with tiny native dwellings lying back in
their clearings and sending up faint blue wreaths of
smoke in the early morning air. This side of the island
has the most population, and one views the rude cabins
of the settlers perched high amongst hanging woods

THE GREAT CLIFF OF CHOKACH

like the peasants' chalets fringing the wooded heights round Altdorf or some Unterwalden hamlet in Switzerland's forest cantons.   On this side of Chokach the groves of breadfruit are magnificent, the greater and lesser banyan, the towering Chatak or Elœocarpus, the Tree-Gardenia, and the Mango, lending their peculiar nuance to a rich panorama of glancing tints of green.

Before us stretches the low mangrove-covered islet of *Taka-tik* or Little Island, and the basaltic round of Langar is emerging in the background with a couple of the German firm's trading vessels lying at anchor in the bay off the long low wharf, and right ahead shows up clear and clearer the long hill-ridge of Not Point and the hulk at her moorings below the little settlement of Villa Madrid, whilst in the centre of the harbour the *Uranus* has just dropped anchor with a host of boats and canoes swarming round her.

Taka-tik once passed, it did not take us long to reach the Santiago wharf, and a busy day of packing we had of it, the boys turning to with a will, as Ponapeans are wont to do for their friends when really wanted.

By sunset all was in order for the departure of the *Uranus* on the morrow at noon.   A farewell visit had been paid to the Spanish Governor, and to my kindly hosts, the captain and officers of the *Quiros*, as well as the priests and the courteous local medico.   I determined to spend my last night ashore with my good old friend Dr Kubary at Mpompo.   So taking with me Kaneki, whom, for his fidelity to me the Spaniards dubbed *El secretario*, I passed through the sentries on watch by virtue of the password for the night given us by the polite captain of Infantry.   Kubary, hale and hearty as ever, had just returned from a long tramp over the hills collecting landshells, his latest hobby.   The reader can guess how two enthusiasts sat far into the night in earnest discussion upon the mystery of the strange lands around them, whilst the faithful Kaneki, worn out with his exertions, curled up in his cloak on the mats and slept peacefully at his master's feet.

In my mind's eye I see my bluff host sitting in his great cane chair, spectacles on nose, with his specimen-cases, instruments, books and pamphlets around him, peering keenly into the hieroglyphs of some huge German tome of science to wrest therefrom some happy illustration of his theme. And this was the last I saw of Kubary, ablest and sturdiest of Germany's pioneers of science in Pacific waters.

The 22nd of October dawns, the last day of my stay in Ponape. The scent of the pandanus flowers hangs heavy on the air as a wreath of incense, and the birds are singing blithe in bush as we walk down through the glades on that fair and golden early morning. I take my final plunge in a cool deep fern-fringed basin where a brawling torrent purls down from its rain-swept home in the cloud-capped hills.

Many and cordial are the leave-takings with native and European in the Colony, but I get away at last with my trusty crew bending sturdily to their oars under the stimulus of the last glass of the good padre's Benedictine. It is now broad noon. The *Uranus*, good old sea grey-hound, is already straining at her leash, black smoke pouring thick from her funnels as she vibrates with the churning of her suddenly-awakened screw. In a trice my boxes are hoisted and handed on board, the word to start is given, and we are off and sweeping out of the bay with the parting cheers of my crew ringing out gallantly in our wake. Little by little the great scarp of Chokach and the cloud-capped peak of Kupuricha sink into grey distance behind, and the lofty island is left ere long a mere blur on the great waters as we tear on into the dark north-west. We are making for Guam (*Guahan*), southern-most of that strange chain of volcanic islands running down into the Micronesian area from out the maze of *shimas* or islets which so thickly sprinkle the ocean south of Japan and the sister chain of the Lew-Chews (*Ryu-Kyu*).

Our voyage to Guam was fair and uneventful. We sighted no land, the captain as usual holding her course well to the north of the reefs and low-lying atolls of the Central, Carolines. The *Uranus* people had much to tell of the progress of the Revolution in the Philippines up to the 8th of October, the day on which she left Manilla. There had been a brisk skirmish at Santa Misa at the north-west suburb of the city, close to the country house of the English Club, on which occasion fifty Spanish artillerymen and about seven hundred loyal natives met and defeated a mob of two thousand rebels. The new rifles employed by the victors inflicted severe punishment. A hundred and four rebels were killed outright, and many more wounded and taken prisoners. A number of the latter were sentenced to be shot, amongst them my poor photographer, who, tired of honest employment, had elected to take part in this his last piece of mischief.

If all reports are true, tortures were freely lavished upon many of the wretched Filipino captives worthy of the most palmy days of the Inquisition—as they lay in the dungeons of the Old town. If so, it must not be forgotten that the rebels had committed horrible atrocities in the rising. One padré at the capture of Imus was impaled, dying in frightful and lingering torments, another was crucified under a blazing sun, and a third chained to a stake, his robes saturated with petroleum and set in a blaze. Unarmed Spaniards were murdered and their corpses chopped in pieces, their wives and daughters reserved for a worse fate at the hands of a dastardly rabble, who at the sight of a dozen English blue-jackets would have run for their lives—aye, and be running still. At the time of the *Uranus* leaving, thirteen of these gentle rebels had been shot in Cavite, and eight on the Luneta esplanade in Manilla. Twenty-one were in safe, but uncomfortable, keeping, waiting to be shot on the day following—a most laudable clearance of worthless ruffians.

The days passed pleasantly enough. The officers were courteous, and all arrangements on board of a distinctly comfortable order. Our hours for meal-times were somewhat curious. Breakfast *à la fourchette* at ten, and dinner at five. Coffee is served in the early morning, supplemented if required by an omelette or rich pancake—eggs being as plentiful on board as they were scarce on Ponape. Reading the Manilla journals and diarios was entertaining work. The style in places was comically bombastic and full of startling drops into pathos and sentimentality. The chief engineer, coming from the Basque country, gave me a number of remarkable words in that tongue, which I shall certainly hand over one day, along with a choice assortment of Pelew and other harsh-sounding dialect forms, to some skilled philologist for dissection. Only I must find one with lips as elastic as caoutchouc, and lungs of brass and leather ; and, above all, a sound dental apparatus, or I should have my fears of his talking-tackle going to pieces in the process.

On the seventh day out the limestone cliffs of Guam were seen emerging on the sky-line, and late at night we lay at the Port Luis anchorage. In the morning I went ashore in the ship's boat, and without waiting for one of the primitive carriages, marched the five miles to Agaña on foot. I proceeded to the house of Henry M., an American resident, to whom I had an introduction, an excellent fellow, who received me most hospitably, and took me round to see the parish priest, Padré José Palomo, who gave me some interesting information about the Ladrone group. To him also I owe a long list of words in the old language of the Chamorros, which now is greatly mixed with Spanish, and rapidly becoming one of the vanished tongues. I also obtained a complete list of the ancient numerals, and all tallied wonderfully with the vocabulary collected by Chamisso in 1814, a fact of which I was then ignorant. The Chamorro dialect in grammar is akin to the Tagala and Pampang of the Philippines, and to the Favorlang of Formosa. In vocabulary and phonesis it has something peculiar to itself. Some of the words much resemble those in the Sulu Archipelago. There are a few Aino traces, and rather a large number of words akin to those current in the Polynesian dialects. There are several clearly-defined cognates with Sanskrit, such as *Falina*, mast ; Skt., *Falan ; Pagua*, areca palm ; Skt., *Pug ; Pupul*, pepper, Kava ; Skt., *Pipal*, pepper ; *Paka*, white ; Skt., *Pak*, bright ; *Lada*, an orange-red dye-wood (Morinda) ; Skt., *Rata*, (1) red, (2) dyed, coloured ; *Luluk, Lulik*, iron ; Skt., *Lauh, Lauk*. Padré José made much of the ruins upon the neighbouring islands of Saipan, Rota, and Tinian, which I much regretted being unable to visit this time, and firmly resolved to thoroughly explore on my return. He told me also of a cave upon Guam, near the village of Ina-rahan, near Agaña, the walls of which are covered with hieroglyphical characters inscribed by one of the ancient queens of the island. There seems no reason why the Chamorros should not have had an ancient written character like their neighbours the Tagals of the Philippines and the allied Malays of Java, Sumatra, Celebes, and Macassar. It does not seem unnatural that owing to long oceanic isolation of the Chamorros, and, *à fortiori*, the Micronesians, who dwell still further away from the civilised Indonesian area, the art of writing during process of long generations, should have more and more fallen into the hands of an intelligent minority who alone could interpret and explain the import of the signs. Finally it would be lost, with the exception of just such traces as the above. Or, again, as in Ponape, the word for writing would be merged in that for tattooing or commemoration. (*Cf.* Ponape *Intin, Inting*, to write, tattoo ; *Intant*, name, fame, renown ; the Lampong of Sumatra has *Untang-untang*, written law ; Sulu Archipelago, *Indan*, to write

or engrave.)   It would thus be very interesting to find
out whether the old Chamorros *did* have an alphabet of
their own, and perhaps even to discover tablets inscribed
with the annals of the olden time and the deeds of native
kings long prior to the Spanish conquest.

Until sunset the good padré sat and conversed, for the
most part in excellent English.   I found to my surprise
that upon the island of Saipan there is a colony of Caroline islanders, mostly drawn from the central groups, and
grievously tantalised I felt at having to return with such
precious ethnographical material almost within my grasp.
But I steeled my heart and took my leave, more determined than ever to revisit the group in a year or two, of
which notion my worthy host M., with whom I spent the
evening, approved, and promised me all the assistance in
his power on my return.

Next morning we drove down to Port Luis together.
The road passes over several small bridges spanning
narrow rivulets (*saddug*) which drain the rich lowlands
stretching back to the line of limestone cliffs through
which the moisture filters down from the moors.   Picturesque native houses, like those in the Manilla suburbs,
peep out on either side of the road amongst taro and
banana plantations.   Coconut palms (*Nidjok*) fringe the
wayside which runs along the sea, separated from the
beach by a narrow belt of palms, hibiscus and pandamis,
with an occasional yam-patch or pineapple clearing.   The
reef only lies some two hundred yards off shore.   Here
very fine specimens of uncommon shells can be picked up
at low tide, but hardly anybody takes notice of them.

We arrived at the village of Asan around which are
beds of a white lily with yellow calix, variously called in
Micronesia *Kiop*, *Gieb*, *Kiuf*, and *Kief*.   To our left lies a
stretch of swampy land, which the local peasantry are
getting ready for the planting of rice (*Fai*).   This was a
well-defined branch of industry of the natives prior to the
conquest of 1570, which the Spanish chronicler remarks

upon as a fact of peculiar interest—as indeed it is. It is doubtless due to the occasional visits in early times of Chinese or Japanese trading vessels. (*Fun-Tan*, the Marianne God of fishermen and sailors, probably is the Japanese *Fune-Dama*, the god of ships and navigation.) A glance at any good chart of this part of the Pacific will show the great probability of such occasional visits, even if they were not regularly kept up. The word *Fai*, rice, like the corresponding word *Mai*, *Komai*, in Yap, where however the grain is not regularly under cultivation, answers to the Chinese and Japanese word *Mai*.

In the background the hill of Nagas looks down upon marsh and meadow. The rounded limestone formation here resembles nothing so much in outline as one of the ancient robber-castles perched on a hillside by the Rhine.

We reach the village of Tipungan embowered in groves of orange-trees (*Kahit*), and load up the trap with a plentiful supply of the fruit thereof, with the aid and entire concurrence of the polite village headman. Hereabouts we met C. on horseback, a lively young American trader, who had been with R. L. Stevenson in the Gilberts, and who now, to his vast content, finds himself located in this pleasant little spot, where, he informs us, the climate is first rate, one's neighbours decent folk, and the lasses wonderfully agreeable, and pretty as a peep-show. Soon after leaving our Bohemian acquaintance we reached Port Luis, and just looking in to see Joe Wilson, the harbour-master, we got a boat and rowed on board the *Uranus*, where we had a very jovial breakfast-party together. We left about noon, reaching Yap the next day but one, where I disembarked bag and baggage, boxes, books and bottles upon Gerard's islet of Ngingich, pending the arrival of Captain O'Keefe, my agent and banker, in whose hands I am to place myself.

PART IV

CHAPTER XVI

DESCRIPTION OF YAP; TOMIL TO LAI

THE following is based on that given by the Spanish historian Dr Cabeza Pereiro, now supplemented by observations of my own made on the spot. The Yap group consists of one main island situated 144° 17' east longitude and 90° 28' north latitude, with the islands of Map and Ramung to the north, which appear to have been torn away by volcanic forces, being only separated from each other by a narrow channel easily fordable at low tide. The other islets are called Tapelau, Engnoch, Tarrang, Obi, and Impakel. Yap is surrounded by a coral reef some thirty-five miles long and some five broad. The main island seems to owe its origin to an elevation of the sea bottom. Towards the north it is nearly cut in two at the isthmus of Girrigir. In the north and central part of the island there is a range of hills of slight elevation which does not exceed 1000 feet, and whose slopes distribute the rain-water to the low-lying districts. Rivulets (*Lul*) are very scarce, and when any considerable time passes without rain the water runs short. The population amounts to some 8000. The folk apparently belong to the Malay race, with a Dravidian substratum, and a slight mixture of Polynesian. Our Spaniard refers them to the Battak type, and declares that they are inclined to be hospitable, but revengeful in character when they conceive that their honour is insulted. Which may very well be so. They are not particularly cordial to strangers, and they often fail to keep their word. Their character is peaceable and apathetic. They are fond of fishing, and their robustness of body and docile nature make them well adapted for all sorts of labour, though in general they are lazy   Socially they are divided into four classes—magicians, nobles, rich men, and slaves.   Their houses are solidly built of breadfruit and callophyllum wood, artistic in form, thatched with nipa palm and pandanus leaf.   The walls are of light canes bound in rows with a cording of cinet or coconut fibre.

Yap does not produce many timber-trees.   The island is surrounded by a belt of coconut palms about half a mile in thickness.   No cereal is under cultivation, and rice cannot be acclimatized.   Maize would apparently yield well, but the Spanish have not tried it.   The country produces in great abundance sweet potatoes, various kinds of yam, giant taro, mammee apples, pineapples, plantains, sugar-cane, breadfruit (" *Thau* ") and the tropical almond (Terminalia Catappa).

Captain Butron of the *Velasco*, sunk in the late action in Manilla Bay, gives the following information on the prevailing winds:—

The north-east monsoon comes on from September to October, veering occasionally to the east, from which quarter its force is increased.   The south-west begins in June and July.

We are indebted to poor Captain Holcombe for a more detailed account of the winds and their seasons.

January and February	Calms and variable winds. Towards end of month cool breezes.
March	Occasional hard squalls. Monsoon loses somewhat of its force.
April	Calm and variable winds. Latter half of month fresh breezes.
May	Calm. Breezes less frequent.

These 3 months form the rainy season. {

June and	July	Calm, occasionally showers of rain. Light and pleasant breezes.
		Calm. Variable towards end. Showery.
August		Season of typhoon (*Yeko*) begins. Yap lies in the very centre of these disturbances which pile up terrible seas, much dreaded by native voyagers.

September and October } are like the three preceding months. With October ends the probable season of the typhoons, though they have been known to occur as late as December.

November   Light and variable winds and calms, and towards end of month north-east, veering to east. The winds hold strong and full, with but little rainfall.

During the south-west monsoon, which begins in June, the days are calm and there are heavy dews and much moisture, and from the middle of July to the beginning of August there are heavy rains. During the north-east monsoon the weather is dry and there is little dew. Typhoons are not uncommon between August and December.

The temperature varies from about 74° to 80° Fahrenheit.

Before describing the architecture of the club houses and the ancient tombs, I must call attention to the peculiar coinage or medium of exchange in Yap. First and foremost comes the stone money, which consists of limestone or arragonite wheels, varying from six or eight inches to twelve feet in diameter. These from their bulk form a most unwieldy medium of exchange. A man who had extensive business debts to meet would need a whole fleet of canoes or some ten yoke of buffaloes or bullocks and a waggon to transport his specie. Generally speaking, however, these stones are more for show and ornament than for use. The village club houses are called *Fe-bai* or stone money-houses, from the wheels of

FÉ, OR STONE MONEY OF YAP

stone which rest against their walls.   In any of the
settlements these great discs or wheels may be seen
outside the houses of the *Madangadang* or plutocrat class,
which here as well as elsewhere enjoy considerable distinction in national councils.

A perfect pair of large shells, the valves of the pearl
oyster, are also highly valued, and used as money.   The
natives call them *Yar-ni-Balao, i.e. Pelew island shells*, for
the early Yap navigators, with the usual recklessness of
folk of Malayan extraction, used to make extensive forays
on the pearl-shell beds of their long-suffering neighbours
of the Pelew group, and were forced at last to make their
title good by many obstinate battles by land and sea.
The smaller specimens of pearl-shell they used to thread
upon strings of hibiscus fibre or cinnet, about twenty on a
line, to be employed as small change.   In these days,
however, bags of copra or dried coconut kernel (*Tutu-ni-
fatuis-a-marau*) are employed as a medium of exchange.
This is produced in great abundance despite occasional
typhoons from the north, which make great havoc in the
palm-groves, and occasions no small rivalry amongst the
trading fraternity.   It may be observed that in the
northern islands of Yap and Ramung and the wilder
parts of the main island the money of the white man,
whether English, Spanish, or American, is hardly ever
accepted as legal tender, and it is only in the settlements
around the Spanish colony in Tomil Bay that the natives
have learned to recognise its value.

There is yet another treasure highly prized in Yap,
but which from its comparative rarity is seldom bartered.
It is a coarse shaggy white mat, resembling nothing so
much as goat or dogskin ; it is made from the beaten-
out bark of the Kal or lemon hibiscus tree.   It is not for
use, but merely for show, and is always kept religiously
rolled up in a safe corner.   It is exactly the counterpart
of the Ie-sina of Samoa, a white shaggy mat made out of
the fibres of the bark of a forest-tree, a species of Ramie.

After setting things in order on Ngingich I visited F. at Rul over the bay and met there his local trader Evan Lewis from Lai on the south coast, a worthy old Welshman who has married a Marianne wife and is blessed with a numerous family. Lewis had been in Lamotrek and Uleai, and readily agreed to put me up for a few days and assist me to gain information both from the Lai natives and from his own stock of knowledge. Next day Lewis brought up his vessel, and after taking in all needful supplies we dropped down the coast with a fine south-west breeze. Our vessel was China-rigged, *i.e.* her mainsail has six or seven supplementary bamboo yards running all the way across it ; this makes the boat sail closer up into the wind, and answer the helm more speedily. This method was introduced into Yap about eighteen years ago by a trading-skipper named Captain Holcombe — murdered a little while ago in a mutiny which arose among his crew off the Gilolo passage. It was not long before Lewis started with reminiscences of the ways of the Lamotrek islanders. "These people," said he, " have a regular grace before meat like Christians. When the fish is taken cooked out of the oven, before they taste a solitary fragment, one of them takes a bit from the head and solemnly mutters, '*Ka Toutop arai*'—'Do thou bless me, oh Toutop.' This Toutop is a Deity greatly honoured in the Lamotrek Pantheon. Then he throws away the bit, and the people immediately begin their meal. But if anyone were to partake of the food before the blessing was asked, the fishermen would have no luck any more, but storms and heavy gales. For Toutop, like the rest of the Caroline gods, is very jealous of any slight put upon him."

We sweep along, tacking every now and then to avoid the numerous weirs of stone and canework (*Thagal* and *Aech*) with which Yap fishermen have industriously filled the shallow lagoon that girdles their coasts. Look-

ing to landward every now and then, one after another
of the great Bachelor Halls or Club-houses with its
peculiar high-pointed gables and projecting eaves shows
up inshore and is swallowed up in the succeeding scenes
of ever-shifting woods and waters.   On either hand
light native craft every now and then pass, hail us,
and shoot away with a flirt of the dripping paddle.
And Lewis, having got fairly upon his hobby, continues
his parable thusly :—

"For four days before a fishing expedition the Lamotrek natives sleep apart from their wives.   They go
out fasting in order to ensure success.   When they
make their first haul they drink one green coco-nut
apiece, and put in shore for the ceremony of *Yaf-ilok*
—*The Coming in of the Fire*.   A fire is made, each
takes a fish, broils it, and eats it.   Each fisherman then
goes down to the sea, washes mouth and hands in the
salt water, and invokes the blessing of Aliu-set and
Sau-lal, gods of the sea.   This ceremony over, the distribution of the heap of fish commences.   If any women
or children come near and break the taboo by helping
themselves, the same will receive swelled ankles or
elephantiasis as a punishment and visible token of the
anger of the spirits." [1]

Just as we are approaching Lai, we run in close to
the seven waterworn islets of Gerem—an aggregation
of odd little pinnacles of limestone rock running up
some twenty feet in height, the resting place of several
species of sea-birds.   We notice two kinds of curlew,
one with curved bill (*Kaku*, Ponape *Chakor*), the other
with straight bill (*Kuling*, Ponape *Kulu*).   There is
also a sort of plover (*Gabachai*).   The islets are covered

---

[1] The same evening he told me of a belief prevalent on Lamotrek in the
existence of a squid that leaves the sea by night, ascends the coconut palms,
and drinks the Kaji or toddy from the calabashes hung to collect it.   The
natives of the Hervey Group have a similar story.—Was Aristotle right after
all in telling us 2000 years ago of an amphibious poulp or squid?

with rushes (*Pipi*), patches of parsley fern and clumps
of the silvery-leafed Heritiera or saltwater chestnut.

After a brief survey of Gerem we push off inshore
towards the *melil* or mangrove clumps which embosom
Lai and her palm-groves. The sun goes down, and
an intermittent gleam of torches shows up the depths
of the dark woods mingled with the coruscations of
the fire-flies floating in and out like fairy lamps in
some Aladdin's cave. A view-holloa greets us from
the beach as we slide into shallow water, and a *Fofod*
or bamboo raft manned by scantily-attired and wild-
looking figures puts off to us, finally landing us on
terra firma under a clump of *Ruai* or white mangroves
close by the copra houses where the cut-up coconut
kernels are stored previously to being put up in sacks
and taken up to the main station at *Rúl*.

We soon found our way to Lewis' house, which only
lies back some 150 yards, in its neat little compound
surrounded by a fence of fine bamboo, and overshaded
by a magnificent grove of areca and coco-palms. After
dinner some of the principal folk of the district called
in. Each carried under his arm a leaf-woven bag containing all the accessories for smoking and betel-nut
chewing, without which a native rarely stirs on a visit.

It would have been an interesting study for a painter,
the group of silent attentive Semitic faces, ebon in their
blackness, alternately rivetted upon my worthy old
interpreter and their new white visitor whom they scan
as if to read his innermost thoughts. Solemn countenances light up bit by bit, and the ice of reserve is
broken up. By and by the House went into a Com-
mittee of ways and means and a rather interesting
session was held. Guides were assigned to the stranger,
likewise tellers of old tales and teachers of that strange
hodge-podge of vowels and consonants which the Yap
folk fondly conceive to represent articulate speech. The
village patriach Gili-megak was told off for duty on

the reef, and undertook to provide at need a trustworthy native to help in specimen-collecting. He received the designation of Minister of the Sea and Reef, and chuckling, hugged the title to himself. His nephew Fatu-mak-ini-chik was appointed Minister of the Woods and Forests, his duty being to teach botany and point out ancient tombs and places of interest in the interior. By this division of labour we gained the goodwill of two powerful district chiefs. It may be remarked here that these very logical arrangements were carried out to the smallest detail at a very reasonable cost without any grumbling or shirking whatsoever, which speaks volumes in favour of certain phases of Caroline Island character when these people are properly directed and treated with ordinary courtesy.

Our plans thus being set in train, we fell to lighter business, and I was soon busily engaged in writing down all manner of miscellaneous and rapidly-volunteered information. Amongst other things, I learn that in a population of some 12,000 there are at least eleven dialects, and the number of different ways of saying *No* would delight a European diplomatist. In order to lose no opportunity for instruction, frequent reference was made to curious native customs, recalling certain restrictions ordained in Leviticus, and shadowed forth in the confessions of Lady Asenath of Fiji, to the natives of which place the Yap folk bear a strong resemblance in many ways. In touching on ancient history, it turns out that the people of Yap were both astronomers and intrepid navigators, extending their voyages far and wide over the great Caroline Archipelago, as far east as *Fanupei* (Ponape), and *Kuthiu* (Kusaie), a distance of some 1300 miles. They appear to have put wholesome fear into the wild folk of *Anangai* (Uleai), and *Pulawat* (Enderby I.), which latter lies about 160 miles west of Ruk, and is apparently a regular nest of Malay pirates. There seems really no reason to doubt the truth of this tradition of former maritime activity in these seas in which the old men of Yap are unanimous. The Ponapeans for their part have a legend about a being named *Chau-Yap*, *i.e.* King of Yap, who brought them the Kava plant. There is a place at the mouth of the Ronkiti River on the south coast named *Chakar-en-Yap*, or the place where Yap men landed. Also the Ponapeans have a small plantain with pink flesh and delicate flavour which they call *Ut-en-Yap*, or the Banana that came from Yap. A species of Eugenia they call *Kamp-en-Yap*. The word *Yap* seems to be used to mean anything foreign, just as the Pelew folk use *Barath* and Malays *Barat*. (*Cf.* Sanskrit *Barata* = India.) These facts appear to greatly strengthen the probability of the early commercial enterprise of the people of Yap.

Next morning we rose about eight. An hour later Lewis departed overland with a retinue of basket-bearing natives, to meet his employer on the other side, and discuss the best means of securing the greatest quantity of coconuts in the shortest time. Now this is the great local industry of Yap, though the natives are apt to work it rather spasmodically. Like the Northampton cobbler who declared there was nothing like leather, even so island traders pin their faith on copra, and appear never tired of discussing this apparently inexhaustible subject. The other day there was quite a row up the coast, so keen is the competition of the rival firms, because one trader boldly and adroitly secured for his employer five or six sacks of particularly fine *tabu* nuts which had been expressly set aside for his rival. This, allowing for shrinking of the copra, would represent no very great gain to the supplanter, but the incident caused a deal of talk notwithstanding. " There's no sound so sweet to me," said one of these keen drivers of bargains, " as the falling of a big ripe coconut, and there's nothing on earth like dollars." And I believe the practical man meant what he said, every word.

Punctually to his appointment the Minister of the Reef bade one of the Pilung or district chiefs to have a *fofod* or raft of bamboos ready that very morning. So about mid-day we started at the ebbing of the tide, my attendant propelling us with vigorous thrusts from a bamboo pole. We floated over beds of sea-grass, stopping every now and then to take note of some curious form of marine life, or to pop some curious crab or fish into the ever ready alcohol-bottle. Our craft was exactly adapted for expeditions in very shallow water, as she only drew some four inches. She was composed of twelve or thirteen stout bamboos, each about fifteen feet in length, lashed rudely together with cinet fibre, forming a framework some five feet in breadth, crossed by four or five transverse pieces of hibiscus wood. A packing-case in the centre served for a seat, and it goes without saying that shoes and stockings were dispensed with, and the oldest and rudest garments donned, for salt water is a grievous enemy to white ducks and broadcloth.

Between Lai and Gerem is a large patch of intensely yellow sand. We punted along in a diagonal direction, keeping always under the tail of the bank. By and by we came to a bed of corals, some foliaform, and some like a forest of minute antlers, with small blue and orange fishes playing in and out of the branches. It was exhilarating in such glorious weather gliding over strange waters, splashed by the sea-spray, played on by the cool breezes that start the ripples glittering under the glow of a tropical sun. The guide points out an old Ponapean friend, which he calls a *Rimich*, a curious form of marine life occupying one of the cracks in the coral—a gelatinous reddish brown creature, stretching out a forest of greedy suckers looking just like a clump of water-weeds. There is also a yellow variety called *Thilthil*. One touch and it shrinks down into its hole like a jack-in-the-box, and there abides safely bottled up until the danger is past.

We are now approaching one of the stone fish-dams or

weirs used for entrapping the unwary finny tribes. Neatly and solidly built of coral blocks, they are generally covered about a foot deep at high tide, and prove the bane of those in charge of trading craft, who are for ever running on them unexpectedly. Some are of considerable antiquity. Tradition assigns their origin to a pupil of the fairy goddess, Lé-gerem. They resemble the *Sai* of Murray Island and the elaborate structures built by early Australian Blackfellows at Brewarrina.

The first one we came to was rather more roughly put together than those we saw later on. Its height was about 3½ feet, breadth of wall about same, length some 15 yards.

My attendant has thoughtfully brought with him some pieces of *Yub* root in order to stupefy the small brilliant-coloured fishes that lurk amongst the branching coral. Catching them with a fine net is hopeless, and with the fingers all but impossible. But the effect of the Malayan root is magical ; the little victims one by one float up on their backs and soon find their way into the alcohol bottle that gapes for them, and is carefully wrapped in damp rags to prevent evaporation of the precious fluid within. But alas, alcohol will not preserve their wondrous hues. In but too many cases the cobalt turns to dull brown, the rose-pink to a brick-dust, and the bright yellow to a dismal gamboge or muddy amber. Specialists now tell me that formyle would have preserved the colours better—a hint that may be useful to future explorers. But the specimen hunter must be guided by successive defeats to ultimate victory, and must often be content to do his best with the materials which lie ready to his hand. We gathered in plenty of shells, for the most part resembling those of the Indian Ocean, and one violet and brown sea-urchin, a hideous sea-spider, a sea-centipede, and various quaint-looking crabs, amongst them a fine specimen of the *Cancrejo pintado* or painted crab of the Mariannes, colours light blue, red, yellowish-brown, and white. We caught sight of a yellow and black-ringed sea-snake (*Lilibots*), but he was too quick for us Our last find was a large sea-urchin, called *Ola'a*, with spines spotted brown and white, for all the world like the quills of a porcupine. We then pushed for shore, and after strolling along the beach a while returned to the house where Juan, Lewis' brother-in-law, a bright sensible lad, had got dinner ready and waiting. The afternoon was spent amongst the books and the animals of Lewis' household, which included a curious specimen of the vampire persuasion, known to the English as *fruit-bat*, and to the Yap people as *Magelao*, a very tame monkey (*Chiek*), a nice little beast, and a great playmate of the native children, a saffron Thomas cat of a saturnine and morose disposition, and a faithful house-dog—hero of a hundred fights, and possessed with the doggy instinct of continually jumping up with muddy paws and soiling spotless white duck suits. Tommy is a famous mouser, and holds his own in the household. Jealous in the extreme of my caresses bestowed on the monkey and the house-dog, he falls tooth and nail upon the old warrior-hound, and spitefully boxes his ears. But the grinning, gibbering and chattering Jacko beats him out of the field in no time ; and, minus some tufts of fur, Tommy disappears to the copra shed to hunt mice, where you can hear the old fellow growling and grumbling to himself for hours amongst the nuts.

Towards evening Lewis returned, and after dipping deeply into Lamotrek and Satawal words, he warned me of the unreliable character of the natives of central Carolines in general. " There's something queer about those Pulawat (Enderby I.) folk. 'Tisn't safe to go in their lagoon. They've cut off several vessels, and about six years ago they did for a trader called Shortman, as well as a Portuguese and a Japanese. The Hall Islanders aren't what you might call safe either, and the people of Losap aren't easy to get on with. In 1882, at a place called Onon, some way north of Ruk, the natives killed a native of Dublin called Edward Vowell, with the object of getting his native wife and going through his store. The Spanish always promised reparation, but it never came. The fact is, they won't punish the beggars, and the natives think they can do as they like. Why, it was only the other day that a Spanish cruiser went down to Tol to punish a chief who had murdered a Japanese trader, with never a reason but robbery. Do you think they punished him? Not much. He climbs on board and looks round him as bold as brass, and the commander gives him a glass of wine and a good dinner, and plenty to smoke, and some dollars as well. If they'd just hang a few of the chiefs it would all come right soon enough. Now the Japs wanted the other day to buy the group, and offered the Spanish six millions of dollars for it, but the Dons wouldn't deal at any price. You may be sure that if the Japs had the group there would be trouble coming pretty quick for some of those chiefs. One day the Spanish will be sorry they didn't fix the bargain when they had the chance. The way they spoil the natives is clean against all reason. A white man's life is worth as much as a native's, or I should say it ought to be. But if he isn't a Spaniard they don't seem to think so." And my host subsides grumbling under his mosquito-bar, and slumbers undismayed by the fierce roarings of the insect host trumpeting without the veil.

CHAPTER XVII

VISIT TO ONOTH AND GOROR

THE day after the trip on the bamboo raft Lewis went across the island again to hunt up more coconuts for the copra-shed, and Fatumak the Minister of the Woods and Interior turned up to take me down towards Goror in the southern promontory, where he said I should find some interesting relics of the olden time. We started out on a well-paved road bordered by areca palms and crotons (*Gotruk*) and by neat bamboo fences, behind which lie picturesque native houses. Passing through the settlement we plunged into a maze of narrow lanes running between high embankments crowned thickly with *môr* or dwarf bamboo, which gives quite a Japanese aspect to the landscape. The whole of the south side of the main island is seamed with a network of these little roads frequently paved with blocks of stone. The path was so narrow that the feathery stalks of the bamboos interlaced overhead in places, but the way was quite clear underfoot. Looking at the abundant ferns and mosses mantling the banks on either side of the path one fancies one's self wandering in one of the deep green lanes of Devon or Somerset. The climbing fern winds her graceful spirals round the stems of healthy young saplings of the forest sprung from the seeds of towering parents which at short intervals droop their shadows athwart our way. We pass bright green clusters of dracæna, with their delicate spikes of lilac bloom, which the Yap folk call *Rit* or *Rich*. (*Cf.* Maori *Rito*, a bud : anything green and fresh.) The pathway leads uphill behind a wide valley decidedly marshy in character, abounding in jungle and dotted with clumps of

Butral or wild ginger, with its purplish-mauve spikes of bloom, and of *Tifif*, a species of *Canna* or Indian-shot, which bears brilliant orange - yellow seeds. The path trends downwards over a little bridge until we reach a paved causeway with a thriving plantation of *Lak* or water-taro (*Colocasia*) with its broad arrow-headed leaves, reddish stems and pale yellow blossoms on our left, which recalls upon a small scale the magnificent lotus-pond in Tokio, the marvel of tourists, and the pride of Japanese landscape gardeners. Here and there a lofty banyan, with its shimmer of small-pointed leaves, looks down upon the rich tropical undergrowth of twining creeper and dense masses of fern, amongst which I discern my old acquaintance the *Nase* or *Nahe* of Southern Polynesia. (*Cf.* Pelews *Ngas*—a tree fern). We pass another *Lak* plantation made by the women of a slave village in the neighbourhood. Deep down it lies in a green hollow extending up the side of the hill in trim and regular beds planted out upon neat little terraces, banked up along the slope in true Japanese fashion. Those who question this may visit the Inland Sea, view the hill-slopes there, and set their doubts at rest. Scattered in the pathway underfoot lie the starry blossoms of the *Tenga-uai* or Cerbera lactaria, exhaling a sweet but heavy and sickly scent. Leaf, bark, and fruit alike contain a deadly poison, with the qualities of which both Micronesian and Polynesian are perfectly well acquainted. In fact, disappointed lovers on suicide intent frequently use the seeds, which, when swallowed, cause deadly spasms, speedily followed, however, by a merciful stupor.

A densely-wooded belt runs along the road some way. I made out the native chestnut (*Voi*), and the *Maluek*, a species of Morinda, closely akin to the plant from which the Malays and Polynesians alike obtain a rich yellow dye —under the shade of which the *Amaral*, a species of heavily-seeded nettle with a fiery sting, springs up amongst the stones. We came into a broad avenue flanked by tall forest trees, conspicuous amongst which is the *Bioutch* or Callophyllum, and the *Abit*, a curious tree bearing large dull-green fruit covered with yellowish patches, and shaped like a mango. The pulp of it is very sweet, but turns bitter on the palate. Natives relish it, but it has an offensive sickly odour that nauseates the European.

Strolling down the broadway in the welcome shade, we enter the long straggling village of Onoth, and come upon an ancient burying-place. By the side of the road stretches a low square pavement faced on each side with erect stone blocks or slabs of various shapes and sizes, generally about two feet in height, most of them slanting forward a little and tapering at the end. According to Fatumak there are two words used in Yap to denote a *pavement*. The platforms or paved floorings of houses or courtyards are *Paepae*—the very word used in a slightly extended sense by Southern Polynesians. Those over graves or marking the limits of burial grounds are called " *Una-pae.*"

We rested awhile, and Fatumak brought out betel-nut, leaf and lime from his ever-ready pouch, without which no native would think of travelling, any more than a Scandinavian peasant on his errands to fjord or sœter would forget his flask of corn-brandy. By and by Fatumak waxes unexpectedly eloquent in broken English, and turns out to have been a protégé of ill-fated Captain Holcombe. Pursuing our way we passed one of the Big Houses, named *Fe-Bai* or Money-Houses, from the massive stone or quartz wheels, the Fé or native currency, piled up against their sides. The sun was very hot, so we turned aside from the road, and sat down on the foundation of an old house over-shadowed by a great *Raual* tree (the *Kangit* of Ponape). Around us thrives a grove of areca palms in all stages of growth, and hard by are some thorny brakes of wild orange (*Gurgur-nu-Uap*) and limes (*Gurgur-morrech* or *morrets*), with globes of golden fruit lying scattered at their roots thick as apples in a Devonshire orchard at cider time. A boy, who met us on the way, and came along for curiosity, climbed a coconut tree, and fetched down some fine green nuts, the cool sweet water of which, with the addition of a few drops from a squeezed lime, made a most refreshing beverage after our hot walk. I complimented Fatumak on the neat roads leading through his parish and the surrounding districts, remarking that we were fortunate not to have made our journey on a rainy day. After heavy showers one would think each of these narrow lanes running between steep embankments must become a flooded ravine. It seems that every now and then in the rainy season a regular washaway occurs, upon which account the sides of the road are sometimes built or shored up with stone blocks. The neatness of the numerous roads intersecting this part of the island is a welcome contrast to the miserable forest trails of Ponape, where axe and knife are called for almost every minute to pass any way into the interior. The thick clumps of bamboo planted along the tops of the Yap embankments doubtless serve the double purpose of binding together the soil with their clinging root-fibres, and at the same time by their steady and vigorous growth of holding in check the everspreading multitudes of weed and creeper. The Hebrew prophet's figure of desolation, "a lodge in a garden of cucumbers," is expressive indeed to one who has viewed and fought with the hosts of the tropical forest. Rudyard Kipling knows and tells us what the *Rukh* of India can do. No vain words were those of Mowgli, Child of the Jungle, to Hathi, the Wild Elephant, when he bids him "*let in the bush*" upon the settlement of the unjust villagers, and blot out gardens, rice-fields, houses and all. The Hindu, fight as he may, but too often fights in vain, but the sturdy man of Yap says to Nature, "Thus far," and rolls back the invading forest from his little domain.

It is really pretty to see some of the paved causeways which are exactly similar to those which so struck Captain Wilson of the *Antelope* in the neighbouring group of the Pelews. When the path takes a steep gradient uphill, little flights of steps ascend it in true Japanese style, and one looks around instinctively to see a stone lantern, a Buddhist image, or the double cruciform outline of a graceful *Torii* confronting one, arching the wayside gateway of some woodland shrine. But here our fancy cheats us, and one wanders on with a sense of something lacking to make up a perfect scene.

Quitting our grove of palms we wend our way through Onoth until we reach the settlement of Goror, where we encounter a curious old mound on the left side of the roadway—the site of the ancient house of a chief of fame called *Tol-Riak*. Below this is a terrace, studded with upright and pointed slabs of basalt standing upon a low platform some three feet above the path with pieces of Fé or stone wheels leaning against the side. The largest of these is seven feet high and over six feet across, the smallest from a foot to two feet in diameter. Facing this is a low flat *Paepae* or platform, length some fifty feet and some forty in breadth, faced by eight erect slabs of black stone, each between five and six feet apart.

Whilst we are examining these odd-looking structures a tall, well set-up young man passed by and paused to wish us good-day. He wore on his neck a strikingly beautiful necklace of oblong scarlet shell-beads, fine at the ends and thick in the centre—a family heirloom which he refused to sell on any terms, probably looking upon it as a talisman. The natives call these *Thauai*, and they are brought up from the Pelew Islands along with the precious stone and shell money. After making a rough sketch of Tol-Riak's house and the platforms, we departed, scrambling over a stone wall of aged and moss-grown appearance, which forms the boundary of the village, and return to Lai in time for the mid-day meal.

That evening about eight o'clock Fatumak appeared to take me to see a native dance, so leaving Lewis busy at his accounts, we started off. About a quarter of an hour's walking brought us to a big house on the outskirts of the settlement of Ngiri, where little groups of folk were sitting on a raised stone platform chatting in the beautiful moonlight. Stopping a few moments to gossip, we leisurely strolled on through the waving shadows to the dance-house at the further end of the village, crossing several *gitrikitral* or little bridges of stone and *Thith*, or single felled palm-trunks spanning ravines or muddy pools which lie in our path. These latter required some effort of balance to negotiate safely. We found some forty persons assembled, and more kept dropping in by twos and threes until behold, a goodly company seated on their mats spread out on the sandy soil. Numbers of dried coconut shells with abundance of dry husk were being piled up into three heaps ready to be set on fire to illuminate the proceedings at the proper moment. A band of intending performers are busy stripping the leaflets from palm-fronds and twisting them up into odd shapes like horns for head ornaments to stick into their bushy periwigs, producing a wild and weird effect in the firelight which now began to flicker. They also bind them like ribands or fillets round their legs, ankles and wrists. At last a row of some twenty figures, all men, forms up with their backs to the stone platform, and a cluster of small boys at the end to the left. After one or two false starts the orchestra gets under weigh. The line of dancers is swaying in rhythm to a wild chant pitched in the dolefullest of minor keys, clapping their hands in time, and slapping their chests and thighs at regular intervals with a report like pistol-shots. Some are garlanded green with fern, others wear bead-necklaces. Some wear bunches of flowers stuck behind their ears ; all of them unclothed save for the usual cincture of grass or leaf-filaments. Some wear *Roai* or carven wooden combs—the emblem of the Pilung or upper classes, stuck in front of their fuzzy chevelure —a motely assemblage. Many of the contortionists wear a slight beard—a thing rarely seen in Ponape, as it is generally eradicated by shell tweezers. The chants, doubtless full of poetic fancy and topical, not to say tropical, allusion, sound like a dismal long-drawn caterwaul to a stranger's ear. Oh for a phonograph or graphophone to bottle up these quaint cacophonies, and photograph the sound of each and every syllable on its unerring cylinders. It would surely create a lively impression and would turn out the most sensational miracle yet performed by a white visitor to these out-of-the-way regions. Imagine the horror of some good old heathen at the uncanny machine all ears and voice, giving back the very words and tone of some wild, rollicking chorus. I'm afraid at first it would prove too much for his nerves, though after a while perhaps the mysterious engine might lose some of its terrors.

The bonfire is now blazing away merrily. Three large piles of the oily shells are crackling, sputtering and pouring out on every side, pungent whiffs and spurts of eddying smoke and trains of hissing sparks, for the wind sweeps freshly through the groves to-night. A simultaneous war-whoop echoes down the line of straining bodies, and the first part of the performance is over.

The antic contingent of small boys who have been chiming in shrilly throughout, disperses, melting off into the dark groves beyond like a troop of chattering little monkeys.

There is a brief interval devoted to betel-nut chewing and smoking *Ligich* or native cigarettes, and shells of *Atchif*, sweet coco-toddy (the *Ati* of the Mortlock islanders), are handed round.

The second performance starts with a prodigious

rhythmic clapping of hands. The chant rises higher and shriller, running up the scales, and missing or jumping several notes of the natural sequence in a manner which to a European ear leaves the strangest sense of something incomplete.   Are these folk tone-deaf?

The central figure in the row is a tall burly native dressed in the scantiest of girdles, bristling with dozens of split and twisted coconut leaflets disposed like streamers shimmering and waving about his person. The chant ends as before in another deep-throated war-cry.

Here a brisk shower of rain drives us indoors for awhile, but the unconquered bonfire burns bravely on.

The third and last scene resembles a Maori *Haka* or war-dance. All stand up in line striking up a livelier chant with a trampling accompaniment which goes faster and faster as the dancers warm to their work. The artists alternately face front and flank, swaying bodies in unison, marking off the cadence with a measured stamping.   This dance is named after that rascally hen-roost robber, the *Galuf* or Iguana, a personage much in evidence in local legend—the sinuous turns and twists and violent convulsions of limb interpreting the stealthy and serpentine movements of the creature prowling on its marauding errands. When the chanting and trampling are at their highest, a long-drawn triple yell marks the climax, and the figure abruptly ends.

Fatumak, sitting close by on his mat, puts in his word. " Galuf he one big thief—all same dog he eat egg (' *hen-fruit*,' *sic*), he steal meat." To the question, " Are the Galuf and the dogs the only thieves in Yap ? " my truthful mentor replies, " Plenty Yap man go steal. First he make pray one god, Luk ; he help him—other man no can catch. All same me think that god plenty busy all the time. Sometimes man he pray—what for Luk no hear ? Thief get punish."

Can the wise and benevolent-looking Fatumak be thinking of some youthful escapade that brought him a smarting skin, or maybe a broken head? He looks away, and promptly turns the subject, and falls to praising the skill of Yap natives in dancing. The performance which we had just witnessed was very much the same as those in vogue in Ponape and the Marquesas. All over the Pacific the pastime has been strongly discountenanced by zealous missionaries as savouring too much of heathenish superstition and laxity. It is true that some of them have objectionable features, yet many of them are graceful and refined, and would prove a decided novelty and attraction in a London drawing-room.

The night's entertainment is over, and the party is breaking up and parting salutations are passing. " Quefel a nep—mol." " Good is the night—sleep! " Followed by a shower of farewell greetings we made for home, gliding over the slippery wooden bridges, striding low walls and trunks of fallen trees, and " padding" through mud and over stones—the cicalas shrilling in the moon-light, and the palmfronds fluttering in the trade overhead, and flinging a thousand waving shadows athwart our path.

A few days later Fatumak and I determined to go across the island to Milai, examine the shrubs, trees and plants, and collect some of the seeds of the more interesting of them. Ngiri lay first on our way with its trim court-yards enclosed by fences of bamboo and thorny acacia, and the inevitable limestone, calcite or arragonite money-wheels propped up against the foundations of the more pretentious dwellings. Our party consisted of five boys carrying baskets, besides Fatumak and myself. We crossed numerous little stone bridges, each composed of a single large flat slab like those of China and Japan, and before long arrived at the structure known as *Fana-Mouk*, the great house of Tanis, a chief of old, whose burial-place lies below. The lower platform is about three feet above the ground, with five Fé or limestone wheels leaning against its front, two of them supported behind between a couple of upright slabs to keep them in place. The upper tier—four feet in height—is ornamented by a line of twelve upright pointed slabs of basalt. Above are still standing the rudely carved pillars—about twenty feet in height—that once supported the edifice, of which a portion of the skeleton only is left. Across the road to the left is a low flat evenly paved platform facing the larger one. Behind this is a flat table of coral called *Rorou*, supported evenly upon four pieces of rock, doubtless for some superstitious observance of olden time. (A similar contrivance is seen upon the site of the Devil-Temple upon Bau in Fiji, and at Gaua upon St Maria in the Banks group.)

Our survey over we climbed the little hill at the back of the settlement, following a narrow pathway neatly paved with level blocks of stone, then after going down a line of cane-fences bordered by palms, crotons and tall dracænas, we passed a little cluster of houses, one of the numerous bush settlements rarely trodden by the foot of a white man. By the roadside growing out by a fence is a species of wild fig, *Ote* or *Wote*, bearing small reddish rough fruits on its trunk after the manner of the Malay apple or Eugenia. Yet another of these *Unapei* or queer stone platforms lies on our left. This the folk call *Koyam*. Our way winds in and out some lovely fresh green lanes, and again I am struck with the luxuriance and beauty of the ferns, the *Lobat*, a delicate species of Adiantum or maiden-hair, being specially prominent. Then our road turns into a high causeway running through a series of swamps with clumps of taro planted thick amongst the plashy hollows. The fertility of the soil must be very great, almost equalling in richness the valleys of Tahiti. Abundant signs of cultivation are seen on every hand in the numerous yam-vines carefully trained and festooned around the protecting trunks and boughs of the trees that overshadow their hidden tubers. We saw on our way three sorts of butterflies, the marsh fritillary, the small

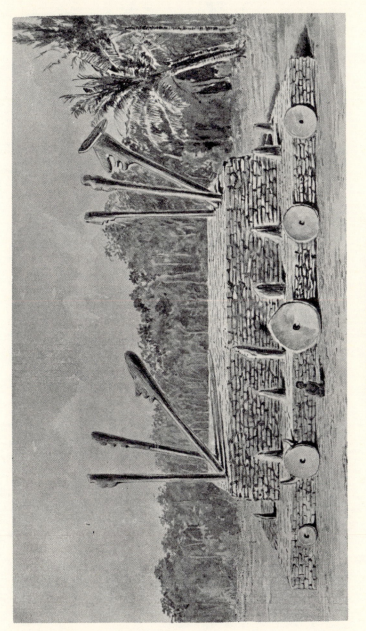

THE RUINED HOUSE OF TANIS

sulphur, and small blue; of other winged life, two or three little dark coloured bush-birds, possibly a species of Myagra or Fly-catcher. Tahiti fully parallels Yap in the scarcity of land-birds, which is rather strange, considering the far superior area of the first-mentioned island. We passed on through Petalan, where there is a small Fe-Bai or Club House, and after climbing another short hill stairway we came to an ancient cemetery where we saw four or five low burial platforms occupying the centre of an open square. Around them were growing various shrubs and saplings, amongst them a sturdy custard-apple tree, which the Yap natives call *Sausau*, and the Ponapeans *Chai* or *prickly* (to which latter root the Yap word " *Choi* " for the pandanus or screw pine is also referable). Along our route we noticed a variety of wild ginger with a dark red spike of flowers, the *Ramilu* with its huge long clubbed leaves (the *Tong* of Ponape), a sort of thornless acacia (*Gumar*), a species of paper mulberry (*Wapof*), a Callophyllum, with pear-shaped fruits, plenty of wild pandanus and arrowroot, and several other shrubs and forest trees well known to me in Ponape, amongst which I recognised the tree bearing the valuable varnish-nut, the *Adidh* or *Adid* of Yap, the *Ais* of Ponape, the *Aset* of the Mortlock Group (*Parinarium laurinum*).

We pass through numerous plantations of swamp-taro, the causeway on either side bordered by a deep cutting. We are drawing near to Milai—Anglice, " *The Plantation or Garden* " (*Cf.* Samoan *Malae*, a clearing, village green). It is well-named. To our right and left is a perfect nursery of yam-vines, holding fast with clinging tendril, and spiral winding stem to the breadfruit trees that shade them. As we marched down the central avenue of the village amidst the yapping of half an hundred *Pillis* or yellow dogs, and the audible comments of a dozen or two idlers, we fancied at first there are two or three sailing vessels in harbour. From a nearer view, however, we sighted a big pile of stones, bristling with tottering poles, the " *disjecta membra*" of an ancient lodge or club house, built on foundations solid as Brighton pier, looking down upon the tides that for many a year have been lapping idly at its base. The natives give the pile the name of *Masisin*. As we halted on the beach a bevy of the local " Bad Boys " pushed forward and displayed a vast interest in the *Obachai* or foreigner. Patiently I sat taking notes, with a crowd of little ebon rogues chattering and gibbering around me. Presently Fatumak dashed in and administered several sounding slaps, which induced the juvenile Hooligans to withdraw to a distance, where they stood hushed in respectful silence, turning up the whites of their eyes in deprecation, like a fox-terrier at the harsh and severe voice of her chiding master. Fragments of subdued chatter presently reach us, *Felagan, felagan, babier,* " Scratch away, scratch away at paper " ; *Machamach tarreb-arragon,* "Magic all same " ; *Dakori i tamadag,* " I'm not scared a bit " ; *Kan, kan, tarreb-arragon a kan,* " Devil, devil, all same devil."

In Milai the Capuchin Padres have a station whence no doubt they exercise much influence for good amongst this simple and primitive folk, whose nature is the strangest medley of conflicting qualities. A truly wonderful indolence alternates with equally wonderful spells of industry. A very remarkable and unique scheme of national morality balances the licensed debauchery of the Big House. Yap men are middling honest, yet they count in their Pantheon a patron saint of Thieves. Once they were great navigators, warriors, and astronomers. Now, instead of taking the trouble of going up to Uleai and Mokomok and Pulawat, they let their tributaries or vassals have the trouble of the journey down. Now and then they indulge in a mild skirmish amongst themselves, generally over the abduction of some local Lady Asenath, or, as the Japanese would term it, *Geisha girl.* The young men only remember astronomy enough to plant yams by and look out for wet weather, but the old men know the

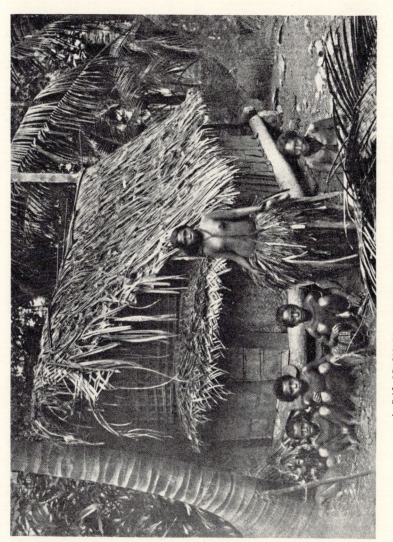

A *PAL* OR SMALL HOUSE RESERVED FOR THE WOMEN

ancient names of the stars from north to south and east
to west (*Cf.* list of Yap star names and days of the
moon's age in Appendix).   Altogether the people of
Yap are a new type, full of interest for the anthropologist.
Their very virtues are as illogical as their vices.

Whilst we were sitting thus moralising on the strand of
Milai in the blazing noontide, one of the village chiefs
appeared on the scene.   I gave him a strong cigar, which,
after puffing some little while, he passed over to one of
the small boys, who fitted the stump into a long bamboo
tube, and thus equipped strutted up and down the beach,
thrusting out his little stomach before him like a pouter-
pigeon.

Fatumak handed some betel-nut to one curious
youngster, who attempted to chew his first quid with
doleful results to himself and to the huge delight of the
mirthful imps, his comrades.

After taking a few more notes on Yap methods of
canoe-building we started to return, passing along a
smooth stone causeway which runs about two miles
parallel with the sea, under an avenue of palms which
leads us up to the settlement of *Gal* or *Kal*.   Soon after
leaving Gal we come to a road cut between two steep
embankments of rich red soil.   This path, solidly and
evenly paved with flat blocks of basalt, leads over the
little hill-rise down to the fertile lowlands of Nimiguil.
A little further on we came to a steep bluff where a *Pal*
or house, tabu to the women, overhangs the road, built
out upon a substantial pile of stones.   As we struck
inland two of the Big Houses came in view with plenty
of stone money as usual piled against their foundations.
Some of these must be very old, as they are all over
cracks, with ferns and weeds actually growing out of
them.   Propped up against a platform on our left we
passed a huge specimen twelve feet in diameter, a foot
and a half in thickness, and the hole in the centre two
and a half feet across.   A little further on we saw a

second platform on the right side of the road. Leaning against it was another piece of these cumbrous tokens of wealth with an inner circle cut lightly round the hole in the centre. These mark the settlement of Ginifai. A brisk shower of rain drove us into the shelter of the nearest house. When the sun shone out again we resumed our journey, crossing a creek by a bridge of felled coconut palm trunks. Another of the Big Houses was passed, the platform below it faced with erect basalt slabs, some inclining to a conical form, with the inevitable wheels of limestone propped up below against its base. Our path lies over another rising bit of ground, bordered with Crotons and Dracænas and bamboo fences. The morning glory runs riot in the brushwood, and here and there in the jungle wave the feathery tassels of the *Rei*, a sort of reedgrass. There we noticed an orange-fruited Canna or Indian shot, and a great quantity of wild pandanus (*N'er*).

We reached the bush town of Tabinif on the top of the ridge. Thence the path trends downhill past a large pond of *Lak* or Aquatic-taro which is blossoming out into large yellowish spathes, the very image of one of our hothouse arum lilies. We caught sight of more ancient stone platforms considerably overgrown with weeds, and found our way down to a primitive sort of village called Balakong after a long tramp along a causeway running through the salt-marshes parallel with the sea. The mudflats on either hand were pitted thickly with the holes of a little black and white speckled crab, each armed with one scarlet claw of a ridiculously disproportionate size. By the wayside we found growing a burr-bearing plant called *Kurrukur* and a curious marsh-weed, bearing on its stem instead of flowers soft red spongy caps like little fungi.

After crossing a shallow creek bridged with coconut trunks we reached the outskirts of Ngiri and so on to Lai, where we found Lewis still busy amongst the coconuts and trading accounts. A venerable old man was with him, whose long black beard streaked with grey gave him a most patriarchal appearance. He was one of the hundred Yap men to whom the King of Korror in the Pelews gave permission in 1882 to quarry out the wheel-money from the limestone rocks of Kokial in the neighbourhood. His name was Takabau, somewhat recalling the name of Thakombau, a former monarch of Fiji. From him I took some lessons in Pelew that very afternoon, and learned some very strange and harsh sounds which would be a wonderful addition to the stock-in-trade of a travelling conjurer-man at a country fair. I subjoin a few of the dulcet sounds taken at random to give an idea of Pelew phonesis. *Parakarakuth* means to adhere ; *Thillakuthuk* is cement ; *Umbebakokle* to go afloat ; Friendship is *Klubbakul* ; Ancient is *Arakwothal* ; To sleep, *Mokoivivi* ; To bake, *Gnulsekkle* ; Bright, *Mongulthoyok* ; Cold, *Kullakult* ; Dark, *Milkulk* ; Dish, *Koknal* ; Ebb-tide, *Krakus* ; Story, *Kulthakathuk* ; Foolish, *Dengarengal* ; Hard, *Tharakarak* ; Hot, *Klald, Kald, Keald* ; Lobster, *Karabrukkle* ; Frog, *Thagathuk*.

Between Pelew lessons and Lewis' Lamotrek yarns and Juan's tales of the Mariannes time passes quickly, and the pencil scampers merrily over paper.

CHAPTER XVIII

TO TOMIL, LAI, ELIK, BY BOAT TO NORTH YAP

IN the morning Gilemegak brought two bits of orange-red rock from Elik, and a peculiar black and white banded species of cray-fish called *Tumal* (Palinurus). About two o'clock in the afternoon we embarked on Lewis' China-rigged sailing-boat—two men, two boys, one Marianne man, Lewis and self. Fatumak we picked up at Ngiri. Tne occasion of our visit to the colony was the marriage of Lewis' employer F., of the German firm at Rul, to a Marianne girl. Now this calls for some little explanation. Traders in Yap seem to find a life of single blessedness tedious, and as white women in these parts are about as rare as snowflakes in summer, it follows that an alliance more or less permanent must follow with the daughters of the soil. But Yap ladies are very, very dark, and by no means remarkable as a rule for personal charms, so it is only rarely that one of *these* is chosen. Moreover, the Yap papas, with more wisdom than one would have expected from them, entertain a decided objection to a white son-in-law. They use a proverb — *Roro fan roro, wetsewets fan wetsewets, rongadu fan rongadu.* "Black to black, white to white, red to red." All the rest is *balebalean* or folly. Now note a beautiful provision of Nature. In the Marianne or Ladrone Group some 450 miles up north, the female native population considerably exceeds the male. There are in consequence many marriageable young girls of the Chamorro or aboriginal race of the group—a handsome debonnair Malayan people of light-brown complexion who do not share the prejudices of the Yap folk against the white man. These Marianne ladies are supposed to make excellent housewives, and in consequence are much sought after by the traders of Yap. But remark here the absence of those irregular alliances so frequent in the Pelew Islands and the Eastern Carolines. The Catholic priests set themselves most strongly against such practices, insisting on an ecclesiastical marriage of the contracting parties. This marriage, moreover, they will not solemnise without first making strict inquiry into the antecedents of the parties, and before the husband, whether Jew or Protestant, becomes formally reconciled to the Catholic Church. I fear, however, that many hollow conversions follow in consequence. I certainly don't think the worthy F. had any very deep convictions.

But to continue. The apparel of our crew was of the very scantiest description and would put a London County Council to headlong rout. The man at the helm, the best dressed of the crew, wore a shabby old brown hat, an equally disreputable jacket of blue dungaree almost dropping to pieces with age, and the narrowest of native girdles of cloth. The crew were dressed in meagre cinctures of coconut leaf filaments or beaten-out fibres of hibiscus bark. Shirts from their rarity are much prized in Yap, and trousers, when worn at all, are used as a sort of shawl, the legs tightly knotted in front and falling over the chest. Every native on board carries with him a basket filled with the threefold apparatus for chewing betel. (1) A stock of betel-nuts which look something like big acorns, the fruit of the Areca palm (called *Pûg* in India, *Pagua* in the Mariannes, *Buok* in the Pelews, *Bu* in Yap, and *Bonga* in the Philippines, the Malay Archipelago and even in the Micronesian area). (2) A bundle of leaves from a species of Piper Methysticum (variously called in Yap *Langgil, Thlanggil,* or *Gabui*). These are used as an envelope for the quid, to which their pungency lends an agreeable zest.   (3) The third constituent is the lime, the *chunam* of the Malays, carried in a bamboo tube sometimes covered with quaint tracery of carved ornamentation.

(The parallel and connection between betel-nut chewing and kava-drinking has been noticed at some length in the description of kava-making in Ponape, and may be of interest to those who study the foodstuffs of native races.)

The betel-nut chewing grievously blackens the teeth, reddens the saliva, and imparts an extra tinge of carmine to the lips, which does not enhance the attraction of these homely ebon countenances.

We reached Gerard's island of Ngingich about midday, and in the afternoon went ashore to attend F.'s marriage, and the feast that followed it.   The wedding went off as such matters usually do, the bride painfully shy, the bridegroom nervous and fidgety, the priest stern and austere. No slippers, no showers of rice, and no wedding cake. The folk who seemed the merriest were the Marianne relatives and the native servants and workmen, who scented goodly pickings to come from bakehouse, oven, and store-room.   Our host indeed gave us a very good dinner, and towards evening things went merrily.   Next morning I found the indefatigable F. had risen early, and was counting over a large number of empty bottles with a thoughtful countenance.   This done he proceeded to stock-taking, entering copious notes in a great ledger—the beau-ideal of a business man—patient, thorough, and minutely exact in all his dealings ; a bit of a slow-coach, perhaps, and lacking his neighbour Gerard's brilliant capacity for native languages, but for all that a fair type of the material from which Germany, if her methods were a little more up-to-date, could build up many a successful colony in the Pacific.   This the Godeffroys of Hamburg in the past sixty years have proved beyond question by the well-educated and industrious type of traders whom they selected to represent their interests in these out-of-the-way regions. And this gives Germany a considerable advantage over her trading rivals in Pacific waters. A glance at any of R. L. Stevenson's or L. Becke's South Sea sketches and short tales will give the reverse of the picture, showing the ungenerous animus felt and shown by but too many English-speaking rivals of these Germans in the wide trading competition in Pacific lands.

Nov. 16th.—Meeting Mr E., O'Keefe's manager on Tarrang Island, I made an agreement to finish my work at Lai with Lewis, and to return in a few days to spend the rest of my time in Yap, under O'Keefe's hospitable roof. Then if I wished to see the northern part of Yap, where many interesting ancient remains were to be found, a boat and crew would be placed at my disposal to take me up to Pilau, where O'Keefe had a station looked after by an intelligent Sonsorol boy who would help me in all matters needful. So on this understanding Lewis and I returned by sea to Lai, putting in for an hour at the wharf at Iloech in order to set down Lewis' son and daughter, who had to walk over to the Catholic school of Santa Cruz, lying about two miles up country from the landing-place.

The wharf lay amongst a belt of white mangroves. It was about two hundred yards long, compactly and neatly built of coral blocks. In Yap, as in the Pelews, these structures are called *Kades* or *Kachers*. A Big House was looking down upon the creek, faced as usual with some limestone wheels. The height of the upper and lower platforms on which it stands was ten feet. The high pointed gable, bisected in the middle by a ridge projecting outwards at an angle at the end, gave it a curious and striking appearance.

We arrived at Lai in the evening, and next day I got Fatumak to fix up another *fofod* or bamboo raft in order to go down to the islet of Elik, near Goror Point, Yap's Land's End, and get some more pieces of the orange-coloured rock. On our way down we examined some stone fish-weirs near the Catholic mission station, as well as a mighty terrace built of basalt and coral blocks running a little way out into the shallow water, the remains of one of the club houses, which, to judge from the loftiness of the ridge-poles with which it bristles, must have been a very conspicuous object out at sea. When the tide ebbed we picked up a good many pink and white spiral shells on the reef, and added some sea-spiders and crabs to the collection of marine creatures, turning over the blocks of coral and disturbing a good many *Goloth* or sea-eels (muræna) from their hiding places. Fatumak, trying to catch a small crab, incautiously put his hand into a deep crack and was instantly seized by the finger with a set of needle-like fangs. With frenzied cries of "*Wei-Wei-Wei*," he danced wildly around in the shallow water with an enraged *Goloth* hanging on tight as a bull-dog, and his rage was not assuaged until he had chopped his foe into little bits with a long knife. The pantomime of his sufferings was noticed by a party of native workmen who were busy near the fishpen loading up a canoe with sea-weed to use as a fertiliser for the local Padre's kitchen garden. In place of sympathy, they greeted my companion's mishap with an unfeeling cackle of laughter, upon which he angrily rebuked the gatherers of vegetable refuse for the menial nature of their employment and their beggarly appearance. They certainly looked a remarkable crew with their *Ruatch* or wide hats of pandanus leaf, shaped exactly like those of Chinese coolies, whilst their ragged attire, lean bodies, and hollow, staring eyes, gave them a distinctly doleful and starveling air.

After this little adventure we made our way down to Elik and chipped off the required geological specimens. I wanted to double Goror Point, but Fatumak advised me not to make the attempt unless in a stout canoe, for the water was deep under the tail of the island, and there were strong currents which might sweep us out to sea.

BACHELORS' CLUB-HOUSE AT LAI, SOUTH YAP

Moreover, the deeper pools in the lagoon at South Point swarmed with sharks (*Aiong*), by no means an encouraging reflection to two navigators in so frail a craft as our bamboo raft.

On my return to Lai, Juan, Lewis' Marianne brother-in-law, told me a tragic tale from Guam of the suicide of two lovers who threw themselves from a cliff overlooking the Diamond Bridge near Agaña. He also gave us an eerie story of the apparition of a spectral white deer to his grandfather hunting in the dusk in the woods above Port Luis. The dog refused to follow, but the hunter went on, and, in his eagerness on the trail, fell over a precipice and got severely shaken and bruised. For my part, I tell Juan that the best method of raising spirits is to pour them down pretty often. According to Juan's account, this is no uncommon trick of the woodland spirits to play on mortal men who rashly invade the mountain wilderness. This superstition answers to the *Bake-mono* of Japan, and to that of the *Puka* of Irish legend, the keynote of many of the fables of the land of Nippon. It seems very deeply fixed in human nature, for we find the idea universal. What first gave rise to so singular a notion is a problem that few would care to solve offhand.

The next two days Lewis, who for a wonder was not chasing after copra, as if the trees would the next minute stop bearing for ever, told me a great deal about Lamotrek star names, which agree very well (1) with some of their equivalents I got in Ponape ; (2) with the list collected by Kubary in the Mortlock Islands ; (3) with those I afterwards obtained in Yap from Lirou, the chief of Tomil ; (4) with the Uleai star names obtained by Chamisso as early as 1815. They illustrate the intelligence, enterprise, and great astronomical knowledge of the early Caroline Island navigators, and agree in a marvellous manner from west to east of the group, which, as aforesaid, embraces over six hundred islands and a total sea and land surface of some 1,800,000 square miles, all along which area the star names are practically the same. The curious reader will see the Ponape, Mortlock, Lamotrek, Yap, and Uleai star-names and days of the moon's age classified together in the Appendix.

On making inquiries about the interesting subject of tattooing, which natives call *Eloi* or *Iloi*, it was found that the ceremony was universally practised and free to all. Compare the Samoan verb *Elei*, to mark or stamp the native cloth with designs from the Upeti or printing-frame, or again the root may be the Maori *Iro* (Whaka-*iro*, to write or carve). The Japanese word *Iro*, colour, may be a remote derivative. Taking Taman, a stalwart native from Goror district for an example, I noticed that on his chest were marked two large representations of the *Roai* or *Ruai*, the native comb of the wood of the white mangrove, the shape of which greatly resembles those from North New Guinea and the Solomon Islands seen in the British Museum. Around the thighs ran a dense fish-tail ornamentation, which, with the chevron, is a frequent feature of Yap designs. On asking whether there are any very aged men upon Yap, my informant replied that there was one in Goror over a hundred years old, by name Giltuk. On arriving at the marriageable age the young Yap native wears a cord dyed a dull red, of the baste of the *Kal* or Hibiscus tiliaceus bark, twisted round his loins or worn around his neck. Like the Ponapeans, they use the bark of the mangrove as a colouring agent, and from it extract a yellow or reddish brown dye.

On the 19th of November I returned laden with curios, and took up my quarters on Tarrang with Mr E. Captain O'Keefe was still an absentee. Mrs O'Keefe, a Nauru lady who speaks excellent English, received me most graciously, and set apart a Sonsorol boy named Matsis to wait on me. Naturally his name soon became corrupted into " Matches," a designation which sorted well with his occasional flashes of ill-humour whenever Mr E., who is a somewhat choleric individual, threatened to lay him out

with a " stuffed club " for carelessness or slurring over his
duties, which in the busiest times were not very onerous.

On Sunday I was staying over at Gerard's island of
Ningich, so on Monday, November 22nd, the sailing boat
Eugenie turned up at the wharf in charge of Xavier, a half-
caste Portuguese, to take me and my belongings up to
Pilau. We started about eight o'clock on a lovely morning with a pleasant breeze, and leaving Tarrang's picturesque
island astern we ran along inshore of Tomil and its bordering of mangrove clumps. After many tacks we got past
Tomil Point, and cracked on all sail, calling to mind E.'s
missive, " Get away quick from Ningich and up coast with
the half-tide, for there is a place up north which the
vessel can only get through at high tide. Whatever
other stores you want, you can get from Gerard's trader,
C. Brugmann, over at Map. If O'Keefe returns whilst
you are away we will send up a boy overland, or the
Eugenie shall come to fetch you back."

Sweeping along towards Gatchepa, one notices the tall
terra-cotta hued gables of the club houses shooting up
between the clustering masses of coconut palm clothing
the lowlands in a waving robe of tenderest green. Behind
them the slopes, clear of bush, lead up to the crowning
plateau some five hundred feet above sea level. The wind
presently fell, leaving us drifting slowly on in the fierce
rays of the noonday sun. On looking over the cargo
I was amazed at the quantity of canned goods, beer,
kerosene and tobacco piled up in the trim little craft. I
felt quite like one of the novelist's traders starting a new
station, and indeed that mode of life was really to be
mine for a week or so, except that curios and not copra
were the objects of my search. Naturally I asked some
questions of the Macao man to guide me in my barter-
ing operations. I found that the natives did not at all
understand the value of foreign money. They seem to
have no sense of proportion whatever. When visiting the
European settlement at Tomil, they have been known to

pay down three or four dollars for a few sticks of tobacco at twenty-seven to the pound. On the other hand, in their simplicity they will tender a meagre half-dollar for a musket or cross-cut saw. Nearly all business there goes by barter. Shells of the pearl-oyster, of which there is a large yearly output from the Pamotus or Low Archipelago, are imported from Tahiti at a moderate rate, and exchanged for copra with the Yap people at a very profitable rate, the natives preferring them to the *Yar-ni-Balao* or Pelew Island shell, which next to the stone money is their most favoured currency. Waist-cloths or *Lablab* (Samoan *Lavalava*) of Turkey red for the young men, and blue or deep yellow for the old men, are held in high estimation ; medium sized fish hooks are also in demand. Tobacco appears to be eagerly sought for, to judge from the following equations :—2 sticks of tobacco = 1 large fowl ; 1 stick of tobacco = 1 small fowl ; 1 box matches + 1 stick of tobacco = 8 fish of moderate size ; 1 pair of coarse blue trousers and 1 Turkey red shirt = 3 weeks' wages ; but this last is looked on as rather extravagant pay, the recipient being greatly envied for his stately trappings, of which one of the district chiefs speedily relieves him.

All this discussion served to kill time, the *Eugenie* continually tacking and tacking, losing two feet to advance three. E. had thoughtfully put in the boat a copy of Thackeray's " Virginians " from O'Keefe's well-stocked library. It seemed very incongruous with the surroundings, and vividly recalled to mind a certain Christmas-tide spent on Washington Island in the North Marquesas, when in my cottage at Vaipae Bay, in the intervals of dictionary - making and fishing, I used to read " David Copperfield " and " Great Expectations," ancient volumes left there by certain dead and gone American settlers. It is wonderful how literature penetrates into this distant corner of the world. In a boatshed on the sands of Hana-mate or Deadman's Bay on Hiva-Oa I actually found a tattered copy of the *Sporting Times.*

"Whence fluttered down this tale of Town, by land or sea or air? How it came—well, I cannot tell, but it was surely there." Thinking of that little bit of pink paper brought back in a moment Ole Brer Rabbit, the Shifter, the Talepitcher, and "pore old Romano in the garb of old gall innercently exhibited"; thence by a natural transition the mind turns to thoughts of restaurants and *lunch.* It is high time, for the sun overhead is looking straight down into the wells or pits in the reef where the octopus lurketh, to borrow a picturesque Samoan metaphor for high noon. "Ua nofo le Fee i le malua, ua nofo-i-fee foi le la." "The squid he sitteth in his cell, the sun he sits on top." All this while we have been slowly getting up to the south end of Map Island (so called, says E., because it wants mapping out again so badly after the incomplete Spanish survey). Close here is a village variously known as Amon, Umin or Amin, where there is a big stockade which the local natives have erected. They have a standing dispute with the people of Rekin, one of the neighbouring settlements, over the carrying off of some *Mespil* or slave-woman. Every now and then an angry band of neighbours come up and try to beat the children of Amon out of their lines. First, so my informant tells me, there is a vast deal of jabbering between the besiegers and besieged, like the noise of a monkey-house in full chatter, as a sort of prelude to serious business, each man vying with his opponent in the choicest native Billingsgate. Bit by bit their feelings are wrought up, and finally a more than usually brilliant flower of speech is the signal for a howling fracas. Spears and stones are thrown, and rusty muskets of ancient model are heard exploding in the din, the latter far more dangerous to friend than to foe. At last a man or two on either side is laid out with a spear through his body, or felled with a rap on the temple from a piece of rock meant for somebody else, and carried home for the *Machamach* men to doctor. The victorious defenders stand up mopping and mowing, and with all manner of ridiculous gestures mocking at their baffled foes. On the last occasion the insulting antics of one of the Amon chiefs, thinking himself well out of range, so irritated a white trader who had joined in the assault out of pure deviltry, that he took careful aim with his Winchester and made the chief's comb leap in pieces out of his fuzzy periwig. The savage still capered away, a glorious mark against the sky, and a second shot stung him painfully on the fleshy part of the thigh, and the poor fellow, roaring like a bull, straightway leaped down on the heads of his fellows below, who like the monks when the Devil lets the squealing lay-brother fall from his red-hot talons amongst them

> "As they up-gazed in sore confusion
> Were all knocked down by the concussion."

This same trader, who was a splendid marksman, of course had not fired to kill. I had met him already myself. He had a touch of grim humour, if the following tale he told me of himself be true. It ran thus, and thus in turn I told it to my comrade in the boat. Whilst this practical joker was on a trading expedition up north, one of the district chiefs, an overbearing sort of man, tried to obtain a large credit with him, and at the same time beat down his prices to nearly zero. Failing in this, he threatened him in a very insolent manner.

"Thing belong you all same belong me. S'pose I kill you I takum quick." "So that's your little game, is it?" coolly observed the trader, drawing his revolver, "I'll teach a darned black nigger like you to know what's what." Now overhead there was a bunch of coconuts dangling from the mother tree. Bang went the first barrel, and out squirted a jet of milk from the nut; a second and a third shot tapping two others of the cluster, which shed their milky blessings on the head of the chief below. "'How d'ye like that,' said the marksman, turning his weapon full on the terrified chief. 'Your head's bigger and uglier than a coconut, eh? and not so far off neither.' I thought that nigger would have dropped for sheer funk," ended this most unpeaceful man of commerce, "and that was the last of any tall talk I got from him or his people, and a good job for them too."

All this while we were making our way through a maze of wooden and stone fish-weirs which lie in the straits abreast of the isthmus of Girrigir. Between Walai and Maki the canal passage runs through clumps of mangroves and other salt water brush nearly dry at low tide —which E. had specially warned us to reach at high water. We passed a fine yam plantation on a hillside on our left, grown by a Walai chief who is said to be a friendly old fellow, and a perfect storehouse of ancient traditions. It soon became certain that we must wait off Walai until late in the afternoon, as the tide was falling fast and the channel rapidly shallowing down. The crew were continually jumping down and shouldering the *Eugenie* over the shoals—but all in vain, for at last we were stranded hopelessly amongst the mud-banks. As the monkish chroniclers of Danish invasions say, " It is tedious to tell how these matters went." At last the tide rose, and cautiously poling up some mysterious backwater or other we got into open water and sailed down, reaching the landing place at Pilau in the early dusk. We found "*Konias*" the Sonsorol boy at his post, who, directly he saw us coming, seized an unhappy fowl by the legs and slashed off its head. " S'pose no kill and eat Yap man he steal," serenely remarks the executioner. " One moon ago Missa Capen he send ten fowl. Him make plenty *sakaigligyaia* (Sonsorol for eggs). Rat he eatem. Three fowl he stop now—me no eat. Yap man he come dark—stelem. You speak Missa Capen he no angry too much." And I believe that the boy, who had a great awe of the redoubtable captain, in his odd fashion was telling the simple truth.

The *Eugenie* sailed away and left me alone with my man Friday, who turned out an amiable, honest and intelligent lad, with a smattering of English. His peculiar Sonsorol accentuation transforming N's to R's, and L to Gl, and Gy was a new philological study in itself. (It is seen in Italian, *cf. Egli* for Latin *Illi*.)

Early next morning I was awakened by a prodigious chattering. Six or seven natives were seated on the floor of the house with their backs to the wall, as if the place belonged to them; others were squatted on the verandah, and others peeping in through the windows. Betel-nut chewing was going on, and the air was thick with the fumes of trade-tobacco. My visitors were evidently making themselves at home. Their cool assurance rather amused me, and I determined to take them in the same vein. " Boys," said I, in my newly acquired Yap—which I have no doubt sounded as queer to them as their pigeon-English to us—" the morning is good and so is our meeting. The verandah outside is also good, and this room is not an oven for baking meat, or a smoke-house where fish are cured. Dead matches and rubbish are not meant to be thrown on the floor, and I pray you mark my words."

In reply to my exhortation—not a word. The smokers smoked on placidly, and the chewers chewed and expectorated by turns in perfect silence—not a word, not a smile or change of countenance. " Friends," said I, " I will make my meaning clearer." Across the room I marched, laid hands on the bag that held the stock of a busy ruminator of betel-nut, walked to the door and tossed it far out into the yard. Returning to the man in the corner with an agreeable smile, " *Mr Man—outside*," said I, extending a hand to assist him to his feet, and pointing to the verandah. Somewhat sheepishly he shambled to the door to pick up his property, and presently the people indoors, all on the broad grin, picked up their belongings and went forth one by one cuddling

their beloved bags under arm. " And now let us talk,"
said I, as I followed them out. " Does anyone here speak
English ? " A handsome, well-built fellow called Gameu
was pushed forward, and the wellspring of his knowledge
once tapped, he launched out into very passable English.
Now in the Pacific the fluent speaking of English by
natives is regarded generally as a danger-signal, a somewhat ominous reflection on the character of the white men
who have taught them. But in this case, at all events, the
rule did not hold. Gameu, though incorrigibly lazy at
manual work, proved neither a thief nor an assassin, and
made a model interpreter to help out the meagre English
vocabulary of Konias. After we had sent away the rest
in peace I set the two of them down to some solid work,
painfully digging out the Sonsorol and Yap equivalents of
English words.

On his departure, Gameu, the teacher of dreadful
jargon, assured me solemnly several times he and two or
three others would be round early next morning with a
canoe to take me to visit Captain Brugmann at Ramung
over the water. The more stress he laid on his certainty
to turn up in good time, the more certain I felt that he
would turn up late. " Now, be off with you, make a
move," cried I at last, " or I shall know that you don't
mean to come at all."

Away went Gameu, and I lay down, but not, alas, to
sleep, haunted by legions of words of the direst cacophony
which have been assaulting my ears for the last two
hours. I lay down, only to rise by and by and wrestle
anew with several Spanish vocabularies of the various
Philippine Island dialects, in which important native key-
words are conspicuous by their absence, and in their
stead any number of Spanish words masquerading in
very odd native guise—and, shade of Sancho Panza !—
what a motley assemblage of proverbs dragged in head
and shoulders ! Part of these precious philological
documents consist of dialogues in Spanish and native,
written in a vein of owl-like solemnity, occasionally

relieved by touches of unconscious humour. " Why haven't you taken part in preparation for the Church festival ? " sternly demands the village priest of some poor ignorant Filipino peasant. " Because, your reverence, I had my own work and lots of household affairs to look after," says the villager. " Don't dare to tell me such a thing," replies the austere pastor. " If you had been a good Christian you could have found time for it all. You are an idle rogue, hardly better than a thief."

Under the heading "*Justice*" may also be seen something startling to those unused to the summary fashion of Spanish provincial rule. " What did you hit the man for ? " says judge to prisoner in an assault case. " I never hit him at all, your worship," says the prisoner, " and I protest before all the saints in heaven that I am telling the truth." " Captain," says the judge to his subordinate, without troubling to inquire any further, " give the prisoner twenty lashes, and to jail with him." And the Spaniards feel deeply hurt at the ingratitude of these rebellious Filipinos, who presume to be discontented under such a just and liberal rule. However, the Filipinos nowadays don't even seem contented with American rule. I wonder why.

A stanza from a late Manilla *Diario* flits across my memory as I struggle through these curious monuments of priestly industry, which may be freely translated

El salvaje del bosque inculto, The savage of the uncultured wood

Odio el progreso, la Luz, Our just rule hath not understood,

Vé indifferente la Cruz He looks indifferent on the Cross,

Deja-lo en la bosque España. And darkling counts the Light no loss ;

The uncultured, culture deems no gain,

To his wild woods leave him then, O Spain.

Another gem in Spanish and Bicol.

A tête-à-tête Dinner.

Scene: A VILLAGE INN.   *Enter Padre and boy.*

Boy.—I am hungry.

Padre.—We shall presently dine, but there must be no extravagance.   What here! ho!   [*Enter servant.*

Servant.—Will it please you to eat, sirs? Will you have meat or fish?

Padre.—Whichever you have handy.   (*Fish is brought in.*)

(*At dinner.*)   The Padre speaks à la Mr Barlow.   " I knew a boy called Juan.   He thought he could swim; he went to bathe in the big river, but the current carried him away, and the fishes ate his body.   *Boy starts up, flings his portion out of the window, then with intense pathos,* " Henceforth I taste no fish."

[*Exit boy tragically, Padre left feeding alone.*]

And then, thank goodness, my dinner comes.   Unlike the trusting pupil, I do not allow his master's shocking tale to come between me and my dish of baked leather-jacket fish, flanked with a regiment of eggs, which Konias has ranged on the table like shot in a pile, and nearly as hard too, for he has industriously boiled them for the last three quarters of an hour in his anxiety to please.

After dinner, more proverbs, more tedious dialogue, more ineffectual search for plain, honest, sensible keywords in these odd little pamphlets, for which the lay author in Spain receives a medal or decoration.   In practical England, dreadful to reflect on, the poor fellow might be taken seriously by some fierce critic, who would fall upon him tooth and nail, and in return for his precious pearls of knowledge rend him piecemeal.

CHAPTER XIX

STAY IN PILAU, FOLK-LORE, LEGEND OF FLOOD, AND THE TABU SYSTEM

NEXT morning no Gameu, no canoe, as I expected. The rogue turned up at last about one o'clock, in the full blaze of one of the hottest suns I ever faced, with the excuse that there was a great feast overnight at the club house, and that being much sought after for his elegance and skill in dancing he had been kept up late. Coconut toddy, he said, had flowed freely, also a Manilla man had sold them many bottles of red wine, of which not one was left. So invoking anything but a blessing on native shiftlessness and unpunctuality I gave the word to start, and under the propulsion of five stout bamboo poles the canoe was soon urged up to the wharf of Maneu, with a banana patch in the background shading off into dense forest, whilst here and there the little clearing is dotted with clumps of the *Môr*, a small species of bamboo, and the *Utel*, a tall graceful species of reed-grass bearing feathery tufts of blossom like the flowers of the sugar cane. Here we take on board a sack or two of coconuts, fully ripe for copra making. For as Gameu says very truly, " It is not good to call on a white man empty-handed."

We passed a double fish-weir, the inner one of stone, the other one of cane. Such structures, as before mentioned, are very common around the shores of Yap. Many a boat has come to grief over these on dark nights, when the man at the helm has been indulging in forty winks or forty drinks, as the case may be. Many of the weirs are in a very dilapidated condition, and long past

use, but still they lie round blocking up the water-ways—
a standing menace to traffic.   Whilst we were painfully
feeling our way along through the labyrinth, I remembered
a tale Lewis told me down at Lai of an accident he had
over one of these structures.   He was in charge of a boat
heavily laden with copra and a trifle late for his rendezvous, and, weary of perpetual tacking and tacking, had
vowed to charge the very next cane weir that came in his
path, cracking on all canvas and flying straight before the
wind to Rul with half a gale behind him.   Somewhere off
Iloech a stoutly-built cane weir showed up clearly in the
moonlight right ahead.   A fine breeze was blowing, and
the boat was slipping through the water as fast as two
broad China-rigged sails could take her.   " Straight
ahead !   Let her go for all she's worth," yelled the excit-
able skipper.   " I'll learn the niggers here to be filling up
all the bay with their blamed fish-traps."   And the boys
on board, *who were not Iloech men*, grinned with delight
at the coming smash.   They hadn't long to wait.   The
boat held on at full speed, and with a mighty impetus
crashed clean through the light cane-work of the hated
enclosure, but, alas, the stout coconut strengthening-piece
or cross-bar on the top proved of sterner stuff.   A smashing sound, a snapping of guy ropes, a rustle of falling
canvas, and bang came a stunning crack over the head of
the captain, causing dozens of bright fitful stars to dance
before his vision.   The rude shock had snapped off the
mast like a carrot, and brought yard, sail and all thunder-
ing down in one disastrous topplement.   The poor old
skipper fairly surpassed himself on this occasion, and there
ensued one of the most brilliant displays of verbal pyro-
technics ever shown on salt water.   The native crew
grinned from ear to ear, as black fellows generally do
when there is damage done or somebody badly hurt, and
chortled away merrily at the excellent joke, until the
injured man felt sufficiently recovered to stumble forward
and take a hand in the game with a belaying pin.

In future the valiant Cambrian will doubtless leave his neighbour's landmark severely alone, and will think twice before he will test the resisting power of mast and tackle against stout logs on the top of light cane fences.

Proceeding leisurely onward we came to the landing place of Talangeth, at the back of which there is a piscina or fish-pond (*Maot, cf.* Samoan *Maota* — a building) where young fish are put in to await development—a sensible piece of native foresight. Here we picked up a few more nuts, and we started off once more. A little further on lay Tabok, where we laid in a supply of green drinking nuts. Yet another stone weir passed and we reached Malaf, which lies on the end of Map Island over against Captain B.'s place across the straits at Tan-ne-Erouach—the land of Departed Heroes. Here was a great heap of stones surmounted by tall poles, the relics of an ancient Big House. In the middle of the channel, between the two islands, stretches a zigzag series of stone weirs,[1] and very solidly constructed, built so that the tops emerge two or three feet at low tides ; at high tides the water covers them about three feet deep. Under the lee of these we cautiously waded over, getting pretty well drenched on our way from slipping into holes, but under a tropical sun nobody minds these little mishaps. The straits here would be some 300 yards across, and the fish-pens are said to be of great antiquity. Reaching the wharf we ascended a steep flight of steps cut out of the hillside, on top of which stands the little trading station. The slope was planted with young coconut trees, and the plateau above dotted with wild pandanus trees (*Choi*), some of them in flower to judge from the sweet scent floating down on the light breezes like the smell of a field of beans in blossom.

Two or three native huts and a boatshed adjoined

---

[1] *Vide* illustration in *The Geographical Journal*, February number, 1899.

the wharf, the only living being around being a melancholy old greybeard, superintending with languid interest the boiling of some sweet potatoes in an iron pot over a fire of driftwood. We found B. at home, one of the sober, thrifty and industrious traders of the new school, and a hospitable welcome he gave us, readily undertaking to point out all places of note. That afternoon and evening it was interesting to hear his pithy descriptions of native customs and modes of life, for ascertaining which his knowledge of the language qualified him so well. I obtained from him some account of the inner life of the Yap people, and from an old chief, Toluk of Omin, the Yap version of the flood.

"Long, long ago, the island of Ramung, now separated by the channel we see before us, was one with the mainland. The land was filled with inhabitants, plentiful as ants. Alok, near Akau on the west side, and Tomil district overlooking the eastern harbour on the other side, were the principal settlements. Now the great God Yalafath abode in the sky looking peacefully down on the labours and pleasures of his people. One of his wives bore him two children, a son and a daughter. (The name of the wife is given variously as Mui-Bab or Mui-Wap.) The heavenly children used to come down to see the village festivals holden at Alok, and other fairy folk from the skies would come down too to view the scene of dancing and revelry. For Yap men—complacently murmurs the old man—were and are the best fighters and dancers in the Sea of Islands, and the people of Alok were the best in Yap. Moreover, the young men were of gallant and stalwart bearing, graceful of form and goodly to look upon when garlanded green, dressed out in yellow leaf-girdles, wearing shell earrings, necklaces strung with red stones, or with the scarlet seeds of the pandan tree, their smooth skins shining with turmeric and scented oil. Now it came to pass that one of these fairies took a fancy to a handsome young man called Maralok, and after the briefest of courtships, agreed to cast in her lot with his for a while, as long as the two parties were agreeable. Accordingly the fond pair eloped. The other visiting bevy of fays went back to the skies and said all manner of unkind things. When Loth, the fairy mother, heard that her daughter had condescended to the love of a mortal man, she was very wroth, and appeared to the newly-wedded wife in a vision. The offended mamma said she would descend to Bulual in Ramung in seven days, and bade her erring daughter meet her there and give some account of her doings and pay penance. After this she would receive miraculous powers and her mother's forgiveness. But the old fairy mother dealt subtly, for well she knew what she would do.

The son of earth and daughter of the skies were going along on the appointed day, when behold! the sea rose suddenly and swamped the lowlands. In fear, mortal husband and fairy wife turned back to flee to the hills of Tomil. Ere they could reach this refuge the angry waters swept away Maralok to death. The woman reached Tomil in safety, and satisfied with their prey, the waves were stayed. In the form of an old woman, Loth the Fairy Mother appeared to her daughter, and the two dwelt awhile together in a cavern underground, shunning the sights and sounds of mortal man. They made themselves wings to escape to the shining regions above, but even as they sat in the sunlight pluming themselves for flight, people from Damachui saw them and snared them in a great net (*Chau*), like butterflies. They were assigned to Igereng, one of the Pilung or aristocracy of Tomil, who determined to marry the two, mother and daughter. A feast was held, and the people brought plenty of coconuts and all manner of food, which the land produced abundantly. The two fairies fell to and polished off the heap of food in quick time, devouring coconut after coconut, husk, shell, and all, continually calling for more and

more. All stood aghast at the marvellous sight. At
length Igereng, fearing a famine in the land from such
voracious appetites, was fain to cry hold! enough! After
a while, the fairies, finding the pangs of hunger insup-
portable, turned themselves into rats, and went up
stealthily night after night to the hill-terraces, and helped
themselves liberally to sweet potatoes, sugar-cane and
yams, causing sad devastation in each plantation. One
night a man on watch surprised the trespassers, hurled a
heavy stone with deadly aim, and there lay quivering the
body of an enormous rat—far, far bigger than any dog
or cat—says the veracious narrator. The gluttony of
Loth the Fairy Mother had brought her thither once too
often. The daughter returned in anger and told her
husband that in seven days the vengeance of Loth would
bring a high flood-tide to overwhelm the land. Meanwhile
she counselled him to build a house on top of the highest
hill to which they could withdraw, and bring with him
some magic herbs with which certain rites or incantations
were to be performed, which might avail against the
inundation. He obeyed, and the two fell to practising
spells and exorcisms. The wife looking out to sea at
dawn of the fatal day exclaimed, "Behold the wrath of
Loth." A typhoon was coming, sweeping down out of
the north, bringing with it a terrible tidal-wave. It burst
over the land. Nearly all Yap was covered under the
raging flood, and all the people perished save one, a slave
man in Unean, and the prudent couple. When the waters
fell the Unean man looking southward saw the lowlands
of Nimiguil emerging from the waste of waters. He went
down upon the newly-risen flats, stuck a bamboo-pole fast
into a crevice of the reef in token of possession, and went
his way to see if any others were alive. Presently he met
Igereng and his wife, and though a slave himself, claimed
from them the lands of Nimiguil, showing the bamboo
landmark in token of his right. And this is the reason
why Nimiguil folk hold their lands by tenure of labour

and military service to the chiefs of Tomil. As the
narrator puts it crisply, " Tomil chief want work he speak.
Nimiguil man he go quick. Tomil man make feast.
Nimiguil man he fetch food."

After this two children were born to Igereng. The
mother one day fell ill and desired to be buried—whether
alive or dead, the narrative did not say. She strictly
charged the children to dig her up again after three days,
promising great and wonderful advantages if they were
obedient. But the boy and girl behaved just like all other
thoughtless children left to themselves with nobody to look
after them. They ran wild all over the country-side,
getting into all manner of mischief, tweaking the tails of
the Iguanas, and teasing the animals and birds. At last
when they did remember to dig up the old lady she was
stiff and dead, and the house of Igereng had lost its
promised blessings. The story doesn't say what Papa
Igereng did to the truants or why he didn't dig her up
himself instead. Probably, as savage as well as some
civilised papas do, he took the matter coolly, and consoled himself in due time with a less exacting mortal wife,
and here Igereng passes out of the story.

Now the great spirit Yalafath, who sits musing in the
sky, and takes a fatherly interest in the land of Yap,
spake one day to his wife Mui-Bab, and said, " I would
know if the flood has destroyed the land as they tell me,
and if any of the people has escaped death. Go down and
see. Return and tell me." And the goddess shot from the
skies in the form of an albatross or, as some say, a frigate-
bird, lighting on Tomil. And she saw how few were left
to till the land now barren of food-bearing plants. Swiftly
returning, she told Yalafath, the Giver of Good, of the
hapless state of the people. And he sent down to nourish
them the areca palm (*Bû*), the betel pepper (*Gabui* or
Kavui), the banana (*Pau*), the plantains (*Irinim* and
Tengera), the yams (*Dol, Dok, Dal*), and the water-taro
(*Lak*).

Therefore to this day, when they see the frigate-bird in the land of Tomil, they say, " Lo, the sacred messenger of the mercy of Yalafath, Lord of the skies."

Now the compassionate goddess, seeing the land again fruitful and fit for habitation, called eight *Kan* or Genii into existence—one female and seven male. The female (*Ngul*) went to Maki in the north, one of the males (*Yangalap*) to Gochepa on the north-east, another (*Toma*) to Omin, another to Gilifith, another (*Ath*) to Goror in Nimiguil, the extreme south point of the island. The fifth went to Akau and the sixth to Obogol. The seventh abode with Mui-Bab in Tomil, who created wives for them by the exercise of her magic will. And these are the generations of the children of Yap.

There appear several familiar threads woven into the fabric of this crude, savage legend. The rather childish version of the origin of the flood is nevertheless a new and naïve contribution to the huge masses of tradition on this point, rescued from oblivion in different parts of the world.

1. The coming down of the fairy beings to earth is the reflex version of the account in Genesis (c. vi. v. 2).

2. The period of seven days is a common Semitic cycle.

3. The device of the fairies changing themselves into rats reads like a Japanese Bake-mono tale, to say nothing of the use of the word *Machamach* to signify magic, which answers exactly to Japanese *Maji* or *Machi*, enchantment, witchcraft, and more strangely still to the Araucanian *Machi*, a medicine man or diviner.

4. Not less striking is the part taken by the celestial messenger, the albatross. Similar, but not quite the same, is the duty assigned to the humming-bird in the Mexican legend, and to the raven and the dove in the ancient Chaldean and Hebrew traditions.

5. The burying and digging up of the mother to obtain certain prospective blessings by her children calls to mind a legend of Rarotonga concerning the origin of Pigs told

by the Rev. Wyatt-Gill, and the Ponapean story of the burying of Kaneki the Leper, from whose poor corpse grew up the Coconut Palm.

Lirou of Tomil subsequently gave me a Southern Yap version, slightly different, but in most particulars harmonising very well. He gives the name of the fairy who came down to see the dances at Alok as Legerem, and that of her husband as Mar-alau. The name of the Fairy Mother is variously given as *Mithigom* or *Michigam*. His account of the flight and pursuit is interesting in its minuteness of detail. " The goddess, chasing them on the wings of the storm, tried to seize them in her talons, but only tore away the island of Ramung. At the second attempt she grasped the tract of land occupied by Map Island. This too she rent away. The third time she succeeded, but in her eagerness nearly tore away another island, the western and eastern portions of the main island being only left hanging together by the narrow isthmus or neck of land at Girigir. Mar-alau is drowned in the welter of winds and waters ; Fairy Mother and daughter hide in a cave ; Legerem is captured by Igereng of Tomil (whom Lirou, with the varying southern tribal phonesis, styles *Eriguk* or *Egeruk*) ; but the Fairy Mother is too wily for her pursuers and escapes, promising, however, to visit her daughter in seven days and bring blessings and not curses upon her new marriage. True to her word she appears, levels and builds the stone wharf called Ochongol running from Dagut to Tomil, and plants all the roads around with avenues of the *Kel* or native almond. The voracity of Michigam, her raids on the plantations in the form of a rat, her ignominious death in a trap, and the flood that follows in seven days, agree closely with the northern version given by Toluk. The name of the survivor from Unean, who had escaped by climbing a tall palm, is given as *Angafau*. This ancient worthy's name appears oddly enough in early Samoan legend as *Ongafau*, coupled with another mysterious personage *Tafitofau*, with-

out whose names no orthodox fairy tale can start—a sort
of traditional introduction.

Legerem creates by magic art five boys and a girl.
To Yangalab, who settled Gochepa, she assigns the
conquest of the eastern islands up to Ruk, and Kuthiu
(Kusaie), and Fanupei (Ponape). Therefore, ever since,
the islanders from the eastward have come down at stated
intervals from Mokomok (*Uluthi*), and Anangai (*Uleai*),
and other places even further, to pay tribute to the *Pilung*
or chiefs of Gochepa. (The name *Yangalab* is probably
eponymous. It means *Trade-wind* or *Great-gale*.)
Yangalab may be taken to represent the restless,
piratical Malay element in Western and Central Caroline
history, his stay-at-home brethren as types of the peaceful,
agricultural instinct of the Dravidian forefathers left
behind them in Southern India.

Now, of course it was necessary somehow for Legerem
to provide wives for these early patriarchs, and Lirou
tells an extraordinary tale of the Machamach or magic
arts of Legerem, reminding one very much of the Mayan
story in the Popol Vuh of the gradual evolution of the
first man and woman.

Seven days wrought Legerem over a tangle of coconut
husk, and the result was (1) the *Ataligak* or black shore-
lizard (*Scincus*). Yet another seven days' incantation,
and (2) the *Athalau* or blue-tailed lizard. Seven days'
more, and, lo ! (3) the *Galuf* or Iguana, a large yellow and
green tree-lizard. The next wonder-working period produced a (4) *Thagith* (in Pelew *Galith*, in Irish *Thivish*),
the spectral or phantom frame of a woman, lacking substance. One last stage of evolution, and there stood (5)
Le-pulei, a perfect woman nobly planned.

By Legerem's unfailing magic *Le-pulei* bears the
following daughters—Tilik, Lé-ngeru, Matenai, Tininga-
mat, Miting, and Rutineg. From these and certain
fairy visitors from the sky, whom Legerem's sons took to
wife, are the people of Yap descended.

Another tale of *Legerem* was told me by Lirou.

The same powerful fairy, to feed her fast-increasing people, went down to the reef, caught a *Goloth* or sea-eel, and cut it in two, carefully planting the pieces. From one half there grew a coconut palm, from the other half a banana tree. By similar means the *Mal* and the *Lak*, two species of Taro, were produced in the land of Yap. Not contented with this, Legerem sent an old man called Galuai, who ascended in a column of smoke to the sky, and there besought the Great Spirit Yalafath to give the Yap people a further supply of food. To him were given yams packed in an enormous hollow bamboo-cane, upon which astride he mounted, with fowls harnessed alongside to bring him in his chariot safe to earth. This is a crude barbarian counterpart indeed to the classical tales of Lady Venus, with her trains of doves and teams of sparrows. And this is how those three useful things, the yam, the bamboo, and the domestic fowl came into the land of Yap.

According to B., after the priestly caste " *Ulu-Uleg* " or " *Machamach*," the two principal classes on the island are *Pilung* or chieftains, and *Pimlingai* or slaves. The latter for the most part dwell in bush villages, such as Damachui and Gatlangal. They are darker in colour than the Pilung, their hair is more curly, and in speaking they have a slightly different pronunciation. It looks as if they belonged to an earlier race, subsequently enslaved by an invasion of fresh settlers. One tradition makes them descended from the crews of certain visiting canoes from one of the neighbouring groups. After Yap had been ravaged with a great and fatal epidemic, the local people determined to seize upon the persons of their visitors in order to restock their land. So they set upon them and killed most of the men, keeping the remainder and the women and children as slaves, and settling them in various inland villages, for fear they should steal canoes and make their escape. These serfs belong to certain district chiefs, and in some cases to chief women. They have to do all the menial work for their masters. They live on poor food, such as the *Kai* and the *Luat*, the greater and lesser squid, which the chiefs do not care to eat. The great distinction between the Pilung and Pimlingai is that the former wear a *Roai* or ornamental comb of white mangrove wood in their hair, the latter none. The slave class are very shy and diffident before their native masters, but in the presence of white men are apt to give themselves airs. "It's because they feel sure of being treated well," says B. "It's just the way niggers have got." Between all the Pilungs there is political equality, there being little or no individual supremacy. The voice of the majority settles the question. The old men act as umpires and spokesmen, their position answering to that of the *Gerousia* of ancient Hellas. With them lies the option of declaring war or peace. These old men form a perpetual court of session, and from their decision or sentence there is no appeal. Murder is generally punished by a heavy fine, by which death by private vengeance is averted. Breaches of the far-spreading Machamach or Tabu were punished by the death of the offender by poisoning or assassination. "In Yap," says B., "bad men never die, but disappear somehow."

In Yap are two great wizards, the head of all the magicians (" *Ulu-uleg*" or "*Machamach*") in the island, both well on in years, who support their dignity under very strict conditions indeed. With them truly it is a case of " *Sagesse*," if not " *noblesse oblige.*" They are only allowed to eat fruits from plants or trees specially grown for them. They may not smoke tobacco, but, subject to the condition above mentioned, may enjoy a quid of betel-nut, the chewed-up remains being reverently collected after them, borne away, and burnt in a special manner, for fear of any ill-disposed person getting possession of the rubbish and doing mischief by uttering a curse over it, a superstition like that of the *Nahak* in the Melanesian area. When one of them goes abroad the other stops at home, for were the two to meet one another on the road, the natives hold that some direful calamity would surely follow. There are plenty of lesser degree Machamach men, who go about always with divers errands in hand, such as recovering missing property, divination, and the like, but all grave and important questions come up before the Mighty Two. To them belongs the power of the Tabu, which applies to places and objects as well as persons. If a village is tabued, no trader or anyone else can take or give anything away from there. It is a very strict rule indeed, and has been known to extend up to six months. It is a very neat savage rendering of the papal interdicts and excommunications of the Middle Ages, to say nothing of the *boycott* of the Emerald Isle and the *picketing* of labour unions. When a canoe is going on a long sea voyage, such as to Ngoli, Uluthi, or the Pelews, they put on a tabu to propitiate the Yap Neptune and the Shark-God. The same before a fishing excursion, during time of drought, famine, or sickness, or at the death of a chief or famous man. In short, any great public event is thus celebrated, and, in fact, there is always a tabu in full swing somewhere or other, to the great disgust of the traders, who only see in those enforced holidays an excuse for idling, drunkenness and debauchery, and I verily believe that they are little better. It is then that the copra-sheds lie empty, and the trader goes about with a surly frown, and the native with a smile you could measure with a foot-rule.

My informant then went on to describe a singular custom similar to that in the worship of Mylitta at Babylon, described by Herodotus. In each of the great club houses, previously mentioned for their remarkable architecture, are kept three or four unmarried girls or *Mespil*, whose business it is to minister to the pleasures of the men of the particular clan or brotherhood to which the building belongs. As with the Kroomen on the Gold Coast, each man, married or unmarried, takes his turn by

A *BAI* OR LODGE IN RUL DISTRICT, SOUTH OF TOMIL HARBOUR

rotation in the rites through which each girl must pass before she is deemed ripe for marriage. The natives say it is an ordeal or preliminary trial to fit them for the cares and burden of maternity. She is rarely a girl of the same village, and, of course, must be sprung from a different sept. Whenever she wishes to become a *Langin* or respectable married woman, she may, and is thought none the less of for her frailties as a *Mespil*. The sign of a *Langin* is a string or cord worn round the neck, hanging down fore and aft, dyed black and knotted. This is called *Mara-fau* (a *Mara* or necklace of *Fau*, the archaic Yap name for the *Kal* or Lemon Hibiscus). But I believe this self-immolation before marriage is confined to the daughters of the inferior chiefs and commons. The supply of *Mespil* is generally kept up by the purchase of slave girls from the neighbouring districts, on which occasion the *Fe* or stone money-wheels are used. The reason that the stone wheels are piled at the foot of these structures is that the *Mespil* may in looking upon them remember that they themselves were bought with great price, and must prove themselves worthy of the honour conferred on them. Therefore these houses are called *Fe-Bai* or *Money-Houses*. Very often a band of *Ufuf* or village mohawks elect to carry off for a freak a *Mespil* from some other village to grace their own. Though an adventure much relished by the local braves, it is considered a most blamable, unclubbable act by their elders, and probably is the most fruitful source of discord on the island. The institution of the *Mespil* is certainly a surprising coincidence with the Yoshiwara of Japan.

It is hardly necessary to state that the good Catholic priests most sternly set their faces against the *Mespil* system, but all in vain. "It is the custom of the land," says the obstinate heathen, and goes his own way—to wake up only too surely to the fact that the young men turn out worthless idle loafers and die early, and many of

the young women after marriage will not bear children.
Padres and traders alike say, and they are probably right,
that this, together with other co-operating influences, has
been the cause of the steady decadence and dwindling
of so many of the Ocean races.   When a *Mespil*
is stolen the aggrieved village declares war, which has
to be staved off by the offending parties sending stone
and shell money in propitiation and by way of a fine.
Sometimes the woman is taken back to her home—
oftener, without doubt, she elects to stay in her new
quarters.

"In Yap," continues B., "men and women cannot
eat out of the same pot.   The women and children
eat together."   Now the women of Yap have rather
a hard time of it.   They have to keep the yam and
taro patches and coconut plantations in order, and do
all the housework into the bargain ; whilst the men's
work consists in building houses and canoes, fishing
and trading.   "Conjugal fidelity," says B., "is not regarded as a virtue"—a rather astonishing statement
which at first sight appears to conflict with the class-
divisions of *Langin* and *Mespil*.   Needless to say, with
excesses in youth and early toil of field-work, the women-
kind age very quickly.   To the Western mind the custom
of young girls about the age of sixteen passing through
such an ordeal as described, is well-nigh incredible.
But the thing is certainly so, and no resident or
missionary will venture to contradict its existence.   It
is one of those startling facts flashing in our face out
of the weird mysterious East, where all things to us
seem turned topsy-turvy, and the fancy reels with the
oppression of a monstrous nightmare.   A similar deep and
chilling sense of the gulf which separates Eastern from
Western thought characterises the solemn imagery in
which De Quincy limns his strange and fitful fancies—
crossed by the still-haunting shadow of China, Rome,
or Egypt.

Have none of my readers felt some vague thrill of
horror lurking behind the jewelled and glorious luxury
of the East—some jarring chord amongst her golden
melodies—a sense of something incomplete where all
seems solid and magnificent, such a union of beauty
and cruelty as seen in the fabled shrub of Java, deep
down in whose gorgeous and fragrant blossoms a little
coral snake lurks coiled whose touch is death. It is
at such times as these that the Western mind turns
thankfully back to those strong, simple, earnest men
—the Germans of Tacitus and the Scandinavians of
the Eddas. These men were our forefathers and theirs
was the better part. It is very well. They are our
fixed stars and shine mildly in heaven. But the others
are ominous lights, these blazing meteors, these comets
that come roaring and raging across our way out of
the chilly gulfs of Time and the black darkness of the
ages. We know our own—these we know not. We
view the Eastern mind as yet in a glass darkly. Our
methods, our planes of thought lie far apart, our notions
of justice, and honour, and all that makes a man, differ
from the very root. Who, after Kipling and Sir Edwin
Arnold, will throw himself into the gulf and bridge it
over?

CHAPTER XX

NORTH YAP—RETURN TO TARRANG

THAT evening we visited the shed where B. is setting up the framework of a trading boat of *tamanu* timber (Yap *Bioutch*). The wood has a handsome reddish longitudinal grain, is very durable, and is said to harden in salt water.

We examined some clumps of a peculiar shrub called *Avetch*. The foliage is like that of the jamboo or Malay apple-tree, each spray terminating in a white petal-like leaf. The seeds are minute like those of the tobacco plant. The flowers are of small size, star-shaped and of a bright golden-yellow hue. From the top of the hill we viewed one of the magnificent sunset effects that are so common here that nobody specially notes them. But in England, I believe, cloud-pictures of green, scarlet and amber are not so common. B. told me of a magnificent club house at Umin on Map Island, also of one at a place called Atelu, which artists, if any should ever come here, would do well to bear in mind.

Next morning B. and I went out early to survey the *Tan-ne-Erouatch*, the land of the Dead Heroes, the district facing down on the straits of Malaf where are the burial places of the mighty men of old.

Tan is the Malay *Tana* soil, or else is cognate with the Polynesian root *Tanu*, to bury; with *Erouatch* cf. the Marshall Island dialect-words for chief or king— *Iroith*, *Uroit*, *Iroich*, and the Marianne *Uritoi*. The whole face of the land is covered with tufts and clumps of coarse grasses, wild sorrel, and the South Sea arrowroot (*Tacca*), diversified by patches of a peculiar pitcher-plant, *At.*

The parcel of land presents the appearance like an old fashioned English orchard, save that instead of apple and pear trees are found growing whole battalions of that quaint and antediluvian looking tree — the wild pandanus. Here and there a graceful climbing fern (*Lygodium*), somewhat resembling the Venus' Hair or Adiantum, curls its delicate green tresses over old and unsightly tree-stumps.

For a long while our search after ancient graves was unavailing, so well had the wild woods kept their secret, and we wandered uphill, through copse, and down dell, until we reached the dense belt of hibiscus running down to the beach, and knew that we had overshot our mark. We found a small rivulet which, in its course to the sea, forms two or three shallow pools ; here we gathered some freshwater shells, exactly like the ones found in the basin of the waterfall at Puia on the Kusaie coast. Retracing our steps, suddenly we came upon a gentle slope covered with little flat platforms built of small blocks of basalt, in many cases thickly overgrown by a dense tangle of climbing fern. These graves are two or three feet in height, in length six feet by four. They belong to the common folk. Those of the chiefs and wealthy men are much higher, and are faced with upright slabs of stone—one in each corner and one in the middle of each side being *de rigueur*. On our way back we fell in with a similar grave near the slave village of *Fal*. In the afternoon we went out again with a small boy and a whale-spade in search of ferns and orchis plants.

Our little guide told us that it was the Yap custom to throw quantities of chewed pandanus fruit upon the top of these graves, apparently as a propitiation to the spirits of the dead. In his quaint and barbarous dialect he tells us of a former island existing to the north of Ramung called *Sepin*, whose people were savage warriors and came across in canoes to fight with the men of Yap. B. says he means a submerged stack of coral, called Hunter's reef, which lies up some thirty miles northwards, about fifteen fathoms deep. But the name to me appears to recall the island of *Saipan* in the Marianne or Ladrone Group. It would only be one more addition to the number of native geographical names repeating themselves with very slight variations over the Micronesian and Melanesian areas. Possibly Favorlana, (Formosa South coast) *Tsipan, " the Western quarter,"* is cognate.

In former times the barren grounds must have been inhabited pretty thickly. Traces of ancient cultivation and the foundations of old houses are numerous on the promontory facing Map. Probably the population perished off in some epidemic, or in some great battle on which history is silent. Now the place is waste and desolate, and the natives fear to come around at night. Only in daytime will they come hither, and then only in company by twos and threes.

That afternoon we stumbled upon another grave, said to be that of Rek, the chief of Umin, the capital of Map across the water. It is surrounded by a narrow trench, and consists of four tiers. Three are of stone and the fourth is of earth. The lowest tier is twenty-five feet in length, breadth twenty-two feet; second tier twenty feet in length, breadth twelve feet; upper tier sixteen feet in length, breadth eight feet. Each of these three tiers is about a foot and a half in height, and the lowest, that of earth, is one foot high. The topmost tier is paved with a layer of flattish blocks of stone. Here are no upright stone slabs as seen in the tomb of Fal, which, though a smaller structure, has eight of these curious erect stones bordering each tier.

On exploring further we found the hillside beyond Fal cut up into a series of terraces and ditches three or four feet deep, very much overgrown with long grass, into which one would occasionally disappear with startling abruptness and a considerable shock. These are the relics of gardens of the olden time, where they used to grow beds of yams and turmeric or wild ginger. Of the roots of the latter they used to make the cones of *Rang, Reng,* or *Taik,* a widely-used cosmetic from one end of the Carolines to the other. (*Cf.* Polynesian *Renga, Lenga,* the turmeric; Javanese *Rong,* gamboge; Hindustani *Rang,* paint, cosmetic; and with *Taik* compare Marquesan *Taiki,* red, orange-coloured.)

We made our way down the hillside through the long lush grasses, which took us up to our waists, until we found ourselves deep down in a green valley, a rich strip of rare old bottom-lands which would have delighted a Whitcombe Riley, with a wee silvery brook singing down with a mellow tinkle seawards amongst the shadowed silence of deep groves. We struggle along through a marshy hollow, and one's thoughts go back to the vales of Thessaly and Lerna fen and the Centaurs or horse-breeders thereof, and thence to Dirk Hammerhand and the rich pastures of Walcheren, whence Hereward the Wake by subtlety stole his mare Swallow. But we meet neither Centaurs nor Lapithæ, and no gainsaying Dirk to challenge rash intruders to a game of buffets. Not a sound save the murmur of the troutless brook, and the gentle sough of the south wind sighing through the ever-glades. " It was all of it fair as life ; it was all of it quiet as death " ; but what a grassy meadow for cattle is lost here, and what a grand retreat for a hermit.

The small boy, bending under a big bag full of plants and seeds, follows gallantly on our track as we go trip-ping and stumbling along through the silent hollow vale, carpeted with matted roots, weeds and creepers. Little by little we win our way out of the valley by a winding trail that strikes upward and along the mountain slopes above. The bright green tints of the grass give way gradually to a light yellowish-brown, where the scorching rays have set their mark all the sultry noontide past. The purple shadows come stealing down from the hollows in the hills, a wonder of amber-flecked cloud-canopy glorifies all the face of the west, and as the sun dips in a sapphire sea, cool, damp, and fragrant closes in the dusk of eventide.

On the slopes above us are crackling little fires lit by the natives to clear the mountain wilderness for the yam-planting, even as their far-off kindred of the South burn off the wild fern which year by year clothes the long hill-sides of New Zealand.

After a longish walk over the hills we returned to B.'s station, and left that night to return to Pilau, where we arrived about midnight, agreeing to pay B. a second visit. We find some natives sitting on the verandah with eggs, yams, and fish for barter, and everything safe as I left it. Visitors and crew were soon paid off, and went ashore well pleased, Gameu agreeing to act as guide for a long walk on the mainland, and the rest promising to bring in any-thing remarkable in the way of sea-shells, lizards, spiders, etc., for the alcohol bottle. One old man and his son undertook to bring in some fine specimens of iguanas (*Varanus*), of which there are plenty in this curious part of the Carolines. This, together with the appearance of fire-flies, the rarity of land birds, and the absence of the horned frog found in the neighbouring area of the Pelews, may afford food for speculation to the naturalist. To the lay mind it seems odd. But then pretty well everything in the Carolines *is* rather odd, and there is plenty to find out still for any energetic scientist who comes along prepared to rough it.

For a wonder Gameu turned up next day in good time and took me over to Gilifith, from which we started about midday. The heat was tremendous, and the stone paved roads with the rain that had fallen overnight, slippery to a degree. Along the road the scenery reminded me of an English country lane. Ferns and mosses were growing everywhere, and the path was frequently intersected by the gnarled roots of the native chestnut. After a long climb we found ourselves on the plateau, from which we had a fine view. The pitcher - plant with its quaint lidded flower-cups grows in abundance on the rich red soil, also another pretty plant, with spotted leaves and violet and mauve flowers. Next we passed through banked-up beds of sweet-potato separated by a series of deep ditches running between them, which gave the place quite the appearance of a market garden. There were also some yam patches, the creepers carefully trained over sticks, like peas or scarlet - runners. Water-melons also were seen growing in great abundance, probably introduced from the Pelews, where the regular Malay name is in vogue (Pelew *Samongka, cf.* Javanese *Samanka*). There were also two small patches of pine-apples (*Ngongor*). We came upon a bush-town called Matreu, and found a party of old men scraping up the *Reng* or turmeric root to make the favourite native cosmetic. From here we followed a causeway on our right running along the side of a pretty little brook flashing at intervals amongst the weeds and grasses that border its course. On our left a stretch of marsh filled with the broad arrow-headed leaves and yellow blossoms of Water-Taro. We arrived at a village, apparently of the same name as my temporary island abode, with its imposing club house and platform studded with upright basalt slabs, overshadowed by a marvel of crotons, papyrus, and areca palms. We saw a fine specimen of the tree called *Kangit* in Ponape, here called *Raual*, with its broad leaves and spherical fruit, containing numerous seeds like those of a mango (*Pangium edule*).

We sat down under the welcome shade of a gigantic native chestnut, and once more Gameu climbed to bring down *Tob* or green drinking coconuts (Hindustani *Dab*, Sonsorol *Sob*, Ponape *'Up*). Ere long a number of people came around us to feast their eyes a while upon the rare spectacle of a visitor from over sea. They were not in the least importunate, curiosity brought them ; and that once satisfied they soon melted away.

Beyond the village the path winds away down seaward, bordered by luxurious clumps of beautiful ferns, amongst which I recognised an old South Pacific friend, the giant fern of Samoa. Here they call it *Mong* or *Mang*. But for the coconut palms around, I could have fancied myself at the Land's End, when I spied a species of Osmunda (*Welem*).

After a slippery descent on the irregularly-paved road we found ourselves at Gilifith, and after resting a while in the house of Yetaman, the chief, we crossed over to the little station on Pilau on a raft of bamboos. Yetaman was a withered old specimen of humanity, who told us tales of *Gaiutch* (Pelews *Gaius*, *Aius*) or stray crocodiles, which had been known to arrive on Yap and the Pelews, drifted on floating logs. Surely some at least of these crocodile stories are founded on fact. On the east coast of Ponape they tell a tale to the same effect, and I have heard a legend of similar type from Lamotrek, where they call the caiman or alligator *Li-karrach-apóm*. The name has a grimly sonorous ring ; my white informant, formerly a resident in Lamotrek, says it means the Saw-toothed Woman. The Polynesian horror of lizards and eels may be perfectly well explained as a traditional recollection of the alligators and venomous snakes left behind them in their primitive homes upon the Asiatic sea-board and the large islands of Indonesia. Their forefathers would have certainly remarked the alligator in the rivers along the New Guinea coast, as their successive streams of migration flowed past. Their intercourse with the islanders of Melanesia, where such saurians abound, would be always reinforcing and keeping alive the old tradition.

That evening the *Eugenie* turned up with Xavier on board to say that O'Keefe was expected very shortly, and asking me to come back on the next day but one at latest. Therefore I determined to pay a last visit to Ramung over the water, and get a few more facts out of the old people. The talk that evening turned upon rats and lizards and the like small deer, and Konias told a heart-rending tale how the Sonsorol people dealt with the rats which were such a plague in the island, and woefully reduced their stores of food, scanty already as they were. " Man catch rat—cut off ear, cut off tail—let 'um go. Him go down hole—fight other rat till him kill."

An old man in the corner began to tell machamach stories about the *Galuf* or Iguana of Yap, which, he declared, was a sacred beast in olden times. A number of these somewhere in Rul district were kept at the present time in a fenced enclosure, and served regularly with baskets of food. One, he said, was very large and fat and exceedingly tame, which it was only lawful for the priests to see. He said that he had seen that day a lizard with wo tails, which he spoke of as an ominous thing. Xavier said that there were plenty of lizards similarly endowed in China, and that the superstition in Macao was that any gambler who carried one of these singular double tails about his person was sure to have a wonderful run of luck. To which the old man in the corner replied that he never gambled ; drinking gin was the only excitement he permitted himself in his declining years. Would the kind Englishman oblige him with a glass of the magical water which made the old feel young and strong again ? On being told the new ordinance of the Spanish Governor prohibiting the supply of gin to the natives, he looked deeply disappointed, but on receiving a tumbler of red wine, which is *not* prohibited, he brightened up wonderfully and promised me a fine large iguana for my collection. I did not put implicit faith in his promises, but sure enough early next morning I beheld the old man and his son seated on the verandah smoking, and two very fine iguanas lying on the ground below tied up and strapped down tightly, paws and tail, to pieces of stick, and their mouths secured with strips of hibiscus bark to prevent their biting. The old man's yellow dog, taking a mean advantage of one of the defenceless saurians, took him gently up by the tail to worry. The iguana's muzzle of bark somehow slipped off, and the assailant found himself seized by the cheek, the lizard in spite of frenzied yelps and struggles nipping him in a vicious hold, until his jaws were forced asunder with a bit of stick. Great was the amusement of the onlookers, and deeply gratified were they a little later at the iguana's plunges and struggles in the uncongenial bath of alcohol. " S'pose Queen Wiktoria him see Galuf, by-im-by him laugh too much," observed the old man. " You stop here more long time. I bring plenty Galuf more. One Galuf, two pieces black tobacco, very good."

And that day, after rewarding the old man, we pushed off for Ramung on our last day's exploration in the north. Soon after our arrival at our friend's hospitable house a chief called Toluk of Omin or Amon turned up again and told us some tales of days gone by.

In the afternoon we walked over the hills to the settlement of Bulual on the north side of the island, passing on our way two interesting graves at a place called Imangangich. The larger of the two had four terraces or platforms ; the lowest of these measured 32 feet long by 26 feet broad; the second 26 feet long by 18 feet broad; the third 22 feet long by 14 feet broad ; the fourth 18 feet long by 10 feet broad. From top to bottom the height was 8 feet. In the centre stood a long thin upright slab of basalt 4 feet high.

Approaching Bulual on the down slope was very slippery work over the paved roads, which on reaching the low level emerge into a substantial causeway with a deep ditch on either side, overshadowed by fine forest trees, amongst which the native chestnut, the banyan and the callophyllum were the most conspicuous. At Bulual we found B.'s sailing boat waiting at the wharf, which he sent round to meet us, and to take in a number of sacks of copra, thus combining business and pleasure in our overland march. After getting back to B.'s station, he

presented me with some pretty good sketches of the
graves which he found time to make.

That evening we got back rather late, and found
things as serene as usual in Pilau. Konias put the
finishing touch on my Sonsorol work, the last of the 450
key-words were carefully gone over, and after supper
notebook and pencil were once more called upon.
Suddenly it was remarked that the east was yellowing
with the coming dawn. So to rest for an hour or two
and away on the incoming tide and down to Tarrang
before the trades. Going down we found a much quicker
business than coming up. Towards sunset E. and I went
over to the Spanish settlement and fraternised with the
doctor of the station and two or three of the officers.
They seemed pleased to see us, and invited us with true
Spanish hospitality to stay and dine that evening, but we
had too much work on hand.

Next day I spent in observing the ways of O'Keefe's
colony of Sonsorol boys on Tarrang, whom he had brought
up from their poor little famine-stricken island, which lies
about half-way between the Pelews and the coast of Dutch
New Guinea. In cast of features they resemble Polynesians much more than the people of Yap or even
Ponape, their quaint dialect in a great measure recalling
that of Uluthi and the Western Mortlocks. They appeared
cheerful and good-humoured, somewhat lazy, but willing
enough to work when called upon. Some while ago,
crazy with pilfered rum, they certainly had pitched into
the man from Macao, chased him into the water, and
beaten him grievously with bamboos. But this was a
very rare exception. The Chinese cook on Tarrang,
according to E., was a strange character, a surly old
devotee of some queer Chinese sect or other, who hated
natives and despised white men. He would gamble all
night with other Chinese from over the water, and would
fleece them of their hard-earned wages. To E.'s sarcastic
rebukes on these goings-on he would give most insolent

replies, careless of the certain punishment in store when
O'Keefe should return. A little accident happened that
day which intensified the ill-feeling on both sides. E.
had just washed his hands before lunch, and threw out a
large basin of dirty water from the second-floor verandah.
The Chinese cook below, returning axe on shoulder from
splitting firewood, was surprised to receive a sudden
shower-bath, and made a great to-do. When E. looked
down to see what had caused the whirlwind of curses
below, he saw his enemy, and the Chinaman seeing *him*
raved worse than ever in his shrill pigeon English. E.
smiled placidly on his victim, and the Sonsorol boys
shrieked in chorus, whilst Milton, the yellow house-dog,
and the two foxy-looking "wonks" from Hong-Kong
swelled the racket with their petulant yap-yap-yapping.

Next day I made a visit to Tomil across the bay, the
abode of the powerful chief Lirou. I went in a dingy
with two Sonsorol boys, carrying with me a two-foot
rule, a measuring tape, and a small box of biscuits and
provender. Landing on the Kades or stone jetty just
below the big club house I saw a number of the limestone or calcite money-stones leaning against the platform
of the club house, whilst others lay in front of the wharf,
some wholly, others partially submerged, with here and
there a rim or a little bit showing above water. Some
fish-nets were hanging up to dry in front of a rude but
lofty boat-house carefully thatched above, but below open
on all sides to the winds and weather. We inquired the
chief's whereabouts, and were directed inland. About a
quarter of a mile up through a narrow stone-paved avenue
shaded on either side by bamboos and crotons, we fell in
with a spacious cane-fenced courtyard paved with stone,
wherein were two or three native houses. There we were
told that the chief was in the house at the end of the
square taking a siesta in the heat of the day. Crossing a
narrow brook spanned by a fallen palm-trunk we went up
to the house which lay embowered in a dense mass of

THE HILLSIDE, RUL DISTRICT

dracæna, crotons, ferns, and giant arum, a pretty little
nook. We found Lirou sitting up, and he received us
graciously, warmly commending my desire to look into
the antiquities, and take notes on the architecture of his
countrymen. He begged, however, for half an hour's nap
to compose himself after yesternight's festivities, and turned
over to sleep, again recommending us to commence with
his house, go on with our measurements, and never mind
him. As in Ponape, the house is closed in at the sides
with shutters of reed-grass cunningly bound up in regular
rows with cinnet fibre, the ends of which are brought down
over the top into a fancy fringe work. Five stout pillars
of *Biutch* wood (*callophyllum*), the favourite native tree in
house-building, each at intervals of five feet, hold up the
house, which in breadth is about sixteen feet. Down the
middle it is divided by a cane or reed partition. The
floor is strewn with *Kini* or rough mats plaited of coconut leaflets. There was the usual angular verandah in front
supported by five pillars, the central one tall and slender,
bisecting the angle of projection. Each side of the house
had two doorways closed by shutters of cane, which can
be raised or let down at will. There were two more at
each end, front and rear. Some bags and baskets were
hanging up inside, and a sea-chest and one or two small
boxes completed the visible furniture.

Lirou was not by any means the only man in the
village suffering the effects of the orgies of the night
before. All the island just then was given up to a
carnival of dancing and drinking, and business in consequence was nearly at a standstill. A man from Rul
came in with a cushion of banana skin, and a betel-
bag under arm, and offered to show us around the
settlement until the chief had finished his nap. So we
followed him a good way along the side of a creek bordered
with masses of asplenium (*Lek*) and parasol-fern (*Kana*),
which I had seen before growing in great quantities on
the plateaus of Hiva Oa in the South Marquesas. (There

the natives used to call it *Manamana-Ohina* or White-fork.)
Presently we came to a Big House, outside of which lay
a highly ornamental column of breadfruit wood (*Thau*)
under preparation, before being erected for a central pillar
of the building. The length of it as it lay on the ground
was 35 feet, and its circumference near the base was 7¼
feet. The base was ornamented by two carved figures of
fishes (*Maltath*) on top, and one on each side. At an
equal distance from either end were two raised representations of the *Kai* or cuttle-fish, separated by a blank space
in the middle. Each had eight legs, four sprawling each
way. The breadth of the ornamental fishes at the base
was 9 inches, their length 4½ feet. A pattern of black
and white crescents was also worked in. The figures of
the *Kai* were rude, consisting of raised white discs, with
two black spots in the centre to represent the creature's
eyes. The larger one was 7½ feet in length, the smaller
6½.

The blank space in the middle was 7 feet long, just one-
fifth of the total length of the pillar. The smaller *Kai*
had its tentacles painted white, the larger one black.

The fishes were black, with the fins and backbone
indicated by lines and dots of white.

Inside the house were several raised platforms of
Bioutch wood, borne up on pillars of the same. The
edges and ends of these platforms were elegantly carved
in chevrons (*wathal*) and crescents. One was graven with
life-like representations of Mui-Bab, the Albatross, the
messenger of the great god Yalafath after the Flood to
his creatures below. The carved figures, of the uniform
size of a foot in height, run alternately up and down, and
are ranged wing overlapping wing, with an upper one in
between two lower ones.

There was another odd design called *Meleol*, of two
segments, which, base to base, actually form a cross of a
rather unusual type.

It goes without saying that a goodly number of

village urchins, and a few curious idlers of maturer age, gathered around with their comments, and more than once our old guide in indignation drove the former back with prods of his staff as they pressed too closely. " Have you anything like that over sea ? " asks some village Caliban. " We do carve a bit, but nothing like that," was the answer given with a certain intonation. " Good carvers are scarce over sea ? " says the village critic. " Aye, and in Yap too," said I, and my facetious friend boxed the ears of a boy for laughing. The old man, our guide, who had been on a trading vessel or two in his time, here improved the occasion by a homily on the wondrous foreign engines and manufactures he had met in his travels. It was the monkey who had seen the world, and found his way back to the forest again.

Next day news came that two canoes from Mokomok, in the Uluthi Group to northward, who, according to ancient custom, had come down to pay their tribute, had arrived in Gachepá. A boy was sent overland to invite down one of the Gachepá chiefs and one of the new arrivals. Pending his return, I resolved to visit the islet of Obi, across the water, in the dingy, and to increase my collection of shells and fishes. Two Yap men were allotted to me, but only one turned up in the morning, his mate having cleared out on the spree. The little craft, though neat and gay to outward view as green and white paint could make her, turned out very crank and lop-sided. Dipping our long, tapering, Sonsorol blades cautiously into the calm water, we paddled up to the mangrove belt which encircled Obi. Unhappily the tide was going out fast and the boat kept grounding amongst the shallows, whilst the boy " poddled " around in the mud seeking some passage, whilst I unwillingly had to keep my seat, owing to an injury received in my foot the month before from a splinter of bamboo whilst climbing up Chila-U above Mutok Harbour. Continual wading in salt water cruelly irritates all such wounds but when interesting work has to be done, and done without delay, one has no time to worry over these little inconveniences.

At last we thrust our craft ashore through an opening in the bushes and landed. We found some swamp-shells (*Botangol*) of dingy hue, and picked up some curious hairy crabs and several sorts of starfish (*Rur*). One of the specimens was brownish-green, studded thickly with bluntish dark-blue points or spikes about ¾ inch in length. Another had red spikes, and a third was brownish-green all over, spikes and body alike.

On Obi we collected seeds of various littoral shrubs, and a bunch of round black berries from an unknown creeper. These, and a large quantity of other seeds, collected from time to time from the Caroline area, I handed over on my return to Mr Holtze, curator of the Botanical Gardens at Port Darwin, who undertook to properly classify them. Unfortunately I have not yet heard from him.

The islet was carpeted with wild ginger and coarse grass, and dotted with clumps of dwarf bamboo (*Môr*) and the peculiar " *Vech* " or *Avetch*, with its clusters of small starry, golden yellow blossoms, with a white leaf petal at the end of the cluster. We also saw a *Wote* or wild fig-tree (Sanskrit, *Vota*). A number of dracænas were putting out their clusters of delicate lilac bloom, overshadowed by a tall *Iriu* tree, the bark and leaves of which recall the *Bischoffia javanica* (the *O'a* and *Koka* of Samoa and Tonga), but instead of little bunches of seeds, it bears long seed-pods. There were plenty of native chestnut and callophyllum trees, and a large bed of yams and sweet-potatoes, and a plantation of Lak or water-taro down in a cool, dark hollow, the work of the slave women of Lirou of Tomil, to whom the islet belongs. We caught a large brown and yellow locust or winged grasshopper, which the Spanish call *langosta*, and saw two kinds of dragon-fly—one was small and of brown and yellow tinting (*Osongol*), the other (called *Galaoleu*) larger, had a red body, and the wings prettily variegated dark blue and white. Returning to our boat we found one of the paddles gone, picked up doubtless in a moment of abstraction by some passing fisherman. We made shift with a bottom board instead of the missing paddle and got leisurely over to Tarrang, where I spent the rest of the day putting my notes in order, and, in the absence of that useful little book *Anthropological Notes and Queries*, thinking over innumerable posers to propound next day to the Gochepá chief and the Mokomok man, who had sent word that they would surely come. That evening the man from Macao presented me with some remarkable shells and the tail of a sting-ray (*Paibok*), with which the Spanish non-coms. are reported to quicken up the intellects of their raw Manilla recruits. Attached to it is the deadly spine (*Ruch*), some six inches in length, used formerly all over the Carolines for tipping arrows, spears, and javelins. But the Age of Bone and Stone has passed away, and the Age of Iron and Steel has come in, and come to stay.

CHAPTER XXI

STAY AT TARRANG AND DEPARTURE FOR HONG KONG

NEXT morning, sure enough, Matuk of Gochepá and a man from Mokomok came down, and a busy time they had of it for the next few days (Dec. 3rd to 8th)—the worthy old Lirou of Tomil coming across two or three times to put in his word about the old traditions. Most learnedly did they discourse about the stars of heaven and days of the moon's age, and the names and attributes of bygone gods and heroes ; how came the gift of fire and the invention of stone and shell adzes, and of the introduction of stone and shell money ; who taught the folk to build fish-pens of cane and stone, of Yalafath the kindly but indolent Creator, and Luk the spirit of Evil, ever nimble and active. They waxed eloquent upon the ancient wars with Anangai and Balao (Uleai and the Pelews), and told strange tales of the vanished land of Sepin or Saiping to the north ; the Yap Atlantis, whence came forth fierce warriors, who fought with the men of Ramung and Map and put certain of them to tribute, in the olden days before the great canoes of the white folk from over sea broke through the sky-line from the worlds beyond. Many such tales did they utter, and stubbornly pencil and note-book toiled behind. The man from Mokomok overcame his bashfulness at the bidding of Matuk, who conjured him to answer all my questions as if I was his very father. Over four hundred Uluthi key-words were added to the table of Caroline Island langu-ages. They much resembled the Lamotrek, Sonsorol, and

Uleai equivalents, but had a distinct and peculiar phonesis of their own, forming a curious and beautiful link in the long chain.

This Micronesian Viking was earnest with me to remain in Yap, for from December to May canoes do not go up from Yap to Mokomok as the wind is contrary. I was then to return with them to Mokomok and enjoy the hospitality of their island. It was a sore temptation, but with a mighty effort I repelled it, for Uluthi is all but a *terra incognita* to the white man. And we went on with the work pleasantly, a trifle slowly, maybe, but surely. For a good interpreter was by, and no pains were spared to make sure of every doubtful or obscure point in each tale. The Mokomok man said that it was like being tried before the council of old men at home, so minutely was his evidence sifted and weighed ; but the man, and indeed all my teachers, had excellent patience, and native curiosity effectually put native indolence to the rout. Moreover, there was plenty of strong tobacco to smoke ; they were not kept at one subject too long, and to relieve the tension, I told them many tales for my part from Ponape and Kusaie, fourteen hundred miles to the east, of which they have perfectly clear record in their traditions as *Fanupei* or *Falu-pei* and *Kuthiu*. In a word, my advice to all who want to collect folk-lore from primitive races is this : (1) First put your native friends at their ease completely and get them to laugh and joke. (2) Tell stories *yourself*, leading up to the point or illustration of the question to be opened up. (3) Never interrupt to break the thread of a tale. You can always hark back after the tale is done and clear up any obscurity or apparent irrelevancy. I say *apparent*, because the Caroline Islander seems to consider side issues more than central facts. This makes his stories a trifle rambling. If taken up and interrupted, he is likely to ask plaintively, like the fuddled man in the story, " *Where was I ?* " A little patience, and the native story-teller will make everything fairly

clear. You can't expect him all at once to have everything cut and dried, bottled up and corked down and
labelled, and laid out neatly into prologue, scene, chapter,
and epilogue like the work of a practised modern essay-
writer. Our inquiry, whilst it lasted, was indeed a stiff
business, and how my method succeeded may be seen in
the Appendix.

On the 8th of December a Fiesta was celebrated in
the Spanish settlement with all solemnity. It was the
date of the Feast of the Conception of the Virgin Mary,
the Patroness of the Colony. We made up a party to go
ashore and view the proceedings, and landed at Tapalau
near the house of the Government interpreter, Doña
Barthola, a worthy old Marianne lady. As we walked
along we beheld at the head of the causeway by the
powder magazine, guarded by a Manilla sentry, cigar in
mouth, an arch erected of branches of croton and palm
leaves adorned with streamers of split coconut-leaflets.
E. and I entered the principal hostelry, "*La Aurora*," and
there played an interminable game of "*caroms*" with
crooked cues and "elliptical billiard balls." There were no
pockets at all, and the cloth was cut and seamed in twenty
different places, showing where *someone* had blundered.
Likewise the table was on a slant, as if a baby earthquake had shaken it up. When we had got heartily
weary of the performance, mine host gave us our
luncheon. To show that Yap is not quite a barbarous place I will even quote the menu. First came
Vermicelli soup, then a dish of beans and turtle, with
the heart and liver taken out, chopped up and made into
little sausages for a side-dish. Then we were served
with a plateful of white radishes each. After that came
fried beefsteak from an animal which had been browsing
on the plateau that very morning. Then an omelette of
eggs (*Fak-en-nu'men* or Hen-fruit), which somehow have
been preserved from rats, pigs, dogs, and iguanas—a very
rare dish in the Caroline Islands, and from its rarity much

prized. A custard and some Spanish sweetmeats, coffee and curaçoa, ended our meal, which was moistened by a bottle of Vino Tinto or rough red wine, and some cider, yclept champagne, from some Spanish village of the ominous name of Villa Viciosa.

Arrived at the blessed stage of coffee and cigars, E. told me of two tragedies of the Pacific—the slaying of a Micronesian trading-skipper by his mutinous crew outside the Gilolo passage, and the murder of a like adventurous spirit, at Tench Island in the Exchequer Group. There is plenty of this kind of raw material going, which I suppose some romancist will one of these days work up into a fascinating boys' book of traders, savages and pirates.

Numbers of natives are passing and repassing on the road, all in holiday best, many of them dressed up in trousers and Turkey-red shirts, looking very self-conscious, and desperately uncomfortable under all their unwonted finery. Some appear to have tasted fire-water, and those who haven't look very much as if they would like to, and are not at all shy of naming their wants either. Every house in the settlement has a Cycas palm (*Fauteir*) planted before it, specially ordered the week before, and brought down by the natives from the hill slopes around the *Magal* or Lighthouse on top of Mount Buliel over-looking the harbour. Four o'clock Mass is over, and at five o'clock the procession is to take place. The whole colony is gay with bunting, and the red and yellow flag of Castile is much in evidence. I observe that the Union Jack is unaccountably absent, and so are the Stars and Stripes. " One of them may be here sooner than the Dons think for," grumbles my prophetic vis-a-vis. By and by the cry arises, " *They are coming.*" Downhill from the chapel marches the procession headed by priests in red robes, and choristers in white coats, bearing crucifixes and pictures and the image of the Virgin. Next marches a body of native converts. Then a band of small boys fitted with tinsel wings to represent cherubs or angels. " I should take them for black-beetles," murmurs my un-poetic comrade in the deck chair.   Then he livens up for a moment, for a bevy of Yap and Marianne schoolgirls follows, some of the latter with undeniable good looks, prettily dressed in the old Spanish fashion, white lace veils and dainty mantillas.   Next come a medley of half-castes.   A group of the officers of the garrison fol-lows, and last of all streams along in loose order a wild looking crew of natives, comb in hair, marching to the accompaniment of bugle, flute and drum.   Observing narrowly the gentlemen bringing up the rear of the motley throng, I observe that many of them can hardly keep their legs.   Evidently the red wine has been going down sweetly.   " I'm sorry for anyone who has a labour contract in hand to-morrow," said I.   " That's so," says the cynic.   " None of the folk ashore will be able to get a native to work for the next week or more.   I wish I could be out at some of them with a stuffed club. They're like a lot of spoiled children, and the Manilla men make them worse every day.   But we're all right on Tarrang.   If any of our Sonsorol boys go ashore on the spree, they know what they'll catch when O'Keefe comes back."

More natives than ever were now crowding around with nimble fingers, seeking to pick up any trifles lying about. Some who had spent their ready money were staggering about the roads offering combs and ornaments, and some their wretched wives and female relatives in exchange for dollars to purchase draughts of red wine to slake their burning thirst.   It is a regular Pandemonium.   " Such a racket that nobody can hear themselves think," is my comrade's terse remark.   A mean-looking Manilla recruit limps along hand to cheek, blubbering like a great baby. A fellow-gambler has smitten him forcibly on the mouth for cheating, and half strangled him into the bargain. Vomiting strange maledictions, his adversary follows with a bitten hand. Things are getting lively, now that fighting has started, so after doing a little barter we start for Tarrang, carrying with us three carven combs, a bamboo betel-box, and a *marafau* or necklace of black hibiscus fibre, the insignia of some adult youth, who doubtless will catch it hot when his grandpapa sees him without it to-morrow.

The day after the Fiesta the white wings of the long-looked for *Santa Cruz* are seen fluttering far out to sea. About noon she sweeps through the narrow harbour mouth, E. and I boarding her whilst she is still under way. I receive a most cordial greeting from the burly and jovial O'Keefe, whom I now meet face to face for the first time. A number of Sonsorol and St David's lads are on board, reinforcements for the band of workmen at Tarrang. Storms have swept their island homes almost bare of coco-nuts, and the poor people are only too glad to take service with the friend and benefactor who had done much for them in past years.

On board the vessel is a prisoner, a Pelew chieftain named Tarragon, a noted homicide. He was one of the prime movers in the cutting-off of the trading schooner *Maria Secunda* and the massacre of the crew in 1894, and had long defied arrest. O'Keefe held him up singly with a revolver in the middle of a menacing crowd, and invested him with the order of the bracelet on the spot. We took him ashore under guard, and what the Spanish did to him I cannot tell, nor do I greatly care to know. He was a sullen looking ruffian enough. I daresay he left some others just as bad behind him. Doubtless the jaws of Justice opened and devoured him even as Alice's walrus swallowed the oysters. That very forenoon O'Keefe and E. had a long interview with the Spanish Governor, who was consider-ably irritated when he heard that the Dutch flag had been hoisted on the little barren isle of St David's, and vowed that they should hear of it at Madrid. O'Keefe was thanked and complimented by the Governor in the graceful and cordial manner in which the Spanish acknowledge a service rendered. There followed a considerable interchange of hospitalities between our island and the shore, in which I unfortunately was debarred from taking a prominent part, my foot giving me much pain, which I endeavoured with some success to charm away by unremitting application to work, the good old Lirou coming over almost every day with some new tale or fresh string of curious facts. " Matches," the Sonsorol boy, was generally at hand to get what I wanted, for I could hardly set foot to the ground for days. However, the Spanish medico gave me relief at last—taking out a deeply-embedded splinter that had escaped notice all this while. The days were tremendously hot, the evenings pleasant and cool, and, thank goodness!—no mosquitoes. There were plenty of books to read, and I was continually busy revising old notes and writing new ones. Mrs O'Keefe also gave me some valuable assistance in getting proper equivalents of my table of key-words in the dialects of Sonsorol, St David's, and Nauru. It was then that I appreciated what hard honest work Konias on Pilau had done for me. " That is a good boy—that Konias," said she. " When you come back again, mind you ask my husband to let you have a Sonsorol boy. They are good boys and always do what I tell them, and I know they would work well for you, because you are not always grumbling at them and finding fault."

And if I ever do get back again to the Carolines I think I will take her advice.

On the 14th December the bi-monthly mail steamer *Saturnus* from Manilla came in with a batch of deported rebels. She was soon coaling at the Tarrang wharf. It seemed odd and incongruous to see numbers of Sonsorol and Yap men scrambling along with great baskets of coal on their heads, like the Egyptians at Port Said, or the Japanese coolies at Moji at the entrance of the Inland Sea. It was ludicrous to see a stalwart native stalking

along the quivering plank, basket on head, mother-naked
under the scorching sun, save for a scanty girdle of red
hibiscus fibre twisted loosely round his loins—his long
hair bound up in a bunch behind, with generally a comb
stuck in it, ornamented by bits of fluttering newspaper
or cock's feathers. Some of the workers were thickly
begrimed with sweat and coal-dust, and presented a very
comical appearance. They did not take any particular
notice of the Manilla men on board. Those of the
garrison ashore they have weighed in their own mental
balance and found wanting, and view the newcomers with
good-humoured indifference and a shade of contempt, as
feeble and unwarlike beings.

The *Saturnus* had left Manilla on the 7th, and consequently brought some interesting news of the progress
of the rebellion. There has been a battle near Cavite,
and a whole villageful of rebels—some eight hundred in
number—have been cooped up by the Spanish reinforcements lately arrived *via* Singapore, and shot down
to the last man. Considering how the rebels behaved
after capturing Imus and Bacor one cannot well blame
the Spaniards for their retaliation. In Manilla just now
there is considerable feeling against Germans and Americans, and by implication of course Englishmen. There
are two German and three English men-of-war lying in
the river, which is just as well in case of accidents.
The morning the *Saturnus* left, six rebels were brought
out and shot on the Luneta esplanade, whilst upwards of
fifty were reported to be lying in jail ready for platoon
practice. Their deaths will leave humanity none the
poorer. Such, at all events, is the opinion of the new
commander lately arrived from Spain—a man of the
Parma or Alva type, who, like one of Carlyle's heroes,
" does not believe in the rosewater plan of surgery."

So the local governor across the water has plenty to
think of, and forty more idle, worthless, mutinous rogues
to house, victual, and discipline.

Just after the *Saturnus* left things went a bit askew in this island of Barataria, and the good governor's noddle was sorely perplexed. A Chinese trader of O'Keefe's came down from the neighbourhood of Girigir in the north in great distress of mind to complain that a party of natives had come upon him and forcibly taken his boat for a fishing excursion. He was thumped and beaten with sticks, and spears were thrown at him, but none of them wounded him. When the report of these doings was laid before the governor he sent up a sergeant and two privates that very day to summon two of the principal natives accused to come down and give an account of themselves. This they very obediently did, for the Spaniards could never have forced them to come down against their will. On examination both accuser and accused managed in the space of about half an hour to involve themselves in such a hopeless fog of lying and perjury, that the governor, losing all patience, settled matters with a vengeance by jailing them all for two days on short commons as an inducement for the future to tell a plain tale plainly. If he had sent the interpreter to join them as well, no great harm would have been done either.

On December 16th I received another visit from Matuk of Gochepá, who told some more odd facts about the Pilungs or aristocracy and the Pimlingai or slave class. (*Pilung*, probably = Sanskrit *Puling*, a male, and means "*The Men*.") The Pilungs were the old settlers —autochthones—and the Pimlingai were castaways from other islands. The latter used to call themselves *Malailai*, which possibly answers to the term *Malaiu* or Malay, in Japanese *Marai*. He gave me to understand, moreover, that an ancient judge called *Magaragoi* introduced the distinction between freemen and slaves by the wearing of the *Roai* or comb of mangrove wood. Lirou came in the afternoon, and as a final *bonne bouche*, served me up further food for thought in the form of the following Yap traditions.

THE INVENTION OF STONE MONEY

There was a wise old man in Tomil named *Anagumáng*, to whom Le-gerem showed all the stars of heaven, and the seasons of their rising and setting. After three months' study this apt pupil took seven men with him (the usual "*perfect number*" in Yap tradition), manned a large Gothamite canoe, and sailed into the unknown southern waters, in quest of the land of Balao (the Pelew Group), under the guiding of the constellation *Mageriger* or Pleiades. Entering the northern reef passage and passing Bab-el-Thaob, he came down to the island of Peleleu. A little to the northward of the last-mentioned island there lie certain conical islets named *Kokial* scattered about the wide lagoon. Here he found a new sort of shining stone (which the men of London call arragonite or calcite), and conceived the idea of hewing it into various portable forms to serve as a rude medium of exchange. There was an abundance of pearl-shell here as well, to which he helped himself liberally for the same purpose. The shining rock he found, and with infinite trouble cut it with his shell-axes into the form of fishes about a yard long. Some fragments, for the sake of variety, his men worked into the shape of a crescent moon. Others again they chipped into wheels of different sizes, rounded like the orb of the full moon. With these last, when they had bored a big hole through the middle of each, Anagumáng was satisfied. So they loaded up their canoe and returned ; the voyage back only taking five days. When they took the stones ashore Le-gerem kept the wheels with the hole in the middle, and threw away the rest as worthless, and put into operation a powerful charm to centre all the desire of the people on the recognised standard coinage.

Before this time, ruefully remarks the narrator, there was no fighting in Yap. Ever since that, however, there have been constant civil wars in the land, arising from the eagerness of each tribe to acquire a large portion of the coveted treasure.

After this there were frequent expeditions going to the Pelews from Tomil, Rul, and Gochepá, and many were the people who lost their lives from imprudently putting to sea in the stormy season. Others, moreover, after reaching the Pelews, perished on their return journey, their vessels swamping or upsetting from carrying heavy or carelessly stowed freight of these precious and fatal stones. Others again were slain in battle by the people of the country, who were valiant men, and resented these uncalled-for visits, and the plundering of their beds of pearl-shell.

A NEW VERSION OF THE PROMETHEUS MYTH

The yam and the taro were in Yap, but as yet there was no fire to cook them. The natives used to dry them in the sand, and, as it were, sunbake them. And the folk suffered grievously from internal pains, and besought Yalafath to help them once more. Immediately there fell a great red-hot thunderbolt from the sky, and smote a Choi tree (Pandanus). At the contact of the fiery element the Choi broke out into a regular eruption of prickles down the middle and sides of every leaf. Dessra, the Thunder god, thus found himself fixed fast in the tree-trunk, and called out in a lamentable voice for somebody to deliver him from his irksome prison. A woman named Guaretin, sunbaking taro hard by, heard the voice, and helped the distressed god. He inquired on what work she was engaged, and when she told him, bade her fetch plenty of moist clay. This he kneaded into a goodly cooking-pot (*Thib*), to the great delight of the worthy housewife. He then sent her in search of some sticks from the *Arr* tree (called *Tupuk* by the Ponapeans), which he put under his armpits and infused into them the latent sparks of fire, and went his way. This is how the art of making fire from the friction of wood, and the moulding of pots out of clay came to the primitive folk of

Yap. Hence two proverbs suggested to the cautious and practical Yap mind.

Moral—" Never refuse to do a good turn to those in need, it may pay you better than you think " ; and " Beware of hidden fire even when you see no smoke."

THE BUILDING OF THE FIRST CANOE

The indefatigable fairy mother Le-gerem prepared to astonish her people with a further display of first-class magical powers. One day a very big canoe was seen slowly floating down from the clouds, let down by innumerable ropes or pulleys, just over the village of Gocham or Gotham in Tomil. The people flocked in crowds to see the wonderful sight. Some inauspicious words of the impatient multitude broke the charm. Before the canoe could be lowered in safety to the earth, the ropes broke, and the wondrous structure was smashed up beyond all hopes of repair. Then Le-gerem hewed a *Voi* tree, measured it out with care, and with infinite pains made another of similar model. The long and somewhat clumsy Yap canoes, running high in bow and stern fore and aft like Scandinavian vessels, with their heavy solid outriggers and the curious fish-tail ornamentation in bow and stern, show how the industry of the Gothamite ship-builders followed the directions of their long-suffering patroness.

After the departure of the *Saturnus* for Guam and Ponape I made busy preparations for embarking myself and my belongings in the *Santa Cruz*, O'Keefe having kindly offered me a passage in her up to Hong-Kong. On the 22nd December, having taken a cordial leave of the Spanish governor, priests, officials, and my native friends, I went on board the little schooner, heavily laden with a cargo of bêche-de-mer, much in request amongst the Chinese for their New Year festivities. I took with me about fifteen boxes of curios in all, which wanted a lot of storing. We left about noon, running Goror Point out of sight before sunset. We passed the Pelews on our right, giving them a wide berth, with a steady north-east monsoon helping us on our way until we were within 150 miles of the Ballintang Straits, which separate Formosa from the north coast of Luzon. We spent a very quiet Christmas at sea, and the day after it a dead calm fell, lasting forty-eight hours just off Duguay Trouin reef. We had a motley crew, two Yap men, one boy from Sonsorol, one from St David's, one half-caste Pelew islander, and two half-wild natives of Ilocan. The first mate was an old Tasmanian, and not a soul on board except O'Keefe had the remotest notion of navigation. So it is hard to conjecture what would have become of us if anything had happened to the captain. But in Micronesia no one bothers his head in discussing what might have been. The last day of the year 1897 we passed through the Ballintang Straits between the Batuyan and Batang Islands. Entering the China Sea we encountered furious tide-rips and very rough water, also occasional squalls with heavy rain, and a considerable fall in the thermometer. Early on the morning of January 3rd the rude rounded and massive outlines of the dreary China coast were sighted. Slowly the distant Peak showed up clearer and clearer out of the banks of cloud-wrack. There fell a spell of light and variable breezes, when to our relief a tug-boat came out and towed us in through the narrow Lyeemoon Pass, past the Quarries and the Sugar Works ; finally, after we had received pratique, casting us off to our moorings opposite the weather-beaten waterfront of Wanchai about three o'clock on a bright and sunny Sunday afternoon. Thence into the bustling streets filled with rickshaws and pedestrians, where one realises that if Europe is still far off the islands are very far off too.

And thus I made my first step back to the civil-isation of the West, carrying with me into the busy streets of great cities and the stirring hum of their marts, thoughts of a strange folk whom my people have not known ; carrying with me, I say, into our island of cloud and mist and fog, memories ineffaceable of tropic woods unscorched by frost, unstripped by rigorous winter, visions of bluest sky and sea, and of a serene, fragrant and lustrous air dreamed of by poets, but as yet unchronicled by artists. And now, weary of our smoky cities, I soon shall be returning to mountain and coral-strand, to a land of hanging woods and singing waters. As carols the settler of Yeat's Lake Isle of Innisfree :—

" And I shall have some peace there, for peace comes dropping slow,
   Dropping from the veils of the morning to where the cricket sings
There midnight's all a glimmer and noon a purple glow,
   And evening full of the linnet's wings.
I will arise and go now, for always night and day
   I hear lake water lapping with low sounds by the shore ;
While I stand on the roadway, or on the pavements grey
   I hear it in the deep heart's core."

APPENDIX

(A) CLAN NAMES OF PONAPE

Called *Tupu* or *Tipu*, also *Chou-tapa*

Note.—The names within brackets are those of the principal chiefs belonging to the several tribes.

1. Tupu-en-Panamai (Noch, in Metalanim).
2. Tupu-en-man tontol (King Rocha of Kiti), patron-saint Ilako, a name that appears in the Yap Pantheon as Ilagoth. The Man tontol, or Dark bird, is the Kau-alik or Blue Heron.
3. Choun-Kaua (The Wachai of Chokach, Lap-en-Not, the headman of Not, and Chaulik of Tomara).
4. Tupu-lap, a Mount Wana clan, allied to Nos. 2 and 13.
5. Lipitán (Nanekin of Kiti).
6. Lachi-aláp (King of U).
7. Tupu-en-Pápa.
8. Tupu-en-Lúk = the children of Lúk, the spirit of guile and mischief.
9. Tip-en-uai, the descendants of Icho-Kalakal's great invading force from the South. (Nanekin in Metalanim, also Lap-en-Paliker, Lap-en-Langar, and the influential chieftain Nan-matau of the Palang valley. The totem of this tribe is the Likantenkap or Sting-ray.
10. Latak.
11. Chau-n-Pók.
12. Tup-en-man-en-Chatau. The children of the Devil-Bird or Native Owl. (Chatau = Pueliko, the Ponapean Inferno.) In Malay the name of the Owl *Burong Hantu* has the same meaning.
13. Tip-en-man-potopot. The Man-potopot or White Bird is the *Chik* or Boatswain bird. Another Kiti tribe.

14. Choun-pali-en-pil.   The people of the waterside.
15. Naniak (Nanchau-Rerren of Roch and Annepein).
16. Chou-n-Chamáki.   Chamáki is the name of a hill near Chap-en-Takai on the south-west coast.
17. Li-ara-Katau.   This tribe is now extinct.
18. Chou-n-mach.   Probably representing the ancient Malay element. Literally. The People of the olden Times.
19. Choun-Kiti.

The old name for a king was *Chau* or *Akata*, and *Icho* meant a prince. The kings of Metalanim and U are entitled *Ichipau*, their queens *Likant*. The king of Kiti is variously called *Nanamareki* or *Rocha*, his wife being called *Nan-alik*. The wife of the *Wachai* or prince of Chokach is styled *Nanep*. The children of a king were called *Cherrichou*. Other chiefly titles were *Taok*, *Noch*, *Chau-wana*, *Nanaua*, *Nanapei*, *Nankerou-n-pontake*, *Nanit-lapalap*, *Nalik-lapalap*, *Nanchau*, *Chautel*, *Lumpoi*, *Auntol-rerren,Mar*,[1] *Au,Au-en-pon-pei, Choumatau,Chaulik*,[2] the smallest title of all. Then came the *Maio* or *Freedmen*, then the *Aramach-mal* or *Common* folk ; and, last of all, *Litu* or serfs, mostly descended from prisoners of war.

Counted equal to the nobles were the two religious bodies, the *Chaumaro* or high priests, and the *Laiap* or priests of the second order. These were of great weight and importance in the land, and united the functions of doctor, magician, rain-maker, and diviner of the future. Theirs was the knowledge of medicinal herbs and poisons, the gift of *Kapakap* or prophecy, of the *Macha-kilang* or second sight, the interpretation of dreams and omens, and the dreaded power of the *Ria* or imprecation of curses. Upon them devolved the ordering of Court ceremonies and public festivals, and the seasonable invocation of the gods of rain and harvest, the staving off of famine and all calamities, public and private, and the maintenance of the

---

[1] *Cf.* Maori, *Mara!* Sir, a salutation of a young man to an older.

[2] Perhaps akin to S.-W. and S. Polynesian, *Taulekaleka, Taurekareka,* and *Taule'ale'a,* a youth, beau. (In Maori, *a rascal.*)

Charaui or Tabu. Theirs were the principal seats upon the Lempantam or high stone platform in the Nach or Council Lodge—theirs, next to the king's, the best portion of cooked food and kava upon the days of solemn festival.

Throughout all the tribes great respect was paid to the chiefs, who were never addressed as " *thou*," but always in the second person plural "*ye.*" As in Malaysia there were many special words used in addressing a chief, and again there was another set form of words for addressing the king, who was looked up to with great awe, and only addressed in the plural of majesty as " *They.*" The chiefs mingle amongst their tribesmen with great familiarity and affability, which, no doubt, forms a fresh bond of sympathy and union. They all hold together loyally ; offend one, and all are eager to take up his quarrel. If the chief be a kindly hospitable man, his people will follow his example. If he be a rogue and a churl, his people will act as rogues and churls too. And this I have observed is a characteristic of Caroline islanders in general. They seem to have little independence of judgment, and love to follow the lead of their chiefs in all things crooked or straight, right or wrong.

(B) NAMES OF NATIVE DISEASES

The miasmas arising from the swampy belt of alluvium surrounding Ponape give rise to various catarrhal and febrile maladies, very fatal to the old people during the rainy season, with its light and variable winds. An important factor in the health of the people is the trade-wind that blows clear and fresh out of the north-east from October to May. Their names for fever are : *Cho-mau-pou* and *Chomau-karrakar*, the first denoting the cold, the second the hot fit of the malady.

They call the smallpox, introduced by a whaling vessel some forty years ago, and which carried off half the population of the island, *Kilitap* or Peeling Skin.

Consumption, for which the natives also have to thank

the whalers, is called by the grim name LI-MONGOMONG or "*The Lady who shrivels men up.*"

The venereal disease, now happily quite of rare occurrence, is called KENCH (Jap. *Kanso*), upon Yap *Rabungek*.

Scrofula (*Pir*) is fairly common, the result of a poor diet.

Leprosy (*Tukotuk*), somewhat rare, and of a comparatively mild type; probably introduced from the East by the early Asiatic settlers (*cf.* Maori *Tukutuku*: a curse, to bewitch).

Rip is the generic term for sores and ulcers (Kusaian RUF) (*cf.* Tahitian; *Ripa*, wasting sickness).

Cough is *Kopokop* (Kusaie *Kofkof*), a cold or catarrh, *Toi* or *Punan*.

Asthma is *Lukoluk*. Hiccough, *Marrer*.

Rheumatism, *Matak*. Vomiting, *Mumuch*. Headache, vertigo, *Maaliel*.

Home-sickness or nostalgia, *Lit-en-chap*. Paralysis, *Li-chongapo*.

Delirium, *Li-aurára*. Insomnia, *Ika-n-pong*.

Itching, *Kili-pitipit* or Quick-skin.

Constipation, *Tang*, *Teng*. Dysentery, said to have been introduced from Manilla, *Pek-en-inta*.

Squint is called *Macha-pali*, or eye on one side.

Blindness is *Mach-kun*. Fainting is *Machapong*.

Lameness is *Chikel* (*cf.* Javanese *Chongkul*).

A swelling of the hands into hard lumps is called *Komut-en-Kiti;* query, *chalk-stones.*

The disease known as *Tanetane* in Polynesia, appearing as an eruption of light-coloured maculæ on the brown native skin, is *Chenchen* (Kusaie *Tantan*, spotted).

The curious furfuraceous disease, mentioned by Guppy as so prevalent in the Solomon and Gilbert Islands called Tokelau Leprosy or Tokelau ringworm, is very common in Ponape, where it is called *Kili-en-Wai* or The Foreign Skin.

Elephantiasis is also common in this group which the ethnic mutilation (*Lekelek*) is supposed to guard against.

(C) PONAPEAN TREES, PLANTS AND SHRUBS

I here give the native names arranged in alphabetical order, and where possible with the botanical name side by side. To each is affixed a description of its economical or medicinal qualities, use, or special virtues. I have sometimes subjoined the neighbouring Micronesian, the Polynesian, or the Philippine Island name, agreeably to the recommendation of Guppy in his book upon the Solomon Islands, pp. 186-190. A more complete dissertation upon the widespread distribution of similar plant and tree-names throughout the great Pacific area will be found in a paper of mine which appeared in the Transactions of the Polynesian Society of New Zealand in 1897.

A

Abit, Abith, Abiut. The Yap name for a bush-tree bearing round edible fruit of a dull green, marked all over with light yellow raised patches. Flavour sweet and mawkish. The pulp has an offensive, sour odour.

Aio. The Banyan-tree of Ponape (Ficus Indica). The *Ao* of the Mortlocks and the *Aoa* of Polynesia. (Also called on the east coast *Oio.*)

Ais. (Parinarium laurinum.) The *Atita* of the Solomon Islands, the *Adhidh* of Yap, the *Aset* of the Mortlocks. In the Pelews known as LAUG. It grows to a considerable height and produces large circular rough reddish-brown fruits about the size of a cricket-ball. A decoction of the pericarp is used for painting canoes red, and the kernel produces a good varnish-oil used in conjunction with clay for caulking seams of leaky boats.

Ak. The generic word for mangroves. (Tagal *Bakah*). The upper branches run into long straight wands or poles which are used for spear-shafts, rafters, punting-poles and husking-sticks. *N.B.*—In Polynesia *Oka* denotes a husking-stick or rafter.

Alek. An elegant species of reed-grass, the slender

stems of which are extensively used for making shutters and floorings.

Aput, Apuit. A white-wood riverside tree used for the *Kerek* or figure-heads of canoes.

Aulong. A species of wild ginger bearing a reddish or crimson spike of flowers called *Likaitit.*

C H

Chai. The Custard-apple (Anona squamosa). In Yap, *Sausau.*

Chaiping, Chaping. (Heritiera littoralis.) The Metalanim name for the *Marrap-en-chet, i.e.* the *Marrap* or chestnut of the salt water, the *sea-side species,* to distinguish it from the *Marrap* of the woods (Inocarpus edulis). The Chaiping has singular keeled seeds. The under part of the leaf is of a silvery whiteness. Wood hard and white, used by boat-builders. The *Pipilusu* of the Solomon Islands (Guppy). In Tagal *Sapang* denotes a hard-wood tree.

Chair-en-uai (*i.e.* The Foreign Flower). The U and Metalanim name applied indifferently to a species of Gardenia, and to the Cananga odorata. (The latter is the *Ylang-ylang* of the Philippines and the *Moso'oi, Mohoki* and *Motoki* of Polynesia.) With *Chair, Sair,* " a flower," compare Javanese *Sari,* " a flower," and Polynesian *Tiare, Siale* id.

Chakan. The Candle-nut tree (Aleurites triloba). Known in the Polynesian area as *Rama, Lama* and *Ama,* also as *Tutui.* The charred nuts used by the Ponapeans for making a black paint.

Chakau, Choko. The kava of Polynesia (Piper Methysticum). From its pounded roots the national beverage is made. It is extensively grown all over the island, except in the Metalanim tribe, where its raising is vetoed. The word is connected with the Japanese *Sake, Saka,* which denotes (*a*) rice-spirit, (*b*) strong drink in general. Compare Kusaie *Seka,* (*a*) the kava-plant, (*b*) the drink prepared from it.

Chalanga-en-ani. A fungus or toadstool. Literally " Devil's ear."

Chapachap, Chap-el-lang.   A sort of rush growing on the plateaus and hillsides.

Chapokin.   A species of wild arum.

Chatak.   The Elæocarpus, and the *Nil-Kanth* of India. A tall forest tree, its trunk supported by wide flanges or buttresses.   The wood is white and firm, much used by the Ponapeans for canoe-building.   The berries are exactly the size and shape of an olive, but of an intense cobalt blue.   They are eaten by the fruit-pigeons.   I have seen the tree also upon Strong's Island (*Kusaie*).   Habitat the upper hill-slopes.   (Perhaps akin to Malay *Jati*, teak.)

Chaua.   The generic name for the *Arum esculentum* or Taro, of which several varieties are cultivated on Ponape. (Compare Motu, Nuku-Oro, and Marquesan *Tao* the Taro, of which word the Ponapean is a harsher Micronesian variant.)

Chenchul (*Ipomea* sp.).   A creeping plant with purple flowers, like a convolvulus, found on all the island beaches. Decoction of leaves drunk by child-bearing women.

Cheu.   The sugar-cane.   (Compare Polynesian *To*, Fijian *Ndovu*, Malayan *Tubu*, German New Guinea *Tab*, *Tup*, *Tep*.)   Called upon Ngatik *Chou*.   In Paliker district the name *Cheu* is tabued, as it occurs in the name of a local chief, and the name *Nan-Tap* or Madame *Tap* is substituted, the older form of the word coming back into life and use in this curious way.   (Varieties : *Cheu-ntâ*, with dark-red stems. *Cheu-puot*, with light-coloured stems. *Cheu-en-uai*, with brownish stems. *Cheu-en-air*, with speckled stems. *Cheu-rei*, with banded stems and dark-coloured juice.)

Choio.   A waterside tree.   Hard white wood.   Drooping habit of boughs.   Longish leaves.   Habitat, the swampy banks near the mouths of the rivers.

Chong, Chom.   A variety of the mangrove (*Bruguiera*). (*Cf.* Polynesian *Tongo*, the mangrove.)   The bark of the root-stems is used for dyeing a brown or reddish-brown colour.   In some Pacific Islands bits of the bark are thrown into the calabashes of fresh coconut-toddy so as to set up a speedier fermentation.

Choun-mal, i.e., " *Worthless fellow.*" The Stinging Nettle.
(The *Salato* of Samoa.   Malay *Jalatan id.*)

Chongut. A bush-tree in Yap with a burning milky sap, which, falling on the skin, produces obstinate and terrible ulceration.

I

Ichak. A wild vine of the gourd family (*Cucurbitaceæ*). The natives use its fruit for calabashes. The name is also used to denote a coconut bottle.

Ichao, Ichau, the *Callophyllum Inophyllum.* The *Fetao, Hetau* and *Tamanu* of the Polynesian area, and the *Bitao* of the Philippines. It is the *Iter* of Kusaie, the *Icher* of the Marshall group. Its wood is firm and durable and of a rich reddish-brown colour, equally good for boat-building or for ornamental work. It produces round fruits with a bitter-sweet kernel, rich in a resinous greenish oil most valuable for rheumatism. It is the *Ndilo* oil of Fiji, which in 1870 commanded such a ready sale in the European market. In 1890 I sent two bottles of the oil from Samoa to Dr Tarrant of Sydney for experimental purposes, but, as frequently happens in these cases, no reply was ever received.

Ikoik. The *Kanava* of Nuku-Oro, the *Tou* of the Marquesas. A littoral tree producing scarlet trumpet-shaped flowers. It has a dark brownish-red wood valuable for boat-building.

Ikol. A small weed with round leaves used for dressing burns.

Ingking (*Compotacea* sp.). A littoral shrub found on the low coral islets in the lagoon bearing crimson fruit, oblong like that of a sweet-briar. Flowers small ; greenish yellow. A decoction of the bark and leaf are used to cure colic and internal pains.

Inot (*Scævola Kœnigii*). A tall littoral tree with large juicy obovate leaves of a bitter flavour and small white cruciform flowers with a violet centre. A decoction of the leaves forms a fine tonic, and the natives say an aphrodisiac. A curious appearance is given to the leaves by the presence of white, raised markings running into a network recalling the maculæ of the Tokelau ringworm on the human skin. I have seen the shrub growing on the roadside near the Quarries and the Sugar-Works in Hong-Kong harbour. Upon Nuku-Oro it is called *Manuka-pasanga*. In the Mariannes it is called NANASO; in Japanese, KUSA-TOBERA.

Ioio. A bush-plant running up to some ten or twelve feet in height, with leaves like a *Canna* and juicy stalks like a ginger plant. It bears white flowers. The fruits are red in colour and oblong in form, growing together in a long bunch or raceme. The juice is aromatic and astringent. A decoction of the pith is used by the natives as an unfailing specific for diseases of the mucous membrane.

Iol, Yol. A species of giant convolvulus growing on the hill-slopes : flowers large, white, with sulphur-yellow centre. A decoction of the leaves and seeds possesses properties akin to those of ergot of rye. Much used by the native women for procuring abortion.

Ita, Ita-n-wal. The wild Ratan-cane (Samoan *Lafo*).

K

Ka, Ke. A shrub cultivated for the sweet cinnamon-scented essential oil extracted from its bruised and crushed bark. The *Ka-en-Mant* is a particularly choice species (Cinnamum Terglanicum ?).

Kalak. A tall bush-tree.

Kalau. The Hibiscus Tiliaceus. (The *Gili-fau* of the Mortlocks, the *Kal* of Yap, the *Lo* of Kusaie and the Marshall Islands.) (The Ponapean name *Kala-hau* contains two elements, the latter the Polynesian *Fau*, *Hau*, Malay *Baru*,[1] Tagal *Bali-bago*.) Strips of the bark form the native cord or string, and was often beaten out into baste to make women's dresses ("Li-kau") in olden times. From the flowers and leaves a decoction

---

[1] The *Varu* of Aurora and New Hebrides.

is made possessing astringent qualities, a great native remedy for urethritis.

Kamp-en-ial, Kamp-en-Yap.   A bush-shrub with long narrow leaves, bearing tiny inodorous white flowers, four or five together on a stem.   The *Seasea* of Samoa. (Eugenia sp.).

Kamuché.   A shrub growing some ten feet high, bearing small bluish-mauve flowers.   Habitat, the low coral islets in the lagoon.

Kanau, Kamau.   A tall bush-tree with pinnate leaves and curious heavy wrinkled seeds like the kernel of a walnut.   Firm white wood.   Habitat, the banks of the Pillap-en-Chakola Creek, Ascension Bay, north coast (Cynometra sp.).

Kanepap.   A tall forest tree bearing minute flowers in panicles.   Wood used in house-building.

Kanepul.   Bush - tree.   (According to Dr Pereiro, a Dracontomelum, order Anacardiæ.)

Kangit.   The name applied indifferently to the true Mango (Mangifera Indica); and to a large tree (Pangium edule), bearing huge round fruits like those of an alligator pear, containing ten or twelve seeds exactly like the single one of a mango, and filled with a custard-like yellowish pulp of delicious flavour.   Upon Yap the tree is called RAUAL. Decoction of the boiled bark valuable cure for urethral troubles.   The kernel of the seeds contains a narcotico-irritant poison.

Kap.   The generic word for the yam, extensively cultivated in all the districts.[1]   (*Cf.* Japanese *Kabu,* a turnip; Philippines, *Gabe ;* Polynesian, *Kape ; Ape* id, the Arum costatum.

Some of the varieties :—

Kap-e-lai, Kape-e-palai.   Sweet variety.   (Samoan *Ufi-*

---

[1] At the planting of the yams at the beginning of the rainy season there was held a singular ceremony.   The chief priest came forward with a digging-stick in his hand, with which he raked about in the ground, with the solemn incantation, " *Champa kota, airi koti,*" *i.e.,* " Good soil rise up, poor soil sink down."

lei, and *Palai* yam. sp., compare Mangaian *Ui-parai*.)
Kap-en-mali : Round, light-coloured skin. *Kap-namu :*
Long. *Kap-en-Ant :* Light-coloured skin. *Kap-mpulam-*
pul : Dark purple skin and flesh. Choice variety. The
potato is called *Kap-en-uai* or the Foreign Yam ; and the
Sweet Potato *Kap-en-Tomara*, or the Yam of Tomara,
from a village near the Palang River on the west coast
where it was first introduced. Similarly the Fijians call
the sweet potato *Kawai-ni-vavalangi*, or the Foreign
Yam ; the Malays *Ubi-Jawa*, the Yam of Java. In the
Pelews the potato and the sweet potato are styled *Tulngut-*
al-Barath, i.e. the Yam from the Westward.

Kara, Kora. A tall forest tree. Hard heavy wood,
white when first cut, but turning red after a few days.
Good for cabinet-making. Habitat, hill-slopes above
Metalanim harbour and around the Kipar and Paliker
district on the west and south-west coast.

Karara. A species of wild nutmeg (Myristica). Fruits
chewed in olden time to make the teeth red. (Query, as a
substitute for betel-nut ?)

Karamat. Species of dead-nettle. Crushed leaves used
for poulticing indolent ulcers.

Karrat. A large plantain with bright orange flesh
(Malay *Kalat*, Kusaie *Kalas*, Hindustani *Kadli, Kela*).

Karrer. The Kiti and Chokach word for trees of the
citrus family, such as the orange, lemon or lime. (The
Kahit of the Mariannes. In Kusaie, *Osas.* In Yap,
Gurgur and *Guerguer*.)

Katai, Kotop. Varieties of areca-palm found on the
plateaus and the upland slopes. Children sometimes
chew the nuts, the adults very rarely. The habit of
Betel-nut chewing practised so universally in the Philippines, the Mariannes, the Pelews and in Yap, somehow
has not taken root firmly amongst the Ponapeans, who
appear to find the stimulus of Kava-drinking sufficient
for their needs.

Katar. The tree-fern found in great abundance in

ravines and clefts of the hills. The trunks are often used for posts in house-building.

Katereng. The sweet basil. Used in soups and for making tea, an excellent fever draught. A decoction of the leaves in boiling water is a capital application to fevered, aching and wearied limbs.

Katiu, Katia. The Ixora. A forest tree of upright and sturdy growth, with long narrow leaves and umbels of brilliant scarlet blossoms with a yellow centre. Spear-shafts are made of the stems, also punting-poles and rafters. This tree also grows in great magnificence upon Kusaie to the south-east and upon the King's Isle of Lele where it is called *Kasiu.* In Yap it is called *Katchu,* and in the Uluthi group *Kathiu.*

Katol. The Paper-Mulberry (Broussonettia papyrifera). The *Pu'uehu* of the Marquesas and the *Lau-Ua* of Samoa. It is not common in Ponape, which may account for the absence of the native cloth called *Siapo, Ngatu* or *Tapa* by the Samoan, Tongan and Marquesan islanders. How-ever, rarity or absence of this fabric in Ponape was compensated by the bast obtained from the bark of the Hibiscus and the *Nin,* a ficoid tree. A curious and instructive word in this connection is the Gilbert Island word for clothes, *Kun-ne-kai,* literally *Skin of Trees.*

Kawa. A tree growing on the mud-flats and salt-water marshes just inside the outer girdle of mangroves that hem in the lowlands. It has narrow, pointed, fleshy leaves growing two and two on a stalk, and bears tufted crimson flowers (Kandelia Rhœdii).

Keiwalu. A wild vetchling. There are two sorts, one resembling an everlasting pea, with pinkish-purplish flowers and broad leaves ; the other, with smaller leaves and yellow flowers of like shape, found creeping everywhere around the beaches just above high water mark.

Ken. A tree found growing on the swampy banks near the mouths of the rivers. It has dark brown wood, used for boat-building and for making posts for the houses.

In the Solomon Islands, KENKEN is the Coix lacryma or *Job's tears.*

Kerari. In Kiti, a shrub with rough leaves like those of a sage-bush and bearing bright blue flowers. On the North Coast, *Maikon.* Upon Yap, *Tenk.*

Kiap, Kiep, Kiop. The native lily, with white petals and yellow stamens and pistils. The *Kiuf* of Kusaie, the *Gieb* of the Marshall and Gilbert Islands. In the Mariannes *Kafo* is the flower of the Pandanus. *Cf.* Maori, *Kopakopa,* the New Zealand Lily. In Japan *Gibo* denotes one of the Liliaceæ.

Kipar. The Kiti name of the Pandanus or Screw-pine (*P. utilis* and *odoratissimus*). The *Fas, Far,* and *Fat,* of the Mortlocks, the *Fala* and *Fasa* of Samoa, the *Hala* and *Fara* of Hawaii and Tahiti, the *Hara-hagh* and *Harassas* of Indonesia. In Japanese *Tako-no-Ki, i.e.,* The Tree of the Octopus.[1]

Kirikei. The old name of the *Wompul, Weipul* or Morinda Citrifolia.

Kiri-n-chom. The rhizome of the mangrove tree.

Kirrak-en-Wal. Lit. *The Kirrak of the Bush.* The jamboo or Malay apple, the *Nonu-fiafia* of Samoa, known in other portions of the Pacific area as *Kehia, Ehia, Ohia, Kahika, Kafika* and *Geviga.* In the central Carolines the name *Kirak* or *Girek* denotes the native chestnut (*Inocarpus edulis*) (*cf.* Maori *Karaka,* a tree with edible seeds).

Kitau. The Polypody fern—much used for garlands. The crushed leaves and stalks are mingled with scraped coconut and a scented oil is expressed therefrom.

Kiti. The Cerbera lactaria and C. Odollam, found on the island beaches. The *Leva, Reva* and *Eva* of Polynesia. Every part of the tree is highly poisonous, and the crushed nuts are all too frequently employed by the women of the Marquesas group for suicide.

---

[1] The natives of the Harvey Group (S.-E. Polynesia) have a strange idea current of a species of octopus that comes ashore at dark, climbs the *Ara* or Pandan tree and devours its fragrant blossoms.

Kom. Cf. Japanese *Kombu*, seaweed. A seaweed with remarkable narcotic properties found growing in little tufts on the edge of the *Mat* or detached reefs in the lagoon. Used by fishermen in capturing the jellyfish *Raraiak* and *Tentumoi*.

Konok. The betel-pepper, a small species of the kava plant which climbs like ivy around the trunks of trees. The *Kolu* of the Solomon Islands. (In Peru *Kunuka* is a climbing plant.)

Korrom. A burr-bearing weed, found on rubbish-heaps and in the neighbourhood of the clearings in rear of each native settlement (*Sida retusa*).

Koto. A species of mangrove with white flowers and circular leaves and rounded seeds. Wood white and firm, good for cabinet-making. It is the *Hali-a-paka* or White Mangrove of the Marianne Group.

Kupu-n-Tanapai, i.e. the plant of the Tiger Shark. The fanciful name of the Osmunda regalis or Royal Fern.

L

Lampa, mould, mildew.

Likaitit. The rose-coloured flower-spike of the wild ginger.

Likam. A climbing plant bearing flowers like a convolvulus in shape—of a light mauve-colour—with a deep purple-mauve eye.

Lim. General term for sponges (Polynesian *Limu*, *Rimu* = seaweed).

Lim-en-kaualik is a scarlet sponge—*Paia*, a yellow one.

Lim-en-tutu. The sponge of commerce, and *Lim-en-auar* a brown and dark-blue species.

Lim-en-Tuka. Lichen or moss growing on trees, which sometimes is wonderfully like a sponge. (Specimen in South Kensington Museum.)

Lim-Par. A long-fronded fern growing on trees overhanging the riverside.

Luach. A tree exactly resembling Callophyllum inophyllum, save that instead of round fruits it bears pear-shaped ones. (Upon Kusaie—*Luas.*) The aromatic rhind used by natives for stringing garlands, and as an ingredient in preparing their *Uchor* or scented oil.

M

Mai. The breadfruit, of which I counted forty-five species.

Maikon. A shrub growing five or six feet high ; rough leaves, blue flowers. Decoction of leaves a blood purifier.

Makiach. A bush-shrub.

Mang. The swamp-taro (Colocasia) with forked roots, whence its name. It bears yellowish flower-spathes. (*Cf.* Samoan *Manga-na'a, Manga-siva,*) species of water-taro.

Mangat. A large species of plantain.

Marachau (*i.e.* the king's garland or necklace). (Dysoxylum or Averrhea, sp.?) A tall and handsome forest tree. The leaves grow by fives together on a stalk, and somewhat resemble those of an English ash.

Marek. The common fern.

Marrap. The Inocarpus edulis, the *Ihi, Ifi* and *Ii* of Tonga, Samoa and Mangaia. In Efatese—*Mabe.* The Tahitian name is *Mape.* In Mortlocks, *Marefa.* It is a sacred tree in which Naluk the God of Thunder is supposed to dwell. Its boiled bark yields a valuable astringent drug. Its firm white wood is much used in boat-building, the root buttresses supplying good material for the bends and strengthening pieces. The large flattish fruits are very much like an English chestnut in flavour, and form a very welcome addition to the native fare. A sucking-pig or fowl stuffed with Marrap fruit and baked in the earth-oven is a dish not to be despised.

Marrap-en-Chet. (In the white man's pidgin Ponapean "Marry-bunchy") is the Kiti name for *Heritiera littoralis,* properly not a *Marrap* at all.

Matakel. The fragrant leaf-like flower of the Pandanus odoratissimus.

Matai. A medicinal bush-weed, decoction of leaves drunk by child-bearing women.

Matal. Applied both to the bush pandanus and to the Freycinetia, the *Salasala* and *Ieie* of Samoa, the *Kiekie* of eastern Polynesia, the *Gire* of the Banks Group, and the *N'er* of Yap.

Matal-in-Iak. A bush-weed. Decoction of leaves good for headache.

Mateu, Matu. The Sassafras or wild Sarsaparilla.

Matil. A long-fronded fern.

Mekei. The old name for the *Kitau* or Polypody fern.

Mokomok. The generic name of the *Tacca* or South Sea arrowroot all over the Caroline area. (In Polynesian called *Pia.*) The *Mamago* of *Mamako* or the Solomon Islands (Guppy). One of the Uluthi or Mackenzie Group gets its name from the quantity of Tacca grown there.

Momiap. The pawpaw, mammee or mummy apple (Carica papaya). The *Ketela* of Malaysia, the *Es* of Kusaie and the *Esi* of Samoa. Introduced into Ponape about 1840 by an old French settler—the recluse of Nan-Moluchai referred to in the account of our visit to the Metalanim ruins.

Mpai. A species of tree-fern.

Muerk (Psychotria). A bush-tree. Decoction of bark used for curing *aphthæ* or thrush in children.

N

Nan-Karu. Name given to plants of the orchid species, which also is designated by the name *Kiki-en-kaualik* or "Blue Heron's claw."

Nan-Tap. The Paliker local name for the *Cheu* or sugar-cane.

Nî. The coconut palm, of which there are several varieties.[1] One has an edible husk (*Nî-atol*, the *Niu-mangalo* of Polynesia). *N.B.*—A curious freak of nature is sometimes seen in a single nut out of a cluster, the kernel of which is divided up into two, three, or four compartments, from each of which a shoot springs.

[1] In Polynesian, *Niu, Nu;* Malayan, *Niyor, Nur;* Philippines, *Niyog;* Skt., *Nariyar.*

This is called in Ponape *Pat-en-parang*. Upon Mokil, *Pat-en-maram*.

The nut has several names according to its stages of development. Small nut just forming, *Kurup* (*Cf.* Maly., *Karapa, Kalapa*). Green drinking-nut, soft kernel commencing to line the shell, *Up* in Kiti, *Pen* in Chokach and Metalanim. Next stage, kernel - thickening, *Mangach.* Stage when the nut is fully ripe and falls down ready for copra-making, *Arring, Arrin.* [Upon Pingelap, *Takatak.*] In the final stage the solid kernel occupying the whole of the interior takes on change, and becomes a soft spongy mass, and the shoot of the young palm sprouts out through one of the eyes. It is then called *Par.* The contents of the sprouting nut, when roasted, are a favourite diet for invalids. The husk is called *Tipanit.* From this the cinnet or cord is twisted. *Inipal* is the name of the natural cloth clinging around the base of the leaf-stalks or fronds. The flower-stalk is *Tangkal ;* the leaf or frond *Paini ;* the sheath of the flower-stalk *Koual ;* the central spine of leaflets *Nok*, and the oil *Le* or *Ler* (when scented, *Uchor.*)

Nin. A ficoid tree allied to the Banyan. It grows abundantly in the valleys and hill-slopes. From the bark the woman's dress (" Li-kau ") was made. (*Cf.* Malay *Nunu*, the lesser Banyan.) *N.B.*—*Nin* in the Mortlock's denotes the Morinda citrifolia (Samoan *Nonu*, Gilberts *Non*, Malay *Nona*, Uluthi *Lol.*)

NG

Ngi (Metrosideros). A littoral shrub, eight to ten feet in height, with very hard but brittle wood, minute leaves, and small delicate flowers like those of a myrtle. It grows in great abundance on the small islands out in the lagoon, rooting itself firmly in between the blocks of coral, its roots washed by the salt water. It bears tiny capsules containing minute dark seeds resembling those of the tobacco-plant. When empty they resemble the bell of a lily-of-the-valley. Decoction of bark a native cure for dysentery. (*Cf.* Pelew Islands, *Ngis*; Lamotrek, *Gaingi*; Pulawat and Satawal, *Aingi.*)

Ngiungiu. The Yap name for a climbing fern (*Lygodium scandens*).

Ngkau. A common bush-weed both on mainland and coral islets in the lagoon. It bears small yellow flowers, like a marguerite or Michaelmas daisy. Leaves heart-shaped, serrated at edges, yielding when crushed a rank and powerful odour. The pounded leaves or a decoction of them are a valuable application to sores and ulcerated wounds.

O

Och. A species of sago-palm (*Metroxylon amicarum*). *Habitat*, the swampy lowlands and the neighbourhood of rivers ; the *Ota* of the Banks Group ; the *Os* or *Rapun* of Ruk and the Mortlocks. It produces large black, round fruits, with a scaly pericarp, which gives them considerable powers of flotation. The kernels are very hard, and exported to Germany for button-making. They are an effective substitute for the ivory-nut or vegetable ivory of South America. Hence the Spanish call the tree *Palma de Marfil* or Ivory-palm. The Ponapeans do not make sago from it, like their Melanesian neighbours to the south and south-east.

Oio. The Chokach and Metalanim name for the Banyan tree.

Oliol. A bush-plant. Decoction of leaves good lotion for wounds and cuts.

Olot. Species of sea-grass, with patches of which the mud-flats appear studded at low tide.

Ong. The wild ginger, of which there are several sorts. (*Cf.* Pampanga, *Ango*, Curcuma ; Samoan, *Ango*, Turmeric ; Javanese, *Wong*, *gamboge*. (Perhaps connected are the Chinese words *Hoang*, *Wong*, denoting a red, yellow, or orange colour.)

Ong-en-Pele. A choice kind.

Ong-en-Pele-en-Uai, i.e. Peles ginger from abroad. The ginger plant of commerce (introduced).

Or. Bush-weed. Decoction drunk to cure sore throat and low fever.

Oramai. Species of Ramie or Kleinhovia. Fibres of bark anciently used in making fish-nets. The *Lafai* of the Solomon Islands (Guppy).

Ot, Wot. The Giant Taro (Arum costatum). In Kusaie, *Wos*. Called in Central Carolines *Pulak* or *Purak*. (In Solomon Island an Arum is called *Kuraka*.) (With *Wot, Wos, cf.* Samoan *Vase*, a species of taro.) *N.B.*—In the Polynesian area *Puraka, Pulaka* and *Pula'a* denote various species of taro.

P

Pai, Pai-Uet. Species of tree-fern.

Par. Two sorts, *Para-pein*, the female; and *Para-man*, the male. Bark of latter in decoction used by natives as a tonic. The Erythrina Indica—the *Ngatae* of Samoa, the *Atae* of Tahiti, the *Netae* of the Marquesas. In India it is called *Pari-bhadra*, the *Par*, or season coming round of the *bhadra* or fifth solar month, August, at which time the tree is covered with scarlet flowers. The Ponapeans divide their wet and dry seasons, which they also call *Par*, from the appearance of these brilliant blossoms. It is interesting to see the Asiatic name retained in this remote corner. (In Kusaie *Pal* also denotes a season.)

Parram. The swamp-palm (Nipa fruticans), the *Ballang* of the Sulu Archipelago; the *Betram* or *Batram* of Java. (*Cf.* Fijian *Balabala*, the Cycas Revoluta. Maori, *Para*, a fern. Marianne (P. to F., R. to D.) FADAN, the Cycas Revoluta. Marquesan *Pa'a-hei* (i.q. *Para-hei*), a tree-fern. An island on the north coast of Ponape is named *Parram*, from the abundant growth of this palm on it. The strange-looking fluted seeds float for a long time in the water without injury. Hence one need not be surprised at the very wide distribution of this palm throughout the

Micronesian and Melanesian area, carried by the ocean currents. I did not notice the *Parram* either in Tahiti or the Marquesas. In the latter group however the fan-palm grew abundantly, especially upon Hiva-Oa and Tahuata, a species that though found in the Solomon Group, unaccountably fails to present itself in the Caroline Archipelago.

Parri, Pearri. The generic name of the Bamboo (Bambusa). (*N.B.*—In Efatese, New Hebrides, *Borai* is the sugar-cane.) In the Favorlang dialect of Formosa, *Borro* is small cane or reed-grass. In Yap, *Mor* is the dwarf bamboo. In Kusaie the bamboo is called *Alkasem*, a word of doubtful derivation. In Hindustani, *Baro* is reed-grass ; and in Malagasy, *Fari* is the sugar-cane. In Nuku-Or, the bamboo is called *Matira*, which word in Maori denotes a *fishing-rod*. The Ponapeans make flutes out of the smaller canes, using the larger ones to store up water in as the Marquesan islanders do. They also employ them as water-conduits (*Kerriker*). Hence the Ponapean verb *Kerrikereti-pil*, to bring down water from the hills for irrigation purposes by a line of bamboo pipes, end on end.

Peapa, Peapea, Peepee. Varying dialect words for a forest tree with fine small leaves like those of a privet shrub. The wood is white, firm in grain. Used for boat-building.

Peipei, Paipai-Ani, i.e. the Peipei of the Gods.

Peipei, Paipai-Aramach, i.e. the Peipei of Mortals.

Two beautiful ferns, closely resembling the umbrella-fern of New South Wales. The name is also applied to a species of Adiantum. *Peipei* is a poetical word, meaning *long tresses of hair.*

Pelak. One of the gourd family, the fruits of which furnish the natives with their calabashes.

Pena, Pona, Pana. The Thespesia populnea, a common littoral tree with a reddish-brown wood. The so-called rosewood of Polynesia. (Samoan, *Milo ;* Tahitian, *Miro* and *Amae ;* Marquesan, *Mio.*) In Kusaie, *Pangapanga* or *Penga ;* in Yap, *Bonabeng ;* in the Gilberts, *Bengibeng.*

Perran, Paran.   The Metalanim name for the orange, lime, or lemon-tree.

Pinipin. One of the gourd family allied to the *Pelak* (*q.v.*).

Poke (*Pandanus inermis*). Upon Lamotrek, *Pogo.* Bush variety—no aerial roots.

Puek. The *Puka* or *Pukatea* of Polynesia. A species of tulip-tree. Wood soft and valueless. (Tongan, *Buka,* Hernandia peltata.)

Pulok (*Carapa Moluccensis*). A tall, hard-wood tree, with curious curving flanges or buttresses. *Habitat* : the salt-marshes, where it occurs mingled with the *Ak, Koto, Kawa,* and *Waingal.* It bears a number of curious polygonal seeds, closely packed together in the pericarp like pieces in a puzzle. The seeds float, and, to judge from the wide distribution of the tree, drift long distances upon the ocean currents. A similar species is found in Africa, the kernel of which yields a useful oil. The wood of the *Pulok* is much used by native carpenters and boat-builders, especially the curious ridges of its root-buttresses, which come in handy for the bends in fashioning the bows of a craft.

Putoput. A shrub common on the low coral islands, recalling the *Tou* of Samoa (*Sponia timoriensis*).

Pur. Flowers in general. In the U and Metalanim districts, *Chair* or *Sair.* (Javanese, SARI, a flower.) The Tree-gardenia is also called *Pur* or *Chair ;* in Yap, ANGAK.

R

Ramak. The Mokil name of the *Inot* (*Scævola Kænigii*).

Rapun. The Mortlock name for the *Och* or sago-palm (*Metroxylon*).

Rara. A species of Freycinetia. Leaves about a cubit long, fluted in the middle by a slightly serrated ridge.

Ratil. A long fronded fern, also the giant fern. The *Nase* or *Nahe* of Polynesia (*Angioptera erecta* and *Marattia fraxinea*).[1]

Re, Rei. The varying tribal and local names for grass. *Reirei* (adj.) denotes a green colour.

---

[1] *Cf.* Pelew Islands, *Ngas,* a tree-fern.

Re-chap, *i.e.*, grass-rush or rush-grass ; a coarse grass. In decoction a vermifuge.

Ro, Rirro, Roi.   A small species of reed-grass, the stems of which are sometimes used for making the native flute.

T

Taip.   The Metalanim name for trees of the genus Pandanus in general. (*Cf.* Gilbert Islands, *Taba*, the flower of the Pandanus tree.) The bush variety is called *Taip-en-wal*, and the seaside species bearing large edible fruits—introduced from the Marshall Group—is called *Taip-en-wai*, *i.e.* the Pandanus from abroad.

Talik.   The Bird's-nest fern, resembling an English hart's-tongue, found on the sides of the stone-work of Nan-Tauach, and at the base of the branches of forest trees. The *Talik-en-wal* or Talik of the bush is a climbing species, forming most ornamental festoons amongst the nurseries of young trees upspringing in the undergrowth.

Tikap.   A species of mountain plantain. (In Samoa, *Soa'a* ; in Marquesan, *Huetu ;* in Tahitian, *Fei.*) Botanical name, *Musa uranospatha*, literally, the Musa (Arabic, *Mawz*), with the spathe pointing heavenward. So called because the leaves of the plantain and its bunches of fruit point upwards, whilst the true banana, leaves and bunch, droops earthward ; *vide* Mr Grant Allen's excellent essay " De Banana."

Ting.   The Dracœna terminalis.   The *Ti, Ji* or *Ki* of Polynesia ; the *Ndili* of the Banks Group ; the *Ndong* or *Andong* of Java.   *N.B.*—In Samoa *Tongotongo* also denotes a species of Dracœna.

Tip.   The generic name for weeds, grasses, creepers, and undergrowth. (*Cf.* Polynesian *Tupu*, to grow ; spring up.)

Tip-en-chalang.   A minute and pretty species of sea-fan found amongst the patches of Olot upon the mud-flats at low tide.

Tipop, Tupap, Tipap.   The native almond (Terminalia catappa). Upon Kusaie, *Sufaf.*   The *Talie* of Polynesia, the *Salite* of the Banks Group, the *Talisai* of the Philippines. Called in Solomon Group *Saori* (Guppy).

Titin. Littoral shrub with soft downy leaves like those of a fox-glove. It bears small white flowers upon six or seven stalks, which grow into a cruciform branch. It is the *Sisin* of Mokil. (Tournefortia sarmentosa.)

Tong. A tall buttressed forest tree. It has long lobed leaves and small seeds. The wood is of a dark reddish brown, hard and excellent for boat-building. The natives also use it for making their *Kachak* or food-troughs, which answers to the Polynesian *Umete* or *Kumete*. Dr Pereiro declares it to be either *Dipterocarpus mayapis* or *Dipterocarpus polispermus*. It is found in the interior of Yap, where it is called *Ramilu*.

Tupuk, Tupok. A tree found on the mainland and also upon the coral islets in the lagoon. It grows from ten to twenty feet in height and bears umbels of greenish-white flowers, and clusters of dark berries, very much like those of our elder tree, which in scent they strongly resemble. The pounded bark is good as an external application to obstinate sores and slowly healing wounds. The wood was anciently used for making fire by friction, and also was employed in the manufacture of the *Aip* or native drum. In the Pelews it is called KOSOM, and is a sacred tree. Upon Yap AR. In the Mariannes ARGAU. In Bisayan a species of Premna is ARGAO, in Tagal AGDAU and ALAGAO.

U & W

Waingal, Uaingal. (Lumnitsera sp.). A tall tree with small oblong leaves, notched at tip, bearing small crimson flowers and roundish flattened seeds. Wood reddish-brown, very hard and durable, used in house-building, and for making keels, masts, and gunwales of boats. Habitat, the salt marshes at the back of the mangrove-belt where it is found side by side with the *Koto*, *Kawa*, and *Pulok*.

Wantal, Uantal (Ipomea pes-capræ). A sea-side

creeper, bearing round black flattish seeds like broad beans, and pinkish purple flowers.

Uch, Uich, Uch-en-ant. Species of rush (Samoan *Utu*, id).

Weipul, Wompul, Umpul. The morinda citrifolia (Lit. Flame tree, so called from the bright yellow dye extracted from its roots and wood). The *Nonu* of Polynesia, the *Wong-kudu* of Java, and the *Tumbung-aso* of the Philippines.

Wet, Wot, Ot. The Giant Taro. In Kusaie WOS. *Cf.* Samoan VASE, a species of taro.

Ui, Wi. The Barringtonia specioso and racemosa. Habitat, coastline of mainland and small islands. A species growing in the bush is called *Wi-en-mar*, or the Wi of the bush clearings. *N.B.*—In Samoan *Vi* is the Spondias dulcis.

Ulunga-en-Kieil. " *The pillow of the Kieil lizard*" (Scincus). The parsley-fern found growing in tufts upon the flower-pot-shaped, limestone islets in the lagoon, also upon the trunks of coconut palms.

Up. A creeper resembling our Wistaria, the pounded roots of which are used for stupefying fish. Yap *Yub.* In Malaysia *Tuba.* Compare Kusaie *Op.*

Ut. The name for bananas in general. (*Cf.* Fijian *Vundi*, Samoan *Futi*, Ellice Group *Futi*, Nuku-Oro *Huti*, etc. etc.)

Varieties :—

Ut-en-wai. The Foreign or China banana with speckled skin.

Ut-iak. Small, deep yellow flesh.

Ut-en-Yap, or Yap banana, a choice species of plantain, pink flesh, very delicate in flavour, and the portion of the priests and high chiefs at a festival.

Other varieties :—*Karrat, Mangat, Tikop, q. v.*

(D) SUPPLEMENTARY YAP PLANT AND TREE-NAMES

Ari-fath., Uatol. Sp. Barringtonia.
Ir-nim, Arai. Species of plantain.

Raual. The *Kangit* of Ponape. Huge spherical fruit filled with delicious creamy pulp, enclosing large roundish seeds which when grated up and mixed with coconut shavings have a remarkable narcotic effect on foods.

Gurgur. The native name for Citrus fruits in general. *Gurgur-nu-ap* is the orange. *Gurgur-morrets*, the lime.

Lur. A weed growing on side of causeways in swampy districts.

Olomar. The sweet basil (Ponape *Katereng*).

Langil, Thlangil. A variety of wild kava, the Avaava-aitu, or Kavakava-atua of south-west Polynesia.

Wote, Ote. Sp. wild fig, bearing small reddish rough fruits on its trunk like Eugenia.

Rtep. A sort of orchid climbing on trunks of coco-palms.

Rumig. A Callophyllum with pear-shaped fruits. The variety with round seeds is known as *Bioutch.* In Tagal *Bitao. Fetao* is the Yap name for the yellowish waxy flower of the tree.

Adid. Bush-tree. Long-ribbed leaves, smooth reddish bark, spherical rough-rinded reddish-brown fruit. The *Ais* of Ponape called *Aset* in the Mortlocks.

Topotop, Talaboi. Sp. Tacca. The *Mokomok* of Central and East Carolines. The *Mamago* of Solomon Islands.

Tenk, a shrub with rough leaves and intense blue flowers. The *Mateu* of Ponape.

Ruai, Tugu. Species of mangrove.

Rung, Voi. Sp. Native chestnut (Inocarpus Edulis). In the Mariannes, *Ufa.* In Polynesian, *Ifi.* In the Philippines, *Dungun.*

Limuet. Creeping plant, small round leaves, good for burns.

Yenuk, Pipi. The common rush.

Uelem. The King Fern.

Re : Lem. Two species of Sea-grass.

Kana.   Parasol fern.

Thengibur.   Sp. fern.

Trath.   Hart's-tongue fern.

Likelike niu.   Var. parsley fern growing on trunks of coco-palms.

Kopokop.   Polypody fern.

Para-lol.   Long-fronded fern.

Lek, Gulugului.   Asplenium.

Likilik-a-voi.   Parsley fern, sp.

Tulubuk, Tilibuk.   Common male fern.

Gumar.   Acacia inermis.

Golat.   Sp. thorny Acacia.

Maikitibum : Mangamang : Mong.   The Giant Fern of the swampy districts.

Talafat.   Sp. grass.

Rangaranga.   Parsley fern growing in cracks of old walls.

Lobat, Talilra.   A delicate species of Adiantum.

Tamagateu.   Large fern resembling Osmunda Regalis.

Orotrol.   Thespesia populnea.   A littoral tree.

Komai.   Rice (introduced).

Yams.   Dok, wild yam ; *Dok-nu-obachai,* variety introduced from Eastern Carolines ; *Bia,* species brought from Ladrone Islands ; *Dal,* short, oval, like sweet potato ; *Dol,* wild yam, small round seeds growing at base of leaves, like Ponape *Likam* ; *Fap,* sp. sub-varieties, *Gote-lap* and *Nanebo.*

Thau.[1]   The breadfruit.   (Artocarpus Incisa.)

Varieties : (1) *Yao-lei ;*   (2) *Yae-reb ;*   (3) *Tagafei ;* (4) *Fanum ;* (5) *Pemathau ;* (6) *Yao-uat ;* (7) *Dapanapan,* (Jackfruit—A. integrifolia)*;* (8) *Yeo-tui ;* (9) *Mai-nior ;* (10) *Luathar;* (11) *Pe-au;* (12) *Yoa-tathen;* (13) *Yu-goi ;* (14) *Yu-ngalu.*

Gotruk.   The Croton shrub of which there are many

_____

[1] *Cf.* Ural-Altaic, *Thav, Thavi,* a head.   *N.B.*—In Polynesian *Ulu* means both *head* and *breadfruit.*

very ornamental varieties with which the village squares and roadsides are thickly planted.

Irich, Rich, Rit.   The Dracœna terminalis, the Ki of Hawaii, the Ti of south-west Polynesia.

Notes on the Coconut.   Flower, *Achabai.*   Small nut forming, *Machal* (Samoan *Aili*).   Green drinking - nut, *Tob, Tub* (*cf.* Hindustani *Dob*).   Kernel thickening, *Manao.*   Kernel further developed, *Agel.*   Fully developed, ready for copra, *Marau* (Samoan *Popo*), Sprouting nut, *Bul* (Tahitian *Uto*).   Old mouldy nut, *Ap.*   Husk surrounding nut, *Kapat, Ling.*   Coconut-toddy, *Achif.*   Stalk of nuts, *Uongoi.*   Copra, *Fatuis-a-Marau.*   Trunk of a tree, *Binal.*

Môr.   The dwarf bamboo, probably introduced anciently from Japan.   Planted thickly on top of the ancient embankments which overlook the paved roads running throughout the southern portion of the island.

Tifif.   A variety of Canna Indica, with bright orange berries.   Found in the bush in the neighbourhood of the taro swamps inland.

Waraburub.   An ornamental fern (Japanese, *Warabi*).

Parafai.   A large tree fungus, dried and used in commerce.

Gathemat.   Sp. Cordia, sweet-scented white flower.

Tingiting.   Species of Taro, yellowish flowers.

Butral.   A scitamineous plant, with purplish mauve spikes of bloom, a sort of wild ginger.

Ao.   The banyan tree (Polynesian, *Aoa*).

Tengauai.   Cerbera Lactaria.   The deadly *Leva, Reva,* or *Eva* of south-west Polynesia.

Amaral.   A heavily-seeded nettle found outside villages near rubbish heaps.

Maluek.   A variety of morinda citrifolia.

Ugina-maluak.   Species bearing long white umbels of flower.

At.   A pitcher-plant, found in vicinity of Tan-ne-Erouach on South Ramung.

Giligil-wath.   Littoral shrub.   Leaves used as medicinal plaster in Samoa.

Tarau.   Meadow-grass.

Pui-wol.   The *Pulok* of Ponape ; a large hardwood tree, with curiously keeled roots and polygonal seeds (Carapa Moluccensis).

Gogoth.   Sp. Betel Pepper.   (*Cf.* Pelew Islands, *Kokuth,* aromatic).

Gonek.   Prickly shrub, edible, oval fruit, turning red when ripe.

The *Banana* grows in great profusion.   Fruit, *Pau ;* Tree, *Denai.*   *Varieties :* (1) *Yereim,* long-fruited plantain ; (2) *Tengere,* yellow-fleshed plantain, roundish (Ponape, *Karrat*) ; (3) *Boul, Voul,* small banana ; (4) *Tafagef,* China banana ; (5) *Fak-e-uel,* small, round ; (6) *Yugo ;* (7) *Ganaeko ;* (8) *Daver ;* (9) *Malukier ;* (10) *Arai ;* (11) *Gumoi ;* (12) *To-nu-Uap ;* (13) *Sakas,* large yellow plantain.

Mal.   The Taro plant.   *Tingiting, Lak,* big, yellow flower, grows in swamps ; *Guiagui,* sp.

Faa.   The wild Pandanus.

Olowalogu.   Bush-shrub.

Uapof.   The Paper Mulberry (Broussonettia Papyrifera).

Ramilu.   Tree with huge long leaves (Ponape, *Tong*).

Arr.   Coarse seagrass.

Tha, Thea.   A common weed, with yellowish flowers and strong-scented, heart-shaped leaves, the juice of which is very healing to wounds and ulcers.   Common on coral islets off Ponape coast, where it is called *Ngkau.*

Otrafangal.   Large convolvulus.

Utel, Roi.   Reed-grass (Samoan, *Fiso*).

Laingen-en-lip-otol.   Curious marsh weed ; soft, red, spongy caps or buttons on stem for flowers.

Kurrukur.   Burr-bearing weed (Ponape, *Korom*).

Thagumut.   Bush-shrub, leaf like coffee.

Fauteir.   A species of cycas ; same name sometimes

applied to the Nipa palm occasionally found in the swamps.

Bû. The Areca Palm. In Pelew, *Buok ;* in Sanskrit, *Púg ;* in Ladrones, *Pagua.*

Chongot. Tall, poison tree ; light bark, long leaves, like *Ramilu.* White acrid juice, producing terrible swellings and sores.

Avetch. Curious shrub, leaf like that of Eugenia or Malay apple in shape. White leaf on end of each bunch of seed capsules, which resemble these of tobacco. Small golden yellow, star-shaped flower.

Choi, Troi. The Pandanus.

Fal. The Pandanus flower. (Ponape, *Matakel ;* Mariannes, *Kafo ;* Samoan, *Singano ;* Tahitian, *Hinano.*

(E) PONAPEAN FISHES, INSECTS, BIRDS, AND ANIMALS

Fishes. Many of these appear in the splendid illustrations of Godeffroy's album of the South Seas.

Ukair. A bright golden-yellow fish about a foot long. (The *Tapereper* of Mokil.)

Kamaik. A species of Parrot-Wrass. The Butter-Fish of New Zealand.

Kapai, Kipai. Small reddish-brown fish with dark spots. Head and tail project out of a most comical suit of defensive armour shaped exactly like the square gin-bottle of commerce (Ostraceon cubicus).

Palat. Length about one foot. Longish nose. Body, light red. Head, salmon-pink. Tail and fins, dark red.

Pako. The generic name for sharks (Polynesian *Mako, Mango*) called *Charaui* on the Ant Atoll, where the name *Pako* is tabooed. Panayan (south Philippines). *Baguis.* Solomon Islands *Pagoa ;* Marshall Islands *Bako ;* Polynesian *Mako, id. ;* Gilbert Island *Bakoa.* It is an Asiatic word, the Sea-Tiger. Indian *Bag, Bagha,* a tiger.

Another shark-name is *Tanapai*. The Tiger-shark, popularly supposed to be deaf. The dreaded *Tanifa* of the Samoans, the *Ndaniva* of Fiji. Compare with this the Maori *Taniwha*, a water monster, or sea-devil. Malay *Danawa* a goblin, evil spirit. Sanskrit *Danawa* id. *N.B.*—One of the words borrowed by the Malays from the Sanskrit, and which has filtered through into Micronesia and Polynesia. Cognate are S. N. Guinea *Dirawa*, an evil spirit. Pelews *Deleb*, *Thalib*, a devil.

A. The mullet.

Karangat. The bonito. From *Ranga*—to rise up, so called from its rising to the surface in great shoals like the English herring.

Ki. A Dolphin or porpoise.

Roch. A whale. (Sometimes pronounced *Rách*). It means the King-Fish. The word also denotes a high chief (*cf.* Malay and Hindustani *Rajah*), and perhaps Fijian *Ratu* a high chief. (*Cf.* Kusaian *Lat*, a whale).

Pup. The Leather Jacket. Silvery-white below ; forehead bright blue ; tip of nose bright blue ; sides and back yellowish brown ; body striped blue and yellow. One long erect spine just behind shoulders. *Habitat*, holes in the reef and in floating logs of wood.

Lioli. Large dark-blue species of Leather Jacket. A deep-water fish.

Paikop. A fish with a remarkably flat face and thick body picked out in chevrons of white and dark olive-green. The people of Palang on the Chokach coast are jocularly styled by their neighbours of Kiti *Macha-en-Paikop*, Paikop-faces, from the prevailing type of features there.

Mengar, Măngar. The Flying-fish, also known as *Mam-pir*.

Mángar. Large brown and white speckled fish with spiny dorsal fin. The Spaniards call it *Garrofa*.

Ikan. Greenish body, brown dorsal fins. Front fins a fine golden-yellow. (*Cf.* Malay *Ikan*, fish in general.)

Tak.   The Gar-fish, which often leaps on board fishing canoes, and inflicts mortal wounds with its sharp lance.

Uat.   The Bladder-fish, so called from its frequently puffing itself up like a balloon. The *Sue* of Samoa, the *Huehue-kava* of the Marquesan Islands. Deadly poisonous.

Pulak.   Large, roundish, dark green body. Flesh firm like a halibut's.

Pulak-tol.   A remarkably handsome brown fish with black and white spiny dorsal fins, two yellow spiny pectoral fins and a continuous row of orange, black and white ventral fins.

Chara.   A pinkish-red fish, small body, large flat head. Row of spines along back. Minute teeth sharp as needles.

Litak.   The Climbing-fish, to be seen hopping and crawling in numbers upon the rocks and stones on the sea-shore. Colour—light green, speckled dark brown.

Toik.   Small red fish.

Potarar.   Small black and white handed fish.

Mamo-tik.   The beautiful little cobalt and orange fish seen playing in and out of the forests of coral in the pools and on the edge of the deep water. Called in Nuku-Oro *Mamo-riki*, and in Tahiti *Mamo*. Also known in Ponape as *Ta-kap-en-taok*. All these three are fond of the pools left in the reef at low tide.

Uakap.   Lower part of body steel blue, upper part dark blue ; black and yellow stripes.

Kir.   Bright crimson fish about 1½ feet long. Spiny row of back fins.

Korikor.   A beautiful fish about 1½ feet long, marked throughout with white and brown lozenges (◇), a band of similar pattern but minute design running round the body. Fins and tail dark brown.

Chaok, Chauk.   Small fish, brown body, speckled white.

Marrer, Merra.   Large, dull, blue fish ; flesh rather

soft and woolly.   Excellent pickled raw with salt water, Chili pepper, and lime-juice.

Li-er-puater (*Chætodon* sp.).   Length five to six inches, circular body.   Large dark brown anal fin, white band round back, surmounted by a ridge of seven small yellowish spines.   The far dorsal fin is edged with rich orange.   Tail light, greenish-blue, sparsely tipped with orange; thorax deep orange.   Slight tinge of orange along belly.   Lower part of face up to the eyes deep orange.   Thin nose, projecting some ¾ inch, orange. Slightly projecting lower jaw.   Rest of body light pale green, streaked with wavy lines of alternating light blue and darker green from back of gills to tail.   Mean thickness of body four inches.   *N.B.*—Another closely related fish of the same name has tail, anal, and dorsal fins banded black and orange.   Perpendicular black stripe down face.   Nose and thorax white.

Lipar.   A flat fish, reddish-brown above.   Meaning of name, *Red Woman*.   Flesh full of small, crooked bones. Of little esteem for food.

SEA-BIRDS

Two species of Sand-piper are found on the coasts, the smaller called *Kulu*, the larger *Chakir*.   The former is the *Tuli* of Nuku-Oro and Samoa, the *Dulili* or *Tulili* of the Mariannes ; *cf.* the Indian *Dulika*, a wag-tail.   The *Kulu* is known in the Pelews as *Golo*, in Yap as *Kuling*, in the Marshalls and Mokil as *Kolech*, and elsewhere in the Carolines as *Kuling, Kulung,* or *Kilung.*   The Malay *Chorling* may be cognate.   In South America we find very strange coincidences — Quichuan, *Chulla ;* Araucanian, *Chili, Thili,* id.; whilst in Aymara *Kullu* means a partridge.

The Ponapean name of the larger variety (*Chakir*) is paralleled by the Hindustani *Chakor* (*Tetrao*); by the Japanese *Shako,* a partridge ; and by the Quichuan *Tsakua,* a partridge.

The most exacting philological critic cannot deny that these far-reaching coincidences are very curious. Many will probably argue that most bird-names are onomatopœic, *i.e.*, imitation sounds, and that the human machinery of speech being cast in a somewhat limited mould, would everywhere produce independently the same or similar results, even amongst remote tribes which have had absolutely no connection with one another. However, when we reach the animal, or, at all events, the tree-names, we shall find ourselves upon somewhat less debatable ground, and these will afford clearer evidence as to the separate waves of population rolling outwards from Indonesia to the farthest isles of the Pacific, up to the very shores of the great continent on the further side.

Akiak, Kake. Varieties of white gull. The latter builds no nest, but lays its eggs in the small brush growing on top of the flower-pot-shaped masses of Takai-Mai or coral limestone which stud the shallow water off the low island beaches. From this habit the observant Ponapeans have deduced a slang word—*Pon-Kake, i.e.* like the *Kake*, to denote any useless, idle, lazy fellow.

There is a large grey gull which they call *Karakar.*

A brown tern with a white head (*Parrat*) is found on the coral islets of the coast. It makes its nests in the tops of the Barringtonia trees. Its young make very good food, albeit a trifle fishy in taste.

Another sea-bird, black and white with two long tail-feathers, is called *Chik* (Phaethon).

There are three sorts of heron, called by the generic name of *Kau-alik.* The first is the *Matuku* or *Matuu*, the common blue heron of Polynesia ; the second is the *Otu* or *Kotuku*, the white heron, a much less common species ; the third is the speckled heron, doubtless a cross of the above two. The *Kau-alik* is jocularly styled in Tahiti and the Marquesas as *Frenchman's turkey* from the skill with which some of their colonial cooks will disguise his fishy flavour.

LAND-BIRDS

Cherret. A reddish-brown parrakeet peculiar to the island (Eos rubiginosa). *Cf.* Maori, *Toreta.* The New Zealand parrakeet. The old name of the *Cherret* was *Terrep-e-icho* or *King Terrep. Cf.* Maori *Tarepa*, a species of bush parrakeet.

Li-maaliel-en-takai. A little brown bird inhabiting the bush. Its name means *Woman-giddy-at-stone.* The natives say that when a stone is thrown near it, it falls down dizzy.

Murroi. Large grey dove. The *Lupe* or *Rupe* of South Polynesia.

Kingking. Small green dove, maroon crest on head, breast maroon (Ptilnopus Ponapensis). *Cf.* Mariannes *Kunao*, a green dove.

Kinuet. Variety of above, but with cream and maroon markings (Samoan *Manuma*).

Paluch. Small dark violet brown pigeon, white breast —a ground pigeon. Peculiar to Ponape. Scientific name *Phlegœnas Kubaryi* from J. S. Kubary of the Godeffroy Firm in Germany who first made it known to science. Habitat, high up on the densely wooded mountain slopes; shy and wild. The Ponapeans have used an ancient generic Malay name to denote a single species.

Compare the following curious and interesting cognates which certainly cannot be mere coincidences ; *i.e. German New Guinea coast*, an area thickly scattered with Malay words : *Palussia, Balus, Balusi, Barussi, Beli,* all meaning dove or pigeon.

Bismarck Archipelago—Palus, Walus, Balus.

Pelew Islands—Bulokol, Pelokol.

Tagala (Philippines)—*Balos, Balod.*

Sulu Archipelago—Baud. (Sulu drops medial *L.*)

Solomon Islands—Baolo.

Malay—Balam.

Hindustani—Palka, Parewa, Parawat.

Latin — *Palumbes* (whence Spanish *Paloma*) and *Columba* (P. to K.).

The above show as well the exceedingly wide distribution of the bird. This is only one of many instances out of the Micronesian and Polynesian to show how tenaciously the early Asiatic and Indonesian names of birds and plants have been preserved in the wanderings of this race over the great waste of waters.

Cheok. A sort of blackbird ; a sacred bird in Ponape.

Puliet (Myzomela rubrata). A red-breasted honey-eater, to be seen hovering round the coco-palm spathes, from which he draws his food.

Kutar, Tirou. Varieties of the king-fisher (Alcedo). With *Kutar* compare Maori *Kotare*, the New Zealand king-fisher ; Tahitian *Otare*, a king-fisher. In Futuna the bird is called *Tikotala ;* in Samoan, *Ti'otala ;* in Tongan, *Sikota'a.*

Possibly in the last three the T or S represents the unconscious article, so frequent in the Gilbert group.

Koekoe, Kuikui. Small, blackish-brown bird ; fly-catcher (Myagra pluto).

Li-kapichir, Li-kaperai. Small cuckoo. Small bird, long tail ; dark colour (Endynamis Taitiensis).

Li-mati. Small green bird, found in coconut groves. Resembles the Samoan *Iao*, but smaller.

Li-porok. Night bird ; black and white. Habitat, mangrove swamps.

Li-kat-e-pupu. The name of several kinds of little bush birds. Breast red, plumage green, wings and tail dark green. Speckled black, white and blue, or white, yellow and blue, or black, red and blue.

Lukot, Likot. The native owl. (The *Pueo* of Hawaii, the *Utak* of the Mariannes.) Dr Gulick in his Ponapean dictionary gives TEIAP, possibly an older word preserved in some of the districts as late as 1870, the date of his visit. For those who love imitative sounds I subjoin the following equivalents :—

An owl is called *Lulu* in Samoa ; it is the *Kasuk* of the Pelews ; the *Zuku* or *Kizu* of Japan ; Timor, *Kaku, Lakuko ;* Indian, *Ulu, Uluk, Ghùghù, Kuchkuchua.*

The South American names have also a pleasing sound : Quichuan, *Chusek, Chaksa, Pakpaka* and *Tuku ;* Aymara, *Choseka* and *Huku ;* and the Araucanian on the south border of Chili has *Nuku.*

INSECTS

Lang, Long. The *Rango* or *Lango* of the south Pacific. The common fly which simply swarms around the huts and cook-houses.

Em-en-ual is the sand-fly, not half so troublesome as his relation in the North Marquesas.

Amu-ché, Emu-ché, Omu-ché. The dialect words for the ever-present mosquito, the *Namukik* of the Mortlocks, the *Namu* of Polynesia, the *Nyamok* of Malaysia, the *Yamuk* of Pampanga (Luzon).

Kat-el-lang, Kiti-el-lang. Lady of the sky or *Dog of heaven* are the quaint native titles of the Looper caterpillar.

The general term for grubs, small caterpillars, or maggots is *Mach, Maach, Muach* or *Much*, without doubt akin to the Japanese word *Mushi*, generic term for worms and insects.

Some caterpillars are called *Mueti*, likewise a small reddish-brown horse-leech, found in great numbers in the bush after rain, and actually applied to the eyes by the natives in cases of ophthalmia.

The common earthworm is called *Kamotal*, sometimes *Much*.

A flat spiral landshell is called *Chepei-en-Kamotal*, the dish or wash-bowl of the earthworm. Drs Finsch and Kubary discovered several curious endemic species. The dense hanging woods of Ponape, with their very considerable height above sea-level, will no doubt yield a fresh curious harvest to the energetic explorer devoted to this branch of natural history.

Ants

The large black ant, the bull-dog ant of Australia, is called *Kakalich*, a large dark brown one *Loi-poro*, and the small red ant *Kat.*

Fleas

Li-karrak, Li-n-karrak. *Woman of Corruption* is the word applied to troublesome insects of the bug and flea order.

Til (Ngatik *Thil*). Applied to creatures of similar type affecting the head. Caucasian dialects, *Til, Tili,* and *Thil.* (Indian, *Dhil ;* Araucanian, *Thin.*)

Solomon Islands *Tel,* Sonsorol *Tir* id.

Beetles

The old word was *Kari.*

Kul is the term applied to the black-beetle of commerce. They have a water-beetle, fancifully called in the Central Carolines " *the turtle of the fresh water,*" and several dull-hued bush-beetles. The sand-hopper is called *Men-en-pik, i.e.,* the creature of the sand.

Spiders

I noticed three sorts, one large and black (*Likan*), the other two small and speckled, called *Chilapani-im* and *Naluk,* the latter also a chief's title. The web is called *Chaling-likan* or *Sal-ing-likan* (Hindu, *Jhâl*).

A small red and black dragon-fly is common, which they call *Man-en-kalip,* the *creature of the pools.*

There are at least three sorts of butterflies : one red, white and black, one sulphur-yellow, and one small blue. There are numerous moths, amongst them the Sphinx. The generic name for all these is *Li-parruru* or the *Fluttering Lady.*

The cicala or cicada (*Tenter*) is very much in evidence in the groves on moonlight nights. Grasshoppers are found, to which they give the name *Man-cheok.*

The name *Tenter* is applied also to any noisy, blustering person, to chattering busy-bodies, and carriers of tales and idle gossips.

In a chant on Paniau we find allusion to the habits of this insect in approved Kalevala metre :—

> " Tititik melakaka-n-tenter
>   Nin chounopong chenchereti."

> " Shrills the chirp of the cicala
>   Thrilling through the silvery moonlight."

Scorpions

A small sandy-hued scorpion is found, but its sting, unlike those of Java, Sumatra, and Timor, is not very venomous. The natives term it *Iki-mang* or *Ikimuang*, *i.e.*, *Fork-tail* or *Branch-tail*, with their minute insight into small things. In Samoa upon Manu'a the centipede or scorpion is called I'UMANGA, word for word the same name as the Ponapean. The Upolu word is *Mongamonga-iu-manga*—the prefix denoting *Beetle* or *Insect*.

Centipedes

Two or three kinds of centipedes (Scolopendra) are not uncommon in the thatch and under the *tet* or floorings of reed-grass in the huts, especially those of old standing. The old Malay name *Alipan* (Formosan *Arripas*) has been dropped—doubtless by some priestly or chiefly taboo, like the *Te-pi* custom of Tahiti. There are two ceremonious names for the creature which go to strengthen the impression. Throughout the central Carolines the custom holds also. By day they call it *Man-en-ran—the Creature of the Day*. By night they call it *Man-en-pong—the Creature of the Night*. If this rule were neglected the careless person would be in danger of a nip from one of these crawling horrors. Similarly the earwig is called in Samoan *Monga-monga-iao* or *The Beetle of the Day*. The centipede's bite is often distressingly painful, though it is not so common here as in Indonesia, and the natives give it a wide berth. The people of Ruk call it *Kutu-mal* or *mischievous insect*, and the Samoans to the south *Atua-loa* or *the long devil*, for which relic of heathenry the missionaries have substituted *Manu-loa* or *long insect*.   (It is the *Saligo* of the Mariannes, the *Lalian* of Timor, the *Nina-kuru* or *fiery worm* of Peru.)

LIZARDS AND SNAKES

Kieil. The skink (Scincus) called *Kiuen* in Ruk and *Gual* or *Kuel* in central Carolines.   *Cf.* Indian *Ghariyal, Gavial*, the crocodile of the Ganges ; *cf. Motu, Uala*, a crocodile. The Kieil is a large black lizard with red spots, slightly yellowish below, and resembles a miniature alligator.   The alligator itself they call *Kieil-alap* or *Kiel-en-pil*, of the arrival of which the natives have some tradition.   Kubary brought a couple of young alligators with him to Mpompo, near the European colony, and for some reason or other let them loose in the Pillapenchakola River.   One of my specimens of these " *Kieil*," as if foreseeing the alcohol bottle, furiously resisted capture, and when hit with a stick fastened to it like a bull-dog.   The Kieil lives in holes in the ground, much preferring the sites of old burying places.   The natives say he feeds on the bodies of the dead, which is very possible.   They call him *Chaot* or " unclean," and view him with dislike and dread as *Likamichik* or " uncanny."   A strange fact about this lizard is that he has established a regular colony on the low coral island of Paniau in Mutok harbour, right off the mouth of the Kiti river, a good two miles from shore, whereas on land he is not so easily seen, generally preferring the thick bush.   On Paniau at first they were very bold, and would crawl close up to us at our meals and eat bits of meat thrown to them, to the great horror of the natives.   But the speedy disappearance of some of the largest and boldest of these intruders soon made them keep their distance.

There is a brownish-black house-lizard with a flattish nose which the natives call *Lamuar.** All night long one might

* [Lipidodactylus lugubris.]

hear them hissing and tchik-tchiking away in the thatch overhead, but they are perfectly harmless, nobody minds them. The same name is also incorrectly given to two small species ornamented with a double row of black and white circular spots down the sides like the eyes on the wings of a peacock-butterfly. Both are only three inches in length ; one dark green, the other light green with faint yellow markings. (The accurate names are *Li-pa-irer* or the *Speckled Lady* and *Li-menimen-en-cherri* or the *Lady who loves little children*, a pretty and poetical idea.) *N.B.*—The former is a curious endemic species (Perocheirus articulatus) and has only four fingers, and the thumb shrunk down to a tiny knob.

There are two slightly differing green and yellow lizards found around the trunks of the coco-palms which they nimbly dart up at the least alarm, called the *Li-teitei-paini* or *Woman rout about or stir up coconut leaf* and *Nan-chelang;* the latter much larger and of more brilliant colouring.

The commonest of all however is the little green lizard with a tail of bright electric blue, so widely distributed over the Pacific area, occurring in the Philippines, Moluccas, New Guinea, Solomon Islands and the Pelews, and even as far south as Samoa and Rarotonga.

Dr Cabeza speaks of a lizard of considerable length which he declares to be the Varanus, known in Yap and the Philippines.

The large green and yellow iguana of Yap I did not meet with here, but the Ponapeans tell of a longish prickly green lizard which may be akin, found on the *Och* or ivory-palm. They call it *Man-tau-och* or *Animal go up ivory-palm tree*, also *Man-kalanga* or *the climbing animal.* Connected with this creature they have an old superstition that anyone who meddles with it will presently be seized with dizziness and fall out of the top—no very pleasant prospect, as the ivory or Sago-palm runs up from forty to fifty feet.

Dr Cabeza gives three species of the *Lygosoma* in scientific form, *L. mivartioc; L. atrocostatum;* and *L. abofasciolatum.*

Dr Cabeza goes on to say that during his stay he saw no frogs or toads, but mentions the interesting fact that a species of horned toad (*Cornufer corrugatus*) is found in the Pelews, 1300 miles distant. He deals in a single sentence with snakes, almost as badly as the historian with the snakes of Iceland. " There are no land-snakes, but some are seen in the sea."

I saw no snakes in Ponape, but I did meet with a specimen of a large pugnacious green eel. The natives called it MACHO to distinguish it from the common river-eel. The *macho* is amphibious and has its habitation in the salt-water marshes behind the mangrove belts, where it lives on the purple and brown crabs (*machat*) crawling on the tree-trunks, up which it writhes itself and coils in the branches waiting for its prey. When I was in Paniau a woman in the Matup district was bitten by one of them and died in less than two days, probably from the shock ; the natives said from its venom. The natives fear it greatly, saying that the fierce creature is the incarnation of the spirit of a wicked and cruel chief who murdered his wife and children, and was chased into the swamp by the avengers and put to death. A specimen was obtained with great difficulty by Kaneke and Nanchom. It was a yard in length, body about the thickness of one's thumb, dark green in colour, the two long projecting fangs much in evidence.

With the Ponapean name *Macho*, compare Japanese *Mushi*, a worm ; Marshall Island *Moch*, a sea-eel ; Central Carolines *Mas*, *Mat*, a worm ; Gilbert Island *Mata*, a worm ; Formosa *Matkad*, a sea-eel.

All the following mean *snake* or *serpent*: German New Guinea *Mot*, *Mat*, *Matsch* ; Bismarck Archipelago *Mote* ; Louisade Archipelago *Mata* ; British New Guinea *Mota*, *Mata*, *Ma* ; New Hebrides *Mata*, *Mwata* ; Malo *Moata* ; Santo *Mata*. In Kusaian, *Mwat* is a worm and *Moet*, *bêche-de-mer*.

There are two sorts of sea-snakes (*Pelamis bicoler*), both called *Na-llupu-loi-loi* or *Nan-li-puloiloi*, *i.e.*, *Lady madam with parti-coloured bands.*[1]   One is banded black and white, and one black and yellow.   Habitat, the beds of *olot* or sea-grass when the tide is out.

Fresh-water Eels

These abound in the creeks and rivers, especially in the deeper pools, and sometimes attain great length and thickness.   The natives hold them in mortal dread, and call them *Kamichik*, that is *Terrible*.   Nothing will induce the Ponapeans to eat their flesh.   The old name, now dropped out of use by the taboo, is said to have been *İt* (Pangasinan *Igat*).   They will sometimes unexpectedly attack people fording the rivers, inflicting very severe bites.   Mr C. F. Wood who visited the Kiti and Metalanim coast in his yacht about 1870 speaks feelingly of the horror he felt of these creatures whilst bathing in the creeks.   Far up in the Kiti highlands on a tableland some 3000 feet above the sea is reported to be an extensive lake filled with these creatures, like the Tahitian lake *Vaihiria* and the Samoan *Lanu-toa.   Tuna* is the name given to the eels in the high basaltic islands of Polynesia (Kusaian *Ton*), either from their dark colour (Micr. *Ton*, dark ; Mangarevan *Tunatuna*, black, brown ; Skt. *Tam, Tan*), or derived from an old Aryan and Semitic root *Tan*, to stretch.   (*Cf.* Hebrew *Tannin*, a water-snake, sea-monster.) The Mortlock islanders call the eel *Tiki-tol*, and use it for the equivalent of the Serpent in the Garden of Eden.   To express the same zoomorphic notion of the Devil the Tahitians have the inimitable phrase, " *Moo-rahi-avae-ore, i.e.*, " The long lizard without paws," or as the French have it, " *Longue lézard sans pattes.*"

It is very remarkable the horror in which Micronesians and Polynesians alike hold lizards and eels, and it certainly seems to point to a traditional recollection of the crocodiles and venomous serpents they left behind them in the great rivers and jungles of Asia and the larger islands of

[1] In Samoan *Puleilei* denotes a necklace of beads strung in alternate colours.

Indonesia. What proves this so strongly is the fact that crocodile and snake names in New Guinea in many instances coincide with lizard and eel designations current in the dialects embracing all the isles of the Pacific.

DOMESTIC ANIMALS

First and foremost is that noble animal the pig (*Puik*), the *Puaka* or *Puaa* of south Polynesia. There are two varieties, one long and thin flanked with a long snout like a greyhound, known to the Australian farmers as *Pangoflin ;* the other with a short snout and serenely-swelling barrel, descended either from the sort introduced by traders and settlers in the last century, or from stray parents deposited in more remote times by Chinese or Japanese trading-junks. The names *Puik* and *Puaka* are certainly the Thibetan *Phuag* or *Phak* with which the Latin *Porcus* is a cognate. Even with the Melanesians who represent the early Dravidian element in these seas, the syllable *Bu, Bo,* or *Ba* underlies their names for pig ; the Malay word *Babi* is one of these primitive forms. In a few of the central Carolines we find the word *Seilo* or *Silo* (Javanese *Chileng*, a pig), which certainly points to the advent of a Javanese prau. In the Paliker district the pig is called *Man-teitei*, or the *animal that grubs in the soil ;* the name *Puik* being tabooed in the district on the death of Lap-en-Paliker's father who bore that name. This is a living instance showing how under our very eyes old words are dropping out of use in these isolated dialects and new ones taking their place, and yet folk thoughtlessly ask, " Why are not all the words in Pacific tongues clearly traceable to India ? " To this the above is partly a reply. In the next place we have not got all or anything like all the Asiatic dialects properly set down so as to form reliable tables of comparison. Moreover there are a good many dialects in Indonesia and in New Guinea, and certainly a few in the central Carolines yet unchronicled, which if set down would add their quota to the continually increasing number already established and brought together. Anyone who has seriously studied the gradual building up of the English tongue from Early Saxon, Norse, Danish, and Latin elements will readily see that tracing the influence of the rapidly succeeding waves of varying stocks is an intricate rather than an impossible task, as some philologists have somewhat supinely been content to call it. In the last place, most Micronesian and Polynesian words *are* very clearly traceable from Asia, though from long isolation they have been greatly planed, chipped, attenuated, and whittled down. A great deal of the rough material out of which the Aryan languages were developed doubtless entered into the composition of the Oceanic tongues which are classified as Melanesian, Micronesian, and Polynesian. Many such common words occur in the languages of the hill-tribes of India, and in the elaborate and probably much later Sanskrit. A more exhaustive study of Micronesian tongues will yield facts enough to prove occasional intrusions of Mongol and later Malay, which latter tongue in vocabulary may well lay claim to possess many Sanskritic affinities.

The next domestic animal is man's faithful friend the dog, *Kiti* (*Cf.* Indian hill-tribes' dialect—Kiranti *Kochu*, Karwa *Kuttu*, Mundari *Kota*, Savara *Kinchoi* id.). *Cf.* Hindustani *Kutta*, Sulu Archipelago *Kitu*, Araucanian *Kiltho*.

The dog is not only valued as a custodian, but for supplying a delicate dish in time of need, especially in the tribe of Metalanim. King Paul, unless report belies him, is particularly fond of the tongue, liver, and entrails, which are always set apart for His Majesty at high feasts.

The native dogs are ordinarily of a dull brownish yellow, the tint of an old copper coin. Their nature is stealthy, sneaking and thievish. They are kept on very short commons, which is thought to increase their vigilance. Many of them—by nature, not art—are entirely lacking in a caudal appendage, which gives the poor wretches a very comical appearance. The unfortunate animal marked out for the feast is either beaten to death with sticks, or seized by the hind legs and its brains dashed out against the nearest stone. Unlike the Japanese the Ponapeans seem to have no consideration for animals. So that the Society for Prevention of Cruelty to Animals is likely to have its hands full for awhile if these islands should ever fall into the hands of John Bull or Brother Jonathan.

Outside the Colony the sheep has not been introduced, though Narhun and the German trader at Chauenting keep a few, and the Ponapeans, like their Polynesian cousins, as a rule hate the taste of mutton whether fresh or preserved. Goats are found on Mutok (Tenedos) and on several places along the coast—introduced by early traders. The natives rather like their flesh, but view the animal with great disfavour for the havoc he makes with their breadfruit trees, ring-barking them as accurately as an Australian woodman clearing a eucalyptus forest.

There is a singular word running throughout the Caroline archipelago which shows that once upon a time their ancestors had a closer acquaintance with the above animals either in Malaysia or India. For the word for feathers or animals' hair all over the group is *Un* or *Ul*. (Compare Sanskrit *Un*, wool, fur, and Turkish *Yun* id).

The domestic fowl *Malek* (*cf.* central Caroline *Maluk*, Pelews *Malk*, Mariannes *Manok*, Malay *Manuk*, Peruvian *Mallko*, a chicken) is well represented in every settlement. Their plumage has a peculiar ruffled and bristly appearance. They are rather shy of approach and remarkably strong on the wing. The cock is called *King* (Peruvian *Kanka*), the hen *Lu-tok* or *Li-tok*, *i.e.* the *Clucking female ;* chickens are called *Purrok*, plural *Purrongko*, *cf.* Malay *Burong*, a bird. (*Cf.* Peruvian *Tokto*, Maori *Tikao-kao*, Ruk *Tukao*.) Their eggs (*Kutor*) are small and not very easy to gather. Directly the cackle of a hen disturbs the air, the pigs and dogs are on the move through the brushwood to secure the precious egg. What they pass over the rats generally secure. Any chickens raised run so many risks in their infancy that it really is a wonder how so many come through with their lives. It is no uncommon thing in some quiet corner of a native hut to come across a mother hen sitting upon her eggs venting her displeasure by a crooning sort of twitter at the approach of a stranger. Fresh eggs are less esteemed than those which have been some time under wing. These the natives consider more savoury. Addled eggs from their delicious odour are called *Puaich-en-uair*, the *inheritance of the bat;* and by the natives of Yap, *Batai.*

Jungle fowl (*Malik-en-ual*) are to be met with on the mountain slopes. Adventurous young cockerels sometimes descend into the valleys and engage in furious conflict with the chanticleers of the settlement, and find their way into the all-embracing ever-ready iron pot, for the watchful native, unlike the effeminate Manilla man, seldom throws away a shot, lead, powder and caps, being so scarce and dear.

Kau (Ang. *Cow*) is the generic word for cattle. Henry Nanapei keeps a small herd in the Ronkiti valley. Like the Japanese, the natives do not particularly relish cow's milk. They fall eagerly however upon the condensed milk, whether the much advertised Nestlé's or some less distinguished brand. It is all the same to them. It is sweet, and they like it. Beef, whether fresh or salt, lean or fat, tough or tender, I had nearly said cooked or uncooked, is devoured with delight, forming a most welcome addition to their frugal fare of shell-fish, fish, and yams. There was a *carabao* or water-buffalo, imported from Manilla, employed in carting earth and stones in the colony at Santiago. He was of a vicious and surly disposition, greatly admired by the natives for his enormous horns, with which he would upset any stranger who came near enough.

The domestic cat is quite a household pet, and often enjoys a hearty meal of scraped coconut when the house-dog goes hungry. Should he presume to actively remon-strate at this one-sided arrangement, he is either seized by the scruff of the neck and dropped out of doors, or kicked into a corner, where, lying supperless, head between paws, he views his hated rival feasting to repletion, growling to himself in a muffled undertone, never once taking his hungry, wistful eyes off the fast-vanishing provender—so near and yet so far.

A kitten is called *Kat-pul* or *Pusa-pul,* " *a green puss.*" The Malays for the same kitten would say *Kuching-muda*, or for a gosling *Angsom-muda*, exactly as in the English phrase, " *a green gosling.*"

CRABS, CRAYFISH, AND MARINE CREATURES

Rokum, Rakum. Generic word for small crabs.

Alimang. Large brown swimming crab, found amongst the roots on the edge of the mangrove swamps (Tagal, *Alemang ;* Samoan, *Alimango*).

Paru, Poru. A digging-crab that throws up little hillocks of sand on the shore.

Karrach. A green rock-crab (*Brachyura*).

Omp. The coconut crab (*Birgus latro* or the Robber Crab). It is of large size, blue with red markings, and is furnished with enormous claws, with which it tears off the husks of coconuts and the tough pericarps of other oily and juicy fruits, and feasts on the kernels.

Li-matal-en-iak. Small marsh-crab, speckled black and white or purple and white, with a disproportionately large red claw.

Umpa. The *Maka-ura* of the Gilbert Islands. The hermit-crab, of which there are several varieties.

Land. (1) Light green, found inside shells of sea-snails.

Sea. (2) Red and white, sometimes with golden splashes on claws, found in purplish or red and white shells.

Sea. (3) Black and purple, claws tipped with red or yellow, found inside old broken shells.

Land. (4) A dark blue sort, with red body and claws, resembling robber crab, wedges his body into old coconut shells or large sea-shells.

Machat, Machaut. A purple and brown swamp-crab seen crawling over the dead timber and on the trunks of trees in the swamp and up the river.

Chiwan, Kopuk. Marsh-crabs related to *Machat.*

Cray-Fish

Urana. The lobster. (*Cf.* Malay *Udang*, a prawn ; Mortlock *Ur*, lobster.)

Inchang (Hindu *Inchna*). Blue and white banded cray-fish found in holes on the mud-flats at low tide especially off Langar Island.

Li-katap-en-chet (Squilla). A small sea - crayfish marked yellow, purple and white, no larger than a good sized prawn.

Li-katap-en-pil (The *Ulavai* of Samoa). The fresh-water shrimp. The name means *Useful Woman of the fresh water*, which it indeed deserves as it is a capital addition to the Ponapean bill-of-fare, sometimes growing to a length of four or five inches. The women dip them out, the boys catch them with minute nooses on the end of sticks.

Tapap. Curious black and white or brown and white banded crayfish. The *Tapapa* of Futuna, the *Tumal* of Yap, the *Thabethabe* of Fiji.

Tarrich. The timber-worm. Frequently mentioned by whaling captains in these seas, but never once with approbation.

Lit. The generic name for sea-anemones.

Ip. A curious slug-like creature of a light blue colour found adhering to the underside of limestone blocks on the reefs at low tide. *Cf.* Samoan IPO, an edible mud-worm. On Yap, *Inap.*

Li-ulul, Lulul. Lady Pillow. A large blue starfish found on the sandy or coralline bottom of the shallow pools in the lagoon. Compare the Japanese term for the creature *Tako-no-makura*, the *Octopus' pillow.* The Lamotrek folk call it *Laul-a-garao* or the *Laul of the skies.* The Ponapeans have a curious superstition about the *Li-ulul* that if taken out of water a heavy shower of rain will soon follow. Called on Ngatik *Kich-el-lang*, *i.e., a little bit of the sky.* There seems to be a hazy sort of connection in the native mind between the colour of the creature and that of the sky, upon which convenient peg some designing medicine-man or rain-maker hung his moral.

There is another species of starfish brownish-red and spiny which they call *Rar.*

Likant-en-Kap. Queen of the sea-bottom. The modern name for the sting-ray or skate-fish, of which there are several species in Pacific waters. The old tabooed name is given as *Pae* or *Pai* (Pingelap and Mokil abbreviated form *Pâ, Pae*), the *Fai* of the Mortlock Islands, the *Hai-manu* of Nuko-Oro (compare Polynesian *Hai, Fai* and *Whai*). In Yap *Pai* appears only in the compound word *Pai*-bok, the *Bok* or tail of the *Pai.* These are all abraded forms of an ancient Sanskrit word. The *Tagala* of the Philippines gives us *Pagui, Pagi*, with its usual change of *G* for Malayan *R.* (*Cf.* *Layag* for *Layar*, a sail; *Niyog* for *Niyor*, a coconut; *Itlog, Telog* for *Telor*, an egg.) The original form appears in Malay *Ikan-Pari*, the *Fairy Fish*, from the Indian *Pari, Peri*, our *Fairy.* (In Sulu the skate is called *Isda-palit*). By some curious chance with us on the Atlantic side, the word has gone through exactly the same process as with our poor relations on the Pacific. Our collateral form for *Fairy*, *Fay*, has also lost the medial *R.*

The names of three varieties were given me by Nanchau of Mutok. (1) *Pae-pai-lik* or *skate-skate-little*, a small sort, (2) *Pata-lik* or *little-tail*, and (3) *Pai-wawa*, the spotted variety known in Kusaie as *Asasa.* The Ray is fond of basking in the muddy shallows, and when trodden on by an incautious foot, it inflicts terrible wounds with the barb of its flexible tail. This the Ponapeans call *Och* (Polynesian *Hoto*, *Foto*, *Oto*). In the absence of iron the Caroline islanders used these barbs as spear or arrow-heads, for which purpose they are eminently adapted. From the rest of the tail riding-whips are made of terrific cutting power. In Samoa the *Foto* or barb was frequently used for secret assassination. The old king Tamasese is reported to have met his death from unexpectedly rolling upon one of these wrapped up in his sleeping mats. A terse Samoan proverb thus runs : " *Ua solo le fai, ua tuu ai le foto.*" " The ray runs off, but leaves her barb behind."

Til-en-Paran, *i.e.*, the orange-coloured louse. A sort of limpet-like slug found sticking to the under part of limestone rocks in the shallow pools on the reef at low tide. Colour, white veined with dark red, with blotches or splashes of vivid yellow and scarlet. It is a Chiton, and I have seen a dull-coloured variety sticking to the sea-washed rocks on the coast of the north and south Marquesan Islands.

Kich is the term for the octopus or squid, *Li-puleio* for the larger kind. With *Kich* compare Kusaian *Koet*, Mortlock *Kis*, Mokil *Kueit*, Pulawat *Kush*, Lamotrek *Kuich* and *Ngit*, Nuku-oro *Kueti*, Marshall Islands *Kweit*, Fijian *Kuita*, Tagal *Kugita*, Malay *Gorita*, Ilocan *Kurita*, Mota *Ugita*, and *Motu* (Pt. Moresby) *Urita*. A line of very curious cognates, showing how rapidly the early Malay word gets attenuated as we get further and further eastward away from Indonesia into the Pacific area and find the word at last down in New Zealand worn away down to *Ngu* or *Ku*.

Bêche-de-mer is abundant in these waters, variously styled the Holothuria, sea-slug or sea-cucumber, which when dried forms one of the staple exports of the great Archipelago.

The generic term for these creatures is *Men-ika* or *Man-ika*, i.e., " *Animal-fish* " or *Man-fish* (*Man* = animal or Man, *Ika* = fish). *Penipen, Pelipel*, and *Periper* is another Caroline name for them, sometimes denoting a species, sometimes the genus. (*Cf.* Polynesian *Penupenu*—tough, glutinous, flaccid). There are a great many species, and the ones most highly esteemed for trade I mention first.

Class No. 1. The most highly esteemed of all, " *Li-machamach-ueipul*," " The favourite wife of the Flame-tree," called by trading-skippers the Tiger-fish, sometimes measuring a foot and a half in length. It is olive-green, covered with deep yellow spots each surrounded by a circle of deep olive. The touch of its tentacles or entrails produces a most violent itching and burning on the skin like the sting of a nettle, and the water it squirts out when taken out of the water if a drop gets in the eyes causes violent inflammation and sometimes loss of sight.

Habitat, the " *mat*," or detached reefs in the lagoon. It mostly lies in the deep water, six to ten feet, on the rocky shelves or amongst the coral lumps.

In cutting up slugs for the try-pot we found inside some of the larger ones minute sea-eels, and small fry, upon which it appears these creatures feed.

Main, the Shoe-fish, so called from its thick-rounded body, of a dark grey colour.

Limach. Teat-fish. Large, black, covered all over with whelks and knobs and projections like a horned frog.

Li-kapichino, Li-kapichinana, also called *Penipen*. Large, thick red, found on the *Paina* or outer reef.

Torono. Large, reddish above, orange below ; found on the outer reefs at low tide.

There are other edible varieties, some of which are put in with the rest as make-weights, or sorted into separate sacks. One dark yellow (*Li-keniken*), one light-coloured, found by moonlight (*Penipen*), one yellowish with black spots called in Kiti by the same name as the foregoing.

There are four varieties sometimes eaten in times of scarcity, the common small thin black sort (*Katup*, in the Pelews *Kasupl*) ; one thick, black, nocturnal in its habits (*Matup*), after which a district in Metalanim is called ; one white, spotted-brown, found at the edge of mangrove swamps (*Longun*) ; and another light-brown above, white beneath (*Kamet, Kamat*).

There are other varieties which the natives do not eat. One large greenish-brown (*Manet*), one light-brown, spotted black, with a black line down the middle of the back (*Uarer*), one long black found under rocks and stones in the shallow pools (*Chaparang*), another long black one of similar habits known as *Keeka* or *Kăkă*, and one dull green mottled dark-brown called *Ul-alap-onge*.

Method of preparing Bêche-de-mer. The slugs are taken straight ashore, split open with a knife, and the viscera (*Wara*) taken out—a most unenviable piece of work—and they are boiled in a deep iron try-pot. A substantial drying shed has already been erected, the framework of stakes of mangrove-wood, thatched and walled in from the winds on every side with solid layers of young palm-fronds cut when the leaflets grow thickest together. Only the narrowest of entrances is left. Within is constructed a platform of shutters of reed-grass raised some four or five feet above the floor. On these the slugs, after the boiling process, are laid out to dry in a dense column of smoke which a carefully tended fire of driftwood below sends up night and day. When thoroughly cured, in course of which process they undergo considerable shrinkage, the fish according to their class are put up into sacks ready to be hoisted on board. They are kept carefully dry, as they spoil very rapidly with the least damp. The Chinese and Japanese value bêche-de-mer very highly as a food, and pay very good prices, as much as £80 per ton having been realised with fish of the best quality.

By a somewhat tedious preparation of stripping and soaking, the bêche-de-mer is made into a delicious gelatinous soup, which has most invigorating properties, and when better known should take its place alongside of beef-tea and chicken-broth in the dietary of invalids, and as an easy rival of the much-vaunted turtle-soup of civic banquets. For the turtle, as every native knows, owes his flavour to the sea-slugs he feeds upon during the breeding-season. In combination with a peculiar vegetable styled Chinese parsley, bêche-de-mer forms a most delicate stew, which I tested one evening at Macao and rendered it ample justice, to the delight of my Chinese entertainer.

(F) MARINE CREATURES OF YAP

Crabs and Crustacea

Small brown—*Tafagif.* The *Rakum* or *Rokum* of Ponape and the New Hebrides. Brownish purple, *Teiteiguluf.*

Large—light blue and red markings (Sp. Cancrejo pintado). *Malööb.*

Small, light brown, long arms. *Or.*

Small, olive-coloured, hairy. *Tamalang, Nomit.*

Small, spotted black, red and white, large red claw, found burrowed in sand and mud near in mangrove swamp. *Gaburrogok.*

Hermit-crab. *Yekayek.*

Burrowing crab. *Kathiu.*

Robber or Coconut crab (Birgus latro) *Aiyui.* (Lamotrek, *Yeffi*). Dark brown, *Kafira.*

Swimming crab. *Arum-a-dai.*

Cray-fish. *Arangoi, Mathithin.* Black and white barred. *Tumal.*

LIZARDS

Gaiutch, Aius, Gaius. An alligator. A word derived from the Pelews, where they are occasionally found. (Malay and Philippine *Buaiya, B* to *G.*)

Atelapok. The skink. A black lizard with red spots,

about a foot in length, called *Kieil* in Ponape, *Kiuen* in Ruk, and *Gual* in the Central Carolines.

Galuf, Guluf. The Iguana (Varanus sp.).

Ataligak, Adaburru, Atarau. Sp. small lizards.

BIRDS

Curlew (*a*) with curved bill. *Kaku* (*b*) with straight bill. *Kuling.*

Plover. Sp. *Gabachai.* Albatross *Mui-bab.* Sacred to the god of war.

Fruit-bat. Magelao, Maguilao

DOMESTIC ANIMALS

In'men, N'min, the domestic fowl. *Pilis,* the dog. [*Cf.* Hindustani *Pilla,* a puppy.]

MARINE ANIMALS

Tai-on. Curious circular medusa, with six tentacles, found amongst the *Lem* or clumps of sea-grass which cover the sandy flats in the shallow lagoon, which the ebbing of the tide leaves with only five or six inches of water to cover them.

Rûr. A brownish-red starfish, studded thickly with bluntish dark blue points or spikes, about three quarters of an inch in length.

Inap (Ponape, *Ip*). A curious bluish annelid adhering to the under parts of masses of limestone rock on the reef.

Rimich. The *Tentumuoi* of Ponape ; a gelatinous reddish-brown creature, living in cracks and fissures of coral reef, stretching out a forest of suckers resembling a clump of water-weeds.

Thilthil. Yellow or orange variety of *Rimich,* called in Mariannes *Dodak-man-yagu, i.e.* the animal that ducks down.

Lon. Sp., jellyfish.

Goloth. A sea-eel (*murœna*).

Mokelikil, Ar, Marabilag. Species of sea-spider.
Lilibots. A species of sea-snake, ringed black and white or yellow and black.

HOLOTHURIA, OR SEA-CUCUMBERS

Daotan. Grey body, whitish below, found on edge of mangrove belt; edible, but scarcely palatable even in famine time.
Buro. Large, inedible, greenish-brown.

INSECTS

Somening. A large brown and yellow-winged grass-hopper.
Osongol. The dragon-fly: one sort large, *reddish-brown ;* the other small, *brown* and *yellow* body.
Galaoleu. Another species of dragon-fly; body red, wings dark blue and white.
Girrigir. The fire-fly, seen in great numbers in the evening darting in and out of the groves of areca and coco-palms like winged sparks of fire.
Ngal. The white ant; very destructive to pillars and flooring and furniture in houses.
Ganau. The house-spider (Aranea).
Riu. The cicala (Malay, *Riang-riang*).
Elolai, Alolai. Worm.
Gorro-mangamang. Caterpillar.

SEA-URCHINS

Buol. The *Cheuak* of Ponape.
Olaa. Large-pointed spines, spotted brown and white like those of porcupine.

FISHES

Aiong, Oiong. The shark, *i.e.* the Hungry One.
Litak. Small cobalt-blue fish, hovering round the clumps of branching coral, familiar to visitors in Pacific waters.

Ngong. Small fish, banded black and white.   Same habitat as *Litak.*

U. The Leather Jacket.

Rul. Sting-Ray.

Kai. Octopus, or squid.   Smaller sort, *Luat.*

Tsinua. Black and white spiny fish.

SHELLS

Botangol. A dingy brown swamp-shell, resembling an elongated whelk.

Dabau. A species of cockle found in mud near mangrove belt.

Sanaf. Black and white speckled shell.

Atam-a-lang. Sp. whelk.

Tinatef. Sp. cockle, speckled red, white and yellow.

Eon. The Tiger cowry.

Furufur. A curiously-shaped shell of the cockle order.

(G) PONAPE ONOMATOPŒAS, OR IMITATIVE SOUNDS

Chakachak. Smashing of glass, rattling, clinking, chinking sound ; ticking of clock or watch ; tolling of a bell.   *Cf.* Persian, *chakachak*, clashing of swords.

Teteng. A slamming or banging sound.

Rarrar : Patapatar. The falling or pattering of raindrops.

Ngirringirrichak. The roar of a waterfall.

Ueichip. To splash about whilst bathing.

Tautau. A splashing noise as of oars or paddles.

Monomonoi. Sound of liquid shaken in a cask.

Rarrar. A rattling, scratching, ripping, grating or tearing sound.

Mpimpering. To flare ; rumble, as a blaze of flame.

Ngorrangorrachak. To jingle ; tinkle ; clink.

Kuku : Kingking. The cooing of doves.

Ketiketikak. To cackle, of fowls.

Tontorrok.   To cluck ; twitter, as a hen over eggs.

Kokorrot : Kokkoroti.   To crow as a cock.

Chinchich.   To skim stones along water ; to play at " ducks and drakes."

Kumukumu-chak.   The croak or grunting of the leather-jacket when taken out of water.   *Cf.* Maori, *kumukumu,* the gurnard.

Uerreuerre-chak : Uerreuer.   To shout ; scream.

Ngirchak.   The noise of rushing water ; fall of cascade.

Terterak.   A scraping or grinding noise.

Tontot.   Cry of *cicala.*

Titik.   Squeaking of rats.

Ichi.   To hiss, as snake or lizard.

Uat.   To hoot, as an owl.

Momant.   To rustle, as a dress.

Kumuchak : Poch.   The detonation of a musket or cannon.

Pungpungak.   The noise of the surf on the reef.

Tui.   The cry of a small black bird of the woods.

Uetle.   The note of the *kinuet,* a small green dove with maroon markings.

Kamakamait : Lokalokaia.   The song of birds.

Tukutukamak.   Squeaking of rats.

Li-aurára.   Indistinct mutterings during sleep ; delirium.

Nannamanam.   To jabber ; speak confusedly.

Kemmemar.   To snore.

Ngiringir.   To growl ; snarl.

Ngarangar.   To quarrel ; scold.

Ngai.   To snap (as a savage dog).

Molipe.   To call out ; summon.

Tantanir.   To lament ; weep.

Melakaka.   The song of a chief.   *Cf.* Hawaiian, *mele ;* Tahitian, *umere.*

Kotuk.   To break ; smash.

Tenterong.   To chatter.   (*Tenter,* the cicala.)

Uerreuer: Uerreuerre-chak.   To   shout ;   scream ;
screech.

Morromor.   A noise ; tumult.

Ngichingich.   To shout (of a crowd).

(H) PONAPE GODS

Kimai.   A Metalanim wise woman of old from the
Matup district, where the *luóu* or ornamental bracelets of
shell were first made.

Chau-te-Leur.   The name of an ancient king or dynasty
of kings in Metalanim, when Ponape was under one rule,
and the great walls of Nan-Tauach, the breakwater of
Nan-Moluchai, and the sanctuary of Pan-Katara and the
walled islets near Tomun were built by the divine twin
brethren—the architects Olo-sipa and Olo-sopa. The
last of them, defeated in battle by barbarian hordes from
the south, under Icho-Kalakal, perished in the waters of
the Chapalap river, near the great harbour, and was turned
into a blue fish, the *kital,* which to this day is a *tabu*
fish.

Chenia and *Monia.*   Two adventurous heroes of old
who explored the northern seas, until they saw the midnight sky filled with fire, and returned home with speed.

Kutun.   God of the reef and all therein, and the little
islands in the lagoon. His totem is the *Li-er-puater* or
black and yellow chœtodon fish.

Rakim.   God of house-building and carpentry. According to Dr Gulick the god of evil, disease, death, and
famine.   In Ruk, *Rakim* = the rainbow ; and Sonsorol,
Glagim ; and on Kusaie, *Nelakem* or *Nlakem* has the
same meaning.   So *Rakim* is probably a sky-god, answering to the classic Iris.

Chou-mach-en-cheu.   The god of the sugar-cane.

Li-kant-en-kap.   The sting-ray (anciently *Pae* or *Pai*)
the totem of the Tip-en-uai tribe, the descendants of Icho-
Kalakal's great invasion.

Changoro.   The god of famine (worshipped in Chokach).

Lumpoi-en-chapal. The name of an ancient hero who built the ancient fortifications at Chap en Takai, above Ronkiti, on the south-west coast.

Nan-chapue. The god of kava and feasting. The *Marrap* or Native chestnut, sacred to him.

Le pépe-en-wal. God of the inland wilderness and jungle.

Nan-kieil-ilil-mau. God of the *Kieil*—a large black lizard with red spots, looked upon by the Natives as " *li-kamichik*," or " uncanny," from its savage disposition.

Chokalai. The " *Kichin-Aramach*," or " little people "— the Trolls, or dwarf goblins, dwelling in the interior of the island. Doubtless here we have the tradition of dwarf Negrito hill-tribes, little by little exterminated by the early Malay settlers.

Kona. The giant race of old. The grave of one of them is shown — an extensive barrow or tumulus at Kipar, near Annepein, on the Kiti coast.

Cherri-chou-lang. *i.e.* The little angel from heaven. One of the lesser divinities who stole the kava plant (*chakau*) from the isle of Koto (Kusaie, or Strong's Island). A piece of the root dropped down from the feast of the gods in the clouds, and thus the kava plant came to Ponape.

Chau-yap. An early navigator from Yap, in the westward, who was directed to Ponape by following the flight of the *kutar*, or king-fisher bird. *Cf.* Maori, *kotare, id.* According to one account, with his *irar*, or magic staff, he dug up the kava plant, and gave it to the men of Ponape, amongst whom he settled.

Li-oumere. A fairy with long iron teeth, who visited Ponape and abode some time ; who was prevailed upon to show them in a ghastly grin, at the sight of the antics of a very ugly and comical buffoon. A man close by in hiding dashed out the coveted iron fangs with a stone, and great was the scrambling of the clan for their new-found treasures.

Ina maram. The moon-goddess. *Cf.* Pol., *Sina,*
Hina, Ina. Cf. Assyrian, *Sin,* the moon.

Tau-koto. One of the gods of Kiti revered in the
kava-drinking.

Chei-aki. An early navigator who landed on the
Paliker coast, from the East Mortlocks, with seven companions, Manchai, Chiri-n-rok, Man-in-nok, Chinchich, Pairer, Roki, and Machan.

Nan-imu-lap. (lit.) "The lord of the great house or
lodge."—The god of dances.

Nan-ul-lap. The Ponapean Priapus, and god of
festivals. Sacred to Nan-ul-lap, who ruled all the con-
tingencies of death, birth, sickness, and good and bad
luck, were the turtle, the *kamaik* or parrot wrass, the
marrer, and the *tep* fishes. They were *chapu,* and only
to be eaten by the chiefs of the tribe.

Likant-Inacho. i.e. Queen Inacho. The presiding
goddess of Chokach Island.

Icho Kalakal. The war-god of Metalanim, *i.e.* Prince
Wonderful.

Icho Chau; Icho Lumpoi. Tribal gods of Metalanim.

Luka lapalap; Luk. The prince of evil. Also, the
spirit that flew over the face of the seas, bidding the
lands rise up, and giving the names to trees and plants.
Cf. Scandinavian, *Lok : Loki,* the prince of evil and
cheatery.

[1] *Li-cher.* Lady of the torch.

[1] *Li-char.* Lady of the knife or sword.

Olo-pat. A demigod. The patron saint of Ngatik.

Olo-sipa ; Olo-sopa. Demigods of the olden time who
constructed the great walls, the stone-water frontages
and wharves upon the islets between Tomun and Leak,
on the Metalanim coast. *Cf.* the two great demigods of
Tahiti, *Oro-tetefa* and *Uru-tetefa.*

Nan-chelang. The god of canoe-building and carpentry
incarnate in a green and yellow tree-lizard of the same name.

---

[1] The female guardians of *Pueliko,* the Ponapean inferno.

Kaneki. God of the coconut palm.

Inacho ; Likant-en-Aram ; Li-ara-katau ; Likant-e-rairai ; Li-mot-a-lang. Fairies—woodland goddesses or nymphs. The emblem of Li-ara-Katau was the *lukot* or Native owl.

Nan-Ilakinia. God of Nan-Tamarui district, on south-east coast.

Maile. A spirit who smites men with dizziness and vertigo.

Li - arongorong - pei. A sea - goddess worshipped on Ngatik, *i.e.*, the Lady who loves the Holy places.

Tau-Katau. The rain-god ; god of the breadfruit-tree.

Li-Au-en-pon-tau. *i.e.*, Lady-chief of the waterway. Goddess of the Palikalao river, on the south-west coast.

Ilako. The family-god of King Rocha, of Kiti, on the south-west coast ; greatly revered in kava-drinking cere-monies. *Cf.* Yap, *ilagoth*, name of a god ; and Tagala, *ilagai*, to command, order, direct.

Nanchau-en-chet. The lord of the morasses and salt marshes, dwelling in the body of the *kaualik* or blue heron.

Kili-unan. A hairy and shaggy goblin of the woods who brings disease and death. (Possibly a faint recollec-tion of the *orang-utan*, left behind them in Java, Sumatra, and other large islands of Indonesia.)

(I) YAP GODS

Yalafath. The Creator ; regarded as a benevolent but indolent being ; incarnate in the bird *mui-bab* (albatross or Frigate Bird).

Nemegai or *Nemegui.* His wife.

Luk. The god of death and disease ; a mischievous and ever-active deity ; incarnate in the *orra*, a black bird of nocturnal habits.

Luk-e-ling. The god of sea-faring men and navigation.

Kuku-balal. The god of cultivation and planting.

Kanepai. The god of the *tsuru* or Native dances.

Ilagoth. The god who blesses and defends folk of good and peaceable life. (Ponape, *Ilako.*)

Marapou. The sun-god.

Urur. The moon-god.

Mukolkol. The god of thieves and robbers, who generally leaves his votaries in the lurch in the long run. The Evil Spirit *Luk* also is a patron saint of the light-fingered fraternity.

Mam. The goddess of childbirth.

Uaga damang. The god of war.

Dotra. The god of canoe-building, house-building, and carpenter's work.

Magaragoi. The god who brings typhoons, gales of wind, and heavy rains.

Madai; Wareleng. The gods of fishes, fishermen, and sailors.

Pof. The god of women and love-making in general.

Koko-galal. God of the *niu* or coconut palm.

Lugeleng. The god of rain.[1]

Tereteth. Goddess of the *atchif* or coconut-toddy.

Mui-bab. The god of war.

Ilu-mokan. God of dances.

Wol Trabab. God of strangers.

Dessra ; Derra. God of fire and earthquake.

Gora dai leng. The avenging deity who punishes bad men after death. A river flows by his abode, running underground. Tortured by fire, the bad spirit falls into the water, and the current takes him along and plunges him down into a deep hole or abyss of flames (*lu-ni-gá*), where he disappears for ever.

Karaneman. The god of whales and sharks.

Ligich. The god of the turtle.

Giligei. A demi-god—the inventor of the *gi* or shell adzes.

Lusarer. A hero of olden time, who taught the men of Yap to build fish-weirs of stone and wood.

Bota-Sunumi. A title of Yalafath, the creator.

---

[1] *Cf.* Lamotrek. *Luk-el-lang.* The god of carpenters.

TRIBAL OR DISTRICT GODS

Yangalav. In Gochepá (central).
Gutherei. In Rúl (central).
Ath. In Nimiguil and Goror (south).
Gatamir. In Map and Ramung Islands (north).
Magaragoi. In Tomil (central).

(J) VARIETIES OF BREADFRUIT IN PONAPE

Mai—Generic name. *Cf.* Tongan, *Mei ;* Marquesan,
   Mei. *Cf.* Chinese and Japanese *Mai*, rice.

1 *En pakot.* Long ; rough rind.
  Pon-panui. Long ; rough.
  Chaniak. Small variety.
  Paimach. Small variety.
5 *Yong.* Small variety.
  En-uaoutak. Small variety.
  Takai. Round ; very hard.
  Impak. Round ; large size.
  En-uchar. Long.
10 *Katiu.* Long.
  Kumar. Long.
  En-machal. Long.
  Niue. Long.
  Letam. Small ; round.
15 *Nakont.* Small ; round.
  En-pol-le. Longish.
  Apil. Round ; small.
  Chai. Smooth.
  En Kaualik. Long ; rough rind.
20 *En-chak.* Longish.
  Nue. Large ; smooth ; round ; the most highly
      esteemed of all.
  En-charak. The mountain variety ; prickly rind.
  Koli. Seeded ; eaten ripe and raw (the jack-fruit).
  Pa or *Mat.* Seeded ; eaten ripe and raw (the jack-fruit).
25 *Kalak.* Smooth ; small.

Taik.   Smooth ; large fruit.
Pulang.   Smooth ; large fruit.

All the following have a Rough and Prickly Rind

Lipet.   Large ; prickly rind.
Uaka.   Longish ; large.
30 *Potopot ; Puetepuet.*   Light-coloured ; long.
En-pon-chakar.   Reddish rind.
Nan-umal.   Longish.
En-paipai.   Long.
Lukual ; Lokual.   Wild bush variety ; very prickly.
35 *Tol.*   Small ; round ; dark rind.
En-patak.   Reddish ; longish.
En-put.   Very small ; round.
En-cherrichang.   Reddish rind ; small.
En-patak,   Long ; thin.
40 *En-par.*   Long ; darkish.
En-kotokot.   Round ; small.
En-monei.   Long ; thin.
43 *Ti.*   Long.

PONAPE

(K) DAYS OF THE MOON'S AGE [1]

First period is called *Rot* or darkness, *i.e.*, nights when there is no moon. *Rot* has 13 days. (*Cf.* Persian, *Rat*, the night.)

1	*Ir.*	8	*Chau-pot-mur.*
2	*Lel-eti.*	9	*Chau-pot-moa.*
3	*Chanok.*	10	*Arichau.*
4	*Chenok-en-komóni.*	11	*Chutak-ran.*
5	*Chanok-en-komána.*	12	*Eü.*
6	*Epenok-omur.*	13	*Aralok.*
7	*Epenok-omoa.*		

[1] Most of these correspond closely to the ancient Tahitian sequence. In this connection *cf.* Appendix A to Tregear's Maori Comparative Dictionary.

The Ponapean *Ir* is certainly the Tahitian *Hiro* ; and the Tahitian *Ari* is clearly the Ponapean *Arichau* with its affixed princely titles.

Second period—new moon—called *Mach ;* contains 9 days, following the sequence of the numerals :—

1	*At.*	6	*Aon.*
2	*Arre.*	7	*Eich.*
3	*Echil.*	8	*Aual.*
4	*Apang.*	9	*Malatuatu.*
5	*Alim.*		

Last period, *Pul*, contains 5 days :—

1	*Takai-en-pai.*	4	*Olo-mal.*[1]
2	*Aro-puki.*	5	*Mat.*
3	*Olo-pua.*[1]		

PONAPE STAR NAMES

1 *Choropuel.*
2 *Mai-lap.*
3 *Mai-tik.*
4 *Tumur.*
5 *Pongenai.*
6 *Li-katat.*
7 *Kien-ua.*
8 *Langemur.*
9 *Li-kamar-en-ich.*
10 *Nach-e-lap.*
11 *Pal-an-tumur.*
12 *Larele.*
13 *Makeriker* (Pleiades).
14 *Uchu-nenek.*
15 *Mel* (The Southern Cross).
16 *Langkoroto.*
17 *Lé-poniong* (seen about time of variable winds).
18 *Katipar* (the blank space in heaven known as the Magellan Cloud).
19 *Aron-mechei-rak* = a comet; also known as *Uchu - pata-iki - mia* = the star with a tail.

(L) LAMOTREK STAR-NAMES

1 *Uiliuil-al-evang.* The Pole-star.
2 *Uiliuil-al-eaur.* The Southern Cross ; also called *Pup*, or the Leather-Jacket Fish.
3 *Tumur*, Antares.
4 *Meal.* Vega and α Lyræ.
5 *Ualego.* Ursa Major. Literally, " The Broom."
6 *Ul.* Aldebaran. Literally, " The Virile Momber."

[1] The Ponapean *Olo* is the Tahitian *Oro* or its equivalent *Roo* (*cf.* Hawaiian *Lono*, Maori *Rongo*) Marquesan *Ono* ; all varying titles of one of the Polynesian ideals of the Supreme Being, *i.e.*, *Sound*.

7 *Evang-el-ul.* Capella ; its appearance denotes heavy gales and bad weather.

8 *Magañgar.* Pleiades.

9 *Oliel.* Orion and Rigel.

10 *Kolong-al-mal.* Sirius ; *i.e.*, literally, " The Body of the Animal."

11 *Ping-en-lakh.* Arietes ; *i.e.*, literally, " The Centre of the House."

12 *Met-a-ryo.* Scorpio ; *i.e.*, " The Two Eyes."

13 *Sor-a-bol.* Corvi ; literally, " The Viewer of the Taro-patches." Shines during Taro season. (*Sor*, to look ; *bol*, a Taro-patch.)

14 *Tchrou.* Corona ; *i.e.*, " The Fowling-net." [1]

15 *Mai-lap.* Althœa and (α) Aquilœ.

16 *Aramoi.* Arcturus. (*Ara*, to conclude ; *moi*, to come.) So called because the rising of Arcturus marks the end of the north-east winds which bring visiting parties to the island.

17 *Yuk-ol-ik.* Cassiopœa ; literally, " The Tail of the Fish."

18 *Mongoi-sap.* Gemini.

19 *Ik.* Pisces.

20 *Mal ; man.* Canis Major.

21 *Ililigak.* Regulus.

22 *Gapi-sarabol.* Speaker.

23 *Ngi-tau.* Piscis Australis.

24 *Gapi-lah.* Pegasi.

MONTHS OF LAMOTREK YEAR

1 *Sarabol.*	5 *Mai-lap.*	9 *Ul.*
2 *Aramaus.*	6 *Seuta.*	10 *Alliel.*
3 *Tumur.*	7 *Lakh.*	11 *Mán.*
4 *Mai-rik.*	8 *Kû.*	12 *Ich.*

(M) MORTLOCK STAR-NAMES

1 *Fusa-makit.* A Ursœ Minoris. " The Seven Mice," *Makit.* *Cf.* Ponape, *Make ;* and Murray Island,

[1] *Cf.* Yap *Chau*, a fowling-net. Ellice group, *Shau, Sheau*, id. ; and Mortlock, *Seu*, id.

Mokis, a mouse. Or it may mean " The *Fus* or Star that moves or changes its position."

2. *Ola.* Ursa Major.

3 *Seu.* Corona Borealis.

4 *Moel.* Lyra.

5 *Manga-n-kiti.* Gemini.

6 *Pou-n-man.* Procyon.

7 *Yis.* Leo. (Lit., The Rat.)

8 *Ap-in-Soro-puel.* Virginis.

9 *Soro-puel.* Corvi.

10 *Eon-mas.* Crateris.

11 *Tanup.* The Southern Cross. (Perhaps " *The Shark*," cf. Polynesian *Tanifa* : *Taniwha*, id.)

12 *Uk-en-ik.* (Unidentified.) Literally, " The Fish-net."

13 *Sepei-ping-en-Sota.* Delphini and Cygni. " The Bowl in the midst of Sota.

14 *Soto.* Equuleus.

15 *Man.* Sirius. The Dog-Star; literally, " *The Animal.*"

16 *Un-allual ; elluel.* Orion and Aldibaran ; *i.e.,* " The Bunch of Three." *Cf.* Maori, *Tau-toru.*

17 *Ku.* Aries.

18 *La.* Pegasus.

19 *Marikir.* Pleiades.

20 *Tumur.* Scorpio.

21 *Mei-sik.* νξo. Herculis.

22 *Mei-lap.* Aquila.

23 *Aramoi.* Arcturus.

(N) YAP STAR-NAMES

Told by Matuk, of Gochepá, on Tarrang Island

Beginning from East to North.

1 *Mai-lap*[1].   3 *Magirigir*[3].

2 *Un*[2].   4 *Moul*[4].

[1] *Mai-lap.* cf. Mortlock, *Mei-lap.*
[2] *Un.* cf. Lamotrek, *Ul* (Aldebaran) ; Mortlocks, *Ola* (Ursa Major).
[3] *Magirigir.* cf. Mortlocks, *Mariker* (Pleiades) ; Ponape, *Makeriker* ; and Lamotrek, *Magarigar, id.*
[4] *Moul.* cf. Mortlocks, *Moel* (Lyra) ; Lamotrek, *Meal* (a Lyræ).

5 *Yigelik* or *Yik-el-ik.*   7 *Mai-le-palafal.*
6 *Ulagok.*

From East to West

8 *Yiliyel*[1].   12 *Matarei.*
9 *Sarabul*[2].   13 *Wonowon-le-yór*, the
10 *Thamur*[3].   southernmost.
11 *Thagalú.*

From South to West.

14 *Tholon-a-Wonowon*[4].   18 *Tholon-a-wún.*
15   „   *matarei.*   19   „   *yiliyel.*
16   „   *sarabul.*   20   „   *mailap*, the
17   „   *thamur.*   westernmost.

From West to North

21 *Tholon-a-magiregir.*   24 *Tholon-a-ulagok.*
22   „   *moul.*   25   „   *mai-le-palafal*,
23   „   *yigelik.*   the northernmost.

LAMOTREK MEASURES

Gat ; Si-gat. A finger's length, *i.e.*, 3 inches.
Rua-gat. Two   „   6 inches.
Sili-gat. Three   „   9 inches.
Fá-gat. Four   „   12 inches, and so on.
Si-ang ; Ang. One span.
Ru-ang. Two spans.
Sili-ang. Three spans, and so on.
Rolibos. A half-cubit.
Gopa. A cubit.
Si-pap. Distance from tip of finger to centre of chest.
Si-ngaf. One fathom.
Si-gip. One foot ; literally, footprint.

---

[1] *Cf.* also Mortlock. *Elluel*: *Allual*, id.
[2] *Sarabul. cf.* Mortlocks, *Soropuel* (Corvi) ; Lamotrek, *Sor-a-bol ;* Ponape, *Choro-puel.*
[3] *Thamur. cf.* Mortlocks, *Tumur* (Scorpio) ; Lamotrek, *Tumur* (Antares).
[4] *Tholon* = facing ; opposite.

(O) LAMOTREK GODS

Aliu-Lap. The Creator or Supreme Being.

Luk-e-lang; Olevat. His sons—presiding over the work of carpenters and boat-builders.

Semili-goror. The wife of Aliu-Lap.

Selang. Her brother.

Saulal. The Prince of Evil.

Alis-i-tet, also called *Toutop.* The Lamotrek Neptune and God of Fishes, called in Satawal *Aliu-sat* or *Ponnorol.*

LAMOTREK

(P) DAYS OF THE MOON'S AGE

Crescent Moon

1	*Sigauru.*	8	*Emital.*
2	*Elling.* (Root, *Ling*, to shine.)	9	*Epei.* (When at sundown the moon is canted over a little to westward.)
3	*Mes-elling.*		
4	*Mis-al.*		
5	*Mesa-fois.*	10	*Rua-bong.* (The joining together (*Rua*) of the nights.)
6	*Meso-ual.*		
7	*Messe-tiu.*		

Full Moon

11	*Yarabuki.*	20	*Evelak.*
12	*Olo-boa.*	21	*Kochalak.*
13	*Olo-mai.*	22	*Karotali-evelak.*
14	*Mares* (= Ripe; developed.)	23	*Saopas-maimor*
		24	*Kili.*
15	*Ur.* (Sun and moon together on sea in the evening.)	25	*Omolo.*
		26	*Romuli-fan.*
		27	*Arafoi.*
16	*Lotiu.*	28	*Eoi.*
17	*Kili.*	29	*Effeng.*
18	*Kalawalo.*	30	*Eráf.*
19	*Saopas.*		

MORTLOCK ISLANDS

[From " Die Bewohner der Mortlock Inseln," by J. S. Kubary ; published in Hamburg by the Geographical Society in 1878-79.]

(Q) DAYS OF THE MOON'S AGE

1	*Sikauru.*	16	*Natiu ; Netiu.*
2	*Allang, Elleng*	17	*Kinnei.*
3	*Mes-allang.*	18	*Ummala.*
4	*Mes-oan.*	19	*Sápas.*
5	*Mes-e-fiu*	20	*Aanak ; Effanak.*
6	*Mes-e-ual.*	21	*Osselang.*
7	*Mes-e-tou*	22	*Aanak.*
8	*Ruapong.*	23	*Sapas.*
9	*Apei.*	24	*Ummala.*
10	*Emátal.*	25	*Ara.*
11	*Aro-puki.*	26	*Roman-fel.*
12	*Olo-pue.*	27	*Aro-fiu.*
13	*Olo-mau.*	28	*Eū.*
14	*Ammas, Emmas.*	29	*Affen.*
15	*Aur, Eur.*	30	*Ese.*

(R) MORTLOCK MONTHS
Named after certain Stars

1	*Yis* (Leo).	8	*La* (Pegasus).
2	*Soropuel* (Corvi).	9	*Ku* (Aries).
3	*Aramoi* (Arcturus).	10	*Mariker* (Pleiades).
4	*Tumur* (Scorpion).	11	* *Un-allual ; elluel* (Aldebaran and Orion).
5	*Mei-sik* (νξο Herculis).		
6	*Mei-lap* (Aquila).	12	*Man* (Sirius, or the Dogstar).
7	*Sota* (Equuleus).		

* *Unelluel* (Orion) = the bunch of three. *Cf.* Maori, *Tautoru ;* Mangarevan, *Toutoru. id.*

(S) MORTLOCK GODS

Rasau, God of war.

Sapinfa; Sau-piong; Ulu-puau; Terie-lap; Piol. Tribal gods.

YAP

(T) DAYS OF THE MOON'S AGE

The Yap month has 30 days counted in three divisions

(1) *Pul* = New Moon

1	*Bungôl.*	5	*Nga-lal-e-pul.*
2	*Nga-ru-e-pul.*	6	*Nel-e-pul.*
3	*Nga-thalib deleb-e-pul.*	7	*Medelib-e-pul.*
4	*Nga-aningek-e-pul.*	8	*Meruk-e-pul.*
11	*Kaiper-e-pul-na-tha-kan-*	9	*Mereb-e-pul.*
	adai.	10	*Aregak-e-pul.*
12	*Nga-logoru-e-pul.*	13	*O-thalib-e-pul.*

(2) *Botrau* = Full Moon

14	*Erebeb-a-botrau.*	19	*Medilib-a-botrau.*
15	*Thalib-a-botrau.*	20	*Meruk-a-botrau.*
16	*Aningek-a-botrau.*	21	*Mereb-a-botrau*
17	*Lal-a-botrau.*	22	*Aregak-a-botrau.*
18	*Nel-a-botrau.*		

(3) *Lumor* = darkness. *Cf.* Pampanga, *lumlum, lumdum,* id. Ponape, *lumor,* the sickness of a chief.

23	*Kaipir-e-lumor-ko-pul.*	27	*Nga-lal.*
24	*Nga-ru-e-lumor-ko-pul.*	28	*Nga-nel.*
25	*Nga-dalib.*	29	*Nga-medelib.*
26	*Nga-aningek.*	30	*Ka-mai-e-pul.*

(U) NAMES OF MONTHS IN YAP YEAR

1	*Maragil.*	5	*Tobil.*	9	*Ambin.*
2	*Paga-ath*	6	*Dunom.*	10	*Yitch.*
3	*Lagu.*	7	*Mathaek.*	11	*Puloi.*
4	*Olo.*	8	*Ya-olang.*	12	*Tchef.*

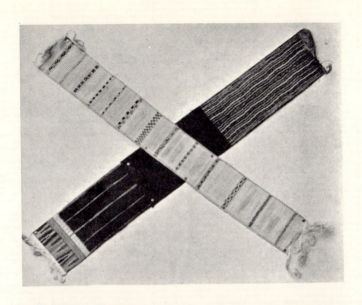

KUSAIAN BELTS

ULEAI

(V) DAYS OF THE MOON'S AGE

An independent list compiled by Chamisso during
Kotzebue's Voyage in these seas in 1815-1818

1	*Lingiling.*	16	*Ladi.*
2	*Sigaur.*	17	*Gilei.*
3	*Mesul.*	18	*Kaira.*
4	*Meseren.*	19	*Gopatemir.*
5	*Meselim.*	20	*Arotevalan.*
6	*Mesaul.*	21	*Olabugi.*
7	*Mesavel.*	22	*Olohue.*
8	*Mesavol.*	23	*Olamahe.*
9	*Mesadu.*	24	*Tamalaval.*
10	*Chabong.*	25	*Ereve.*
11	*Alabugi.*	26	*Eii.*
12	*Olobao.*	27	*Erevi.*
13	*Olomoal.*	28	*Eūū.*
14	*Alat.*	29	*Evan.*
15	*Ir.*	30	*Etav.*

Observe the wonderful coincidence with the Mortlock
and Lamotrek equivalents with a mere change from N. to
L. and T. to R.   G. to K. and T. to S.

This shows very clearly the minute and accurate astronomical knowledge possessed by the early Caroline Island
navigators, and the very considerable range of their maritime activity in generations past.

(W) SOUTH KENSINGTON MUSEUM NOTES

(a) The following is the result of a preliminary inspection
of some dredgings taken by the Spanish Cruiser *Quiros*
in the Ant Lagoon to the west of Ponape Island, East
Carolines.

The washings consist chiefly of Foraminifera, in addition
to which may be noted Alcqonarian spicules, spines of

several genera of echinoderms, numerous pteropods, hetero-
pods, and ostracoda (including *Bairdia* and *Loxoconcha*).
The most conspicuous foraminifera are :—

> *Spiroloculina impressa*, Terquem.
>   „   *grata*,   „
> *Miliolina agglutinans* (d'Orb).
> *Pelosina variabilis*, Brady.
> *Textularia concava* (Karrer).
> *Globigerina bulloides*, d'Orb, var. *triloba*, Reuss.
> *Truncatulina rostrata*, Brady.
> *Calcarina spengleri* (Linn.).
> *Amphistegina lessonii*, d'Orb.
>   „   *radiata* (Fich. & Moll.).
> *Operculina complanata* (Defrance).
>   „   „   „   var. *granulosa*,
>   Leymerie.
> *Heterostegina Depressa*, d'Orb.

(β) The stone money of Yap is merely crystallised carbonate of lime (calcite), and is probably from a vein of that
substance filling cracks in limestone or other rock.

(γ) A microscopical examination of a thin slice of the
limestone from Gerem Islet, Lai, South Yap district, West
Carolines, shows the rock to have been a calcareous sand
composed of molluscan shell fragments, echinoderm spines
and plates, foraminifera such as *Orbitolites complanata* Lam.
Textularia barrettii I. and P., and *Amphistegina lessonii*
d'Orb., also numerous pieces of *Lithothamnion* and joints of
Halimeda. These organic fragments are firmly compacted
by a dolomitised matrix with some cavities in the rock.
The matrix is probably the result of crystallisation and
subsequent dolomitisation [1] of a calcareous mud.

(δ) The reddish rock from Elik seems to be an impure
limestone stained in bands by iron oxide.

Kindly supplied by F. CHAPMAN, A.L.S., F.R.M.S.

[1] Dolomitisation is the partial replacement of the carbonate of lime in a limestone by carbonate of magnesia.

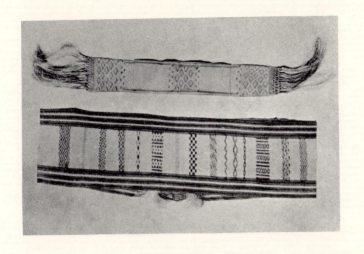

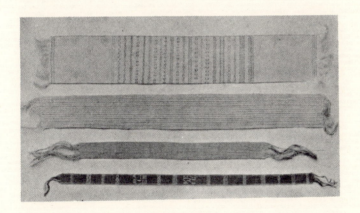

KUSAIAN BELTS

(X) KUSAIAN TEXTILES

Four photographs—(a) Two "*Tols*" or woven belts of banana fibre crossed, one dark, one light coloured; (β) eight Kusaian "*Tols*" in line on screen; (γ) two finely finished specimens of same; (δ) four ditto from the King's House.

Notes on Photo (a).

Black "*Tol*," Length, 4ft. 9½ ins.

Width, 7¼ ins.

Ends terminating with fringes knotted—stained salmon-pink. One end has five particoloured bands in various designs, each about ¾ in. wide.

In line with the length of the "*Tol*" the space is occupied at regular intervals by three particoloured stripes and borders of various widths extending into the body of the "*Tol*" for a distance of ten inches. Colours in stripes red, dark-blue, purple, yellow, pink and brown.

The central portion is stained a glossy black, the texture having the appearance of horse-hair cloth.

The upper right-hand end is woven in eighteen bands similar to those previously described, and of the same colours, save that the red and the blue are not found. The design is uniform but not continuous, the colours of each band running in broken lines.

Light-coloured "*Tol.*"

Length, 3 ft. 4½ ins.

Breadth, 5⅜ ins.

Made from natural coloured banana-fibre—fringed at each end. At varying intervals across the width, and almost uniformly disposed, are bands of interwoven ornament in dark red and black, forming diapers, ornamental chequers and diamonds variously disposed. The outer edges are bordered by two narrow lines in dark red.

Notes on Photo (β).

These "*Tols*" sustain the character of the two described

above, but are less elaborate in pattern, and woven in plain lines or checks. The natives use them for sashes and sometimes as a hat-ribbon. In Honolulu the curio-shops used to receive regular small consignments of these from the Boston mission at Mout on Ualan, and they were quite the fashion amongst the society *belles* of that city.

Notes on Photo (γ).

Two exquisitely finished belts given me by Likiak-Sā. The upper one has a lozenge ornamentation in a lovely electric blue. The delicate designs of the one below are traced in brown, dark-red and dark-blue upon a sheeny white background.

Notes on Photo (δ).

Four delicately finished Tols of the finest sort. The top one picked out in graceful patterns in blue, black, crimson and brown. The second striped light blue and white. The third striped reddish-brown, yellow and white. The lowest red-brown, with white perpendicular ornamentation with the names of the weavers, *Kenie* and *Malem*, in broken lettering.

Similar woven belts of the same fibre, frequently of very fine design, are found throughout the Melanesian area.

In Aneityam (N.H.) they are called "*N'etu.*" They are found in Santa Cruz, where they call them "*Neveia-nikapu*," specimens of which, brought by Mr Jennings, may be seen at the Liverpool and British Museum, and the Rev. Codrington showed me some very fine specimens which he said came from the Banks Group.

One is reminded somewhat of the *Basho-fu* or banana-fibre fabric of Japan, said to be derived mainly from the Ryu-Kyu or Lew-Chew Islands.

The same industry is seen in Sumatra, and I believe in many other islands of the Malay Archipelago.

The loom is a simple hand-loom. In Ponape they call it *Tantar*, in Kusaie *Puas*, in Bencoolen (Sumatra) *Pisa*.

SPECIMENS OF SHELL-ADZES FOUND IN THE GREAT CENTRAL VAULT
OF NAN-TAUACH IN THE NAN-MATAL RUINS

In the Malayan area the Rainbow is called *Bahag-Ari* or *Pinang-Rajah*, both of which names denote the belt of a great lord. Possibly some such elaborate and beautiful fabric as this was worn by the great chiefs of Malaysia in early days, before the Arab merchants plied, and before cheap tawdry cotton goods came in from Manchester.

(Y) PONAPEAN ADZES

Notes on Ponapean Shell Adzes.

Seven adzes and gouge ground down into present shape from central shaft or hinge of the Tridacna Gigas or Giant Clam. Found in the central vault called the Tomb of Chau-Te-Leur upon Nan-Tauach Island in the Island City of Nan-Matal, Metalanim district, Ponape, east coast. The five first named are now in the British Museum.

				WEIGHT.
No. I.,	.	.	.	1 lb. 6½ oz.
No. II.,	.	.	.	1 lb. 2 oz.
No. III.,	.	.	.	— 11 oz.
No. IV.,	.	.	.	7 lb. —
No. V.,	.	.	.	— 7½ oz.
No. VI.,	.	.	.	— 13½ oz.
No. VII.,	.	.	.	— 6½ oz.

Scale of measurement in illustration calculated in centimetres.

F. W. CHRISTIAN.

	English	North.	South.	East.	West.
Eastern Carolines	Ponape, Kusaie, Mokil, Pingelap, Ngatik,	Pali-Apong, Epong: Yepong,	Pali-Air, Eur: Eir,	Pali-Macha-n-lang, Kát-alap: Eir-lap	Pali-Kapi: Kapi-lang. Roto.
Central Carolines	Mortlock Islands, Ruk (Hogeleu), Pulawat, Uluthi, Lamotrek and Ifalik, Satawal, Uleai,	Pali-apong: Apang, Effeng: Afong, Effeng, Euang, Yivang, Evang, Evang: Efang: Ma-efang,	Pali- er, Aur, Yer: Or, Ar: Or, Eür, Jur: Yur, Eaur, Eür, Oru, Eaur: Ma-Yur,	Pali-mácha: Machal-lang, Etuu: Masa-i-lang, Mása, Koteu, Máta-ral, Kotiu, †Koteu, Kotiu: Koto: Mata-ral,	Pali-Kapi: Kapi-lang: Api-lang. Loton: Apeilang. Apeilang. Iloto. Malethao. Ilotiu. Iloto. Iloto: Lotu: Ma-lesu.
W. & S.W. Carolines	Yap and Ngoli, Sonsorol and Tobi, St David's, Nuku-Oro, Marshall Islands— (Ralik and Radak) Gilbert Islands or Kingsmills,	Leloch: Laloch: Laelot, Yevaeng, Evong, Tua, Wasog-i-eng, Eang: Eung, Me-ang,	Imuch: Emuch: Imut, Eürgl, Ior, Tai, Wasogi-rik, Irok: Ruk, Aiaki: Me-ak: Maiaki,	Ngak: Ngek: (Tomil, a district name), Gatiu, Rák, Ngangake, Kasu, Rear, Mainiku: Niku: Naku: Tan-rako: Me-inuk: Aka-potai,	Ngal: Ngol. Iroto. Lito. Ngangaiho. Kasus-o-Kepileng. Kabi-lang. Maiao: Tan-rio: Me iao: O-pungi-tai.
	Nauru, German New Guinea,	Pueu-a-po, IAORTE: Kakua: Sangu,	Puiu-mako, Ambi: Bubere:	Puiu, Sarlu: Karaka,	Puca-ua. Talem: Dadau.
	Bismarck Archipelago, British New Guinea,	IAWAR: Malol, Atobar: Lombur, Suroma: Mirigini,	Jouon, Ataberu: Atombar, Seipi: Diho: Gaburigo: Ahi-daina,	Laur: Taubara, Kaeaona: Maireveina: Tototaina: Walau: Vacau,	Meli: EWAR. Telwat: Labura. Taradiho: Diho: EAVANA: Tivo-taina.

ENGLISH.	NORTH.	SOUTH.	EAST.	WEST.
Louisade Archipelago, Pelew Islands,	Waiyek, Delokus : Thilugus,	Rorau, Dimus : DIMIS,	Nati, 'Ongos : Kongos : Gongos, San-Katan : *Manun,*	Paii, Barath : Barth : Anga-*barath.*
Marianne or Ladrone Islands,	San-Lago : TIMI,	San-Hadja : Seplun,		San-Lichan : Fanu-ipan.
Sulu Archipelago,	Utala : Siguiran,	S'latan : Satan,	TIMOL,	Lalamaddan : *Bagat* : Sedlfipan.
Tagal, *(Philippines Dialects)*	Hi-Laga : Hi-Lagaan,	Ha-*Bagat,*	Si-*Langanan,*	Ka-Lunuran : Kakalong nangalin. Albugan. Kalondan. S-i-alpan-sang-adlao. *Laud.* Sagud.
Pampanga, Bikol, Panayan, Ilocan,	Pangulu,	A-*Bagat,*	As-*lagan,* Silagnan, Sidlangan, *Daia,* Bukuig,	
Pangasinan,	Amian,	A-*Balat*-an,		
Kabaran (N. Coast), Pepo-Hoan (S. & W.), Favorlang (E.), Pilam (E.), Timor, Malay, *(Formosan Dialects)*	Amisan, Loud : *Laud,* Feto, Utara : (J) *Lor,*	Wannan : Soan, *Daiak,* Mane, *Selatan* : (J) Kidul,	Bajan, Ameh, Loro-sae, Timor : *Masrak* : (J) WETAN, Intik-Iloksimunan, sekomunan,	Zipan : Tsipan. TIMOR. Loro-mono. Barat : (J) KULON.
Quichua (Peru),	.	.	Intik-Iloksimunan, sekomunan,	Intik-yaikunan.
Aymara (Peru), Araucanian (Chili),	Piku,	HUAVHUEN : GHUYLLI, Muliken,	Inti-halsu, Antu-UUTHAN,	Inti-halanta. GULL.
Futuna,	Tokelau,	.	Sasake : (*Kake*=to go up),	Sisifo (Ifo = to go down).
Solomon Islands, Indian,	Uttar : Shimal,	Dakhan : Ju nub (Sanskrit, *Evara,* the S.W.),	(*Lanka*=Ceylon) : Purab : *Mashrik* : Shark : Khawar,	Pachcham : Maghrib : *Ghurub* : Gharbi. Barata = India.

* The Micronesian forms in *Pong, Feng, Vang,* and *Vong* denote "the quarter of the N. Trade Winds." *Cf.* Mortlock *Le-feng,* a year; *i.e.,* the Season of the *Feng,* or trade wind. *Cf.* Japanese *Fū,* wind; Chinese *Fung, Fun,* wind. Term doubtless introduced from early Chinese trading vessels.
† With Central Carolines *Koten,* the East, compare Polynesian *Katiu, Kotiu, Atiu* and *Tiu,* the North-East.

INDEX

A.

AGAÑA, Metropolis of Mariannes, 53, 55, 250.
Albany Pass, 28.
Alek, carver 'n native woods, 207.
Aleniang Station, 110, 176.
Alligators, 18.
Amaral Nettle, 248.
Amon, Umin or Amin Village, 271.
Amoy, coolie traffic, 42.
Ancestral worship, 75.
Ani, gods, 74, 84, 117.
    Present at kava making, 191, 193.
Ant Islands, 22, 118, 210.
    Account of, 70.
" Arbungelap " feast described, 95.
Areca Palms (*Katai* and *Kotop*), 61, 114, 189, 249.
Arnold, Sir Edwin, 293.
Aru Island, 76, 202.
Arum (*A. Costatum*), 64.
Asan village, rice planting in, 232.
Atua on Eastern Upolu, kava drinking at, 191.
Au of Marau—
    Gives author information, 211.
    On Palang people, 111.
    On tradition of Nan-Matal, 81, 83.
Augustino, Padre, 57.
Aulong (*see* ginger, wild).
Author (F. W. Christian)—
    Arrives at Yap, 233.
    Ast Nalap, 63, *seqq.*
    Collection of seeds, 33, 46, 120, 175, 308.
    Curios, 322.
    Extract from diary, 155.
    Interview with Don José Pidal, 57.
    —— Ichipau, 105.
    —— the Nóch, 203.
    Learns Kusaian dialect, 155.
    Leaves Manilla, 48.
    Leaves Ponape by *Uranus*, 228.
    On Washington Island, North Marquesas, 270.
    Returns to Colony, 175, 197.
    Starts for Manilla, 42.

Author (*continued*)—
    Sonsorol work, 303.
    Starts from Sydney, 27.
    Studies Ponapean language, 67.
    Visits Barrow of Kipar, 69.
    Visits native markets, 47.
    Visits ruins of Nan-Matal, 76, 85, 89.
    Visits Shanghai and Japan, 41.
Avetch shrub described, 294, 308.
Avira, Tahitian sage's prediction, 169.

B.

BABELTHAOB ISLAND, 17, 18.
Balakong village, 260.
Ballintang Straits, 322.
Bamboos, 343.
Bananas, 334, 351.
Banka, native craft, 39, 42.
Banyan trees (*Nin* and *Aio*), 111, 177, 227.
Barringtonia or Wi, 159, 181.
    Described, 182.
Barter, Yap system of, 237, 270.
Bats (*Kalekaf*), 161.
Bêche-de-mer, 374 ; method of preparing, 375.
Beck, Louis, opinion of Likiak-Sa, 154.
Belolach Island, 51.
Betel-Nut chewing and kava drinking, 189, 263.
Bird's nest fern (*Talik*), 114, 182.
Blanco, General, gives credentials to author, 47.
Boating accident near Tapak, 201.
Bolinao, 45.
Bows and arrows, 136, 137.
Bracelets, shell, 90.
Bread-fruit groves, 149, 227.
Bread-fruit wood, 306.
Brugmann, Captain, at Ramung, 275, 280.
Bulual, graves at, 302.
Butron, Captain, of the *Velasco*—
    On prevailing winds in Yap, 235.
    Opinion of Pelews, 17.